GW01186372

Revolution and Reaction

Why did so many Latin American leftists believe they could replicate the Cuban Revolution in their own countries, and why did so many rightists fear the spread of communism? Cognitive-psychological insights about people's distorted inferences and skewed interest calculations explain why the left held exaggerated hopes and why the right experienced excessive dread. The resulting polarization provoked a powerful backlash in which the right uniformly defeated the left. To forestall the feared spread of revolution, the military in many countries imposed authoritarian regimes and brutally suppressed left-wingers. Overly worried about the advance of Cuban-inspired radicalism as well, the United States condoned and supported the installation of dictatorship, but Latin American elites took the main initiative in these regressive regime changes. With a large number of primary and secondary sources, this book documents how misperceptions on both sides of the ideological divide thus played a crucial role in the frequent destruction of democracy.

Kurt Weyland utilizes a distinctive theoretical approach that draws on cognitive-psychological insights to elucidate crucial political phenomena. He is the author of four books and approximately fifty journal articles and book chapters. His previous book, *Making Waves* (Cambridge University Press, 2014), won the book award from APSA's Comparative Democratization section.

Revolution and Reaction

The Diffusion of Authoritarianism in Latin America

KURT WEYLAND

University of Texas, Austin

CAMBRIDGE
UNIVERSITY PRESS

CAMBRIDGE
UNIVERSITY PRESS

University Printing House, Cambridge CB2 8BS, United Kingdom

One Liberty Plaza, 20th Floor, New York, NY 10006, USA

477 Williamstown Road, Port Melbourne, VIC 3207, Australia

314–321, 3rd Floor, Plot 3, Splendor Forum, Jasola District Centre,
New Delhi – 110025, India

79 Anson Road, #06–04/06, Singapore 079906

Cambridge University Press is part of the University of Cambridge.

It furthers the University's mission by disseminating knowledge in the pursuit of
education, learning, and research at the highest international levels of excellence.

www.cambridge.org
Information on this title: www.cambridge.org/9781108483551
DOI: 10.1017/9781108692823

First published 2019

Printed and bound in Great Britain by Clays Ltd, Elcograf S.p.A.

A catalogue record for this publication is available from the British Library.

ISBN 978-1-108-48355-1 Hardback
ISBN 978-1-108-72883-6 Paperback

Contents

Tables

Graphs

Acknowledgments

One book leads to the next! After I finished *Making Waves: Democratic Contention in Europe and Latin America since the Revolutions of 1848* (Cambridge University Press, 2014), I noticed that like most scholars who examine the diffusion of political regime change, I had investigated attempts to spread "good things," namely political liberalism and democracy. Obviously, it is more pleasant to analyze progressive changes and their proliferation. We all root for the social and political forces that try hard to effect improvements.

But because I am German, I am painfully aware of the fact that during certain time periods, it were the nasty, violent, and (self-)destructive innovations that held a great deal of ideational appeal and that spread. The prime example is, of course, fascism during the interwar years. What the monumental catastrophe caused by Italian and especially German fascism makes many observers forget is that Mussolini and even Hitler for years drew a great deal of admiration and emulation. As many liberal democracies crumbled, fascism seemed to be the wave of the future.

While an analysis of the autocratic riptide of the interwar years will have to wait for my next book, this was not the only reverse wave of democratic breakdown that the modern world has seen. Political liberalism came under renewed assault in Latin America during the 1960s and 1970s, when right-wing military regimes spread. The present book focuses on this proliferation of autocracy, which preceded the "third wave" of democratization in the region that my 2014 study sought to elucidate. Why did so many countries, including the longstanding democracies of Chile and Uruguay, fall to conservative dictatorships? Why did nations that had significant experiences with liberalism come to suffer under regimes that were unprecedented in their repressiveness and cruelty?

In light of scholars' understandable preference for explaining progressive changes, these questions about the causes of consequential political reversals hold considerable intellectual interest. Why does history sometimes move in the wrong direction? Investigating these dark issues is not a very uplifting task, however. The fears and resentments of reactionaries do not make for pleasant reading. One marvels at the exaggerated threats they perceived and cringes at the drastic countermeasures they regarded as necessary. What a chilling experience, for instance, to peruse the reasoning of Argentina's former dictator Jorge Videla in explaining why the military junta came up with the idea of simply "disappearing" opponents (which meant killing them in a clandestine fashion and disposing of the corpses secretly; see Reato 2012: 52–3, 58–61, 92–3, 149–52). Yet, to help prevent recurrences, understanding the causes underlying the waves of political regression that brought such atrocities is important.

When researching and writing a wide-ranging study, one incurs innumerable intellectual and personal debts; after all, a book is the individual product of collective efforts. I thank the librarians and archivists at the Biblioteca Nacional de Chile in Santiago, at the Pontificia Universidad Católica del Perú in Lima, and at the Centro de Pesquisa e Documentação de História Contemporânea do Brasil (CPDOC) of the Fundação Getúlio Vargas in Rio de Janeiro. Special thanks go to Francisco Bulnes of the Centro de Investigación y Documentación, Universidad Finis Terrae in Santiago de Chile, who gave me access to a wealth of oral history transcripts. I am also grateful to the librarians in the Rare Books and Manuscript Division of the Benson Latin American Collection of the University of Texas at Austin.

I am thankful to Daniela Hernández and Fernando Rosenblatt for excellent research assistance. Conference presentations at annual meetings of the American Political Science Association and at international congresses of the Latin American Studies Association, and workshops at the German Institute of Global and Area Studies (Hamburg), Harvard University, the Max Planck Institute for the Study of Religious and Ethnic Diversity (Göttingen), Oxford University, Princeton University, Sciences Po (Paris), Universidad Diego Portales (Santiago de Chile), Universidade de São Paulo – Leste, Universitat Pompeu Fabra (Barcelona), and the Wissenschaftszentrum Berlin proved highly stimulating and productive.

For excellent comments on draft chapters and thorough discussions about topics related to this study, I thank Zoltan Barany, Mark Beissinger, the late Ana María Bejarano, Daniel Brinks, Jonathan Brown, Jason Brownlee, Celso Castro, Ruth Collier, Eduardo Dargent, Carlos de la Torre, Henry Dietz, Zachary Elkins, John Gerring, Johannes Gerschewski, Fabrizio Gilardi, Kenneth Greene, Seva Gunitsky, Frances Hagopian, Bert Hoffmann, Rose McDermott, Scott Mainwaring, Marcos Novaro, David Pion-Berlin, Kenneth Roberts, Fernando Rosenblatt, Andrew Stein, and Laurence Whitehead. Wendy Hunter, Fabrice Lehoucq, and Raúl Madrid have been particularly patient in listening to my ideas, insightful in making suggestions, and helpful in offering advice. Moreover, I am full of gratitude to the three anonymous reviewers enlisted by Cambridge University Press for their wealth of incisive comments and useful suggestions. And I thank Robert Dreesen and Cambridge for shepherding this project through the review and production process so smoothly and expeditiously. Moreover, I am grateful to Matthew La Fontaine for his careful copy-editing.

Chapter 8 draws on two of my published articles, namely "Fascism's Missionary Ideology and the Autocratic Wave of the Interwar Years" (*Democratization*, December 2017) and "Crafting Counterrevolution: How Reactionaries Learned to Combat Change in 1848" (*American Political Science Review*, May 2016). I thank these journals and their publishers for their permission to use this material.

With their wild games and insane jokes in Austin and with their serious questions, for instance during our trip to Chile in mid-2017, during which we visited several sites associated with the atrocities of the dictatorship, my sons Andreas and Nikolas provided a wonderful family atmosphere for this study. This book is dedicated to Wendy Hunter: *¡Muchas gracias por acompañarme en toda esta aventura!*

PART I

THEORETICAL CONSIDERATIONS

I

Introduction

THE PUZZLE OF REACTIONARY DIFFUSION

Why do regressive changes sometimes spread across states and countries? What makes "bad" innovations attractive to emulators and prompts their adoption? Social scientists commonly assume that it is modern, progressive innovations that exude strong appeal and therefore diffuse inside countries and from nation to nation. In this vein, modernization theory postulates that new, rational ways of organizing politics and exercising authority have a clear advantage in efficiency and legitimacy and therefore displace tradition and religion; accordingly, political liberalism pushed aside the divine right of kings, and democracy has more and more displaced the rule of traditional elites. With similar optimism, many currents of constructivism tend to claim that advanced, universalistic norms and values sooner or later win out against personalism and arbitrariness, leading, for instance, to the growing protection of human rights (Risse, Ropp, and Sikkink 1999; Finnemore and Sikkink 2001: 403–4). These progressivist premises also inform large parts of the burgeoning literature on diffusion in comparative politics.[1] Authors often assume that improvements such as political liberalism and democracy spread (Simmons, Dobbin, and Garrett 2008) – not repression and authoritarian rule. Therefore, studies of novel, beneficial reforms far outnumber analyses that examine "the political power of bad ideas" (Schrad 2010).

But twentieth-century history calls this progressivism into question. Modern, forward-looking innovations are not always the models that most decision-makers find appealing and therefore adopt. Instead, reactionary institutions and policies can diffuse as well. Most jarringly, authoritarianism and fascism spread during the interwar years, in Europe and Latin America. Squeezed between

---

[1] The field of international relations, by contrast, features many analyses of the spread of war, terrorism, civil war, etc. – a point I owe to Fabrizio Gilardi.

communism with its world-revolutionary ambitions and this upsurge of right-wing regimes, liberal, pluralist democracy was on the defensive – contrary to the hopes of modernization theory and constructivism (see graphs in Huntington 1991: 14–15, 26; Gunitsky 2014: 562). Democracy came under renewed assault in Latin America during the 1960s and 1970s, when a rash of military coups rippled through the region; shockingly, these authoritarian takeovers often found broad civilian support (a fact downplayed in retrospect). The result was a pronounced, deep reverse wave that overwhelmed many liberal regimes, especially in South America;[2] even the longstanding democracies of Chile and Uruguay fell prey to this riptide (see graphs in Smith 2012: 27, 35; Mainwaring and Pérez-Liñán 2013: 3, 73–4; see also the coup data in Powell and Thyne 2011: 255).

While a future volume will examine the massive, complex autocratic wave of the interwar years, the present book seeks to explain the latter, regional process of reactionary diffusion, one of the most clear-cut and striking instances in which modern history seemed to move "in the wrong direction." The atrocities committed by the Latin American dictatorships, which continue to cast a dark shadow long after re-democratization, highlight the historical significance of these regressive regime changes. In light of the progressivism prevailing in the academic literature, the proliferation of reactionary rule over the course of fifteen years constitutes a puzzle. It is therefore crucial to investigate why authoritarian regimes spread from country to country. What causal mechanisms propelled this surprising reverse wave? This study assesses the main approaches applied in the diffusion literature, which highlight great power pressure and imposition; normative appeal; and rational learning (Weyland 2005: 268–71).

THE MAIN ARGUMENT

Extant approaches cannot provide convincing explanations for the Latin American reverse wave of the 1960s and 1970s, as Chapter 2 demonstrates. The great power in the Western hemisphere, the United States, did not impose dictatorship; instead, its influence on democratic breakdown was limited, as Chapter 7 shows in depth. Similarly, the normative appeal of authoritarianism was low; military rule was seen as the lesser evil, tasked with forestalling a descent into disorder and chaos. As reactionary diffusion was not driven by coercion or moral attraction, it resulted mainly from interest-based learning. But this learning systematically deviated from standard rationality, as Chapters 4, 5, and 6 demonstrate.

---

[2] Most of Central America was chafing under repressive authoritarianism, as thoroughly explained in Lehoucq (2012); because there was little progress to reverse, this subregion was therefore not much affected by the Latin American reverse wave.

TABLE 1.1: *Military Dictatorships in South America, 1960–1980* (Institutional military regimes marked in bold)

1962	Argentina, Peru
1963	Ecuador
1964	Bolivia, **Brazil**
1966	Argentina
1968	**Peru**
1970	Bolivia
1971	Bolivia
1972	**Ecuador**
1973	**Chile**, Uruguay
1976	**Argentina**
1978	Bolivia
1979	Bolivia
1980	Bolivia

Cognitive-psychological mechanisms, especially inferential shortcuts and the skewed weighting of gains versus losses, shaped and distorted the perceptions and decisions that drove the remarkable spread of autocratic rule in the 1960s and 1970s. By applying cognitive heuristics and acting out of disproportionate loss aversion, sociopolitical elites, common people, and their organizations overreacted to perceived revolutionary challenges to their core interests; driven by excessive fear, they installed and supported repressive authoritarian rule to protect order and hierarchy. Thus, the central mechanism that produced the proliferation of autocratic regimes was a backlash effect. Left-wing efforts to spread revolution, inspired by the epic Cuban Revolution of 1959, prompted determined counterrevolution, which forcefully sought to immunize the region against the communist virus. Radical diffusion, which started with a rash of guerrilla movements, provoked reactionary counterdiffusion, which led to the installation of military dictatorships in country after country.

With these arguments, the book substantiates and further develops the bounded rationality approach to diffusion studies that my earlier work has introduced (Weyland 2014). In particular, the new study conducts an "out of sample" assessment of this theory by going beyond the analysis of democratizing changes and investigating authoritarian waves, which were pushed forward by different types of actors. After all, elites are the protagonists in autocratic regression, not the masses, which play crucial roles in struggles over democratization (Teorell 2010: chap. 5). Do these elite sectors operate in fundamentally similar ways as their progressive, pro-democratic adversaries?

Moreover, the present study enriches the bounded rationality framework by highlighting the decisive role of asymmetrical loss aversion, a mechanism rarely invoked in political science. As a wealth of psychological experiments and field studies show, humans attach much greater subjective weight to losses than to gains. Therefore, they are zealous in stemming deterioration, while pursuing improvements with much less energy (Kahneman and Tversky 2000: chaps. 7–11; Zamir 2014; for an application to contentious politics, see Bergstrand 2014). This skewed choice mechanism is crucial for explaining the backlash driving the reverse wave of military regimes. In particular, loss aversion accounts for a striking feature of Latin America's autocratic regression, namely the enormous brutality with which military generals imposed and exercised their rule. In dislodging tottering democracies, suppressing their political enemies, and extending their hold on power, dictators employed an unprecedented degree of violence. They overshot beyond any conceivable political need and engaged in "unnecessary" overkill, as evident in the heinous, large-scale human rights violations committed by these autocracies, such as the infamous "caravan of death" in Chile (Verdugo 2001). This paroxysm of cruelty reflected excessive threat perceptions derived via cognitive heuristics, which triggered disproportionate loss aversion, the main impulse behind authoritarian crackdowns.

To explain this violent reflex, the study argues that Latin America's main wave of autocracy emerged from a strong reaction against apparent threats (see for democratic breakdown in general, Linz 1978: 14; and more broadly Stenner 2005). The rash of military coups constituted exaggerated responses to the danger that important sectors saw emanate from the radical left, which had received an enormous political and ideological boost from the Cuban Revolution. As radicals inspired by Fidel Castro's surprising success sought to promote similar profound transformations in a wide range of countries, right-wingers cracked down exceptionally hard to block these emulation efforts. Loss aversion explains why left-wing efforts at diffusion provoked massive counterdiffusion. This interactive dynamic, through which incessant attempts to spread revolution prompted determined counterrevolution, is central for the present study.

Historical analysis shows that the main motive for adopting reactionary regimes was a pervasive fear of the radical, revolutionary threats emanating from communism. To many observers, the Cuban Revolution demonstrated the striking ease with which a determined minority could grab power, impose total control, and overturn the sociopolitical order (Wickham-Crowley 1992: 30–7). Jumping to the conclusion that this unexpected, dramatic revolution could well find replication in their own countries, conservative and even centrist sectors did everything in their power to forestall such diffusion, which left-wing extremists and revolutionary Cuba actively promoted (Wright 2001; Brown 2017). The perceived danger of communism's spread – which was in fact quite unlikely – induced many political forces and organizations to seek refuge in the strong arms of anticommunists. Therefore, they demanded, supported, or accepted the brutal repression of left-wing revolutionaries and the imposition of harsh autocratic rule. Of course, the destruction of political liberalism and democracy exposed these sectors themselves to the arbitrary abuse of power by unaccountable dictators. To escape from the overestimated specter of the communist fire, they jumped into the reactionary frying pan, which really did burn, though not as badly as the imagined Marxist inferno. Disproportionate loss aversion drove this precipitous choice.

The threat perceptions and the reactionary reflex that produced the Latin American wave of autocracy did not emerge from thorough assessments and rational evaluations, but from the hasty, problematic inferences and unbalanced cost-benefit analyses of bounded rationality. Instead of rational learning, heuristic shortcuts governed information processing (Kahneman, Slovic, and Tversky 1982; Gilovich, Griffin, and Kahneman 2002), and asymmetrical loss aversion deformed political decisions (Kahneman and Tversky 2000; Kahneman 2011). Specifically, people relied on inferential heuristics to assess the impact of the Cuban Revolution. Therefore, they greatly overestimated the chances of communism taking hold in their own country. Because the resulting threat perceptions fueled outsized loss aversion, important sectors took excessive countermeasures to defend themselves against this menace and fortified their polities through autocratic rule. Chapter 3 develops these arguments in greater depth and specifies their cognitive-psychological underpinnings, which Chapters 4, 5, and 6 then substantiate with ample documentary evidence.

One point bears highlighting: asymmetrical loss aversion played such an important role because communism promised a profound, dramatic, and all-encompassing transformation of the socioeconomic and political order; consequently, both the supposed benefits and the likely costs of revolution were huge. Due to the enormous magnitude of these prospective gains and losses, asymmetrical loss aversion produced deviations from conventional cost-benefit assessments that were substantial, consequential, and clearly noticeable, despite the messiness and "opacity" of the political world (cf. Pierson 2000: 259–62). Because losses have much greater motivating force than gains, defenders of the established order tended to outnumber promoters of revolution and to act with particularly strong determination, including the willingness to employ brutal violence. By contrast, steps toward democratization (as analyzed in Weyland 2014) constitute less drastic change: They offer benefits – increased political rights and liberties – to large segments of the citizenry without imposing great net costs on other segments.[3] Therefore,

---

[3] While there often are powerful sectors that benefit from autocratic rule, the concentration of power and lack of accountability exposes them to the risk of losing these benefits and even suffer costs. For an interesting recent analysis of these risks and of elites' resulting ambivalence toward autocracy, see Albertus (2015).

loss aversion often does not spur a surplus of stubborn resistance that permanently blocks advances toward freedom.

The exceptional case of democratization in Chile, where the military coup of 1973 had evicted the only Marxist government that ever won a democratic election, demonstrates this difference. In the initial stages of the democratic transition during the 1980s, the depth of prospective change was unclear: significant sectors feared that the end of dictatorship would result in the dismantling of General Pinochet's market model and his rigid 1980 constitution and bring socialism back to power (Weyland 2014: 193). Therefore, resistance fueled by loss aversion for years prevented pro-democratic sectors from achieving inroads. The authoritarian regime finally relinquished power only after the main opposition groupings credibly promised moderation, accepted the market model, acquiesced in the constitutional framework (cf. Fuentes 2012), and thus strictly limited the change they sought and the cost it would entail for Pinochet's supporters. That is, democratization only advanced after the opposition largely deactivated loss aversion (Roberts 1998: chap. 5; see in general Drake 2009: 204, 214; Schmitter 2010: 19–20; Mainwaring and Pérez-Liñán 2013: 36–9, 77–80, 104–14). This case shows that the fear of profound socioeconomic and political transformation, especially revolution, triggers loss aversion to a much greater extent and in a more observable way than most efforts at democratization, in which only a political regime change is at stake.

In sum, when ample sectors see a serious risk of communism, loss aversion severely skews their political choices and prompts an urge to adopt strong countermeasures. Accordingly, the spread of autocratic rule in Latin America primarily constituted counterdiffusion: because radical leftists were captivated by the "success" of the Cuban Revolution and made incessant ill-considered attempts to imitate this precedent in many countries, ample rightist and even centrist sectors felt the need to combat these efforts at any price, including their own liberty. Left-wing hyperaction prompted right-wing overreaction. Thus, the riptide of autocracy during the 1960s and 1970s constituted a backlash phenomenon. As the example of the Cuban Revolution helped to fuel widespread radicalization during the 1960s, this reverse wave assumed a reactionary character, in the literal sense of the term. These clustered regime changes tried to stem the historical advance of mass mobilization and restore the stability that had prevailed in the past (cf. Mayer 1971: 48–9; Hirschman 1991: 8–10; Lilla 2016: xxii–xxiii).

DIFFUSION AND COUNTERDIFFUSION

The power and significance of the backlash driven by asymmetrical loss aversion have broader implications for diffusion studies, starting with their conceptual foundation. Diffusion is usually defined as the process by which an innovation or precedent in one unit increases the probability of its replication in various other units; by providing positive reinforcement, diffusion brings the spread of similarity amid diversity (cf. Elkins and Simmons 2005: 36; Weyland 2007: 19). But a broader conceptualization is required for investigating the feared spread of revolutionary change and its reactionary repercussions. Facing an externally inspired challenge that would entail exorbitant costs for them, status quo-oriented sectors often go beyond defensive efforts to avert such a profound transformation. Instead, they counterattack, repress their radical adversaries, and destroy revolutionaries' capacity to seek an overhaul in the future. Thus, political groupings cannot only refuse to follow a precedent, but try to turn the clock back. Attempts to force revolutionary change can thus provoke serious setbacks.

Consequently, the diffusion of radical contention tends to galvanize pronounced polarization. Initiatives to emulate a revolutionary precedent usually provoke counteracting efforts to suppress these challenges and prevent their recurrence (Beissinger 2007: 268–74). Ambitious transformational impulses thus have a cleaving impact: they stimulate initiatives toward imitation but also moves in the opposite direction. Attempted advances serve as a deterrent and trigger a backlash. These contradictory effects, which are both causal products of the initial precedent, complicate diffusion studies (Gunitsky 2013). Statistical analyses, for instance, are only starting to grapple with the possibility that such opposite repercussions cancel out (Pengl 2013). By looking primarily for direct replication, scholars may miss the contradictory effects of the triggering impulses and overlook powerful counterdiffusion. Whereas the diffusion literature has focused on positive stimuli for replication, such as contagion and demonstration effects, this study demonstrates the importance of repulsion by powerful deterrent effects.

Due to this backlash, the net outcome of diffusion impulses can in fact be negative (Weyland 2010: 1158–9). The more drastic and radical the change sought, the more likely it prompts an aggregate move away from the initial model or precedent, rather than toward it. Communist revolution promised great gains for some, and corresponding losses for others. Yet disproportionate loss aversion means that subjectively, losses clearly outweigh gains of equal magnitude. This asymmetry was a principal reason why the leftist quest for deep-reaching change remained much weaker than the rightist efforts to squash this quest at all cost. As a result, radical efforts to spread revolution were mostly unsuccessful, whereas reactionary counterattacks, which included attempts to seek refuge under authoritarian rule, advanced much farther. Consequently, the Cuban Revolution did not prompt the spread of communist transformation from country to country, but the proliferation of right-wing authoritarian regimes that sought to immunize countries against the revolutionary virus.

This remarkably lopsided distribution of outcomes reflected not only obvious resource advantages, especially the command over economic clout, political influence, and military might that established elites held. Instead, even in popular support, antirevolutionaries usually bested revolutionaries.

As the available evidence suggests, conservative military coups that ousted leftist governments in Latin America often found majority acceptance, as in Brazil in 1964 and in Argentina in 1976 (Brands 2010: 111, 116, 120; Cohen 1989: 41–6; Potash 1996: 508; Novaro and Palermo 2003: 23–33; Finchelstein 2014: 124–5; Motta 2014: 11–13).[4] In fact, Argentine society in 1976 even "justified [the military regime's] ruthless repression" of urban guerrilla groupings and "vigorously supported their elimination" via forced disappearances and assassinations (Moyano 1995: 96, 152; see also 98). Thus, loss aversion induced ample sectors to reject radical left-wingers with fervor and to embrace reactionary forces that sought to forestall the risk of revolution through the installation of autocracy.

This stark asymmetry suggests that deterrent effects can be stronger than contagion and demonstration effects. Because the diffusion literature has focused primarily on the positive boost emanating from novel models and precedents, it has largely overlooked this possibility (Gunitsky 2013), which arises from high-stakes innovations with huge repercussions. By calling attention to the double-sided impact that external stimuli can have, this book tries to broaden the focus of this important body of scholarship.

THE RELEVANCE AND CONTRIBUTIONS OF THE STUDY

Investigating Latin America's reactionary wave holds great substantive and theoretical relevance. This cluster of liberal breakdown and autocratic imposition constituted a watershed in the political development of many countries. The military regimes of the 1960s and 1970s left lasting legacies. The dictatorships in Brazil, Peru, and – more disastrously – Argentina used their unaccountable power to impose profound transformations on economy and society, create a host of new state agencies, and, in the lusophone country, totally restructure the political party system. The imprint of autocracy is most thorough in the Chilean case: the Pinochet regime decreed a neoliberal economic model and a power-concentrating constitution (Garretón 1983), whose basic parameters have remained in force to the present day, significantly shaping the new democracy (Fuentes 2012). Thus, although the autocracies installed during the reverse wave did not endure and sooner or later gave way to renewed democratization, this reactionary diffusion process proved hugely important for countries' political trajectories.

With its extensive narrative analysis, the study seeks to capture the distinctive politics of this unusual time period, in which the political world seemed upended and profound uncertainty reigned. The Cuban Revolution shook up the established sociopolitical order like an earthquake and shattered the parameters of political thought and action throughout the

---

[4] While these coups did not result from popular clamor (Bermeo 2003), they seem to have found widespread popular endorsement.

region (cf. Kurzman 2004). Suddenly, longstanding structures and institutions that had persisted for decades seemed open to change, causing excitement and exorbitant hope on the left, and perplexity and fear on the right and among the center. This outpouring of enthusiasm and idealism, yet also of paranoia and resentment gave this epoch a distinctive flavor. The unexpected appearance of drastic new options – revolution and counterrevolution – shattered actors' system of political coordinates and made the ground crumble under their feet. The so-called backyard of the United States was turned upside down by the surprising irruption of Castroite communism. The following groundswell of radicalization that swept across the hemisphere transformed politics into a new kind of epic struggle: instead of adjustments and reforms of limited magnitude, politics now focused on millenarian visions with huge stakes.

By drawing on core insights of cognitive psychology, the study elucidates the uniqueness of these excessively "interesting times," which ended up in such tragedy and heartbreak. Standard rationality cannot explain why so many young people suddenly believed that "a new society was possible," and why so many conservatives took these unrealistic and naïve hopes so seriously that they smashed them with the sledgehammer of brutal repression. Strikingly, political actors of all stripes did not respond with the poise and prudence that guides so much of political behavior in normal times. Instead, they were all "bent out of shape" by dramatic events, which they processed with the distortionary mechanisms of bounded rationality. As the left got carried away by inferential heuristics, the right plunged into the depths of loss aversion and starkly overreacted. These dramatic experiences of abortive revolution and bloody counterrevolution can serve as deterrents for any new efforts to design grand visions, which the hypercomplexity of the contemporary world would probably make even more disastrous.

In theoretical terms, this study contributes to the burgeoning literature on nondemocratic rule, one of the most vibrant areas of comparative politics in the new millennium (see, e.g., Gandhi 2008; Levitsky and Way 2010; Svolik 2012; Schedler 2013). One important group of writings has focused on the genesis of autocracy, usually as part of broader theorizing about regime change in general (seminal: Acemoglu and Robinson 2005; similar Boix 2003). These authors have mainly employed a distributional approach, deriving regime developments from the material interests of socioeconomic collectivities in a rational-choice version of Marxian-style class approaches (cf. Acemoglu and Robinson 2005: 20). In some ways, this body of literature offers a formalization and generalization of theories propounded originally by Moore (1966), and especially Rueschemeyer, Stephens, and Stephens (1992).

Like Acemoglu and Robinson (2005: 25–8), the present book finds that the threat of revolution and the resulting prospects of losses provided crucial stimuli for the imposition of dictatorship. But whereas these models invoke material interests as driving forces, my research suggests that struggles over political power and control of the state proved much more central, as the classical studies of Samuel Huntington and Theda Skocpol already highlighted (Huntington 1968: 264–78, 308–15; Skocpol 1979: 24–32, 161–8). In line with the thorough and systematic criticism of the distributional approach by Haggard and Kaufman (2016; see also Albertus 2015), my research shows that the main protagonists in the conflicts over revolution and regime change were not socioeconomic categories or classes, but political actors such as parties, movements, leaders, and especially the military (similar Mainwaring and Pérez-Liñán 2013). The armed forces, in turn, pursued primarily the institutional interests of their organization and of the state as a whole, focusing on the maintenance of sociopolitical order and the preservation of their own monopoly over organized coercion.

With these findings, my study confirms the validity of a Weberian approach, rather than the Marxian-style reasoning informing the recent rational-choice models. While socioeconomic factors mattered, politics proved much more important, in a variety of ways. As regards the main protagonists of the Latin America coup wave, an extensive literature established the crucial role of the military as an independent actor (most important: Stepan 1971, 1973, 1978b; see also Potash 1980, 1996; Rouquié 1985, 1987; Hunter 1997). In general, political forces and their (mis)calculations, rather than structural factors and socioeconomic actors, primarily shaped the processes of democratic breakdown, as a longstanding stream of writings has shown.[5] For instance, radical political movements exerted a deleterious impact on liberal democracy, as Mainwaring and Pérez-Liñán (2013: 36–9, 77–80, 104–14) emphasized in their major recent analysis. All of these studies demonstrate the importance of political factors and forces, rather than socioeconomic collectivities.

The book also diverges from the rational-choice models of Boix (2003) and Acemoglu and Robinson (2005) by relying on solid empirical findings about bounded rationality. Whereas those authors assume that regime developments reflect the optimal choices made by self-interested actors, my explanation captures the tragedy of the Latin American reverse wave much better by demonstrating the importance of misperceptions, miscalculations, and distorted choices (see also Gimpelson and Treisman 2015). Due to cognitive shortcuts and asymmetrical loss aversion, rash actions and exaggerated reactions prevailed on both sides of the ideological divide, causing a great deal of ill-considered, "needless" violence that rational assessments would have avoided.

After all, how can it be rational for radical left-wingers to start rural guerrilla movements over and over again, despite numerous earlier efforts having ended in catastrophic failure? Certainly, widespread poverty and profound social inequality seemed to clamor for urgent alleviation. But of course, pressing needs and long-neglected grievances do not make it rational to embark on

[5] See, for instance, Linz 1978; Linz and Stepan 1978; Valenzuela 1978; Cohen 1994; Novaro and Palermo 2003; Haslam 2005; De Riz 2010; Harmer 2011; Ferreira and Gomes 2014.

bold, risky remedies such as armed uprisings spearheaded by small groupings of activists. The basic commands of prudence would insist on assessing the feasibility of countermeasures and their likelihood of success – which was infinitesimal, as any cost-benefit analysis would have suggested. Thus, notwithstanding the idealism that helped to motivate extremist challenges, they were marred by striking deviations from standard rationality. Tragically, status quo defenders suffered from equivalent distortions. Because they overestimated radicals' chances of success, they employed unnecessary brutality in combating these ill-considered and ill-planned challenges. Why this overkill? Exaggerated fears of the extreme left also drove the imposition of autocratic rule, which ended up exposing even many coup mongers to the risk of arbitrary oppression, a suboptimal outcome. Standard rationality would not predict this slew of political mistakes, which had such dire consequences for thousands and thousands of people.

Moreover, rational-choice models would have difficulty explaining the stark unevenness in regime outcomes that underlay the Latin American reverse wave. Rationalists treat benefits and costs as equivalent. They thus overlook the intensity of people's urge to avoid losses, which skews aggregate political results when high-stakes issues are on the agenda. In Latin America's starkly unequal societies, where the profound transformations sought by left-wingers promised substantial social gains for large majorities of the population, rational-choice models cannot easily account for the frequent numerical predominance of opponents of change (see, e.g., Sigmund 1977: 199–201; Lavareda 1991: 156, 159; Bermeo 2003: 173; Navia and Osorio 2015: 126–7). The strong motivating force of loss aversion is crucial for explaining why relatively few actors mobilized on behalf of left-wing revolution in most cases, whereas a broad phalanx of forces combated these efforts – and employed all means at their disposal. These massive, resolute counterattacks universally squashed the diffusion of revolution and brought right-wing repression and autocratic rule instead. While the resource advantages of elites contributed to the victory of reaction, the skewed choice mechanisms of bounded rationality also played a significant role in producing these strikingly lopsided outcomes.

By highlighting uneven political processes and results, the study addresses a broader debate over structure versus agency in political regime change. O'Donnell and Schmitter (1986: 19) claimed that democratic transitions differ fundamentally from democratic breakdowns in this respect. While the construction of an open, participatory regime with its complex institutions and norms is a precarious project shrouded in uncertainty that requires prudent leadership, structural obstacles and acute crises can irreparably undermine a democracy and push it into almost inevitable collapse. By contrast, Linz (1978: 4, 75–8, 90) and Stepan (1978a) postulated the contingent nature of democratic breakdown, which apt decision-making could have avoided. These authors highlighted political mistakes and faulty leadership.

The present study traces a new path in this structure – agency debate. By employing an actor-centered approach that rests on the firm empirical regularities documented by cognitive psychology, it shows that in major postrevolutionary conjunctures, predictable, systematic distortions in decision-making cause a powerful reactionary backlash from which political actors have difficulty escaping. Disproportionate loss aversion thus gives rise to the asymmetry in the politics of regime change postulated by O'Donnell and Schmitter (1986). While the gains promised by democratization have limited motivating force and induce tentative and uncertain advances, the losses threatened by radical revolution provoke drastic countermeasures that only strong, consolidated democracies can survive. While not unsalvageable and condemned to death, as the cases of Colombia and Venezuela prove (see Chapter 4), problem-plagued democracies swept up in an antirevolutionary riptide have a high risk of failure. Reactionary counterdiffusion causes whirlpools that powerfully drag countries toward autocracy. Contrary to Linz and Stepan (1978), political actors cannot easily forestall democracy's breakdown in such an unpropitious context. As leaders are constrained by cognitive structures and their rationality has more or less tight bounds, agency has limited room of maneuver. Systematic calculations and prudent decisions are often conspicuous by their absence, especially during crises and other critical junctures.

At the most general and abstract level, my study also seeks to make a small contribution to the theoretical development of political science as a discipline. After the monumental debate over rational choice during the 1990s, the field has entered a post-paradigmatic phase in the new millennium. Nowadays many scholars draw eclectically on a variety of approaches and try to synthesize diverse elements in complex edifices (captured well in Lichbach and Zuckerman 2009). This pragmatic tendency has the benefit of avoiding the paradigmatic battles of the 1990s, which consumed enormous energy and caused a good deal of bad blood. Instead of attacking other approaches, scholars now concentrate on solving specific puzzles and explaining substantive phenomena. But the disadvantage is that this pragmatic focus on limited issues leaves the big questions about basic premises and underlying assumptions unaddressed. In their focus on substantive issues, academics disperse, concentrate on smaller topics, and tend to their niches of specialty rather than engaging the broader scholarly community.

To help counteract these disaggregative tendencies, the present study centers on a major theoretical topic, namely the role and nature of political rationality. The theoretical reasoning and the ample historical analysis further develop and substantiate a bounded rationality approach to political macrochange. While my earlier work (Weyland 2007, 2014) built this approach in direct contrast with rational choice, the present book dialogs more with constructivism as well. After all, the puzzle of historical regression is most acute for conventional currents of constructivism, which tend to believe in normative advance. How, then, to account for reverse waves and the repression and atrocities they entail? As Chapter 2 discusses, a historicist version of constructivism, which highlights changes in the Zeitgeist during certain time periods, also has explanatory problems. Both of these ideational lines of reasoning overestimate the causal impact of ideas. History is not guided by the unfolding of a reasonably coherent set of principles and norms.

My bounded rationality approach better captures the actual twists and turns of history, the false starts and overreactions, the mistakes and tragedies. Political actors often pursue self-interests that are at odds with norms and principles, and they do so in suboptimal and problematic ways. As a result, their decisions often lack coherence and historical direction. My reliance on cognitive psychology does more justice to the uncertain course of history, the problems and risks along the way, than do constructivist alternatives.

Certainly, political actors are influenced by ideational developments, which shape their perceptions and interest definition to some extent. But rather than simply acting out given values and norms, political groupings have choices to make and face options among various possible, ideationally suggested, and culturally legitimate courses of action. In fact, the more modernity advances, the more diversity and heterogeneity there is among the prevailing ideas. The Zeitgeist itself is never uniform, and it gives rise to countercurrents and new challenges.

Moreover, the pursuit of self-interest often marginalizes or overrides norms and ideas. This tendency is especially strong in crisis situations, when threats seem to loom and intense loss aversion comes to the fore: norms can rarely tame the desperate defense of fundamental goals. Consequently, political interactions and their complex repercussions produce strings of historical events that do not reliably reflect the prevailing ideas and norms. As the Latin American reverse wave analyzed in Chapters 4 to 7 and similar counterrevolutionary processes examined in Chapter 8 provide a great deal of sobering evidence, the study takes a clear position concerning the relative importance of ideas and norms versus interests. By addressing this debate, the book helps to focus the attention of political scientists on a major topic, and thus seeks to counteract the dispersive tendencies pervading the discipline in recent years.

RESEARCH DESIGN

To disentangle the complex interplay of revolutionary diffusion and reactionary counterdiffusion that fuels authoritarian reverse waves, this book engages in comparative historical analysis and relies on qualitative research. This methodological approach is unusual in diffusion studies, where statistical investigations predominate. Quantitative analyses have made essential contributions, especially by documenting the prevalence of temporal and geographic clustering in political regime change. Examinations of various waves of democratization have been particularly common (Brinks and

Coppedge 2006; Gleditsch and Ward 2006; Teorell 2010: chap. 4; Mainwaring and Pérez-Liñán 2013: chap. 7; Wejnert 2014; Gunitsky 2014, 2017; see also Elkink 2013; mixed findings in Houle, Kayser, and Xiang 2016).

Despite their impressive and increasing technical and theoretical sophistication, however, statistical investigations of diffusion run up against important limitations. Many of these analyses draw on large-scale, cross-sectional and longitudinal data sets that have significant conceptual problems (see Munck and Verkuilen 2002; Bowman, Lehoucq, and Mahoney 2005; Lehoucq 2016). Moreover, diffusion processes are often highly complex, shaped by multiple intersecting and counteracting impulses. Whereas contentious cascades (cf. Hale 2013) triggered by a single outstanding precedent, such as the revolutions of 1848 or the Arab Spring of 2011, advanced in crisp, tight waves, many other clusters of regime change, such as the democratizations at the end of World War I or the "color revolutions" in the postcommunist world, have arisen from a variety of interacting influences and have unfolded in much slower, more complex ways.

The third wave of democratization, for instance, played out differently in different regions of the world. This wide-ranging process advanced slowly but with great success in Latin America, while sweeping across Africa and especially Eastern Europe much faster, yet with more varied outcomes (Weyland 2014: chaps. 6, 8). Inside Latin America, this wave gathered steam from a confluence of demonstration and contagion effects and gained further momentum from great power promotion, such as US human rights pressures. But regime change also provoked resistance and reactions; the Pinochet dictatorship in Chile, for instance, dug in its heels to avert the kind of trials that the perpetrators of atrocities were facing in the new democracy of neighboring Argentina (Weyland 2014: 208–10). Statistical models, which have inherent difficulties modeling complex interactions and multiple paths (cf. Ragin 2000: chaps. 1, 4), cannot easily capture these diverse influences and effects.

As this study shows, autocratic diffusion is especially complex. Fueled by reactions to a dramatic revolution, it is triggered by a deterrent example, which, however, stimulates emulation efforts as well. In fact, the very attempts of imitative revolutionaries to follow the Cuban precedent aggravated the fears of status quo-oriented sectors and strengthened their determination to forestall such replication at all cost. Thus, counteracting impulses lie at the root of reactionary waves; yet because their variegated effects can partly cancel out, they are not easy to detect with statistical techniques (cf. Pengl 2013). As the initial revolutionary precedent causes concerns among conservative sectors about the stability and resilience of the status quo, fears of subversion prompt a search for alternative regimes that offer reliable protection against the perceived threat. These concerns create receptiveness for new political models, such as the Brazilian prototype of developmentalist, institutionalized dictatorship. Thus, the deterrent effects of revolution and the appeal of new types of reactionary rule interact to propel the proliferation of autocracy.

These complex, multifaceted processes of diffusion and counterdiffusion often take substantial yet varying amounts of time to unfold and come to fruition. After all, many of the relevant actors subject to diverse external influences were not unorganized masses of citizens, which tend to respond precipitously and quickly to foreign stimuli (Weyland 2014: chaps. 2, 4). Instead, political organizations such as conservative parties, business associations, and the military took the lead in the imposition of authoritarian rule. Due to more experienced leadership and to institutional mechanisms for information processing, these organizations did not as easily fall prey to cognitive shortcuts. Instead of acting immediately, organizations tend to wait for promising opportunities before following foreign precedents and models (cf. Weyland 2014: chaps. 2, 5). As a result, external stimuli often have a delayed impact, which can operate across a much longer time span than statistical studies model with their short-term lags (cf. Elkink 2013). Indeed, the Cuban Revolution inspired new guerrilla challenges in Argentina from 1959 to the late 1960s (Brown 2017: 380–3, 388–91, 395–404, 408). Brazil's model of fortified authoritarianism, built in the mid- to late 1960s, had an impact on the installation of the Argentine autocracy in 1966 (De Riz 2010: 29, 38) and the Chilean dictatorship in 1973 (Harmer 2012; Burns 2014). Thus, demonstration and deterrent effects operated over the course of many years, with varying intervals between the original stimulus and the eventual outcomes.

Together with the "contradictory" mix of contagion and repulsion, the irregular timing of diffusion and counterdiffusion creates enormous obstacles for statistical investigations. What quantitative variables and models could capture these complex influences in a valid fashion? Qualitative research with its thorough investigation of specific cases and its controlled comparisons (Slater and Ziblatt 2013) can track these inspirations and deterrents with greater accuracy and assess their impact on political decision-making whenever it occurs. By reconstructing the perceptions, judgments, and calculations of important organizations and leaders, process tracing can demonstrate the linkages between political phenomena and developments in different countries. Qualitative analysis is especially well suited for documenting the deliberate import of political institutions and regime types across countries. Political forces often observe or even study foreign models and invoke them to justify their domestic adoption decisions. In fact, countries that designed the initial innovation often try to export it to other nations and thus extend their international influence or their ideological project. Castro's Cuba, for instance, was notorious for its incessant promotion and support of guerrilla struggles all over Latin America throughout the 1960s (Brown 2017).

Qualitative research, comparative analyses, and historical investigations are ● particularly good at reconstructing these processes of borrowing and sharing. They search for evidence about visits and study missions, reports about other countries' innovations, and proposals that copy and adapt some of these foreign models. In these ways, scholars open up the black box of decision-making and reveal who promoted and who opposed an external innovation; how these groupings pursued their goals; and how these efforts interacted to produce adoption, adaptation, rejection, or backlash. By examining similarities in political style and behavior between the precedent and potential emulators, qualitative research also seeks to capture influences of which political actors may not have been fully aware.

Methodologists have in recent years clarified "the logic of process tracing tests" (Mahoney 2012; see also Collier 2011; Beach and Pedersen 2013; Bennett and Checkel 2015; Beach 2017). These contributions highlight the distinction between evidence that is necessary versus sufficient for supporting an argument. For the sake of narrative flow, I avoid a formal application of these types of tests (e.g., "hoop tests" versus "smoking gun tests"), which can get stilted and clutter up a book-length study. But my research took inspiration in the principles highlighted by these methodological discussions and searched for documentary evidence that would be necessary or sufficient for substantiating processes of diffusion and counterdiffusion.

Specifically, to establish that a demonstration or deterrent effect occurred, it is necessary to document that foreign political actors had knowledge of a precedent; that it affected their thoughts, dispositions, or actions; and that they were attracted or deterred. The more a researcher can then dig up evidence of actual steps toward political action, such as proposals for emulation or the preparation of countermeasures, the closer one moves to establishing sufficiency as well. If a scholar can reconstruct the complete sequence of decision-making and document a strong push for imitation that carries the day, then a diffusion argument can count as corroborated.

Accordingly, causal process observations that are necessary for establishing diffusion include references to foreign precedents or models that political actors make in their speeches or writings. The copying or usage of foreign texts, such as the widespread reliance of Latin American insurgents on the guerrilla manual of Che Guevara ([1961] 2007) or the manifesto of Régis Debray (1967), also proves this point. While not necessary, assessments of foreign innovations, evaluations of the likely benefits and costs of their emulation, and discussions of potential adaptations to the specific needs of the importing country offer strong additional evidence. The next step concerns the elaboration of proposals to follow a foreign precedent or adopt an external model. If organizations participate in a diffusion process, they are likely to leave a paper trail, which scholars can access via archival research; informal decision-making processes are harder to piece together and require in-depth interviews or, for historical cases, the reading of letters, diaries, or memoirs.

Documenting these steps in the emulation process is also crucial for ruling out the purely strategic use of a foreign precedent for legitimating a political initiative that actors had already planned to undertake beforehand. When foreign innovations carry special prestige or when a gathering wave of emulation efforts suggests their unusual appeal, domestic actors have incentives to invoke these models in order to justify changes that they had decided to promote for other reasons. In these instances, external precedents do not provide the real impulse, but serve merely as a legitimating fig leaf for initiatives that have domestic motives; they play only an instrumental role, as especially adherents of rational choice or Marxian critics of "ideology" would postulate.[6] To rule out this alternative argument, it is necessary to assess whether a foreign innovation made a real difference in reshaping actors' beliefs, judgments, and dispositions: Did it trigger a new initiative that was not in preparation and that would not have been pursued otherwise? In other words, did knowledge about a new foreign precedent or model transform the thinking, feeling, or actions of domestic political forces?

For this purpose, it is important to go back in time and examine actors' thoughts and ideas, goals and plans before the appearance of a new international precedent or foreign model. Were Latin American left-wingers, for instance, itching to start insurgencies during the 1950s, waiting only for a propitious opportunity? Or did the unexpected success of the Cuban revolutionaries suddenly suggest the promise of a new option for effecting sociopolitical change and prompt a clear change in posture? Because the established left, especially communist parties, had not regarded Latin American conditions as ripe for socialist revolution and because they severely criticized the "adventurism" of Castro's enthusiastic disciples during the 1960s (Goldenberg 1971: 408; Lamberg 1972: 217–18), it is clear that the Cuban precedent caused a stark, genuine inflection in perceptions and dispositions among the left. Without the inspiration emanating from the Cuban precedent, • the unexpected rash of guerrilla uprisings that started immediately in 1959 and continued until Che Guevara's death in 1967 remains totally inexplicable (Wickham-Crowley 1992: 30–3; Wright 2001; Mainwaring and Pérez-Liñán 2013: 45, 60, 73, 218–24).

The issue is less clear-cut on the right side of the spectrum, however, where a mix of interests, attitudes, and principles prevailed. Hard-core reactionaries had long been hostile to liberal democracy and waited only for a pretext to push for its overthrow; for this purpose, they highlighted and exaggerated the threat of communism exacerbated by the Cuban Revolution. By contrast, many other elite sectors accepted or preferred liberal democracy as long as their fundamental interests and causes seemed secure. Among these moderate conservatives and centrists, genuine albeit distorted perceptions of the danger eradiating from revolutionary Cuba led to a decisive change in posture. The more intense their authentic fears became, the more they turned against democracy and sought protection in authoritarian rule (see, e.g., for the Chilean

---

[6] For an argument that Argentine elites during the violence-prone 1970s "constructed" an enemy on the left and promoted perceptions of "subversion," a term she tellingly puts in quotation marks, see Franco (2012). Similarly, Leacock (1990: 109, 132, 170) argues that domestic and foreign elites used the "red scare" for instrumental purposes in Brazil during the early 1960s.

right, Jarpa 2002: 113–16, 145–6, 162, 183–202; see also Mainwaring and Pérez-Liñán 2013: 91–2). Thus, for a good part of the elite, deterrent effects made a substantial difference and caused a transformation in their regime preferences.

Yet who exactly were these hard-liners, and who the soft-liners (cf. O'Donnell and Schmitter 1986: 15–17)? "Preference falsification" (Kuran 1995) forestalls the candid expression of actors' views and makes it difficult to ascertain this issue precisely. Under a democracy, for instance, reactionary generals may well hide their contempt for civilian authority and their goal to engineer an autocracy. But while the precise stance of specific actors can be difficult to identify, there is strong aggregate-level evidence that genuine concerns prevailed and prompted the conditional abandonment of democracy during the Latin American reverse wave. After all, the dictatorships installed in the 1960s and 1970s did not claim inherent legitimacy for their autocratic regime type. Instead, they claimed to serve as protective shields against the communist threat,[7] and depicted themselves as temporary expedients that, after a thorough cleanup, would restore some form of democracy. Once these dictatorships had crushed and eliminated their left-wing enemies, the soft-liners indeed promoted liberalization and thus initiated processes of regime change that culminated in the transfer of power to elected civilians (seminal: O'Donnell and Schmitter 1986: 15–17; see recently Mainwaring and Pérez-Liñán 2013: 119–23).

The lack of a fundamental rejection of liberal democracy and its restoration after the military had accomplished its supposed rescue mission suggest the predominance of genuine fears of communism, rather than firm autocratic values that used the red scare only for strategic purposes. Thus, while it can be difficult even for qualitative and historical analysis to identify the exact interests, ideas, and goals of specific actors, the aggregate picture offers greater clarity. Among much of the right side of the ideological spectrum, the Cuban Revolution and the widespread emulation efforts it inspired seem to have made a great difference for perceptions, dispositions, and actions.

In sum, qualitative analysis and process tracing of diffusion phenomena require thorough field and archival research, which investigators need to conduct on their own or access by drawing on the rich historical literature. After all, historians specialize in the careful reconstruction of past decisions and events and thus offer a wealth of materials that political scientists can use. Certainly, reliance on historical accounts can have theoretical biases if political scientists read mainly those historians whose approach they share; in that case, they use selective evidence and risk artificially "confirming" their

---

[7] A coin minted by the Pinochet regime in Chile shows an angel who is breaking shackles and features the inscriptions "liberty" and "11 September 1973," the date of the coup against the Marxist government of Salvador Allende (www.pinterest.com/pin/489273946995085224/, accessed April 26, 2018).

hypotheses (Lustick 1996). But this problem does not plague the present study: I have found no historian who applies a bounded rationality approach! Because reliance on cognitive psychology does not shape and skew historians' investigations, references to rash judgments or to disproportionate, excessive reactions to perceived threats constitute powerful evidence for the arguments advanced below. For instance, historians who are aghast at the fierce, unnecessarily harsh and widespread repression unleashed during and after the Latin American military coups provide evidentiary grist for my theoretical mill.

Historical studies also help with one of the hardest problems facing an explanation that draws on cognitive psychology, namely, how empirically to demonstrate the postulated deviations from full rationality. Proving these distortions is easy in psychology laboratories, where decision parameters are given in the experimental setup; consequently, researchers can incontrovertibly ascertain the distortions arising from inferential shortcuts and asymmetrical loss aversion (Kahneman and Tversky 2000; Kahneman 2011: part 4; Zamir 2014). In the real world, however, political actors' cost-benefit calculations and probability assessments are much harder to gauge, and impossible to pin down with precision. Therefore, conclusive proof of problematic inferences and skewed choices is elusive; scholars have to content themselves with plausibility claims. But inspired by innumerable experiments that have documented the prevalence of cognitive distortions in people's information processing and decision-making, a growing number of field studies has gathered a strong body of evidence that corroborates the bounds of human rationality (Hafner-Burton, Haggard, et al. 2017; Jones and Baumgartner 2005; McDermott 2004; Redlawsk and Lau 2013; Stein 2013, 2017).

The difficulty of determining the nature of political rationality is exacerbated by the interpretive flexibility of rational choice, which often retro-infers actors' preferences from their actions – and which in this way makes a vast range of actions look rational. Due to the lack of a firm reference point, it is inherently difficult to demonstrate deviations from conventional rationality. Interestingly, however, the investigations of historians help mitigate this problem by indicating how a theoretically unbiased, reasonable observer would assess and judge these situations in a careful and systematic way. Accordingly, when historians uniformly bemoan the exaggerated threat perceptions of conservatives and their resulting overreactions and "unnecessary" brutality, they establish the plausibility of the divergence from rational standards hypothesized by my bounded rationality approach. For this reason, I often complement my own efforts to demonstrate these deviations with the evaluations of other observers who are uninvolved in political science's debates about the nature of rationality, and who can therefore count as neutral sources on this complicated issue. The in-depth discussion of the rational-choice framework in Chapter 2 shows how I bring these sources to bear.

For all of these reasons, the present book draws on countless studies penned by historians, sociologists, and political scientists.[8] Reliance on the ample and thorough secondary literature is indispensable for making the analysis of a broad regional reverse wave practically feasible. In addition, I read large numbers of primary sources, especially testimonies, eyewitness accounts, and memoirs. Given the nature of this project, I deliberately consulted works by actors from across the ideological spectrum, ranging from left-wing *guerrilleros* (e.g., Guevara [1961] 2007; Béjar 1970; Sirkis [1979] 2008a; Marambio 2007) to right-wing generals, whose perceptions and assessments – however distorted they may be – ended up being particularly consequential (e.g., Lanusse 1977, 1994; Pinochet 1990; Merino 1998). Oral history transcripts also proved very rich and instructive (e.g., Julião 1982; Tello 1983; Muricy 1993; D'Araujo, Soares, and Castro 1994; Prieto Celi 1996; D'Araujo and Castro 1997; Jarpa 2002; Arancibia 2006; Reato 2012). The many confidential transcripts of interviews with leading politicians and generals that the Centro de Investigación y Documentación at the Universidad Finis Terrae in Santiago de Chile generously made available, but that I am not allowed to cite or quote, were very helpful as well.

Furthermore, I collected original documents about the Brazilian dictatorship of 1964–85 in the Centro de Pesquisa e Documentação de História Contemporânea do Brasil (CPDOC) of the Fundação Getúlio Vargas in Rio de Janeiro and read many interview transcripts in the John W. F. Dulles Papers Relating to Brazil, 1920–1979, at the University of Texas at Austin. Several of the interviews with leading politicians that I conducted for my last book (Weyland 2014), especially in 2007 in Chile, yet also in 2008 in Brazil and in 2009 in Peru, provided relevant information for the present study as well (e.g., interviews with Cáceres 2007; Fernández 2007; Jarpa 2007; Molina 2007; Morales-Bermúdez 2009; Palmeira 2008; Rodríguez 2007; Sirkis 2008). By processing this wide range of sources, I have sought to capture the diversity of actors' perceptions and assessments and to give the volume a solid and balanced empirical foundation.

CASE SELECTION

This study focuses on the most clear-cut, wide-ranging wave of democratic downfall and the imposition of reactionary dictatorship that swept across Latin America during the last century. The riptide of military coups displayed distinct temporal clustering. From 1963 to 1977, liberal democratic breakdowns and installations of autocracy clearly outnumbered transitions to

---

[8] Even biased sources can have a valuable aspect. For instance, James Whelan's (1989) in-depth but Pinochet-friendly account of the overthrow of Chile's democracy drew on close access to a host of leading right-wingers, and thus reflects their distorted perceptions and exaggerated threat assessments.

democracy, which had prevailed before (Mainwaring and Pérez-Liñán 2013: 74). Following Huntington's conceptualization of waves and reverse waves (1991: 17–21; see also Kurzman 1998), many scholars have highlighted this turnaround in the regional trend (Drake 2009: 199–200; Smith 2012: 27–9). Whereas the secular advance of democracy can make it difficult to identify and delimit waves of democratization, as the continuing discussion about Huntington's "first wave" suggests (Weyland 2014: 18; Gunitsky 2017: 62), authoritarian regressions are more visible because they run against longstanding historical tendencies; the inflection points at which these reverse waves surge and then dissipate stand out fairly clearly. Indeed, the rash of coups caused a stark trough in Latin America's overall movement toward democracy (Smith 2012: 27, 35; Mainwaring and Pérez-Liñán 2013: 3, 73).

As the concept of reverse wave implies, this investigation focuses on countries that at some point from the late 1950s to 1970s enjoyed liberal democracy (or at least came close to it); only in those nations can a democratic breakdown occur and can the imposition of autocracy bring a change in regime type. Consequently, the dictatorships of Central America and the Caribbean,[9] the longstanding authoritarian regime of Mexico, and the tyranny of General Stroessner in Paraguay are not directly relevant for this study. Effectively speaking, then, the book focuses on South America; and for reasons of source availability, it pays special attention to the major nations of the subcontinent.

This analytical focus, logically derived from the notion of reverse wave, means that the following investigation concentrates on countries with political regimes and states that differed significantly from Cuba's prerevolutionary polity. Consequently, the fears of falling to emulative revolutions were particularly far-fetched – and in need of theoretical explanation, which my bounded rationality approach can provide. The dictators of Central America, the Caribbean, and Paraguay, especially autocracies with pronounced Sultanistic features such as Haiti and Nicaragua, had good reason to fear following General Batista into the dustbin of history. By contrast, the (semi)democracies of South America, which governed fairly institutionalized states and well-organized, competent militaries, commanded much firmer bases of sustenance. That nevertheless, worries about the revolutionary spark ignited in Cuba were intense and that these concerns prompted the downfall of liberal democracy in so many countries, constitutes the puzzle that this book seeks to elucidate.

---

[9] Lehoucq 2012: 19–24. On the rare occasion that a Central American country experienced a spell of political liberalism, as Honduras did in the late 1950s and early 1960s, the downfall of this semidemocracy in 1963 resulted largely from threat perceptions exacerbated by the Cuban Revolution (Bowman 2002: 143–4, 171–4), conforming to the backlash argument of this book. Note also that in line with Chapter 7, the United States did not foment this military intervention, but "actively discouraged the coup" and threatened to "suspend economic aid" (Bowman 2002: 174).

While this volume examines the regional reverse wave as a whole, some countries receive special attention. This in-depth focus is crucial for assessing the operation and impact of cognitive mechanisms such as inferential heuristics and asymmetrical loss aversion, and for analyzing the way these microfoundational factors shape organizational action and political decision-making. Therefore, Chapter 6 investigates the emblematic cases of Brazil, Argentina, and Chile to examine how the fear of radical-left threats prompted military coups and the installation of bureaucratic-authoritarian regimes. Yet because the reverse wave did not engulf the whole region uniformly, Chapter 4 probes why democracy survived in Colombia and Venezuela. Moreover, I investigate the decision-making, actions, and impact of the great power that used to be depicted as a major instigator of the coup cascade, namely the United States. Based on recently declassified documents and major historical studies, Chapter 7 shows that the northern "hegemon," whose political leadership acted with distinctly bounded rationality as well, had only limited influence and involvement in the downfall of democracy across South America. Through this combination of breadth and depth, the empirical chapters seek to assess and substantiate the theoretical ideas of this book.

ORGANIZATION OF THE STUDY

This book consists of three parts, namely a theoretical discussion in Chapters 1 to 3; the in-depth examination of the Latin American coup wave in Chapters 4 to 7; and a comparative and concluding assessment in Chapters 8 and 9. After the present introduction, Chapter 2 assesses the main explanations for reverse waves and demonstrates their limitations and problems. Chapter 3 then presents the theoretical approach of the present study in a systematic fashion by embedding cognitive-psychological microfoundations, with a special emphasis on asymmetrical loss aversion, in macro-organizational structures. This bounded rationality theory explains how reactionary counterdiffusion advanced in two stages. First, isomorphic attempts to imitate the Cuban Revolution through innumerable guerrilla struggles prompted determined, often brutal repression. Yet the strategic defeat of the rebels showed that established regimes were capable of containing the danger. As a result, conservatives did not see the need for overthrowing democracy. Second, however, Castro's success inspired a broader process of radicalization that swept up a wide range of leftist and populist forces. This groundswell of pressures for a profound transformation of the sociopolitical order seemed to pose more serious threats to status quo sectors, and therefore prompted the installation of anticommunist autocracies across the region.

Part 2 then analyzes in depth how this two-step backlash to the Cuban Revolution unfolded and how it led to the proliferation of military rule in Latin America. Chapter 4 examines the region-wide impact of Castro's striking precedent, the riptide of guerrilla movements it spurred, and their almost uniform suppression. The chapter also analyzes the preemptive reform efforts undertaken under the Alliance for Progress, with which a wide range of Latin American governments sought to block the feared spread of communism. While this containment strategy often did not achieve its goals, it did help Colombia and Venezuela preserve democracy, as the end of this chapter argues.

Chapter 5 first highlights the massive radicalization of politics that the Cuban Revolution helped inspire in Latin America during the 1960s. Discussion then turns to the reactionary backlash that was driven by the fears of status quo defenders and that fueled the regional reverse wave. Chapter 6 focuses on the resulting imposition of authoritarian rule in Brazil, Argentina, and Chile. Given the historical significance of these cases and the need to reconstruct complex demonstration and deterrent effects, these case studies go into some depth.

Chapter 7 probes additional external influences on the autocratic reverse wave, discussing first the inspiration and support provided by Brazil's new model of developmentalist, institutionalized authoritarianism. Thereafter, I investigate the involvement and impact of the United States, which encouraged and condoned the installation of dictatorships. But a wealth of documents and historical studies show that domestic forces took the initiative and played the main role in these reactionary moves. While complicit, the northern superpower does not hold primary responsibility for the downfall of liberal democracy in so many Latin American countries.

After Part 2 substantiated the main arguments of this study through wide-ranging narrative analyses, the concluding part first offers comparative perspectives. Chapter 8 analyzes reactionary waves across three centuries. It starts with the backlash against the French Revolution of 1789 and the revolutions of 1848, moves to the autocratic responses to the Iranian Revolution of 1978–79, and ends with the reaction to the postcommunist "color revolutions" of the early 2000s. Finally, Chapter 9 summarizes the book's central findings, draws out their broader theoretical implications, and offers reflections about the topic of historical progress. The book concludes with some thoughts about the current prospects of liberal democracy, which again seems to face risks of backsliding and regression.

2

The Difficulty of Accounting for Reverse Waves

What explains the reverse wave of reactionary autocracy in Latin America? The present chapter shows that a variety of established approaches do not provide fully satisfactory explanations. First, domestic structural and institutional factors create vulnerabilities and undermine political liberalism and democracy, but an internally focused approach cannot account for the clustering of autocratic installation during the 1960s and 1970s; powerful external influences, especially demonstration and deterrent effects, shaped these regime changes, as my research shows. Second, common-cause arguments do in principle predict temporal clustering, but they have difficulty explaining this reactionary wave in a consistent fashion. No severe economic shock rocked the subcontinent during the early 1960s, when the proliferation of authoritarianism gathered steam; instead, such a painful challenge, namely the regional debt crisis, erupted in the early 1980s – and contributed to the (re-) establishment of democracy!

Theory assessment therefore focuses on diffusion approaches. But frameworks that invoke the coercive imposition of autocracy by great powers, the normative appeal of reactionary rule, and rational learning from failures of democracy and the success of dictators cannot convincingly explain the massive spread of authoritarianism. The present chapter substantiates these claims with a good deal of evidence.

Chapter 3 therefore develops a theory that rests on mechanisms of bounded rationality and embeds them in an organizational framework. By highlighting the impact of asymmetrical loss aversion, my argument explains how the revolutionary challenge emanating from Cuba prompted a reactionary backlash which provided a strong impulse for the proliferation of autocratic rule. In a nutshell, the reverse wave constituted a process of right-wing counterdiffusion, driven by the urge to forestall left-wing efforts at the diffusion of radical change. As Chapters 4 through 6 then document, this interactive dynamic lies at the core of democratic regression in Latin America during the 1960s and 1970s.

A VARIETY OF THEORETICAL ARGUMENTS

Can extant theories convincingly account for the spread of reactionary rule during the Latin American coup wave? Scholars have proposed a variety of explanations, which, depending on their analytical scope and approach, can be classified into three groupings. First, structural and institutional arguments emphasize domestic variables that lead to regime changes in a group of countries. According to this framework, the imposition of autocracy resulted from some combination of developmental problems or requirements and of institutional vulnerabilities. Underlying material factors and historical legacies made nations susceptible to reactionary rule.

Second, common-cause explanations point to a single external impulse that pushed a broad range of countries directly toward autocracy. In this view, a dramatic challenge, such as a global or regional economic crisis, undermined existing regimes and prompted the installation of dictatorships in a number of polities – independently of developments in other nations.

Third, diffusion arguments conceive of the reverse wave as a cluster of interconnected phenomena. According to this approach, a precedent in one country triggers contagion, demonstration effects, or deterrent impulses that snowball and push more and more other countries toward regime change as well. Thus, events and developments in various nations affect each other because political actors take inspiration or engage in learning across borders. Depending on the specific nature of these cross-national connections and influences, diffusion arguments come in several versions, which embody different theoretical paradigms. The present chapter examines these three groups of approaches, including the set of diffusion theories, in turn.

STRUCTURAL AND INSTITUTIONAL EXPLANATIONS

Theories that emphasize the material or historical-institutional foundations of politics highlight domestic challenges or vulnerabilities that contribute to regime change. To have analytical bite, these hypotheses invoke fairly specific factors and developments, for instance, a certain stage in industrialization, a constellation of class forces, a mismatch between nation and state, or an entrenched institutional defect, such as the alleged "perils of presidentialism" (Linz 1990; Linz and Valenzuela 1994). These risk factors certainly created weaknesses here and problems there, contributing to the downfall of democracy, which was rather frequent in Latin America during the first three quarters of the twentieth century (Drake 2009; Smith 2012).

But the very specificity of structural and institutional arguments makes it difficult to account for the wide-ranging, wave-like spread of authoritarian rule during the 1960s and 1970s. After all, autocrats took power not only in backward countries such as Bolivia, but also in modern, more developed nations such as Argentina; not only in countries at more advanced stages of import-substitution industrialization such as Brazil, but also in countries with less developed economies such as Ecuador; not only in ethnically heterogeneous countries such as Peru, but also in homogeneous nations such as Uruguay. And while the Latin American reverse wave toppled presidential systems, the even more wide-ranging and profound spread of authoritarianism and fascism during the interwar years affected many parliamentary systems as well, in Central and Eastern Europe (e.g., Metcalf 1997: 317–18).[1] Because nations with diverse internal characteristics fell under reactionary rule, domestic structural variables, institutional parameters, and historical legacies do not offer sufficient explanations for the broad sweep of autocratic reversal.

The most influential structuralist explanation of reactionary rule in Latin America, for instance, Guillermo O'Donnell's (1979) theory about bureaucratic authoritarianism, cannot explain the imposition of dictatorship across a variety of countries. O'Donnell attributed authoritarian reversals to the socioeconomic problems erupting during the "deepening" of import-substitution industrialization. But democracy also broke down at significantly lower levels of economic development in Bolivia, Ecuador, and Peru. Moreover, O'Donnell's economic-structuralist claims that the "requirements" of industrial development drove the installation of autocracy drew devastating empirical and theoretical criticism (Collier 1979). The present study agrees, however, with O'Donnell's (1978) more general argument that severe threat perceptions prompted the imposition of dictatorship. I defend this fundamental insight against criticism (Remmer and Merkx 1982) by providing a new, more solid microfoundation.[2]

The major historical-institutional account of Latin American regime developments, David and Ruth Colliers' (1991) comprehensive analysis of countries' distinct trajectories, also fails to capture the commonality of dictatorship across the region. By highlighting the different paths that eight major nations followed, this thorough, massive investigation makes it difficult to explain why a similar type of autocracy emerged across these diverse trajectories around the same time. Moreover, why did some countries that had long followed the same path, such as Colombia and Uruguay, end up with strikingly different regime outcomes? After all, Colombia's problem-ridden democracy survived, whereas the seemingly more consolidated regime in the "Switzerland of South America" collapsed and gave way to a harsh autocracy.

As regards institutionalist arguments, the main risk factors highlighted in this ample literature concern the rigidity of presidentialist systems of government, the power dispersal they promote, and the resulting tendency toward gridlock

---

[1] I owe this point to a conversation with Lee Metcalf many years ago.

[2] For an important study that demonstrates the causal connection between threat and authoritarianism in very general terms, see Stenner (2005). Stein (2013) offers an interesting discussion of threat perceptions and their impact on international affairs.

and stalemate,[3] which discontented sectors then try to break through authoritarian imposition. But the initially stark warnings about these dangers (Linz 1990; Linz and Valenzuela 1994) soon dissolved into more differentiated assessments that stressed conditioning factors, such as the structure of the party system.[4] In fact, empirical investigations did not find any systematic association between presidentialism and democratic breakdown.[5]

As regards Latin America in the 1960s and 1970s, while many presidential systems collapsed, one of the most immobile exemplars, the consociational regime of the National Front in Colombia (1958–74), survived, and that despite the persistent festering of various guerrilla challenges. Last but not least, the institutionalist argument can certainly not explain why short-term interruptions of presidential democracy, which had long been common in Latin America, were after the Cuban Revolution replaced by coups that sought to institutionalize autocracies with long-term development goals. In other words, why did authoritarian reversals become more profound and ambitious, causing a deep, lasting trough in the region's regime development?

In sum, structural and institutional theories point to factors that are too specific to account for the broad sweep of autocracy's spread. While they usefully highlight various vulnerabilities that afflicted Latin American democracies, their domestic focus neglects international factors, which are crucial for understanding the wave-like nature of the proliferation of dictatorship. Attention therefore turns to common-cause arguments and, thereafter, to diffusion theories.

COMMON-CAUSE ARGUMENTS

The international factors that seem crucial for explaining the Latin American wave of autocracy can operate in different ways. One approach emphasizes an external impulse or shock that directly undermines democracy in a wide range of countries (cf. Houle, Kayser, and Xiang 2016). But such theories, which invoke a "single cause" to explain a riptide (Huntington 1991: 31–2), are not very persuasive. The impulse that this line of reasoning most commonly invokes

---

[3] In an interview with this author, Arriagada (2007) highlighted the contribution that "presidentialism with a double minority" made to the downfall of Salvador Allende in Chile, who had won the presidency with little more than 36 percent of the vote and whose support coalition did not command a majority in Congress either. But of course, the main reason and "moving cause" for the breakdown was Allende's decision to push for a determined transition to socialism despite this weak political starting position, that is, the radicalization highlighted in Chapter 5.

[4] Mainwaring 1993; Mainwaring and Shugart 1997. For a case study of the Brazilian coup of 1964 that highlights party system fragmentation and polarized pluralism in a presidential system of government, see Santos (1986).

[5] See, e.g., the in-depth case study by McClintock (1994: 367–87) and the book edited by Mainwaring and Shugart (1997); and the statistical analyses by Power and Gasiorowski (1997) and Cheibub (2007).

is an international economic crisis, which simultaneously shakes a multitude of nations and thus prompts regime change across the board.

This kind of explanation is especially prominent in accounts of the reverse wave of the interwar years. Scholars have highlighted the devastating impact of the Great Depression of 1929, which, for instance, allowed Adolf Hitler to re-emerge from virtual obscurity and contributed greatly to the eventual takeover (*Machtergreifung*) of National Socialism in Germany (discussion in Mann 2004: 56–8). But a broader view suggests that this economic shock was not the root cause for the riptide of democratic breakdown that swept across Europe during the 1920s and 1930s. Instead, the rise of Italian fascism in 1922 and a number of authoritarian coups, for instance in Spain in 1923, Lithuania, Poland, and Portugal in 1926, and Yugoslavia in 1929, preceded the eruption of this economic catastrophe. Thus, the common-cause argument cannot really explain the autocratic cascade for which it is often invoked.

This line of reasoning is even less persuasive for elucidating the Latin American reverse wave. The rash of coups in the 1960s and 1970s occurred in the absence of a region-wide economic crisis. There simply was no wide-ranging bout of hyperinflation or mass unemployment afflicting the subcontinent at that time. Moreover, where specific countries did suffer from serious economic difficulties, such as Salvador Allende's Chile with its exploding inflation and spiraling scarcities (Sigmund 1977: 172–7, 195–6, 228–9, 234–6), these problems were largely the product of political conflict, especially ideologically driven polarization, and cannot be regarded as an "independent variable." Thus, economic crisis was not the root cause of authoritarianism's spread.

In fact, the gravest economic challenge facing the whole region during the second half of the twentieth century, the debt crisis erupting in 1982, coincided with the subsequent wave of redemocratization. Contrary to widespread fears, this dramatic problem, which eventually plunged several countries into hyperinflation, did not prompt a relapse to authoritarian rule. This striking nonevent casts further doubt on the causal impact of economic crises and their contributions to the rise of autocracy. For all of these reasons, common-cause arguments cannot offer convincing explanations for the spread of reactionary rule during the 1960s and 1970s in Latin America.

Interestingly, the Cuban Revolution, which this book highlights as the root cause of the autocratic reverse wave, did not operate in the way of a common cause either; instead, this political challenge prompted demonstration and deterrent effects that set in motion processes of counterdiffusion. After all, Castro's success did not directly provoke a reflex of autocratic imposition across the board, as a common cause would do. Dictatorship did not sweep through Latin America like a tsunami in the early 1960s – despite the Cuban communists' incessant efforts to export revolution throughout the region (Wright 2001; Brown 2017). Instead of embarking on a panicked, headlong flight into the strong arms of autocratic rulers, many liberal democracies first tried out a more thoughtful and sophisticated strategy. They combined the suppression of violent leftist uprisings with preemptive reforms, supported by the United States via the Alliance for Progress. Only after these differentiated responses did not seem to eliminate the perceived threat of communism, and after left-wing radicalization continued to advance in many countries, did right-wing forces sooner or later combat the feared diffusion of revolution with the counterdiffusion of dictatorial imposition.

The complex processes through which the Cuban Revolution exerted its contradictory repercussions diverged from the straightforward logic of common-cause arguments. Instead of one powerful impulse producing a set of direct effects, it stimulated interacting processes of diffusion and counterdiffusion. Because Castro's success provided inspiration for some yet instilled fear in others, and because different political forces tried out various political strategies and tactics, the impact of this striking revolutionary precedent was mediated by intersecting demonstration and deterrent effects. Attention therefore turns to theories of diffusion, which highlight these kinds of mechanisms.

DIFFUSION THEORIES

Considering the limitations plaguing the preceding approaches, can diffusion arguments provide a more persuasive account of Latin America's autocratic reverse wave? These theories see temporal and geographic clusters of regime change as interrelated events and developments. Various mechanisms of contagion, inspiration, or learning can create connections among the installation of dictatorship in different countries. Because the diffusion literature has not examined the spread of reactionary autocracy specifically, this section derives potential explanations from the broader approaches to diffusion studies.[6] The focus on political, not economic innovations makes classification schemes that give a prominent place to economic competition (Simmons, Dobbin, and Garrett 2008: 9–40) less useful. A typology centered on politics seems more promising. This study therefore distinguishes external pressure, normative appeal, rational learning, and cognitive inferences (Weyland 2005). This classification of the literature is organized around three sequential research questions.

First, given that there is a global hierarchy of countries, is diffusion primarily a vertical phenomenon, or do horizontal processes prevail? That is, does the spread of innovations result from a powerful third party using clout or coercion to push a regime change on weaker, subordinate countries? Or do the adopting countries have considerable latitude to make their own emulation decisions? Second, to the extent that diffusion reflects domestic initiative, is it driven mainly by normative or symbolic concerns, or by interest calculations?

---

[6] An exception is Ambrosio (2010), who takes inspiration in the theoretical approaches discussed in the present section.

Do other-regarding motives such as modern principles and advanced values play a crucial role, or are self-regarding goals and drives decisive? In theoretical terms, is constructivism or some form of rationalism more persuasive? Third, to the extent that interests matter, do actors pursue these self-regarding goals in a careful, systematic, fully rational fashion, or do they apply cognitive shortcuts and other mechanisms of bounded rationality which facilitate decision making, but at the risk of distortions and biases? Thus, do they draw careful lessons from foreign experiences and act on these insights in prudent ways? Or do they jump to conclusions about the replicability of precedents or panic about the threat emanating from them – and then act in ill-considered, precipitous ways?

External Promotion and Imposition

As regards the issue of vertical versus horizontal impetus, several scholars argue that great powers commonly impose their political regime preferences on countries in their sphere of influence (Owen 2010; Boix 2011; Narizny 2012; Gunitsky 2014, 2017). According to this approach, transformations in the international constellation of power, especially hegemonic transitions, drive the spread or retreat of specific regime types. If prodemocratic nations are ascendant, political liberalism and democracy advance in a region or in the world as a whole; by contrast, if countries with autocratic regimes gain international power, democracy recedes (Huntington 1982: 25–35; Gunitsky 2017).

The historical record shows, however, that forceful promotion by great powers was not the main driver of the dictatorial wave of the 1960s and 1970s. Despite the predominant clout of the United States in the western hemisphere, Latin American military coups and the establishment of longer-lasting authoritarian regimes did not result from hegemonic imposition. While Washington certainly facilitated and supported the overthrow of left-wing governments, especially in Brazil in 1964 and Chile in 1973, domestic sectors took the main initiative even in these cases (Brands 2010; Brown 2017).

After all, Latin American elites, middle classes, and broader sectors of the population had their own strong concerns about the dangers of communism and needed no encouragement from the United States to combat left-wing radicalization. In spearheading coups, the Brazilian and Chilean militaries, for instance, sought to protect their institutional interests and preserve internal order; conservative politicians and clerics wanted to safeguard their interests and values; business and landowners defended their property and political influence; and many citizens, even from the working class and especially the peasantry, yearned for stability. Internal decisions, not great power pressure led to the installation of authoritarian rule in those two emblematic cases, as Chapters 6 and 7 demonstrate below.[7]

---

[7] This is true even in the much-discussed Chilean case (see assessments ranging from Valenzuela 1978 to Harmer 2011 and Shiraz 2011).

Domestic political forces clearly held the primary responsibility in many other cases as well, such as the Argentine coups of 1966 and 1976, which happened without US involvement. The crucial role of autonomous decision making is especially clear in the overthrow of Peruvian democracy by a group of left-leaning, nationalistic generals in 1968, who immediately proceeded to nationalize a major US company. Only in an exceptionally weak and underdeveloped country was the United States – and Brazil! – more directly involved, facilitating the eviction of a military socialist in Bolivia in 1971 and supporting his replacement by an anticommunist dictator (Malloy and Gamarra 1988: 63–4, 68, 80). In sum, the wave-like spread of authoritarian rule in Latin America did not result from imposition by a great power, as Chapter 7 documents with ample evidence below.

In particular, the United States did not advocate the institution of harsh dictatorships that intended to transform their countries' socioeconomic development profoundly and therefore sought a lengthy stay in power. Instead, soon after military takeovers, Washington's envoys called for redemocratization and encouraged the convocation of elections (see, e.g., *FRUS 1964–1968*: 317–22, 489–90, 493–4). Moreover, they complained about human rights violations and tried to reassert the rule of law (*FRUS 1964–1968*: 317–22, 459–60, 489–90, 493–4; Leacock 1990: 215–17, 221–30, 236). It came as a surprise to them that hardline sectors pursued ambitious plans to monopolize power long enough to reshape their countries thoroughly and thus forever forestall the resurgence of left-wing radicalism, in part via large-scale repression. Strikingly, the supposed "hegemon" proved unable to block this unexpected turn of events, which caused so much of the shocking regression during the Latin American reverse wave. While the United States acquiesced and ended up backing these durable dictatorships as the lesser evil, compared to the perceived threat of communism, the northern superpower had clearly preferred a more moderate, transitory form of authoritarian rule.

In sum, great power influence was not the driving cause behind the proliferation of autocracy in Latin America. While putting pressure on left-wing governments and helping to create propitious conditions for their overthrow, the United States did not play a major role in the organization and execution of the rash of coups. The hemispheric giant held even less responsibility for the brutal nature and the unusual duration of the authoritarian regimes that emerged from these coups. Great power arguments are not very convincing.

Moreover, the reverse wave of the 1960s and 1970s did not conform to theories about international hegemonic transitions. The Cuban Revolution and the subsequent intrusion of the Soviet Union in the western hemisphere made a dent in US influence, but no country in the whole region followed Castro's path into communism; even the Nicaraguan Revolution, which occurred much later in 1979, did not veer nearly as far to the radical, totalitarian left. Furthermore, by any economic, political, or military measure, US clout over most of Latin America remained strong. In fact, the challenge emanating from the Castro regime induced the northern giant to exert its influence more actively than before. It is noteworthy that this concerted effort started with President Kennedy's Alliance for Progress, which sought to protect and promote reformist, liberal democracy. Thus, the United States first attempted to spread its own regime type with greater determination and voluminous resources. Yet in many Latin American countries, this ambitious project did not come to fruition and sooner or later failed to achieve its progressive goals. These disappointing results suggest that international power constellations do not directly and reliably shape political regimes in weaker, subordinate countries. Liberal democratic "hegemons," in particular, face limitations in exerting their own clout.

In conclusion, vertical influence played some role in the Latin American reverse wave. After all, the United States promoted the region-wide fight against Cuban communism and offered encouragement and support for the installation of right-wing dictatorships. But US influence did not provide the principal impetus for the rash of coups, and especially the rise of longer-lasting authoritarian regimes. The proliferation of reactionary autocracy resulted mainly from domestic initiatives, which reflected horizontal processes of diffusion and counterdiffusion.

Normative Appeal

As vertical pressures were not decisive, what drove the horizontal diffusion of right-wing regimes? Did domestic decision makers mainly respond to normative appeal or did they pursue their political interests? In other words, does constructivism or some form of rationalism offer a more persuasive account of the proliferation of autocracy?

As mentioned in the introduction, predominant versions of constructivism cannot account for reactionary waves. The spread of regressive regime types flies in the face of their optimistic premises (cf. Risse, Ropp, and Sikkink 1999; Finnemore and Sikkink 2001: 403–4). History can move in the opposite direction from the progress that conventional constructivism expects. With the spread of authoritarianism in Latin America, political liberty, human rights, and personal dignity suffered enormous damage. After the modern principles and norms on which democracy rests had advanced in preceding years, the imposition of right-wing autocracy brought a whole series of unexpected setbacks that ran counter to constructivist assumptions. The overthrow of the apparently consolidated democracies of Chile and Uruguay, where sophisticated public spheres and vibrant civil societies had flourished, was especially shocking.

As the universal progressivism that underlies conventional constructivism is problematic, perhaps a historicist version of normative appeal arguments can offer a convincing account of the pronounced political retrogression that occurred during the 1960s and 1970s in Latin America? Progress may lie in the eye of the beholder; the prevailing norms and principles may change, depending on the historical era (Weber 1976: 446). The *Zeitgeist* can shift; sometimes it advances toward political liberalism and democracy, but at other times it runs in the opposite direction.

In this vein, the late nineteenth century saw a profound, comprehensive turn to cultural pessimism, which came to displace the belief in rationality and progress that had reigned in earlier decades (Burrow 2000). An intellectual climate spread that nostalgically extolled traditional "life" rather than efficient, calculating modernity; that valued emotion, myth, and sheer willpower over reason; and that depicted the world as ruled by conflict and struggle, rather than deliberation, negotiation, and compromise. The strong would carry the day!

This antiliberal *Zeitgeist* took root especially in Europe and influenced the reverse wave of the interwar years. Yet it inspired right-wing circles in Latin America as well, particularly in Argentina, where the intellectual climate during the 1920s turned distinctly nationalist and traditionalist, if not reactionary (Deutsch 1999; Spektorowski 2003). While the global defeat of fascism and the victory of the United States in World War II brought a resurgence of liberal democratic ideas from the mid-1940s onward, some of the ultraconservative undercurrents persisted and still had echoes during the 1960s and 1970s (Finchelstein 2014). Political and military hardliners embraced these reactionary types of *Weltanschauung*, which condemned liberal democracy as feckless, decadent, and doomed. These voices called for much stronger forms of authority and sought to preserve deference to elites while keeping popular demand making and political participation under control.

These authoritarian views and values lacked the magnetic appeal that fascism had exuded during the interwar years, however. Rather than promoting an exciting mission of existential redemption and political salvation, they focused on preserving traditional arrangements. Consequently, this ultraconservative *Weltanschauung* had limited motivating force and did not win many new adherents. Even among right-wingers, more moderate, cautiously liberal currents often prevailed, which sought to advance their interests and defend their causes against the perceived threat of communism, but which did not want to spearhead a crusade on behalf of the traditional values enshrined in "Western, Christian civilization."[8]

Due to the limited appeal of hard-right ideas, the military regimes of the 1960s and 1970s did not claim inherent legitimacy for authoritarianism as a permanent alternative to democracy (O'Donnell and Schmitter 1986: 15–17). Instead, they merely announced a more or less profound revamping

---

[8] These disagreements were especially pronounced in Argentina, even inside the military, giving rise to armed confrontations among different currents (Potash 1980: 378–9; Potash 1996: 19–28, 34–8, 51–61).

of economy, society, and polity, after which they would restore a stronger form of democracy, immune to the virus of communism (Rouquié 1987: 345–50). Certainly, this rhetoric covered up some not-very-liberal goals; for a number of conservatives, "strong democracy" was probably a euphemism for what contemporary political science classifies as competitive authoritarianism. But the perceived need to use such deceptive rhetoric and the lack of a distinctive legitimacy claim betray the striking weakness of the normative foundation underlying Latin America's military regimes. Whereas interwar autocrats proudly adopted the title of dictator (see, e.g., Ferro 1939: 32, 41, 99, 134, 157, 176–7), the dictatorships of the 1960s and 1970s angrily rejected this label;[9] instead, they depicted themselves as the founding fathers of a future democracy.

For these reasons, even the relativistic, historicist version of normative appeal arguments cannot convincingly account for the reverse wave sweeping across the southern subcontinent. During the 1960s and 1970s, there simply was no *Zeitgeist* strong enough to bring about the regional turn to authoritarian rule. The intellectual influence of the liberal United States in the western hemisphere posed an additional obstacle to the flourishing of hard-right, militantly antidemocratic ideas. Because the military coup makers depended on support from the northern powerhouse, they certainly did not publicly promote such a provocative discourse to motivate the institution of longer-lasting autocracies. Instead, their interests in US assistance carried the day, overriding the reactionary ideas that inspired hardline factions. Calculations of costs and benefits won out over right-wing values.

The limited effect that ideas and norms exert on political regime developments is also evident in the subsequent time period, after the authoritarian riptide in Latin America crested. Interestingly, in the Western world the *Zeitgeist* darkened in the 1970s, when longstanding expectations of infinite progress ran afoul of economic crises, governability problems, and the ecological "limits to growth" (Meadows, Meadows et al. 1972). Yet although liberal democracies suffered from "malaise," in Jimmy Carter's memorable term, and although prominent scholars questioned their governability, if not sustainability (Crozier, Huntington, and Watanuki 1975), it was precisely at that time that the "third wave" of democratization started to advance in Latin America and then progress across the globe.

In sum, ideas and norms matter because they create a substrate of interpretive schemata and predispositions that can shape the appealing and legitimate options considered by actors. But because these orientations are fairly broad and general, they exert a loose type of influence that does not foreordain actual political decisions. Political agency and pragmatic calculations play a more important role. While ideas matter, interests seem to matter much more.

---

[9] Accordingly, Gaspari (2002), who drew on unprecedented access to regime leaders in researching his massive, multivolume analysis, calls the Brazilian regime after the 1964 coup "the bashful/ ashamed dictatorship."

Rational Learning

The predominance of self-regarding motives and utilitarian calculations raises the third question mentioned above: when pursuing their political interests, did decision makers mainly follow the postulates of standard rationality, or did they resort to the shortcuts and skewed choice mechanisms of bounded rationality? This debate, which has faded in much of political science as many erstwhile advocates of rational choice have recognized humans' cognitive limitations (e.g., Levi 2009: 117–18, 127, 130), has maintained its relevance in the study of regime change because the bold rationalist model of Acemoglu and Robinson (2005; similar Boix 2003) has drawn enormous attention and scholarly interest. This seminal contribution forcefully raises the question whether the major political actors engage in systematic information processing and careful, balanced cost-benefit calculations. As a result, scholars have conducted a new round of investigations about politically relevant perceptions and misperceptions (see recently Gimpelson and Treisman 2015).

In this continuing debate about the nature of political rationality, my research suggests a clear answer: while learning from the success of outstanding precedents was crucial for the spread of reactionary regimes, this learning did not proceed in conventionally rational ways. As regards the assessment of reactionary regime models, observers in other countries were too easily impressed with the political stability and "economic miracle" engineered by Brazil's military regime after 1964 (e.g., Silveira 2016). Lesson drawing from this precedent did not follow the standards of conventional rationality.

Moreover, the main impetus for the diffusion of right-wing regimes was not the positive lessons suggested by precedents such as Brazil's developmentalist dictatorship, but an overriding defensive goal, namely to forestall the spread of leftist extremism (see recently Brown 2017). For years after the Cuban Revolution, most elites and many common citizens lived in fear of radical subversion; for that reason, sooner or later they sought protection in the strong arms of reactionary autocrats, as Chapters 5 and 6 show below. The crucial role of this deterrent impulse becomes obvious in "unlikely cases" such as pre-coup Brazil, where communism commanded limited support and where left-wing and populist sectors were fragmented and divided. But nevertheless, conservative politicians, generals, businesspeople, clergymen, and ample middle sectors were afraid of revolution (Brasil 1964; Pinto 1964; Dulles 1978; D'Araujo, Soares, and Castro 1994; Ferreira and Gomes 2014).

The question of rationality therefore hinges largely on the realism of these threat perceptions. Did decision makers assess the danger posed by communism in a systematic and unbiased fashion, or did they significantly overrate the menace by relying on information processing shortcuts that caused distortions and biases? The historical evidence suggests a clear overestimation of the radical-left peril and a pronounced overreaction to this threat. Since Castro's revolutionaries had grabbed power with surprising ease, rightist and centrist sectors rashly concluded that their own governments were also fragile and precarious and that radical stirrings had good chances of success. Panicked, they went to great lengths to battle this threat. In reality, however, the chances of a revolutionary wildfire were low, as the consistent failure of Cuba-inspired and Cuba-supported guerrilla struggles during the 1960s shows. Right-wing fears and the defensive measures they prompted were clearly disproportionate, sometimes bordering on paranoia.

The professional expertise of scholars who are uninvolved in political science's ongoing debates about the nature of rationality corroborates these claims about actors' systematic deviations from rational cost-benefit calculations. Based on their painstaking, thorough research, historians commonly bemoan the exaggerated nature of conservatives' threat perceptions. These investigators marvel that ample political sectors were gripped by fear, overreacted, and employed excessive brutality in responding to left-wing challenges. For instance, analyzing the run-up to the 1964 coup in Brazil, Thomas Skidmore (1967: 282–3) judges that conservatives' tendency "to refer to 'Communist' infiltration in order to explain the new life on the left was seriously misleading." Similarly, Hal Brands (2010: 27) highlights how "the radicalization of the Cuban revolution and the outbreak of insurgencies across Latin America [were] causing near-panic in official circles" and fueling baseless warnings about "communist agents" even in the firm dictatorship of Paraguay. And Jonathan Brown (2017: 333) reports that in the fight against sporadic and weak guerrilla movements in Peru, "the indigenous *campesinos* suffered disproportionate losses – eight thousand killed," partly from the army's use of napalm against the civilian population!

In general terms, threat is a product of cost and probability of occurrence. While communism would have imposed severe losses on "bourgeois" groupings, middle sectors, and status-quo defenders in general, the likelihood of a revolution was in fact low. As world-historical experience and a long line of scholarship shows, major revolutions are rare (Skocpol 1979; Goldstone 1991; Katz 1997; Goodwin 2001; Foran 2005; Wickham-Crowley 1992). Even the epic Russian Revolution, which drew enormous attention across the globe, did not set in motion a riptide of socialist transformations. While the takeover of Lenin's Bolshevists demonstrated the feasibility of a communist overhaul, it did not inspire a spate of emulative revolutions, but instead provoked a powerful backlash that brought the most massive wave of reactionary autocracy in modern history, as my next book project tries to show.

Similarly, after the Cuban Revolution, radicals and communists rarely had a real chance to take control of other states. Clearheaded assessments of the power constellation would have suggested that despite their activist stirrings and grandiloquent calls for revolution, left-wing extremists usually commanded little mass support. Moreover, radical challengers lacked the capacity to defeat the forces of organized coercion, especially the military. Whereas the old regime in Cuba had been weakened by Sultanistic tendencies (Domínguez 1998) and the dictator's military had therefore crumbled under a comparatively weak assault (Wickham-Crowley 1992: 158, 166–73, 191), the liberal or democratic regimes in South America commanded fairly institutionalized states with well-organized, disciplined armed forces that could easily withstand radical challenges and guerrilla uprisings. Due to the resilience of the established order, the political opportunity structure was unpropitious for revolution, as the uniform failure of guerrilla movements all over Latin America demonstrated. Weak to begin with, left-wing extremists were easily defeated.

Yet even this quick failure of radical adventurism did not end up putting conservative sectors at ease, which continued to overestimate communists' ability to grab power. The asymmetry of their inferences and the stickiness of their fears is striking. Revolutionaries' one "success" in Cuba sent shivers down their spine; by contrast, the defeat of emulative rebellions across the region did little to calm their nerves. Thus, overlearning from the single failure of status-quo defenders on the Caribbean island was quick and powerful, whereas learning from the defensive prowess of established regimes in so many other countries took years to have an equivalent impact. These distortions in information processing are difficult for conventional rationalism to explain.

Moreover, as right-wing and even centrist sectors sought protection under autocratic rule, they sacrificed their own liberty. The dictatorial concentration of power posed considerable risks, even to elite groupings such as business and conservative politicians. Who can control tyrants and their repressive agents and prevent them from abusing their unlimited might (cf. Svolik 2012: chap. 5)? Autocrats may even turn against their erstwhile supporters. Indeed, Latin American military regimes experienced numerous internal coups and purges, and sometimes imposed costly reforms on defenseless elites (Albertus 2015). The abolition of liberal safeguards exposes all sectors to substantial danger. The willingness to accept these risks arose from the intense fear of communism, which was exaggerated given the improbability of revolution. Choosing a lesser evil is not very rational when the greater evil is so unlikely to occur.

To account for the widespread overestimation of the far-left menace, standard rational choice would suspect that right-wing forces deliberately exaggerated the leftist danger to justify their own power grab. But historical evidence suggests that these expressions of fear were mainly sincere, rather than constituting manipulative efforts to use the scarecrow of Communism for elite self-interests. While there certainly was some strategic usage of anticommunism (see, e.g., Leacock 1990: 109, 132, 170), ample testimony shows that many conservatives and centrists really believed in the peril posed by the radical left; these sources include private documents, the best available evidence for actors' authentic viewpoints.

In this vein, Marshal Humberto Castello Branco, a leading Brazilian general and later post-coup president, in the early 1960s marked up books in his private library with notes that revealed his concerns about communism (Dulles 1978: 253–4), a fundamental thread in his whole thinking (Dulles 1978: 265–6,

270–2, 313–14, 323). Similarly, every single one of the fourteen generals asked decades later about the reasons for the 1964 coup emphasized fears of communism.[10] The confidential discussions among Chile's military leaders that culminated in the overthrow of democracy in 1973 also reveal the strength of genuine fears about left-wing subversion and communist threat (Merino 1998: 204–38; González 2000: 202–7, 221–3, 304–10), which civilian right-wingers shared (Jarpa 2002: 115, 135, 143, 183). Thus, the available evidence suggests a great deal of real dread about the menace of left-wing revolution.

Moreover, even where conservatives invoked the danger of communism for strategic purposes, these appeals presupposed receptivity and resonance among their target audience, based on strong currents of anticommunism among elites and the broader population. This argument, developed by Carlos Waisman (1987: 165–6) for the middle of the twentieth century in Argentina, *a fortiori* applies to the time period after the Cuban Revolution, when concerns about left-wing radicalism were much more widespread and acute.

As most right-wingers and many moderates truly saw a "clear and present danger," even moderate left-wingers such as Venezuela's Acción Democrática (Levine 1973: 47–53) sincerely perceived a serious radical threat. These wide-ranging sectors were convinced that communists had an uncanny ability to take advantage of any opportunity; therefore, even small groups of extremists endangered sociopolitical stability. Interestingly, left-wing extremists shared these beliefs in the ease of revolution, which diverged from a systematic evaluation of effective chances and risks, as Chapter 4 shows below. As a result, radical left-wingers undertook incessant efforts to ignite guerrilla struggles, even under distinctly unpropitious circumstances – as they "learned the hard way" when their efforts to emulate the Cuban Revolution dramatically failed. As leftist hopes paralleled rightist fears, these shared yet problematic perceptions of impending revolution did not arise from motivated reasoning, but from heuristic shortcuts that yielded a remarkable overestimation of the significance and replicability of Castro's success.

As these historical and systematic assessments suggest and as Chapters 4 to 7 corroborate, bounded rationality provided the principal causal mechanisms that drove the diffusion of reactionary regimes. Inferential heuristics distorted perceptions and interpretations of the Cuban Revolution and stimulated both the illusions of the radical left and the worries, if not panic among the right and center. As their unfounded hopes induced left-wingers to engage in insurgent hyper-activism, frightened status-quo defenders combated them with exorbitant force and sooner or later imposed dictatorships in many countries to block the feared advance of radical extremism. By developing these points

---

[10] Interviews in D'Araujo, Dillon Soares, and Castro 1994: 11, 40, 46, 60, 91, 95, 126–7, 142–3, 155, 161, 175, 190, 206–7, 214–15, 230–1; and in D'Araujo and Castro 1997: 162, 168; and Muricy 1993: 442–5, 456–67, 460, 482, 505–6, 514–15, 525.

step by step, Chapter 3 shows how core insights of cognitive psychology offer the best foundation for explaining the striking spread of right-wing authoritarianism all over Latin America.

CONCLUSION

This chapter demonstrates that a variety of theoretical approaches have difficulty accounting fully for the region-wide reverse wave of the 1960s and 1970s, which undid a great deal of liberal progress and swept away even seemingly stable democracies such as Chile and Uruguay. As reactionary autocracy advanced across the southern subcontinent, domestically centered arguments that emphasize structural and institutional factors usefully point to internal vulnerabilities but fail to capture the regional and temporal clustering of regime change. Conversely, common-cause arguments do expect wave-like change, but there was no severe crisis at the inception of this riptide that directly propelled the widespread downfall of democracy. Of course, my own theory stresses the importance of the Cuban Revolution, but this radical challenge did not operate in the way that a common cause does. Rather than stimulating an immediate tsunami of autocratic imposition, the diverse impulses unleashed by Castro's dramatic precedent unfolded via complex, intersecting, and partly counteracting demonstration and deterrent effects.

Theory assessment therefore turns to the burgeoning diffusion literature, which highlights a variety of causal mechanisms, especially vertical imposition, normative attraction, rational learning, and bounded-rational inferences. Interestingly, great power promotion played a limited role in the reverse wave, despite the preponderance of the United States in the western hemisphere. Washington used its clout only to support the panicked moves to authoritarian rule that local actors, especially the military, spearheaded on their own initiative. Domestic forces, not the northern superpower, held primary responsibility for the proliferation of anticommunist autocracy.

As regards normative appeal, the progressivist assumptions of conventional constructivism preclude a convincing account of the Latin American reverse wave, when history lurched backwards. Historicist versions of constructivism that invoke the specific *Zeitgeist* of each era cannot persuasively explain the proliferation of authoritarianism either, as the dictators' bashful promise to prepare the eventual restoration of democracy suggests. Autocratic regimes inspired by strong normative appeal would have claimed genuine legitimacy as a superior alternative to democracy, as the dictators of the interwar confidently and loudly did. In general, ideas and norms were variegated and fluid. Therefore, they only provided some loose conditioning and did not determine specific political actions. Interests exerted much stronger motivating force.

Did political actors pursue their interests in line with the postulates of standard rationality and push for reactionary autocracy on the basis of careful, systematic cost-benefit analyses? This kind of rational-choice explanation runs afoul of a vast body of historical research which documents the disproportionate, almost paranoid fears that often drove the overthrow of democracy, and that bemoans the excessive brutality and unnecessary violence employed in the attack on presumed enemies and the imposition of dictatorship. My own research accounts for these notable deviations from standard rationality by documenting that many relevant actors resorted to cognitive shortcuts and acted out of asymmetrical loss aversion. As a result, they vastly overestimated the threats they faced and then responded with exaggerated determination, employing all the means at their disposal, including massive coercion. Chapter 3 develops this cognitive-psychological line of reasoning in systematic depth and embeds these boundedly rational microfoundations in macro-organizational structures.

3

A Theory of Reactionary Waves

Chapter 2 showed that extant theoretical approaches cannot fully account for the reactionary wave examined in this book, namely the rash of institutionalized, development-oriented military regimes in Latin America during the 1960s and 1970s. Domestic structural and institutional factors miss the clustering of these democratic breakdowns, and there was not the kind of exogenous shock and severe economic crisis that common-cause arguments would invoke to explain this riptide. Diffusion arguments that stress coercive imposition, normative appeal, and rational learning are not fully convincing either. The main cause for the proliferation of dictatorship was neither US pressures nor the normative appeal of autocracy, which was in fact low. Moreover, my research shows that relevant political actors learned from foreign precedents in ways that diverged significantly from the postulates of standard rationality.

This study therefore proposes a theory that draws on central insights from cognitive psychology, and thus rests on the microfoundation of bounded rationality. This distinctive explanation starts from the observation that fundamentally, the wave of autocratic rule arose from panicked reactions to the threat of left-wing revolution spreading across countries. The specter of radical diffusion prompted reactionary counterdiffusion (cf. Mainwaring and Pérez-Liñán 2013: 36–9, 77–80, 104–14).

Aroused by the Cuban Revolution, the fear of communism became so intense that it provoked disproportionate, excessive responses. Information processing and decision making did not follow the systematic, optimizing rules of conventional rationality, but reflected the substantial deviations documented by cognitive psychologists. Political actors of all ideological stripes assessed revolutionary precedents via cognitive shortcuts that overweighted the significance of these dramatic events, exaggerated the similarities to their own countries, and thus inspired strong beliefs in the replicability of revolution. While leftist radicals therefore undertook many precipitous emulation efforts, conservative sectors were struck by fear, defended the existing order at all cost, and crushed extremist stirrings, often brutally.

This unnecessarily harsh reaction was driven by the intense loss aversion that shapes humans' cognitive architecture. As psychological experiments and field studies show (Kahneman 2011: chaps. 26–28; Zamir 2014), people weight costs much more heavily than gains of objectively equal magnitude. Driven by the resulting urge to avoid losses, establishment sectors tended to combat the perceived threat of communist revolution with full force, and sooner or later sought reliable protection by advocating autocratic rule, sacrificing freedom, and exposing themselves to the arbitrariness of right-wing dictators. As asymmetrical loss aversion has rarely been highlighted in the field of comparative politics,[1] my study makes a contribution by analyzing the operation of this skewed choice mechanism and demonstrating its momentous impact.

After discussing these microfoundations, which are crucial for understanding the reactionary wave in Latin America, this chapter explains how cognitive-psychological mechanisms play out in the political world. After all, most political forces are not individuals – the primary subjects of psychological research – but collectivities or organizations. Thus, it bears examining what aggregate effects psychological mechanisms produce at the collective level. This impact depends on the organizational characteristics of the relevant political forces, as theorists of bounded rationality emphasize (Simon 1976; March and Simon 1993).

Accordingly, pluralistic, internally democratic organizations such as broad-based political parties can mitigate misperceptions and rash judgments (cf. Weyland 2014: chaps. 2, 5). But important organizations involved in the installation of autocratic rule had a closed, hierarchical structure that limited these beneficial effects. The military, in particular, seeks to forge internal unity and homogeneity (Pion-Berlin 1988: 383). Such close-knit organizations can turn into hotbeds of groupthink, reproduce cognitive distortions, and exacerbate deviations from conventional rationality (McDermott 2004: 249–55). Therefore, inferential shortcuts and skewed loss aversion shape – and bias – not only individual perception and choice, but also the decision making of many organizations.

Based on these organizational arguments, the chapter's third section then discusses the two processes through which status quo-oriented actors responded to the perceived threat of communism. First, after the Cuban Revolution, cognitive shortcuts reigned supreme, both among the radical-left sympathizers of this dramatic precedent and among the many sectors that were determined to forestall a violent overthrow of the sociopolitical order. For these reasons, the extremist left spearheaded a wave of emulative contention and in many countries tried directly to repeat Castro's success through rural guerrilla

---

[1] For a rare application to contentious politics, see Bergstrand (2014).

movements. Yet due to loss aversion, defenders of the existing system decisively squashed these armed insurgencies, often with overwhelming force and blatant disrespect for human rights.

The uniform defeat of these precipitous revolutionary stirrings suggested, however, that the established order would not simply crumble under the most immediate, isomorphic challenge. These experiences prompted political learning on all sides, sooner or later. Because counterdiffusion clearly defeated diffusion, democratic regimes survived the guerrilla attacks. Above all, pluralistic organizations that engage in more thorough information processing, such as broad-based political parties, updated their beliefs, drew inferences from the debacle of left-wing radicals, and lowered their concerns about the danger of communism. Therefore, pluralist democracy demonstrated particular resilience where fairly well-organized parties dominated the political and electoral arena, as in Venezuela. In sum, Cuban-style guerrilla struggles induced established regimes to bloody their hands, but did not set in motion a wave of autocratic regime changes.

Second, however, Castro's success also had a broader effect by suggesting the feasibility, if not ease of structural change. This overoptimistic inference inspired radicalization among a wide gamut of political forces, which in several countries was channeled through leftist and populist parties. Their insistent demands for profound transformations provoked grave concern among establishment sectors. In particular, tight-knit organizations such as the military, which tended to remain under the spell of cognitive heuristics, feared the advance of revolution. Moreover, the loss aversion activated by calls for radical change reached particular intensity among the right, which would bear the highest cost from a systemic overhaul. Indeed, the communist regime in Cuba survived US hostility and kept up its efforts to export revolution, turning conservative worries even more acute.

For all of these reasons, the groundswell of left-wing radicalism, which was especially pronounced in countries such as Brazil, Chile, Argentina, and Uruguay, instilled great fear among powerful sectors, especially conservative politicians, businesspeople, and the military. The perceived threat of revolution fostered doubts in the defensive capacity of liberal democracy, which in the underdeveloped countries of Latin America faced structural and institutional problems as well. The widespread sense of insufficient protection from the danger of communism prompted the imposition of autocracy across the subcontinent, most brutally in the Southern Cone. Consequently, the initial rash of repression was followed by the gradual advance of authoritarianism, which unfolded sequentially in a region-wide wave.

These regime changes drew additional inspiration from the emergence of a reactionary regime model, which right-wing sectors saw as particularly strong armor against the threat of leftist extremism. Brazil's developmental dictatorship looked like a promising recipe against instability and left-wing agitation. This new form of autocracy seemed to guarantee immunity against the virus of communism. The institutional mechanisms designed by the lusophone autocracy and the accomplishments it achieved during its first decade in power, including an "economic miracle," provided an additional impetus for the reactionary wave.

With these arguments, the chapter outlines a comprehensive theory of reactionary cascades, which the remainder of the volume substantiates. This theory rests on solid, empirically corroborated microfoundations and is adapted to the organizational macrostructures characterizing the world of politics. By developing these arguments, the study adds to the construction of a bounded rationality approach for political science.

THE CRUCIAL ROLE OF BOUNDED RATIONALITY

The preceding Chapter 2 has shown that political actors of all ideological colors, especially the proponents of reactionary autocracy as well as their radical-left enemies, deviated significantly from standard rationality; they instead employed basic mechanisms of bounded rationality. Above all, the Cuban Revolution activated inferential heuristics, which made people assign disproportionate significance to this striking precedent and induced them to overrate the ease of its replicability in other countries. These distorted perceptions then stimulated asymmetrical loss aversion among status quo defenders, which prompted right-wing and even centrist sectors to fight left-wing efforts at spreading radical revolution. The following subsections explain these cognitive-psychological mechanisms in turn and highlight the resulting importance of deterrent effects, which contributed mightily to the victory of reaction over revolution and thus fueled the Latin American reverse wave.

The Importance of Inferential Heuristics

People tend to process political information not in careful, systematic ways, but rely instead on inferential shortcuts, which facilitate information processing, yet at the risk of distortions.[2] The two shortcuts that have drawn most attention in psychological research (Kahneman, Slovic, and Tversky 1982; Gilovich, Griffin, and Kahneman 2002; Kahneman 2011) and that have proved most useful for political analysis (see, e.g., Kuran and Sunstein 1999; McDermott 2004: 57–69; Mercer 2005; Levy 2013: 310–12, 316–17; Redlawsk and Lau 2013: 137–40; Weyland 2007, 2014) are the heuristics of availability and of representativeness.

Due to the availability heuristic, which shapes memory recall and attention, drastic, vivid, directly witnessed events make a disproportionate impression on people's minds; by contrast, less stunning information is neglected even if in objective terms it is equally or more relevant. As people overweight striking

---

[2] This subsection draws heavily on Weyland (2014: 49–50).

appearance relative to actual importance, they deviate from rational calculations. Dramatic events have an excessive impact on people's perceptions and thinking, leading to an overestimation of their likelihood. As a real-life example, most drivers hit the brakes when they see a car accident – although in rational terms, a single event should not significantly affect the systematic risk assessment of speeding.

The distorted inferences derived from the availability heuristic are not just psychological curiosities, but can have serious, even tragic consequences for people's lives. Under the impact of 9/11, for instance, many Americans avoided plane rides and went long distances by car – although highway travel is, in fact, much more dangerous: scholars estimate that approximately 1,500 people died as a result (Gigerenzer 2006)! Thus, the availability heuristic seriously skews people's information intake and probability estimates, and distorts the input side of decision making.

This inferential shortcut also affects the perception of political events and shapes the actions that people take in response. For instance, the unexpected, dramatic overthrow of Tunisia's long-ruling dictator Zine El-Abidine Ben Ali through mass demonstrations in January 2011 grabbed observers' attention across the globe and exerted unusual weight on their beliefs, especially in the region. Within minutes (!) of receiving confirmation of this outstanding event, oppositionists in Cairo began to tweet, "VIVA LA REVOLUCION !!!" and "WE WILL FOLLOW! . . . Tunisians are the heroes of the Arab world" (Idle and Nunns 2011: 27; see Weyland 2012a: 925). Thus, due to the availability heuristic, the striking feat achieved by Tunisian protesters immediately transformed the probability assessments and political calculations of their potential counterparts in Egypt.

The representativeness heuristic then aggravates these distorted views of reality, including the political world. This heuristic induces people to draw improperly firm conclusions from apparent, superficial similarities while disregarding relevant information, such as statistical base rates and the possibility of chance factors (Kahneman, Slovic, and Tversky 1982: chaps. 2–6; Gilovich, Griffin, and Kahneman 2002: chaps. 1–3). People tend to overrate commonalities between different experiences and overestimate the significance of these parallels; conversely, they disregard underlying, relevant differences and neglect the likelihood that similarities – to the extent they do occur – result from accidental coincidences. One manifestation of this cognitive shortcut is that people often derive excessively strong conclusions from small samples. They attribute too much significance to patterns that appear in limited sets, although these patterns could well be due to chance; they improperly assume that small samples are representative of the whole population.

Accordingly, a dramatic event overweighted by the availability heuristic appears to foreshadow similar events elsewhere. The representativeness heuristic then leads observers to overestimate the commonalities between the precedent and the situation that they themselves confront; conversely, they underestimate the differences and their significance. These facile judgments make domestic circumstances look equivalent to those that allowed for the original occurrence. Accordingly, actors jump to the conclusion that the conditions for replication are given in their own country.

In the world of politics, the two heuristics lead people to infer from a striking precedent of regime change that the political situation prevailing in their own polity is similar, and that they can follow the frontrunners' footsteps and achieve the same feat. When citizens of one nation manage to drive out their corrupt, oppressive ruler, for instance, people chafing under autocratic regimes in other countries come to believe that their own governments are also weak and that oppositionists have sufficient willpower and clout to evict those dictators as well (Weyland 2012b: 29–37). Among critics of the established regime, these rash inferences stimulate quick imitation efforts, which can sweep across a wide range of diverse nations; and among defenders of the existing order, the same cognitive shortcuts instill fear, which then motivates efforts to forestall replication.

Inferential heuristics thus spur overreactions on both sides, yet in opposite directions: Opponents of incumbent rulers fall prey to ill-considered, excessive optimism, whereas defenders are gripped by fright and therefore react to challengers' enthusiasm by trying to foil these hopes. Thus, despite their divergent interests, the opposing sides share the same sudden belief – derived from the distorted processing of a foreign precedent – that the established regime is brittle and in a highly precarious position. Cognitive shortcuts, not wishful thinking, drive this commonality among political enemies.

In the world of international affairs, the two shortcuts had their most extreme manifestation in the domino theory, namely the expectation of status quo forces – such as US foreign policy-makers of the 1960s – that a communist takeover in one country would quickly spread to a number of other countries. Specifically, as the dominos tumble unencumbered, this metaphor embodies the fear that revolutionary diffusion advances in a rather automatic and not easily stoppable way (Shimko 1994: 666–7). This concern reflected the representativeness heuristic, namely the overestimation of similarities across nations and the corresponding overrating of external impulses of change; domestic differences, which might make other countries much less vulnerable than the frontrunner and which might give rise to preventive and defensive countermeasures, were discounted (Shimko 1994: 666–7). Thus, the two cognitive shortcuts shaped the thinking of important international decision-makers.

The Impact of Asymmetrical Loss Aversion

Interestingly, this commonality of perceptions and the opposed courses of action that it stimulates can produce starkly skewed outcomes. After all, the bounded rationality approach follows the broader family of rational frameworks in emphasizing that perceptions and beliefs interact with people's interests and preferences. As actors pursue to a good extent self-regarding goals, cost-benefit analysis predicts that those who foresee net gains will promote a change, whereas those who anticipate net losses will seek to prevent it. Yet whereas conventional rational choice postulates the equivalence of gains and losses, cognitive psychology has documented a fundamental asymmetry in human calculation and decision making.

People subjectively weigh losses much more heavily than gains of objectively equal magnitude (Kahneman and Tversky 2000: chaps. 7–11; Kahneman 2011: chaps. 26–33; Zamir 2014; see also Kahneman and Renshon 2009). Accordingly, a gain does not directly offset a loss of identical size, as standard rationality assumes. Instead, the human mind employs differential valuation and weights losses much more heavily than gains. Consequently, those who lose something are more dissatisfied than those who win the same thing are happy. Because people perceive the status quo as an entitlement that they legitimately deserve, they strenuously defend it against threats; yet they are distinctly less zealous in striving for further gains above and beyond their current endowments (Thaler 1992: chap. 6).[3] Due to this stark asymmetry, fear constitutes a much stronger motivation than hope.

Loss aversion shaped people's responses to dramatic assaults on the status quo, such as the Cuban Revolution, which promised substantial gains for the masses while threatening significant costs for the numerically limited elite and middle class. Accordingly, the projected beneficiaries should far outnumber those who would pay the price for this redistributive transformation. Indeed, the law of diminishing marginal utility – a central postulate of conventional rational choice – suggests that the poor would value their gains more highly than the rich would resent the curtailment of their privileges. Despite these apparently favorable prospects, however, the small groupings on the radical left who pursued immediate gains and actively tried to replicate Lenin and Castro's revolutionary success in their own countries found strikingly limited support; prospective gains did not motivate many people to join efforts to overturn the unjust status quo. Instead, large segments of the citizenry seem to have anticipated net losses and therefore feared revolution. Accordingly, majorities usually rejected emulation attempts and backed crackdowns on far-left uprisings and guerrilla movements. Status quo defenders clearly outnumbered promoters and supporters of profound change.

Loss aversion makes sense of this fact, which diverges from the premises of standard rationality. The asymmetrical valuation of gains and losses – and not only elites' resource preponderance – helps explain why leftist efforts to replicate revolutionary precedents and bring progressive transformations ran afoul of a broad phalanx of conservatives and suffered one defeat after another.

---

[3] For additional cognitive mechanisms and biases that contribute to this "endowment effect," see Morewedge and Giblin (2015).

As a result, it was reactionary counterrevolution that diffused broadly, not left-wing revolution.

Asymmetrical loss aversion, the basic impulse behind counterdiffusion, adds a major component to the bounded rationality approach to political regime contention (see especially Weyland 2014). Because steps toward democratization usually do not entail a profound restructuring of state, economy, and society that would threaten serious costs for elites,[4] political challenges to autocratic regimes tend to trigger intense loss aversion primarily among a limited group of government officials.[5] By contrast, radical revolutionary overhauls as in Cuba foreshadow enormous gains or losses for large parts of the population. Consequently, loss aversion comes to the fore and heavily skews the calculation of net benefits; after all, the specter of communism scares a broad range of sectors, especially powerful elites, yet also middle classes, farmers, and even better-off workers. Thus, when a particularly high-stakes transformation is on the agenda, this skewed valuation mechanism plays a clear, visible role, shapes the constellation of supporters and opponents, and drives outsized reactions to perceived threats. In the research for the present study, disproportionate loss aversion therefore appeared as a central factor for explaining the uniform failure of radical-left diffusion and the remarkable prevalence of right-wing counterdiffusion.

The Disproportionate Strength of Deterrent Effects

Taken together, cognitive shortcuts and loss aversion elucidate the backlash mechanism that drove the Latin American reverse wave. Essentially, the perceived threat of communism prompted the imposition of conservative authoritarianism.[6] Thus, the preponderance of deterrent effects emanating from the Cuban Revolution and from the efforts at its emulation account for

---

[4] In considering these cost-benefit calculations, it is important to keep in mind that with their concentrated and largely unchecked power, autocratic regimes can impose serious losses on elite sectors, as for instance Peru's military dictatorship did (Albertus 2015). Contrary to the claims of Acemoglu and Robinson (2005; similar Boix 2003), it is therefore simply not true that democracies pose greater redistributive threats to elite interests; instead, the checks and balances and the constitutional safeguards of liberal democracy often serve as crucial protections for elite interests (see also Ansell and Samuels 2014). Accordingly, Brazilian businesspeople, who feared the "statization" of the economy promoted by the conservative (!) military regime, were at the forefront of the push for redemocratization in the 1970s (Cardoso 1986).

[5] Given their atrocious human rights violations, mainstays of Chile's military regime, for instance, most prominently President Augusto Pinochet himself, were scared that a withdrawal from power would expose them to judicial prosecution and serious punishment, as had happened to their colleagues in neighboring Argentina. Consequently, loss aversion induced them to extend their dictatorship as long as possible (Weyland 2014: 208–10).

[6] On the impact of threat perceptions on authoritarianism, see in general terms Stenner (2005); for a thoughtful analysis of the impact of threat perceptions in international relations, see Stein (2013).

the proliferation of reactionary autocracy and history's turn in a regressive direction.

Specifically, while inferential heuristics led both the radical left and the conservative right to overestimate the chances of communist revolution, the political responses to these perceptions displayed a strong interaction as well as a clear asymmetry. On the one hand, because left-wingers sought to imitate the revolutionary precedents, right-wingers forcefully combated these contentious efforts. Extremist diffusion bred defensive counterdiffusion, in a reflexive move. As radical hyperaction provoked forceful reaction, the "contradictory" repercussions of communist revolution, namely the emulative inspiration it provided for the far left and its deterrent effects on the right and center, were causally linked.

On the other hand, the resulting conflicts were lopsided. In most cases, limited numbers of leftists – small minorities in the case of guerrilla movements – tried to emulate revolution, but a much wider range of conservatives, centrists, and even moderate leftists fought radical subversion and insurgency. Moreover, these defenders of the established system used any means at their disposal, including harsh repression and the installation of dictatorial rule. They did not only crack down on radicals, but many were willing to abdicate their own political rights, live in a police state, and submit to an unaccountable, uncontrollable Leviathan (cf. Svolik 2012: chap. 5). As mentioned in Chapter 2, historians have been astounded by the overreaction of status quo-oriented sectors and have condemned their countermeasures as excessive. It is noteworthy that reactionaries often mustered surprisingly broad support, which helped them defeat extremist subversion. Their victories resulted not only from the predominant power capabilities commanded by elites, but also from their massive effort, which reflected the intensity of their preferences and the wide-ranging backing they received.

These skewed outcomes show that among the divergent repercussions of communist revolution, deterrent effects proved much stronger than the forces of attraction; they overpowered contagion and demonstration effects. This finding suggests an important correction to the diffusion literature, which has mostly highlighted factors of propulsion by examining how precedents and models unleash stimuli for replication. The present study shows, by contrast, that certain precedents operate mainly as forces of repulsion. They provoke a great deal of rejection and induce most actors to block emulation efforts. Graph 3.1 depicts this backlash dynamic, marking the uneven strength of demonstration versus deterrent effects through the differential width of the causal arrows.

In conclusion, my book enriches the analysis of diffusion by documenting the importance of deterrent effects, which are driven by the causal mechanism of asymmetrical loss aversion. Overall, cognitive-psychological findings provide promising building blocks for explaining the proliferation of reactionary autocracy.

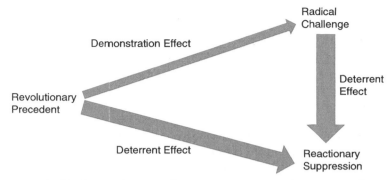

Radical
Challenge

Demonstration Effect

Deterrent
Effect

Revolutionary
Precedent

Deterrent Effect

Reactionary
Suppression

GRAPH 3.1: Backlash: Revolution and Its Demonstration and Deterrent Effects

THE ROLE OF POLITICAL ORGANIZATION

Political Organization and Bounded Rationality

As the preceding section argues, fundamental cognitive mechanisms offer solid microfoundations for understanding the politics of reverse waves. Yet, how do the distortions caused by inferential heuristics and by asymmetrical loss aversion affect the world of politics, where organizations, not individuals, make many of the relevant decisions? In principle, organizations can compensate for the cognitive limitations of individuals; their collective mechanisms of information processing and decision making can guarantee much better results than people on their own would likely achieve. The scholar who introduced the framework of bounded rationality, Herbert Simon, emphasized that organizational structures are often designed to overcome the shortcomings of individuals and to loosen the bounds of rationality. Accordingly, collective decisions tend to come closer to the standards of conventional, full rationality (Simon 1976; March and Simon 1993; similar Jones 2001: chap. 6; Bendor 2010; Hafner-Burton, Haggard, et al. 2017: S5, S20).

Organizational theory has indeed demonstrated the benefits arising from the division of labor, from specialization and expertise, and from experience, derived from the training and testing of organizational leaders during their lengthy ascent to major positions of power (Payne, Bettman, and Johnson 1993: 3, 35–6, 199–201, 206–7; Jones 2001: 23, 82, 131; Bendor 2010: 28–9, 36–44, 163–9; Saunders 2017).[7] Consequently, organizations can have

---

[7] As Frey and Gallus (2014) emphasize, however, there have been surprisingly few scholarly efforts to examine the "aggregate effects of behavioral anomalies," such as the extent and way in which individual-level cognitive distortions affect the world of politics with its predominance of collective actors.

advantages in the aggregation of information and the formation of overarching decisions. Organizational subunits provide different perspectives, and in this way allow for a more comprehensive, thorough assessment of problems and a wide-ranging discussion of possible solutions. Internal competition breeds accountability and can keep mistakes in check. For all of these reasons, officials of organizations often perform better than individuals would on their own. Organizations thus have the potential of alleviating the problems that cognitive limitations create for individuals.

Besides facilitating the task of actors to deal with their environment, organizations also make this environment itself more orderly and predictable. Institutions create regular patterns of behavior that are much easier to discern and understand than an uncontrollable "free-for-all." Institutionalized parties, for instance, give popular mobilization and electoral competition a good deal of stability (see recently Mainwaring 2018). Whereas in fluid, inchoate party systems, outsider candidates can arise, dramatically shake up politics, and stun observers, institutionalized party systems feature established politicians who draw from a well-known repertoire of strategies and tactics; new leaders are socialized into this system or weeded out, making surprises rare. Given these long-standing patterns of political behavior, even boundedly rational actors, despite their cognitive limitations, can get a reasonable grasp on current developments and likely future trends. Thus, strong organizations reduce the risk of perceptual mistakes and problematic choices not only by improving information processing, but also by ordering politics and thus simplifying the information to be processed.

Whether organizations can actually fulfill these beneficial functions, however, especially by bettering the quality of perceptions and decisions, depends on their nature and internal structure (Zamir 2014: 30–1).[8] Broad-based organizations that comprise various sectors, are internally pluralistic, and represent this diversity in mechanisms of discussion and deliberation hold especially good prospects for loosening the bounds of rationality and for keeping the limitations and biases at bay that regular individuals face on their own (see Weyland 2014: 53–6). Organizational leaders of different backgrounds and viewpoints tend to question and cross-check each other's perceptions, inferences, and propensities and thus diminish the risk of rash judgments and unthinking mistakes.

As an example from the world of politics, Venezuela's center-left Acción Democrática (AD) was a wide-ranging organization with internal mechanisms for debate and deliberation (Levine 1973).[9] Consequently, its leaders responded

---

[8] Analyzing heterogeneity, especially the degree to which different individuals or groupings approximate or diverge from the standards of comprehensive rationality or – by contrast – display cognitive distortions and biases, constitutes the current research frontier in the application of psychological insights to political science (Hafner-Burton, Haggard, et al. 2017: S4–S5, S13–S21; Stein 2017: S250, S256, S258).

[9] On the ossification of this party in later years, see Coppedge (1994).

to the Cuban Revolution with greater prudence and success than the closed, hierarchical military with its advocacy of simple repression would have achieved (see Brown 2017: chap. 9). Based on discussions among its leaders, this broad-based organization elaborated a comparatively sophisticated strategy for coping with a range of tenacious efforts to spread communism. Above all, AD-led governments combated Castro-supported guerrilla movements not only with counterinsurgency, but also by enacting social reforms and by offering left-wingers opportunities to reintegrate into democratic politics, as Chapter 4 later shows. Due to this savvy approach, Venezuela managed to preserve democracy at a time when excessive reactions to the overrated specter of communism drove many other South American countries into military dictatorships. Thus, organizations comprising variegated sectors that engage in discussions and deliberation can indeed extend the bounds of political rationality and trace courses of action that diverge less far from rational cost-benefit calculations.

But there are also organizations with very different characteristics – close-knit and unified by strong ideational commitments. Organizations that forge a uniform mindset forego the information processing benefits arising from diversity and debate; therefore, they are fully subject to cognitive shortcuts and their problematic effects. Their internal homogeneity precludes the cross-checking of problematic perceptions and rash inferences. In the extreme case of narrow sects that revolve around fervently shared viewpoints and causes, groupthink can prevail: members reinforce each other's misperceptions and biases and thus exacerbate misjudgments (Esser 1998; McDermott 2004: 249–55; Schafer and Crichlow 2010; see also Bendor 2010: 179). Left-wing radicals often assembled in such sect-like groupings, which fomented the operation of cognitive shortcuts; therefore, these extremists rushed into ill-considered efforts to emulate the Cuban Revolution and started innumerable guerrilla struggles under unpropitious conditions, as Chapter 4 documents.

As broad-based, pluralistic organizations and narrow ideological sects mark the extreme poles, other political groupings line up along this continuum of organizational openness versus closure – and of looser versus tighter bounds of rationality. The military, for instance, which often took the lead in instituting reactionary regimes, falls toward the closed side of the spectrum. The armed forces try to forge individuals into a collective unit, entrench hierarchy and discipline, and limit internal disagreement and criticism.[10] To instill in young

---

[10] Needler 1975: 69–70. Sometimes, however, even militaries create mechanisms for broad, structured deliberation. During the severe crisis caused by sociopolitical polarization in Chile in 1972–73, for instance, the Chilean armed forces formed a committee in which an equal number of representatives of the three main branches regularly debated the political situation (Arriagada 1988: 90–1). In the early 1960s, the notoriously divided Argentine military had a similar committee for interbranch discussion and coordination (Potash 1980: 361–4).

men the willingness to die for the fatherland, military leaders foster a strong esprit de corps, often by discrediting or even demonizing an emblematic enemy.

After the Cuban Revolution, the targeted enemy[11] included domestic radicals who sought to emulate Castro's precedent. Because extremists often operated under the cloak of clandestinity, this subversive threat was difficult to identify and pinpoint. Facing an "invisible" adversary during times of turbulence and confusion, many officers relied heavily on cognitive shortcuts and ended up drawing problematic inferences. Conformity pressures inside the military then limited debate and deliberation that could have filtered out misperceptions and rash judgments. As a result, the armed forces often embraced a worldview that seriously overestimated the communist threat, which in turn activated intense loss aversion. Because left-wing revolution jeopardized the very survival of the military, as the mass executions of old-regime generals in Cuba glaringly showed, officers were determined to combat this danger wherever it seemed to rear its head – and in their eyes, that happened in many places!

In sum, organizations in which ideological uniformity, a strong esprit de corps, or hierarchy and rigidity prevail do little to loosen the bounds of rationality; in the extreme, they can provide a hotbed for groupthink, which fosters reliance on cognitive shortcuts and aggravates their problematic repercussions. For these reasons, the beneficial effects of political organization, which can in principle loosen the bounds of rationality, were mixed and overall limited. While pluralistic organizations reached higher standards of information processing and decision making, homogeneous groupings remained exposed to biased inferences and skewed choices. Because many relevant political forces, including the principal protagonists of revolutionary diffusion and reactionary counterdiffusion, remained in the throes of cognitive shortcuts and asymmetrical loss aversion, the mechanisms of bounded rationality shaped a good deal of aggregate-level decision making and political action.

Situational Problems, Political Organization, and Bounded Rationality

Another factor that affects the bounds of rationality are the situational challenges that political organizations face. By nature, organizations are best at processing issues that arise under normal circumstances. After all, their standard operating procedures are designed to deal with recurring tasks. Political parties, for instance, know how to select candidates and run electoral campaigns – but they may not know how to respond to the outbreak of a revolution. A sudden shock can unsettle an organization and leave it at a loss. As confusion erupts and profound uncertainty reigns (cf. Kurzman 2004), it becomes doubtful whether long-standing procedures can cope with the new

---

[11] What Germans call *Feindbild*, the concept or image of the foe that one seems to face.

threats and opportunities. Organizational leaders and specialists may be dumbfounded by the unexpected turn of events.

To deal with this uncertainty and crisis, even the officials of broad-based, pluralistic organizations are likely to resort to the fundamental mechanisms of cognitive psychology. Pluralistic organizations with established structures of information processing and decision making may therefore see the normal improvements in their performance erode under the pressures of unusual circumstances. The need to respond to unforeseen problems and dangers tends to compress their bounds of rationality. Whereas under regular conditions, these organizations keep reliance on cognitive shortcuts in check and filter out many misperceptions and distortions, in crisis situations they cannot help but employ inferential heuristics, and thus risk operating on the basis of problematic judgments.

When these organizations see threats emerge in the fog of political turmoil and trouble, they act out of intense loss aversion and launch resolute, even fierce counterattacks against their presumed enemies. In those situations, broad-based, pluralistic organizations may close ranks with close-knit organizations that always operate with tighter bounds of rationality, such as the military. All of these problems affected pluralistic organizations such as Venezuela's AD after the unexpected, stunning revolution in Cuba. The use of massive armed force with which the AD government combated the initial Castroite guerrilla groupings in 1962–3 (Wickham-Crowley 1992: 199; Brown 2017: 259–62) exemplifies the temporary convergence resulting from situationally compressed bounds of rationality, as Chapter 4 analyzes.

In the absence of an acute threat of armed revolution, by contrast, cognitive shortcuts operating at a time of heightened uncertainty and consternation can push broad-based parties into emulative radicalization. In this vein, the Cuban precedent had striking and consequential repercussions for Chile's Socialist Party. After this organization had for decades embraced a reformist, parliamentary route, in the 1960s it fell under the spell of Castro's revolutionary success and surprisingly declared its commitment to armed struggle! In fact, an experienced mainstream leader like Salvador Allende drew on the violent Movement of the Revolutionary Left (MIR) to provide his bodyguards (Haslam 2005: 64; Marambio 2007). In conclusion, under conditions of uncertainty and confusion even the organizational leaders of broad-based, institutionalized parties are susceptible to inferential heuristics and the resulting distortions and biases.

These problems then diminish again as the situation normalizes and as political leaders adapt to the changes that have occurred. After the shock caused by the Cuban Revolution slowly faded, it became ever clearer that other regimes were not nearly as brittle as the representativeness heuristic had made it appear in the immediate aftermath of this stunning upset. Correcting the initial overestimation of similarities, observers noticed the differences between the Caribbean island and many other Latin American countries. Due to its Sultanistic tendencies (Domínguez 1998), the old regime of General Fulgencio Batista had been unusually vulnerable (Wickham-Crowley 1992: 158, 166–73, 191), whereas the institutionalized states prevailing in South America rested on significantly firmer, more resilient structures. Furthermore, status quo defenders learned from Castro's frightening success. Therefore, they fought radical leftists in resolute ways and thus made the sociopolitical order even safer.

For these reasons, the political earthquake triggered by the Cuban Revolution eventually subsided, and the leaders of pluralistic organizations recovered firmer ground under their feet. As a result, they were swept up less by cognitive shortcuts, and their internal discussions and debates became more successful again at sifting out distortions and biases. Consequently, these parties returned to fairly sophisticated political strategies. Venezuela's AD, for instance, embraced democratic reformism and drained support away from Castroite guerrilla movements with political means, rather than relying on coercion alone (Brown 2017: 272–8). In particular, the government offered capitulating insurgents the opportunity to return to civilian life and enter electoral politics, thus weakening the revolutionary impulse. These political moves, which reflected the recovery of wider bounds of rationality, helped to prevent Venezuelan democracy from falling prey to the coup wave that was sweeping through South America.

In conclusion, profound political tremors temporarily reduced the beneficial impact that pluralistic organization normally exerts on information processing and decision making. As the bounds of rationality narrowed, even broad-based organizations came to act in problematic ways. Yet once confusion and crisis eased; once politics moved into more regular patterns again; and once relevant actors came to understand the new constellation of forces, pluralistic organizations managed to improve their performance and recover greater rationality. While never living up to the standards of full rationality, they acted with renewed prudence and avoided striking mistakes.

Overall, organizational macrostructures mediate the impact of cognitive mechanisms on political decision making, and can in principle mitigate the problematic impact of inferential shortcuts. But this improvement of information processing depends on the type of organization. Broad-based, pluralistic organizations that engage in internal debate and deliberation indeed loosen the bounds of rationality. But close-knit or hierarchical organizations that seek ideational uniformity lack this salutary effect; where groupthink prevails, actions largely reflect the rash judgments derived via cognitive heuristics. Furthermore, situational uncertainty and profound confusion can prompt even the officials of pluralistic organizations to rely heavily on inferential shortcuts. When they face sudden shocks, their bounds of rationality tend to narrow considerably. During unsettled times, even experienced political actors have difficulties coping.

As a result of all these factors, fundamental mechanisms of cognitive psychology mold a great deal of organized action on the political stage. The microfoundation of bounded rationality therefore forms a solid base for understanding the intersecting processes of diffusion and counterdiffusion that gave rise to the Latin American reverse wave.

REACTIONS TO REVOLUTION: REPRESSIVE CAMPAIGNS AND THE IMPOSITION OF AUTOCRACY

The interaction of cognitive micromechanisms and organizational macrostructures which evolved with the irruption of situational challenges made the reactionary responses to drastic revolutionary precedents quite complex. Different from the way in which a common cause would operate (see Chapter 2), the Cuban Revolution did not propel the immediate proliferation of autocratic regimes. While stricken with fear, and while fighting left-wing revolutionaries ferociously, many status quo defenders did not succumb to panic, despair of the resilience of liberal democracy, and seek protection in the arms of right-wing dictators. After all, bounded rationality does not predict full-scale paranoia, which could have triggered a reflexive flight impulse and a lemming-like plunge into the sea of autocracy.

Instead of falling prey to real irrationality, a majority of political actors pursued their interests and causes with more or less tightly bounded rationality. Many promoters of profound change, as well as many opponents of deep-reaching transformations, therefore engaged in some degree of productive information processing and learning. Rather than attempting the isomorphic emulation of the Cuban Revolution, a wide range of progressive political forces assessed the political opportunity structure more carefully and employed political and electoral means to effect profound transformations. Similarly, their adversaries did not rush into drastic countermeasures, but more or less carefully prepared major initiatives, especially risky moves such as efforts to spearhead military coups and install anticommunist dictatorships.

Accordingly, while direct attempts to replicate Castro's takeover through guerrilla struggles erupted all across Latin America, they largely spared the few countries that featured particularly institutionalized states or stable regimes, such as Chile, Mexico, and Brazil. Where in those nations democracy prevailed, however, as in Brazil and Chile, the resilient institutional setting allowed for a broader radicalization of political and electoral forces, fueled by democratic competition in societies suffering from serious economic and social deficits. Across Latin American countries, there thus was a certain trade-off between the two types of radical challenges inspired by the Cuban Revolution, namely Guevarist insurgencies and the political push for drastic transformation. Many countries primarily experienced either one of those two left-wing efforts, not both (with exceptions such as Argentina, however). In fact, the more prolonged and sustained the guerrilla challenge was, the less likely was the spread of extremism in the partisan arena, as the experiences of Colombia and Venezuela suggest. Armed assaults on the government ended up hurting the left's political quest for capturing power; and as guerrilla movements did not provoke the overthrow of democracy, whereas broad-based political radicalization did, they paradoxically helped to immunize liberal regimes against the political danger emanating from right-wing backlash.

After all, reactionary countermeasures to radical challenges also unfolded in different ways and clustered into two distinctive types of conservative response to the perceived threat of revolution. As Castro's feats inspired a rash of isomorphic imitation efforts (examined in Chapter 4), these innumerable guerrilla uprisings immediately drew a coercive response from democratic incumbents, and especially the military. But these repressive campaigns, which violated human rights and thus deviated from liberal democratic norms, did not bring political regime change and provoke the imposition of reactionary autocracy. Instead, a wide range of establishment forces, led by broad-based political parties in a number of countries, learned from the clear defeat of radical left-wingers, lowered their estimates of danger, and believed in the defensive capacity of liberal democracy and social reformism. Depending on the political strength of these parties, democracy therefore had a chance in quite a few Latin American nations during the 1960s.

Strong fears of communism persisted on the right side of the ideological spectrum, however, especially among the armed forces, as Chapter 5 documents. Where established elites and conservative groupings lacked broad-based, pluralistic organizations, they tended to face tighter bounds of rationality. Moreover, they would have borne the greatest cost from a radical transformation. As Castro's Cuba survived US strangulation efforts and continued to promote communist subversion, right-wing sectors doubted democracy's capacity for resistance. In fact, in a number of countries the Cuban Revolution inspired a broad radicalization among left-leaning and populist sectors, which greatly exacerbated the concerns among the civilian right and the military. Because revolution seemed to be on the agenda, fear spread among conservatives and, increasingly, among centrist sectors as well. Liberal regimes therefore lost support, most clearly in the Southern Cone. Reactionary forces sought safety from the specter of communism by pushing for the installation of dictatorships, as Chapter 6 shows for the cases of Brazil, Argentina, and Chile.

Accordingly, the proliferation of autocracy proceeded in a complex fashion, driven by various demonstration and deterrent effects and mediated by boundedly rational learning. The Latin American reverse wave resulted from processes of diffusion and counterdiffusion that advanced and intersected in variegated ways. To provide a clearer picture and set the stage for the in-depth analysis of Chapters 4 to 6, the present section examines the two main backlash dynamics that drove the reactionary wave in turn.

Crackdowns against Isomorphic Emulation – and Democratic Survival

The wave of repressive backlash was triggered by radical-left attempts to replicate Castro's revolutionary success directly. During the decade after the Cuban Revolution, extremist groupings initiated rural guerrilla struggles across most of Latin America, in some countries over and over again; only a few nations with particularly capable states, where armed uprisings were totally unrealistic, such as Brazil and Chile, escaped largely unscathed (Goldenberg 1971; Lamberg 1972; Wickham-Crowley 1992, 2014; Gott 2008; Brown 2017). Driven by the heuristics of availability and representativeness, the radical fighters sought to follow the exact recipe that had supposedly worked on the Caribbean island, as codified by Che Guevara ([1961] 2007). That left-wingers spearheaded new insurgencies repeatedly, although earlier attempts in the same country had failed (see, e.g., Brown 2017: chaps. 9, 13), shows the tight bounds of their political rationality.

These impetuous challenges, their frequent recurrence, and their cross-national linkages, especially to the new hotbed of communism in the Caribbean, reinforced the fears of conservatives, centrists, and even some center-leftists, who had been shocked by the dramatic events in Cuba. A broad phalanx of status quo defenders therefore reacted to the outbreak of imitative guerrilla struggles with considerable concern. Because their political universe had been shaken by Castro's stunning revolution and because the existing order now looked precarious, they resorted to cognitive shortcuts to make sense of the unclear situation.

As a result, political forces initially overrated the threat posed by the rash of insurgencies and confronted these isomorphic imitation efforts forcefully.[12] Militaries were at the forefront of this overreaction because their internal hierarchy and quest for uniformity gave cognitive shortcuts relatively free rein and thus activated loss aversion. Due to the representativeness heuristic, it weighed heavily on their minds that the Cuban revolutionaries had summarily executed old-regime generals. Yet even some broad-based, pluralistic organizations, which have mechanisms for better information processing and thorough deliberation, relied on inferential shortcuts during this phase of heightened uncertainty. Because a center-left party like Venezuela's AD overestimated the radical threat as well, its government led the charge to squash communist uprisings.

This repressive backlash in Latin America is shown in Graph 3.2, which indicates the uneven constellation of the contending forces through the differential width of the causal arrows. In particular, the demonstration effects of the Cuban Revolution inspired only small minorities of extremists to

---

[12] My research did not find instances of preemptive repression, as postulated by Danneman and Ritter (2014). Boundedly rational elites do not seem to anticipate the potential eruption of rebellion, but respond only in the face of open insurgencies.

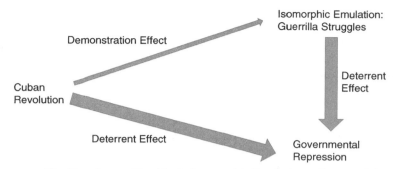

GRAPH 3.2: The First Stage of Backlash: Isomorphic Emulation Efforts and the Repressive Response

initiate guerrilla struggles. By contrast, the deterrent effects of Castro's precedent and of radicals' emulation efforts induced a much broader range of status quo defenders to mobilize their ample power capabilities and crush these ill-considered insurgencies. These counterinsurgency campaigns entailed atrocities and thus violated liberal rights – but they did not provoke the downfall of democratic regimes.

After all, due to the starkly uneven constellation of forces, Castroite guerrilla struggles suffered strategic defeats, in most cases total extinction. Isomorphic emulation efforts clearly proved ineffective, as Che Guevara's disastrous campaign in Bolivia eventually confirmed. Therefore, broad-based parties started to update their inferences and arrive at a more accurate assessment of the danger arising from radical left-wingers. As the unexpected tremors caused by the Cuban Revolution faded, pluralistic organizations relied less on inferential heuristics. Consequently, they ascertained the constellation of power more thoroughly, which was clearly unfavorable to extremist insurgents. Therefore, center-left parties like Venezuela's AD distanced themselves from their military allies and returned to their emphasis on human rights, the rule of law, and other democratic principles. In other words, they resumed their normal position in support of political liberalism and democracy. Depending on the political weight that these forces commanded, political freedom gained a lease on life in a number of Latin American countries.

As isomorphic attempts to replicate the Cuban Revolution uniformly failed, conservative elites and military generals eventually lowered their estimates of the immediate danger arising from communism as well. They noticed that their own power capabilities still held considerable sway. While civilian right-wingers and especially the armed forces often lacked well-performing structures of discussion and debate, they did slowly engage in learning. As a result, in many cases they came to support, accept, or at least acquiesce in the liberal democracies that had proliferated in South America from World War II onward.

Thus, repressive counterdiffusion, which squashed the left-wing attempts directly to repeat Castro's armed assault on power, brought the excessive use of force and entailed many human rights violations, that is, deviations from liberal norms. But this fierce backlash against Guevara-inspired rebels did not go hand in hand with the imposition of autocratic rule. None of the often fragile democracies of South America collapsed due to the guerrilla uprisings inspired and supported by the Cuban Revolution. The counterinsurgent backlash focused in a targeted way on the limited groupings of extremists who spearheaded ill-considered efforts at isomorphic replication. Consequently, these crackdowns did not destroy the political regime. Precisely because the insurrectionaries had acted in precipitous ways and were rather easy to defeat, liberal democracy survived the temporary usage of military force. Thus, this wave of reaction did not cause a series of democratic breakdowns.

Political Radicalization and the Imposition of Reactionary Autocracy

While surviving the armed uprisings that directly sought to repeat Castro's takeover, liberal democracy fell in numerous countries as a reaction to sustained efforts by a broader range of left-wingers to promote radical causes. Colombia and Venezuela with their stronger party systems contained radicalism, but in other countries leftist and populist forces took tremendous inspiration from the Cuban Revolution and came to promote ambitious goals of profound sociopolitical transformation. This push for drastic change, which gathered steam especially in nations that had not experienced rural guerrilla struggles, induced powerful elites and substantial parts of the citizenry to doubt their democracies' resilience and capacity for resistance. Because they feared that as in Cuba, the call for economic nationalism and major social reform would end up in communism, they often embraced autocratic rule to guarantee their safety.

Graph 3.3 depicts this momentous backlash dynamic, which was mainly responsible for the autocratic reverse wave in Latin America. As indicated by the width of the causal arrows, a much larger number of leftists pursued profound reforms than the small groupings that had started guerrilla struggles (compare Graph 3.2). But these broad-based transformational efforts also prompted strong repulsion, reinforced by the deterrent effects emanating from the Cuban Revolution itself. As a result, status quo defenders in most cases held numerical superiority over left-wing challengers, whom they clearly bested through their command over preponderant power capabilities. The following paragraphs examine these political impulses behind the proliferation of autocracy in greater depth.

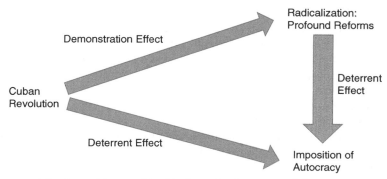

GRAPH 3.3: The Second Stage of Backlash: Radicalization and the Imposition of Reactionary Autocracy

The Cuban Revolution had a dual impact on the Latin American left. Besides inducing small numbers of extremists to undertake isomorphic emulation efforts, Castro's success inspired a much broader gamut of progressives to embrace transformational causes and promote them in more realistic and promising ways. Many of these new radicals rejected the idea of immediately initiating violent assaults on power, especially via Che Guevara's voluntaristic rural *foco* approach. The sobering conclusions suggested by the disastrous balance sheet of guerrilla struggles reinforced their preference for political, electoral, and mass mobilizational strategies, which might eventually culminate in revolutionary violence in the future, but only after a lengthy phase of political preparation.

Interestingly, this upsurge of political ambition tended to be especially pronounced and widespread in countries that had not experienced significant guerrilla uprisings, such as Brazil and Chile. By contrast, persistent pockets of insurgency, as in Colombia and Venezuela, helped to discredit the legal left and to forestall widespread radicalization. Thus, there was a negative correlation between the two types of efforts to follow in Castro's footsteps. Some countries, however, were swept up in both of the repercussions of the Cuban Revolution. Argentina, in particular, witnessed a series of rural guerrilla uprisings from 1959 to the mid-1970s, when urban terrorism also spiraled out of control; in addition, the country underwent a massive process of extremist mobilization from the second half of the 1960s onward.

In sum, while much of the Latin American left rejected the guerrilla strategy, Castro's success offered tremendous inspiration and encouragement for progressive forces and unleashed a groundswell of radicalization in a number of countries. The ability of the Cuban communists to revamp their island under the nose of the United States prompted an upsurge of voluntarism across Latin America. The Caribbean precedent stimulated demands and campaigns for massive land reform, for the control or takeover of foreign businesses, for the empowerment of popular sectors, and for the corresponding elimination of elite influence and US interference. Thus, although the violent means of the Cuban revolutionaries proved unworkable in the rest of Latin America, their heroic goals and seeming accomplishments drew widespread admiration and stimulated a host of emulation efforts. As a result, many political forces, ranging from Brazilian populists to Chilean socialists, experienced a process of thoroughgoing radicalization.

Consequently, left-wingers came to pursue ambitious goals via a multifaceted approach that emphasized party organization, mass mobilization, and electoral participation, but that could also include clandestine preparations for violent action, designed to defeat the likely resistance of reactionaries. Communist, socialist, reformist, and populist parties started ceaseless recruitment drives and indeed won growing support in a number of countries. Where communists faced governmental bans or prohibitions, they created innocuous front organizations and sought to infiltrate established associations, especially parts of the labor movement. At the same time, the most radical groups of left-wingers anticipated repression and prepared for revolution. For these purposes, they created armed formations that operated more or less openly, such as Chile's Movement of the Revolutionary Left (Movimiento de Izquierda Revolucionaria – MIR).

In addition to the radical activism of domestic left-wingers, communism also maintained an international foothold from which it kept spreading its ideological projects. After all, Castro's revolutionary regime withstood constant US suffocation efforts, which backfired by inducing Cuba to align ever more closely with the Soviet Union. Thus, the font of extremism persisted, executed fundamental transformations at home, and continued to serve as a powerful inspiration for revolutionaries abroad. In fact, the Caribbean regime actively promoted the spread of extremism; besides aiding guerrilla movements for many years, Castro also supported many other left-wingers across Latin America, ranging from the leader of Brazil's peasant leagues to the presidential candidate of the Chilean socialists, Salvador Allende.

This external promotion of communism seemed to pose a common danger that affected the widest range of countries, regardless of the specific strength of domestic left-wingers. As Castro's own success weighed heavily on their mind, status quo defenders feared that with Havana's help, even a small nucleus of radicals could turn into a serious menace. The backing of internal revolutionaries by the "international communist movement," which included the provision of funds and weapons, was substantial. But its strength remained unclear because many of these flows and connections occurred in secret, to avoid discrediting its beneficiaries as "foreign agents."

In the world of bounded rationality, the hidden nature of this external support, combined with the clandestine approach of domestic radicals, aggravated the concerns of status quo defenders. The uncertainty that shrouded extremist agitation and subversion fueled concerns by hindering systematic rational assessments and opening room for cognitive shortcuts. The military, for instance, is trained to combat external enemies marked by distinct uniforms. How to deal with internal adversaries who conceal their identity and try to blend in with the general population? The Cuban experience served as a particular warning: After all, Fidel Castro had not led the revolution as a self-proclaimed Marxist (as Lenin, for instance, had done in the Russian Revolution). Instead, he had appealed to broad sectors of Cuban society as a democratic reformer and nationalist – only to betray these promises after taking power by embracing communism and imposing a totalitarian dictatorship (Guerra 2012).

Concerned about these "invisible" enemies and alert to the risk of deliberate deception, conservative forces and the military watched ample sectors of the left with grave suspicion.[13] What if nationalist reformers revealed themselves as Marxist subversives or quickly mutated into communists? Whereas center-left parties had a closer understanding of their radical comrades and knew better how to distinguish inflammatory rhetoric from true intentions and realistic projects, ideological distance and unfamiliarity with the left-wing milieu instilled in conservative forces much greater uncertainty, prompted heavy reliance on cognitive shortcuts, and – due to loss aversion – produced a tendency to think in worst-case scenarios.

Furthermore, right-wing sectors often had relatively weak organizational mechanisms for filtering out the misperceptions and problematic inferences that resulted from the availability and representativeness heuristics. Many elites did not advance their interests via broad-based political parties, but via smaller, more homogeneous groupings, such as business associations or informal coteries. Moreover, the military commanded a particularly close-knit, hierarchical organization. By limiting diversity and engaging in truncated deliberations, these groupings and organizations had little capacity to correct distorted judgments. Consequently, fear of the left continued to run rampant among the right. Of course, right-wing forces also faced the highest stakes. After all, conservative and reactionary sectors would bear particularly high costs from left-wing revolution, which would take away their political power, social clout, and property, if not their life. For all of these reasons, substantial concerns about communism persisted long after the Cuban Revolution. Powerful status quo defenders, in particular, tended to overestimate the danger emanating from the radical left and to fear enormous losses.

These exaggerated threat perceptions turned intense in countries plagued by institutional fragility and acute socioeconomic problems. In the unstable

---

[13] In the research that Wendy Hunter conducted on the Brazilian military from 1988 to 1990 (cf. Hunter 1997), she still encountered these kinds of strong fears, which by then were particularly excessive.

settings prevailing in much of Latin America (outside Mexico and Venezuela, for instance), right-wing sectors came to doubt democracy's capacity to contain and combat the danger presumably posed by the radical left. Did the guarantee of political liberty not allow "communists" to undermine the established system from within? Democracy's moral relativism and excessive toleration seemed to create an inner contradiction, jeopardizing freedom by conceding freedom of maneuver to the enemies of freedom. This sense of vulnerability eroded the already limited support for liberal regimes that existed among the right and bred growing advocacy of autocratic rule. A regime commanding concentrated power would protect the citizenry from extremist subversion and forcefully resolve the abovementioned problems as well. Anti-communism thus provided a fundamental motive for the abolition of liberal democracy and the imposition of military dictatorships in country after country. Consequently, left-wing radicalization inspired by the Cuban Revolution provoked a series of right-wing backlashes across Latin America.

The Emergence of a New Type of Autocracy

While the diffusion of reactionary rule gained its fundamental impulse from the deterrent effect of the Cuban Revolution, it gathered additional steam from the emergence of a new type of authoritarian rule that seemed to hold greater promise for fortifying the polity against the communist threat than political liberalism and democracy did. Brazil's bureaucratic authoritarianism had more institutional solidity than traditional, personalistic dictatorships; and with its determined quest for development, it went beyond sheer repression and sought to overcome the poverty and social deficits that could provide a fertile ground for communist subversion. In the eyes of many right-wingers, this autocratic model therefore offered a viable solution to the challenge arising from left-wing radicalism.

Brazil's innovative dictatorship seemed to fill the political needs that the specter of radical revolution made urgent. After all, this national security regime instituted firm authority that reliably commanded and projected political power and coercion. Through a professional military supported by a government party, the autocracy established control over the citizenry. Corporatist mechanisms of interest intermediation contained conflict between business and labor and guaranteed the political platform for a state-directed strategy of economic development. At the same time, political censorship, systematic vigilance and espionage, and targeted repression kept serious opposition from coalescing and threatening regime stability. The new version of authoritarianism thus had the institutional means to guarantee political order and neutralize the enemies of the state.

Accordingly, while the diffusion of autocratic rule drew its main impetus from the repulsion against leftist revolution, the attraction of this rightist innovation contributed as well. The deterrent effects of communism and the demonstration effects of bureaucratic authoritarianism went hand in hand. Jointly, these interlocking forces provided a powerful impulse for the proliferation of reactionary rule.

By highlighting the interaction of diffusion and counterdiffusion, the theoretical analysis of the present chapter corroborates the main methodological point of Chapter 1: the complexity of autocracy's spread would make it exceedingly difficult to unravel this process with statistical models. Given the limited number of cases, the variety, intersection, and irregular timing of deterrent and contagious impulses would preclude clear, meaningful results. To avoid these problems, Chapters 4 to 7 employ qualitative analysis and process tracing to substantiate and assess the theoretical ideas advanced above. The book draws on ample historical research – some primary, most of it secondary. Yet as a work of social science, it tries to identify common patterns and processes in the welter of particular developments that played out across Latin America during the 1960s and 1970s.

CONCLUSION

To explain Latin America's momentous reverse wave of reactionary rule, this chapter has designed an explanation that rests on bounded rationality and embeds cognitive microfoundations in organizational macrostructures. Specifically, inferential shortcuts that propel the spread of prodemocratic regime contention (Weyland 2014) also provide crucial impulses for the diffusion of reactionary autocracy, yet with a serious twist arising from asymmetrical loss aversion.

The heuristics of availability and representativeness drew the attention of observers in a wide range of countries to the dramatic precedent of radical revolution that occurred in 1959 in Cuba. That a few rebels could succeed in toppling a US-supported dictatorship suggested to political actors across the ideological spectrum that the incumbent rulers of their own nations might also be giants on feet of clay. While the radical left therefore initiated precipitous attempts at imitative revolution, status quo-oriented sectors combated these efforts with full force. In this way, conservative groupings acted out of the same belief as their leftist foes, namely the inference that the established system was precarious. But given their opposite ideological preferences and political interests, they of course sought to stabilize what their enemies tried to topple.

This reactionary determination was fueled by the intense fear and repulsion that revolutionary precedents triggered among status quo-oriented sectors. The perceived danger of communism's spread activated the asymmetrical loss aversion that fundamentally skews human cost-benefit analysis. As a result, left-wing diffusion prompted powerful right-wing counterdiffusion. By documenting the important impact of disproportionate loss aversion, the present study adds a crucial element to a bounded rationality approach for understanding politics.

This skewed choice mechanism explains the interactive dynamic of revolutionary challenges and reactionary responses as well as their lopsided outcomes, namely the uniform defeat of the left by the right. Because people weight losses much more heavily than gains of objectively equal magnitude, the defenders of the established order significantly outnumbered emulative revolutionaries; and they went to great lengths to defeat and forestall attempts at communist revolution. Therefore, a wide range of forces squashed leftist uprisings. And when despite these early victories, the danger of radicalism nevertheless seemed to persist, especially in the eyes of right-wingers, these sectors promoted or supported the imposition of autocracy in order to immunize the body politic against the communist virus.

These cognitive-psychological mechanisms shaped political action because important organizations involved in struggles over the political regime lacked the internal pluralism and deliberative mechanisms that can mitigate the impact of inferential distortions and unbalanced decision weights. In particular, uniformity-seeking groupings on the right, such as the military, overestimated the communist threat. In the initial perplexity and confusion caused by Fidel Castro's unprecedented revolution, even broad-based organizations of the center and center-left relied on cognitive shortcuts and shared the excessive fears of conservatives. As a wide range of political actors overrated the danger of communism, intense loss aversion prevailed. Consequently, a broad, ideologically diverse coalition of forces combated the rash of guerrilla efforts that sought to emulate the Cuban Revolution directly.

As these ill-considered insurgencies suffered defeat after defeat, broad-based parties that can process political information relatively well updated their threat perceptions and arrived at more realistic assessments of the actual danger posed by communism. As their fears eased and loss aversion turned less acute, these groupings reaffirmed their commitment to liberal democracy and the rule of law. Conservative forces, by contrast, who tend to have less well-established mechanisms for information processing and deliberation, continued to see communism as a grave risk. In fact, Castro's success had set in motion a broad process of radicalization in much of Latin America which seriously seemed to jeopardize the sociopolitical status quo. Because a radical transformation would hurt the core interests of establishment sectors, loss aversion continued to prompt enormous concern among their ranks. Therefore, as radical reformism and conservative resistance brought growing polarization and conflict, these sectors pushed for the installation of authoritarian rule in order to fortify the established order and finally eliminate the danger of extremism.

By complementing cognitive microfoundations with arguments about organizational macrostructures, my theory provides an explanation for the most striking wave of reactionary autocracy that the western hemisphere has seen. Moreover, this theory adds another important piece to a bounded rationality approach to politics. The following chapters substantiate and assess these arguments through an in-depth examination of the twists and turns in the proliferation of long-lasting military regimes in Latin America during the 1960s and 1970s.

PART II

REVOLUTION AND THE REACTIONARY BACKLASH IN LATIN AMERICA

In line with the theory developed in Chapter 3, the surprising success of the Cuban Revolution provided the main impulse for the Latin American reverse wave. The perceived threat arising from the irruption of communism in the western hemisphere prompted a regional backlash that propelled the riptide of authoritarianism. An interactive sequence of revolution and reaction, of diffusion and counterdiffusion fueled the proliferation of military coups during the 1960s and 1970s.[1]

Fundamental mechanisms of bounded rationality, especially cognitive heuristics and asymmetrical loss aversion, shaped the repercussions of Fidel Castro's unexpected revolutionary precedent, which stimulated both precipitous emulation efforts and determined countermeasures to forestall the spread of left-wing radicalism. People's disproportionate aversion to losses is crucial for explaining why a broad phalanx of status quo defenders combated the specter of communist revolution and employed full, often excessive force. As a result, both Castro-inspired guerrilla struggles and broader leftist transformation efforts suffered uniform defeat. Revolution lost to counterrevolution. In these struggles, reactionaries overreacted and committed unspeakable atrocities, which reveal the intensity of their loss aversion.

Producing the first communist regime in Latin America, the "backyard" long claimed by the United States, the Cuban Revolution inflamed leftist radicalism and inspired and supported an upsurge of guerrilla movements across the continent (Castañeda 1993: 67–8, 74; Marchesi 2018: 23–5, 28–31, 37–9, 58, 69–95). These variegated attempts at diffusion provoked a powerful response from right-wing and even centrist sectors (on the impact of radicalism, see Mainwaring and Pérez-Liñán 2013: 218–24). Out of inordinate fear of Castroite communism, perceived as a mortal threat to weak, unstable civilian regimes, takeovers by the armed forces proliferated sooner or later.

---

[1] For a theoretical explanation similar to my own, yet based on somewhat different psychological mechanisms (namely empathy), see Waisman (1987: 231–4, 249–52, 263–4).

The heuristics of availability and representativeness fueled these perceptions of imminent danger arising from leftist radicalism. On this basis, loss aversion then prompted lopsided reactions. These cognitive-psychological mechanisms explain the disproportionate response to leftist challenges that in most cases had, rationally assessed, fairly low chances of success. The perceived danger from the extremist left, aggravated by Cuba's alignment with the Soviet Union, also induced the regional hegemon United States to support the installation of conservative authoritarian regimes as the lesser evil and as a necessary protection against communist revolution. This vertical backing, molded by the abovementioned cognitive mechanisms as well, facilitated and bolstered the spread of military rule, but was not its principal cause, as Chapter 7 shows below.

Thus, the Cuban Revolution supplied the crucial stimulus for the rash of military coups in Latin America and provoked the proliferation of a new form of institutional dictatorship with long-lasting developmental ambitions. Certainly, fledgling, fragile civilian regimes were likely to break down here and there, for various reasons. But the broad advance of authoritarian rule and the strong predominance of liberalism's demise over instances of redemocratization – that is, the wavelike character of this regional reverse movement – reflected the shock caused by the Cuban Revolution. The ability of an initially small band of rebels to topple an established regime, take power, and initiate profound transformations aroused inordinate expectations of success among the far left, which therefore initiated isomorphic emulation efforts across the region.

This wave of guerrilla movements exacerbated concerns among the right and center, which were also swept up by distorted inferences from the Cuban "success" and which jumped to the conclusion that existing regimes were fragile. Yet while sharing the radical left's belief in the easy replicability of the Cuban precedent, ample status quo-oriented sectors held opposite interests and value judgments. Among them, the prospect of communism activated pronounced loss aversion, which made these powerful sectors support determined efforts to stem communism's spread. The expectation of revolutionary diffusion, shared by the left and the right, aroused profound fear and sometimes panic among reactionaries, conservatives, and even centrists, and induced them to forestall this prospect with all means. Therefore, they marshaled their ample sociopolitical resources and squashed extremist stirrings with full force.

These quick victories calmed the worst fears. The pure revolutionary voluntarism derived from the Cuban Revolution (Goldenberg 1971: 372–3, 383–4, 539) and codified in the guerrilla manuals of Che Guevara ([1961] 2007; see Wright 2001: 73–6) and later Régis Debray (1967) had clearly failed reality checks. Obviously, Latin America's established regimes were not nearly as precarious as the most extreme groupings of the left had assumed in their isomorphic emulation attempts. These experiences stimulated learning and eased the fears prevailing among status quo defenders. In particular, broad-based organizations such as centrist political parties came to proceed with greater political rationality again. As revolutionary Cuba survived US aggression and continued to inspire and export radicalism, centrists and center-leftists sought to counteract this continuing danger with preemptive social and political reforms, encouraged and supported by John F. Kennedy's Alliance for Progress. In many South American countries, however, this innovative approach, which US officials saw as "a necessity if Latin America was to be preserved as part of the Free World" (May 1968: 25; similar 37, 164), did not manage to achieve its goals. In some countries, democracy with its dispersal of power hindered social reform; in others, change did advance, but democratic competition often fueled radicalization rather than moderation.

These setbacks discredited the preemptive reform strategy and made liberal democracy look incapable of coping with the communist threat effectively. Political polarization resulted: conservatives dug in their heels, whereas leftists pushed hard for profound transformation. As radical pressures seemed to grow and the advocacy or use of violence increased, rightist forces and some centrist sectors embraced authoritarianism as a lesser evil. To put an end to growing conflict and instability, the military promised to eradicate the danger of communism with a combination of systematic repression and determined developmental efforts designed to undermine and deplete support for radicalism permanently. Thus, the persistent left-wing threat and the perceived weakness of competitive civilian rule induced more and more actors to seek refuge in the strong arms of autocrats. What proliferated were new types of authoritarian regimes: institutionalized, and therefore more powerful and resilient than the personalistic rulers who had run many Latin American dictatorships, most notably Cuba's prerevolutionary regime, before. These high-capacity autocracies undertook ambitious projects to transform politics, economy, and society, and thus immunize the polity against radical threats. Accordingly, only after the coercive organs of the state had – with brutal means and terrible atrocities – rooted out the specter of leftist violence completely did South American militaries agree to relinquish power and slowly (re)institute democracy.[2]

In sum, Cuba's revolutionary precedent triggered waves of ill-considered imitation attempts and repressive backlash, of radical reform efforts and reactionary countermeasures, culminating in the imposition of anticommunist dictatorships. In these epic struggles, the right consistently beat the left, often with cruel means. What spread across Latin America was not Castroite

---

[2] Peru's last military dictator, Francisco Morales-Bermúdez, emphasized (interview 2009) that if the Shining Path guerrilla movement had begun its campaign of violence under his rule, he would have retained power until the military defeated this threat. But the Shining Path struck first on the day of the transitional election, when such a move was politically no longer possible, especially because the organizational strength of this terrorist network was far from clear.

communism, but conservative authoritarianism. The shock wave emanating from the Cuban Revolution gave rise to a powerful, wide-ranging reverse wave of counterrevolution.

The following four chapters substantiate these points step by step. Chapter 4 examines the most immediate diffusion effects of the Cuban Revolution, which inspired ill-fated attempts at isomorphic emulation, namely a rash of guerrilla movements all over Latin America. These radical-left adventures drew a repressive response, but they also stimulated socioeconomic and political reforms designed to forestall revolution. While these measures, coordinated by the United States via the Alliance for Progress, managed to stabilize new, fragile democracies in Venezuela and Colombia, they did not achieve their intended outcomes in many other countries.

Chapter 5 examines the groundswell of radicalization that was reinforced by the perceived failure of preemptive reform and that inexorably seemed to push large parts of Latin America toward the left. To block these powerful transformational impulses, conservative sectors spearheaded by the military sought refuge in authoritarian rule, which unleashed a ferocious counterattack against revolutionaries and suppressed broader sectors of leftism and populism as well. In Chapter 6, case studies of the installation of autocracy in Brazil, Argentina, and Chile demonstrate that these breakdowns of democracy constituted backlash phenomena. They reflected the profound fear derived via cognitive heuristics from the Cuban precedent and were driven by the resulting loss aversion.

While Chapters 5 and 6 examine how the diffusion and counterdiffusion triggered by the Cuban Revolution affected domestic regime change, Chapter 7 highlights additional external influences. First, the imposition of military rule created its own demonstration effects, which helped to propel the riptide of coups across the region. The Brazilian putsch of 1964 and the subsequent formation of a bureaucratic-authoritarian regime constituted a new model of repressive developmental autocracy that promised to insulate countries against contagion from communism. The lusophone precedent influenced coup mongers all over Latin America and set in motion horizontal diffusion processes.

Second, the superpower United States exerted vertical influences. Deeply preoccupied by the Cuban precedent, the United States responded to the meager success of the Alliance for Progress with ever stronger support for reactionary autocracy as the necessary evil for precluding the much-feared spread of communism. The regional "hegemon" thus contributed to the downfall of democracy in much of Latin America. It is noteworthy, however, that the US role in these regime changes was much more limited than many observers used to suspect. Latin American conservatives, especially the military, acted with considerable autonomy, and had their own very clear and powerful reasons to block escalating radicalization with full force and guarantee sociopolitical stability through the overthrow of democracy. Thus, the main responsibility lay with domestic actors.

4

Diffusion Effects of the Cuban Revolution

Guerrilla Struggles, Repression, and Preemptive Reform

The present chapter examines the most direct impact of the Cuban Revolution, which set in motion the interactive dynamic of diffusion and counterdiffusion and thus paved the way for the autocratic reverse wave of the 1960s and 1970s. Fidel Castro's armed takeover in Cuba and the subsequent socialist transformation stimulated a large number of isomorphic emulation efforts. All over Latin America, guerrilla movements launched violent assaults on the established order. Deeply shaped by the distortions arising from cognitive shortcuts, these risky attempts to spread emulative revolution were ill-planned and uniformly failed, as Section 1 explains.

Weak to begin with, radical insurgencies ran afoul of state repression, as discussed in Section 2. After all, the Cuban precedent sent fear down the spines of status quo defenders and induced them to combat the rash attempts at replication with full force. Powerful, institutionalized militaries easily extinguished most of the beginning brushfires. Incumbent regimes went beyond mere counterinsurgency, however, as the last part of this chapter shows. Supported by the United States, many Latin American governments also embraced a reform strategy in order to alleviate the socioeconomic and political problems that Cuba-inspired radicals could exploit. This Alliance for Progress indeed helped to consolidate liberal democracy in Venezuela and Colombia. In other countries, however, preemptive reforms were blocked, or they fueled the very radicalization that their proponents had intended to avert. Thus, this sophisticated effort to contain the political fallout of the Cuban revolution inadvertently helped to set the stage for the downfall of liberal democracy in country after country, which Chapter 5 will examine.

REVOLUTIONARY DIFFUSION: ISOMORPHIC INSURGENCIES

The Cuban Revolution, occurring in the context of other revolutionary advances in the global South (see, e.g., De la Puente 1964b: 1, 5–6, 12–13), had a striking impact that set in motion the interactive dynamic by which left-wing challenges prompted right-wing reactions. Most importantly, extremist groupings quickly started attempts to repeat Fidel Castro's success and initiated a welter of violent guerrilla movements in most of Latin America. Predictably, the political establishment, especially the military, responded with force and extinguished these flickering flames. Yet in addition to repression, incumbent governments soon adopted a more sophisticated strategy. With US support, they tried to enact a reform program designed to overcome long-standing socioeconomic and political problems. In this way, they sought to alleviate discontent, leave no room for leftist agitation, and guarantee sociopolitical stability. The fate of these reform efforts was crucial for subsequent regime developments, as the second half of this chapter shows.

The surprising collapse of the US-supported Batista regime, which crumbled under a militarily weak challenge, drew widespread attention due to the availability heuristic. The representativeness heuristic then suggested to sectors across the ideological spectrum that their own governments might also be precarious, which could enable revolutionaries to take power. Strikingly, both leftists and rightists held these views, despite their fundamental ideological differences. This commonality demonstrates that these perceptions did not result from wishful thinking by the left or from fear mongering by the right, but from heuristic inferences drawn from Castro's success. Observers of all stripes processed the Cuban events not with the logical tools of standard rationality, but with the cognitive shortcuts of bounded rationality. As a result, both sides of the ideological divide acted in ways that deviated starkly from conventional cost-benefit assessments.

In fact, the force of these cognitive shortcuts could override prior ideological predispositions. In both Argentina and Brazil, the "overwhelming" impact of the Cuban Revolution, together with other precedents such as the Chinese Revolution and the Vietnam War, turned a number of right-wing youths into radical left-wingers. Making an about-face by abandoning their initial anticommunism, these turncoats ended up participating in armed struggle for the socialist revolution.[1] Some of these converts became "super-radical" to prove their devotion to the new cause (Sirkis 2005: 5, 7).

The problematic inferences derived from the Cuban precedent had their most direct repercussions among the far left, unleashing a burst of revolutionary voluntarism all over Latin America (Gott 2008: 103–4, 111, 163, 221–2, 227, 244, 322–4, 330). Certainly, this enthusiasm for following in Castro's footsteps was driven in part by the serious social problems afflicting Latin America, especially deep inequality and mass poverty. But of course, pressing needs do not make drastic countermeasures rational, especially violent assaults on the

---

[1] See especially Goebel (2007, particularly 368, 372, 374) and Finchelstein (2014: 95–6, 107, 112); see also Sirkis ([1979] 2008a: 56, 102); Ridenti (1993: 125–6); Ollier (1998: 98, 114); Reis (2005: 9); Langieri (2013: 165–7); Brown (2017: 391–5, 405, 408).

established order. Instead, it is crucial to ascertain the feasibility and promise of remedial action. On this decisive issue, cognitive shortcuts misled many left-wingers, who jumped to the conclusion that they could spearhead emulative revolutions, and in this way replicate the profound redistributive changes imposed on the Caribbean island. This problematic short circuit resulted from the cognitive shortcuts highlighted in this book.

Ample evidence demonstrates how the heuristics of availability and representativeness reshaped and distorted the thinking of many leftists. As a Colombian guerrilla leader reported, for instance, "The triumph of the Cuban Revolution caused a tremendous stir among revolutionaries in our country" (quoted in Gott 2008: 244). A Brazilian militant highlighted that due to "the impact of the Cuban Revolution . . . there was tremendous optimism . . . History was in our favor" (Reis 2005: 7; see also Langland 2013: 69). And an Argentine insurgent stressed the attention that the striking events in the Caribbean attracted immediately, thousands of miles away: "In the year 1959, the Cuban Revolution awakened in me an unusual interest . . . Fidel Castro was a popular hero" (cited in Ollier 1998: 86). A Venezuelan fighter also emphasized "the tremendous encouragement of [provided by] the Cuban Revolution" (Prada 1999: 78).

In line with the availability heuristic, Castro's success drew enormous attention "because the Cuban Revolution is still the most recent revolution and is geographically the closest to us," a Peruvian radical stressed in the late 1960s (Béjar 1970: 10). Demonstrating the monumental significance attributed to this precedent, Brazil's Organização Revolucionária Marxista – Política Operária (POLOP – Revolutionary Marxist Organization – Worker Politics) declared in 1967 that "The history of Latin America, today, is divided in two phases: before and after the Cuban Revolution" (document reprinted in Reis and Ferreira de Sá 2006: 123). As this radical organization explained: "With this [Castro's accomplishments], all the class struggle in the continent was raised to a higher level. A return [reversal] is not possible" (ibid. 124). The conclusion, in line with the representativeness heuristic, was that "What the countries of Latin America have in common today is, above all, a similarity of conditions of struggle that creates an active solidarity among the masses of the continent" (ibid. 124). As an Argentine fighter reported, "I read about the triumphs of Fidel Castro, the mountains, the people involved there; and I said, 'We can do it.' A few years later I went to the mountains [as a guerrilla commander]" (interview in Salas 2003: 44).

Peruvian guerrilla leader Luis de la Puente (1964b: 5–6) was particularly emphatic: "The Cuban Revolution is nothing but the beginning of the Latin American Revolution, the triumphant beginning of the second great heroic deed in the emancipation of Latin America." After outlining a guerrilla strategy that closely followed the approach advocated by Che Guevara (similar De la Puente 1964a: 11–15), this ill-fated imitator, quickly killed by the Peruvian army in 1965, added: "The Cuban Revolution is invincible . . . The Cuban Revolution has revealed up to what point the supports [of the established order] are already insecure. It has put in evidence that they . . . incubate a time bomb that threatens to blow the whole system to smithereens" (De la Puente 1964b: 12–13). Lacking in realism, these rhapsodic beliefs reflected the distortions arising from inferential heuristics.

Even left-wingers who did not fall for these kinds of inferences highlighted the powerful impact of cognitive shortcuts on important sectors of the left. For instance, Waldir Pires, a leading Brazilian reform advocate, reports about the early 1960s: "The idea of an easy political voluntarism was very strong. There was a whole tendency that one could repeat in a country like Brazil the democratic episode of the Cuban Revolution . . . The idea that a solution [along the lines] of the revolutionary *foco*, a movement of the Cuban type, would be possible was very widespread in that epoch" (1987 interview cited in Moraes 2011: 219–20). Peruvian peasant organizer and guerrilla fighter Hugo Blanco (1972: 74), who disagreed with the specifics of the Cuban-inspired *foco* strategy (Blanco 1972: 62–3, 75), also stressed, "The Cuban Revolution opened a new chapter in Latin America. It was a tremendous blow not only to imperialism and all exploiting classes, but also to reformism of all varieties . . . also, it signified a milestone with regard to the tactic of guerrilla warfare."

Among the most radical observers of the Cuban Revolution, these cognitive shortcuts stimulated replication efforts. After all, "Fidel Castro had made the revolution with 56 people, and the [Cuban] state had just crumbled"; consequently, guerrilla struggles "looked so doable, so easy," as a former urban *guerrillero* in Brazil explained (interview with Sirkis 2008). According to the Brazilian Communist Revolutionary Party, "The grandiose example of socialist Cuba . . . inspires the people of Latin America to the revolutionary struggle" (document in Reis and Ferreira de Sá 2006: 217–18; similar for Argentina, Langieri 2013: 159). And former fighter Héctor Béjar (1970: 60–1) commented on the "adolescents [who] . . . joined the ranks" of Peru's guerrilla groupings: "They were united in their admiration for the Cuban Revolution and its desire to follow that example" (similar Béjar 1970: 10, 47). Che Guevara's *guerrilla foco* idea, in particular, "inspired wild voluntarism," as a Brazilian student activist remembers (interview with Van der Weid 2008).

In a similar vein, Francisco Julião, the leader of Brazil's peasant leagues, which soon prepared a guerrilla challenge, commented on his visits to Fidel Castro: "I returned from Cuba impressed . . . I imagined that . . . in Brazil . . . we could follow the Cuban experience. Thus, in a certain way, I committed this distortion, when I let myself guide, with a certain romanticism, by the great revolutionary process in Cuba, which ended up filling the whole Latin American continent with enthusiasm" (1983 interview cited in Moraes 2011: 85; see also 84).

Inspired by these distorted inferences, the radical fringe sooner or later started imitation efforts which also benefited from Castro's encouragement and support. From 1959 onward, a rash of guerrilla movements sprouted up and affected most of Latin America during the subsequent decade.[2] Insurgencies erupted right after Castro's takeover of power, beginning in 1959 in Argentina,[3] the Dominican Republic, and other circum-Caribbean countries.[4] The wave then extended to Colombia, Paraguay, and Venezuela in 1960 (Mercier Vega 1969: 127, 144), to Guatemala in 1961 (May, Schneider, and González Arana 2018: 26), and to Nicaragua (ibid. 68; Gambone 2001: 32, 56–7, 139–40) and Peru from 1963 onward (Béjar 1970). This riptide found its high-profile culmination in Che Guevara's Bolivian campaign of 1966–7 (Brown 2017: chap. 14). There were significant preparations in Brazil in 1962 as well, which governmental repression aborted (Azevêdo 1982: 93–5, 102–3; Rollemberg 2001: 21–6; Sales 2007: 42–54). The lusophone country also experienced a strikingly late emulation effort. The Araguaia guerrilla of the early to mid-1970s, while officially inspired by the Chinese Revolution (Genoino 2006: 69, 86–7), in fact followed the Cuban *foco* model very closely (Ridenti 2007: 44, 47).[5]

Several countries, such as Argentina, Colombia, Peru, and Venezuela, saw a variety of insurgencies, which in Argentina and Venezuela erupted over the course of many years and which in Colombia kept festering in marginal areas of the far-flung country. Leftist groupings initiated these small-scale uprisings in different parts of the national territory, often without much coordination (Béjar 1970: 68–73, 79; Brown 2017: 314–34). Thus, extremists inspired by Cuba tried over and over again to replicate Castro's success, despite a long string of earlier failures. The inferences derived from this striking precedent evidently had such weight that they blocked the realistic processing of experience and hindered prudential learning. Rebels operated with very tight bounds of rationality and persisted in their unpromising efforts. Even in the mid-1970s, after fifteen years of insurrectionary failures across Latin America, an Argentine guerrilla group hoped "to recruit more than 1,000 men," establish a "liberated territory" in the rural interior, and thus provoke a direct military intervention by the United States (Marchesi 2018: 152, 166–7). Based on an "assessment of the situation . . . [that] was very far

---

[2] Wickham-Crowley 1992: 16–18; Wright 2001: 42–5, 76–80; comprehensive overview in Lamberg 1972: 65–224; see also Gott 2008: xxiv, xxviii, xliv, 111, 221–7.

[3] On this early guerrilla effort and the inspiration from Cuba, see Salas (2003: 19, 44, 52, 84, 125).

[4] Lamberg 1972: 187–91, 196–98; eyewitness account in Diederich 2009: 131–4, 141–7.

[5] In line with the main argument of this book, even this late challenge by a mere seventy fighters in a fairly remote part of this huge country still caused considerable concern among political elites. Allegedly, this ongoing challenge prevented outgoing dictator Emílio Garrastazu Médici from nominating a civilian as his successor (Soares, D'Araujo, and Castro 1995: 261).

removed from . . . reality" (Marchesi 2018: 157), this plan resulted in another disaster for the radical left.

These ill-planned, rather indiscriminate, and obstinate emulation attempts betrayed the distortions of bounded rationality, especially the exaggerated perception of similarities derived from the representativeness heuristic.[6] This belief in the replicability of the Cuban precedent could not withstand rational scrutiny. The settings of this multitude of guerrilla challenges differed greatly from Castro's homeland. Most Latin American states boasted much higher levels of institutionalization than the Batista dictatorship with its Sultanistic tendencies (Domínguez 1998; Wickham-Crowley 1992: 166–73). Their bureaucratic machines and professional militaries predictably maintained control and avoided collapse in a guerrilla war (Rouquié 1987: 239; Wickham-Crowley 1992: 166, 169, 173, 184–92).[7]

Moreover, many South American countries were living under liberal, democratic regimes which allowed for peaceful reform and limited support for armed attacks among the citizenry, as even some left-wing radicals recognized after their defeat (for Peru, e.g., see Béjar 1970: 86–7, 104, 123). In fact, Guevara himself ([1961] 2007: 8) had counseled against a guerrilla challenge under these circumstances: "Where a government has come into power through some form of popular vote, fraudulent or not, and maintains at least an appearance of constitutional legality, the guerrilla outbreak cannot be promoted, since the possibilities of peaceful struggle have not yet been exhausted." But Che's overeager disciples disregarded their idol's advice, started armed uprisings in many (semi)democratic countries – and suffered dramatic defeat, often quickly.[8]

As the fundamental reason for the failure of the Peruvian guerrilla movements of 1965, for instance, analyst Lamberg (1972: 161–2; see also Rénique 2006: 93, 96) highlights "the exact copying of the Cuban example." This isomorphic emulation resulted from the unthinking tendency to "identify [Peru's democratic president Fernando] Belaúnde with [Cuba's corrupt dictator] Batista, the well-equipped, experienced Peruvian army with the demoralized Batista soldiers," and various socioeconomic characteristics of this Andean nation with the very different features of the Caribbean island.

---

[6] Where there were debates about the proper tactics and strategy to follow, they focused on abstract and abstruse theoretical issues, such as the role of the proletariat in underdeveloped Guatemala, that were "only marginally relevant to [the specific country's] situation" (Mercier Vega 1969: 128). After all, how many real "proletarians" were there in Guatemala at that time?

[7] Because bounded rationality differs from full-scale irrationality, however, significant rural guerrilla movements did not erupt in countries with particularly strong states and with seemingly consolidated democratic regimes (see next paragraph), such as Chile. Thus, in clear-cut cases, the distortions arising from cognitive shortcuts did not overwhelm basic probability assessments.

[8] Typical of bounded rationality, only in extreme cases did these considerations influence potential insurgents. Thus, Chile with its institutionalized state, its professional military, and its long-standing democracy was largely spared rural guerrilla movements à la Che Guevara.

All of this facile equating which "sovereignly disregarded the openly evident political, social, power-related, civilizational, and psychological realities of their homeland" (Lamberg 1972: 162), reflected the representativeness heuristic.[9] Similarly, a Venezuelan fighter in retrospect attributes the "errors" dooming insurgencies in his country to the prevailing belief that "the issue would be resolved in 'the easy way,' in the Cuban way" (Prada 1999: 102–3).

The strictures of bounded rationality are especially obvious in the fact that radical emulators did not learn from the actual historical experience in Cuba itself. Instead, they fell for the Castroite misrepresentation of this success, as enshrined in the guerrilla manual of Che Guevara ([1961] 2007). This misconception was reinforced by the later manifesto of Régis Debray (1967),[10] which according to Brazilian fighters was "advocating a servile imitation of the Cuban experience" (Quartim 1970: 69), "evoked more or less blind obedience" (Gabeira [1979] 1996: 48), and made revolutionary challenges "look so easy" (interview with Sirkis 2008).

Contrary to this *foco* theory, what succeeded in Cuba was not an armed challenge by a small band of fighters promoting Marxist revolution, but a broad-based, heterogeneous opposition movement pursuing democracy, social reform, and nationalism (Wickham-Crowley 1992: 174–8, 183; Guerra 2012). In the effort to win power, Castro himself had not advocated communism, but explicitly denounced it and embraced moderate, much more widely appealing goals. By contrast, the guerrilla groupings sprouting up all over Latin America proclaimed the radical goals that revolutionary Cuba eventually adopted. Ironically, these emulators were deviating from the very precedent that they sought to imitate (Lamberg 1972: 12–16, 227–30; Wickham-Crowley 1992: 183, 271). Due to their limited, distorted processing of the relevant information, they followed the official codification of this success, rather than the actual reality – a striking misunderstanding that betrayed a great deal of "irrationality" (Lamberg 1972: 51–2).

Thus, despite the obvious differences in local settings and despite the fundamental misunderstanding of the Cuban precedent, cognitive shortcuts inspired many isomorphic emulation efforts across the continent. Resting on clear departures from standard rationality and on unrealistic assumptions, most of these guerrilla campaigns utterly failed and quickly fell to governmental crackdowns (Gott 2008: 112–14, 120–1, 131, 146–7, 152, 156, 191–5, 289,

---

[9] On the Peruvian guerrilla movements' lack of planning and misunderstandings, see also Campbell (1973: 46, 54) and Rénique (2006: 90, 93). Béjar (1970: 84-5) denies the exact copying of the Cuban example, but at the same time shows that the Peruvian guerrilla followed the *foco* approach propagated by Che Guevara (Béjar 1970: 64-6, 71-72, 81).

[10] On the simplifications in these texts, see Wickham-Crowley (1992: 32) and Wright (2001: 73–76). For the impact of these texts on young activists, see Marambio (2007: 57–60), Sirkis ([1979] 2008a: 51, 81-2, 97, 141-2), Campos (2013: 80), Marchesi (2018: 37–40), and interview with Palmeira (2008).

358). In particular, by raising the scary banner of Marxism – rather than the nationalism and democratic reformism that Castro himself had advocated before 1959 – they aroused strong rejection from a wide range of status quo-oriented sectors, legitimated determined repression, and practically set themselves up for failure (Brown 2017: 207–9, 256).

These revolutionary stirrings were not based on careful cost-benefit calculations, but on rash inferences derived from the Cuban success and, especially, its official (mis)representation. Impressed by Castro's takeover, radical left-wingers jumped to conclusions about its replicability. Scholars regard the resulting imitation wave as "quixotic" and "naïve" (Wright 2001: 76; similar Levine 1973: 161–2, 205, 227) and emphasize its disastrous failure (Goldenberg 1971: chap. 17; Lamberg 1972: 153–62, 171–82, 229–30). In his particularly careful and systematic investigation, Wickham-Crowley (1992: 30–6, 41–3, 48) highlights how illusionary these adventures were, driven by "inflexible awe for a new [doctrine, namely the Cuban-inspired *foco* approach], whose superiority lay more perhaps in its psychological immediacy and temporal proximity than in its political efficacy" (Wickham-Crowley 1992: 33). Accordingly, in a recent study this expert invokes the availability and representativeness heuristics to account for these ill-fated emulation decisions (Wickham-Crowley 2014: 226).

Specifically, Castro's accomplishments, processed via cognitive shortcuts, led left-wing extremists to overestimate the success of imitation efforts and automatically discount failures. As a Chilean radical reports, "The [temporary] victories of *guerrilleros* in Venezuela, Colombia, Peru and Guatemala turned into news and their debacles were regarded as simple accidents on the road toward certain triumph" (Marambio 2007: 40). Thus, the distortionary impact of the Cuban precedent skewed the assessment of actual experiences. Miller (2016: 140) marvels, for instance, that Venezuela's guerrilla fighters "continued to behave in a curiously paradoxical way: the more they failed, the more they insisted that they were on the path to victory if only they would try harder." In the minds of Brazilian fighters, "defeat was not [regarded as] possible." Any setback was dismissed with the claim, "we lost one battle, but we will win the war," as a former insurgent records (Gabeira [1979] 1996: 69). The Uruguayan *Tupamaros* went even further and boldly "declare[d] in 1969 that they were 'invincible'" (Marchesi 2018: 56). Soon thereafter, however, they suffered "a resounding military defeat" and "had been dismantled" by the end of 1972 (Marchesi 2018: 107–8; see also Rey Tristán 2005: 45, 319, 323, 427–8).

For many years, learning, a central mechanism of standard rationality (Tsebelis 1990: 34), was deficient and often conspicuous by its absence. No wonder that due to these kinds of "errors" the particularly persistent insurgents in Venezuela, who kept fighting for nearly a decade, suffered "disastrous," "shattering" defeats (Ellner 1988: 40, 46–8, 50; see also Levine 1973: 161–2, 188, 205, 227). In fact, guerrilla groupings often made the most basic mistakes. As former fighter Héctor Béjar (1970: 79) bemoans, "The guerrillas . . . forgot that the Peruvian army has more than 50,000 men under arms and that it can fight on several fronts."[11] And with respect to some insurgents' trust in the safety of their "security zones" in remote mountain regions of the high Andes, Béjar (1970: 83) comments: "Only excessive naiveté could have led to the belief that where the guerrillas can go, the army can't." Due to this misjudgment, the rebel column suffered quick annihilation. Similarly, a former militant of Brazil's revolutionary "Bolshevist Fraction" reports, "As far as I remember, the political scenery, the correlation of forces was never discussed," which led to "out-of-control activism" (Falcão 2013: 309).[12]

Most of these emulation attempts suffered from deficient planning. Often, the main protagonists were middle-class intellectuals, especially university students (Béjar 1970: 60, 96, 110–11, 116–17; Ridenti 1993: 71–2, 159). Lacking a track record of personal experience and displaying particular receptivity to novel ideas (Marambio 2007: 38–40, 61–2), students were highly susceptible to the inferences derived from cognitive heuristics (cf. Wickham-Crowley 1992: 33–4, 46–8). But the realities of armed insurrection quickly revealed their Cuba-fueled hopes as illusions. As sympathetic observer Richard Gott (2008: 120; similar 107, 111, 121, 357, 483) notes, for instance, "all those who were involved in this early guerrilla venture [in Venezuela in 1962] have indicated that it was ill-planned, the guerrillas for the most part consisting of enthusiastic students who were in no fit state to bear the rigours of guerrilla warfare." Peruvian radical Héctor Béjar (1970: 60–1, 97–8, 110–19) highlights similar deficiencies, including students' lack of preparedness for his country's forbidding terrain, to explain the quick failure of the guerrilla uprisings of 1965. Similarly, one of his former comrades emphasizes the lack of fighters' military training (cited in Rénique 2006: 93; similar for Argentina, Salas 2003: 60–4; 81–5).

Besides their limited stamina for the hardships of fighting in steamy jungles or remote mountain ranges, students also lacked the capacity to reach out to the popular majority and win recruits. Poorer sectors had more pressing interests and concerns than the quest for the socialist revolution and rarely provided significant support for Castroite guerrilla struggles. For workers and peasants, immediate material needs took precedence over broader ideological goals inspired by a foreign success (see Béjar 1970: 116–18). The organizers of

---

[11] Similarly, Peruvian guerrilla leader Luis de la Puente (1964a: 14) regarded "the repressive solidity . . . [of the army and police as] very debatable," clearly underestimating the institutional cohesion and hierarchical discipline of his country's military.

[12] This striking divergence from reality also characterized one of the last major guerrilla campaigns in Latin America, namely the outburst of urban terrorism in Argentina during the mid-1970s. Even when one militant group after the other was decimated and massacred under the post-1976 military dictatorship, fighters continued to plan a full revolutionary war and to expect impending success (Novaro and Palermo 2003: 77–9).

armed *focos* therefore found little resonance among the popular sectors that were supposed to provide the foot soldiers for their insurgencies and to end up as the main beneficiaries of revolutionary transformation. In several countries, such as Venezuela, Colombia, and Peru, most rural dwellers hoped to benefit from land reform and therefore refused to participate in risky efforts at radical transformation.[13] Moreover, in nations where good parts of the peasantry, especially in peripheral areas amenable to guerrilla efforts, were indigenous and spoke native languages, middle-class intellectuals had great difficulty entering into communication with their presumed popular base (Béjar 1970: 96, 110–11). This problem was particularly pronounced in Bolivia, where Che Guevara, the main propagandist of the *foco* theory, failed to win over a single peasant recruit in nine months of effort![14]

Most of these guerrilla groupings also lacked a solid organization, as evident in their frequent defections and splits. Coordination among parallel efforts remained very limited and different groupings often operated at cross-purposes (e.g., Béjar 1970: 68–73, 79–80; Rénique 2006: 86, 88, 92; Brown 2017: 274–7). Material sustenance was often precarious as well. To alleviate this problem, a number of guerrilla movements received financial subsidies and arms from Cuba (Gott 2008: xliv–xlviii; Goebel 2007: 372; Sales 2007: 48–50), which for many years kept training thousands of Latin American fighters (Rollemberg 2001: 18, 65). Venezuelan *guerrilleros* benefited from especially ample assistance by Castro, which even included the deployment of Cuban militants, a bold and risky type of interference in a foreign country.[15] But these kinds of support depended on the unconditional commitment to follow the Cuban approach to revolution – in its abovementioned misrepresentation – and thus exposed the insurgents to accusations of serving as foreign agents. After all, "the pro-Cuban *guerrilleros* were under the direction of Cuba," as a former *guerrillero* in Venezuela reports (Prada 1999: 90).

Notwithstanding their limited manpower and resources and their problematic starting conditions, radicals were eager to risk their lives by trying to replicate the Cuban success across a wide range of countries. Their

---

[13] Alexander 1964: 182-3, 190–91; Chaplin 1968: 410–11; Weitz 1986: 410; Wickham-Crowley 1992: 44, 120–4, 196; Gott 2008: 151, 297, 370–71. Even Peru's radical peasant organizer Hugo Blanco (1972: 121, 124) recognized that "The previous agrarian reform law … [adopted by the Fernando Belaúnde administration, 1963–68] had succeeded in bridling the upsurge of the peasant impetus" and "alleviated some of the tensions in the countryside, decreasing thereby the possibility of armed struggle." Peru's military leaders recognized this pacifying impact as well (e.g., Mercado Jarrín 1974: 198, 209–10), and therefore spearheaded an ambitious reform drive after their takeover of power in 1968 (ibid. 194–95; Tello 1983, vol. 2: 128–9, 286).

[14] Lamberg 1972: 170-3, specifically 173; see also Quartim 1970: 67, 72; Wickham-Crowley 1992: 53; Lyles 2016: 280. Guevara acknowledged "the lack of popular response from the Bolivian campesinos" when questioned right before his execution by the Bolivian military in 1967 (*FRUS 1964–1968*: 384).

[15] Prada 1999: 84, 86–9. 91; Miller 2016: 94, 100–1, 111, 133, 143, 157, 161–2, 168, 180, 182, 190, 216; Brown 2017: 90, 250–1, 256–7, 260, 262, 268–9, 273–79.

reliance on tightly bounded rationality is evident in their stubborn clinging to isomorphic replication, namely the simplistic application and unthinking repetition of the (alleged) Cuban strategy. Whereas rational choice predicts that high stakes, namely the serious risks of violent contention, should induce careful, systematic cost-benefit calculations (Tsebelis 1990: 33-4), *guerrilleros* displayed remarkably deficient adaptation and weak learning.[16] For example, where can rural fighters hide in the open landscapes prevailing in much of Argentina (Lamberg 1972: 191; for Chile, see Marambio 2007: 61)? Yet despite unpromising preconditions for the *foco* approach, the countryside saw armed attacks in 1959–60, 1963–64, 1968, and 1969. Predictably, all of these unrealistic insurgencies failed (Lamberg 1972: 186–91; Brown 2017: chap. 13). Even in the plains of Uruguay, Guevara disciples scoured the landscape to find potential sites for guerrilla *focos*. Under the sway of cognitive shortcuts, they identified one of the country's few mountains, the Cerro Betete with its altitude of a mere 1,332 feet, as their own Sierra Maestra (Rey Tristán 2005: 177–8)!

After the decade following the Cuban Revolution had seen an outpouring of rural guerrilla struggles that affected most countries of the region, the disastrous outcome of Che Guevara's ambitious attempt to use Bolivia as the base for promoting armed uprisings across South America[17] finally prompted some rethinking (see, e.g., documents in Reis and Ferreira de Sá 2006: 197–8, 292–3, 351–4). A Brazilian radical, for instance, was shocked: "It is difficult to believe that so many mistakes could have been made by a group commanded by the greatest hero of the Latin-American revolution. Not only errors of preparation . . . but also errors of conception" (Quartim 1970: 67; see also 67–78). Thus, it took the indisputable falsification of the rural *foco* strategy to make an impact on sectors acting under the spell of cognitive shortcuts.

Interestingly, however, in a number of countries this reconsideration remained remarkably limited, confined to the "unavoidable," minimal adjustments predicted by bounded rationality, especially the theory of incrementalism (Lindblom 1965: chap. 9). Accordingly, extremists in the Southern Cone simply relocated their insurgencies by operating in the main cities rather than the countryside.[18] From the late 1960s onward, they employed an urban guerrilla strategy, which often was as voluntaristic, militarized, and delinked from political preparations as the rural approach preached by Che Guevara had been (see, e.g., Ridenti 1993: 45; Moyano 1995). Demonstrating the limited nature of this

---

[16] Interestingly, an Argentine radical questioned the usefulness and prospects of the rural guerrilla strategy, but was overruled by Che Guevara, who participated in the planning of some insurgencies in his homeland (Salas 2003: 112–13).

[17] *FRUS 1964–1968*: 369–88; Gott 2008: 399–472; Lust 2016: 226–9; see also Rollemberg 2001: 35–6.

[18] Lamberg 1972: 201–3; Gillespie 1982: 76–79; Rey Tristán 2005: 177–79; Sales 2007: 70–72; Brown 2017: 394, 398, 404–8; Marchesi 2018: 23–5, 36–7, 46–59.

adaptation, many advocates of this reorientation depicted urban attacks as the first step toward later rural guerrilla movements, which they continued to regard as decisive.[19] After all, "guerrilla [war] had to be in the countryside . . . [it had to be] created, as Che Guevara taught, via a rural *foco*" (Sirkis [1979] 2008a): 141-2).

This partial adaptation of the Cuban approach via the transfer of guerrilla struggles to urban settings produced more lasting challenges and caused great upsurges of violence from the late 1960s until the early to mid-1970s, especially in Argentina, Uruguay, and Brazil (Lamberg 1972: 201-4; Gillespie 1982; Ridenti 1993: 30-72; Rey Tristán 2005; Marchesi 2018: 23-5, 46-59). But urban fighters also proved incapable of taking national power. Instead, the ever more indiscriminate violence meted out by the insurgents turned increasing numbers of citizens against this terrorism (Moyano 1995). Urban guerrillas thus provoked a profound reactionary backlash which favored the imposition of brutal military regimes in Argentina and Uruguay and the hardening of autocracy in Brazil, as discussed in Chapter 6. Radical hopes that massive state repression would soon play into their hands by spurring popular revulsion, sparking mass uprisings against reactionary autocracies, and finally usher in the socialist revolution (Brown 2017: 203, 256-7; see also Shapiro 1972: 102) failed to materialize. Asymmetrical loss aversion clearly worked against the challengers of the status quo and stacked the deck in favor of its defenders. Therefore, harsh institutional dictatorships, which counted on majority acquiescence and a good deal of support,[20] proved powerful and determined enough to eradicate the extremist threat and inflict a terrible price on most of its protagonists. Thus, the limited modification of attempts to emulate the Cuban Revolution offered no greater chances of success than the initial reliance on isomorphic imitation.

Radicals' propensity to engage in guerrilla warfare depended in part on organizational structures. Most communists were affiliated with established parties, which – while far from being paragons of pluralistic deliberation – had organizational mechanisms of internal debate and decision making. These parties disagreed with the voluntaristic inferences that weakly organized students derived from the Cuban success. Instead, they highlighted that Latin America's social and institutional structures precluded successful socialist revolutions at the time. In line with this reasonably well-founded diagnosis, they severely criticized the activist fervor of *guerrilleros* as irresponsible adventurism (Goldenberg 1971: 408; Gott 2008: 188, 369-77). Accordingly, communist parties in most countries refused to participate in armed insurgencies. In the rare case in which they did temporarily support guerrilla

---

[19] See, e.g., Ridenti 1993: 40-1, 46-9; Marchesi 2018: 102; documents in Reis and Ferreira de Sá 2006: 220, 266, 272, 280, 345-6.
[20] O'Donnell 1983; Moyano 1995: 96, 98, 152; Novaro and Palermo 2003: 23-5, 30-3; Brands 2010: 111, 116, 120; Schmidli 2013: 8.

movements, namely Venezuela, they withdrew fairly soon, when indications of failure became hard to ignore for any reasonable observer (Levine 1973: 53–5, 188, 199, 203, 227, 236; Ellner 1988: 44–8; Prada 1999: 93; Gott 2008: 159–75, 183–90).

The strong disagreements between traditional communists and Castroite *guerrilleros* also suggest that fundamental ideological goals were not decisive for radicals' propensity to initiate armed challenges. Communist parties shared the firm commitment to socialism, that is, a total transformation of economy, society, and politics. But they diverged in their feasibility judgments, seeing minimal chances of achieving this ideological quest under present conditions, especially via direct armed attacks. The difference lay not in values and principles, but in estimates of the chances for realizing these values and principles. Via the representativeness heuristic, Castroites derived from Cuba's success the belief that the *foco* strategy was generally replicable and broadly applicable. Based on their established organization and long-standing political experience, by contrast, mainstream communists stood on firmer ground, were less susceptible to cognitive shortcuts, and put much greater emphasis on the structural obstacles to socialist revolution. Thus, the widespread eruption of guerrilla struggles was due neither to ideological goals as such nor to simple wishful thinking; instead, feasibility judgments derived via cognitive mechanisms, whose operation was mediated by organizational patterns, played a major role as well.

Because they acted on tightly bounded rationality, the rash, direct emulation efforts spearheaded by Castro's disciples uniformly fell victim to the coercive forces directed by incumbent governments; in most cases, these precipitous insurgencies suffered total eradication. By any objective standard and rational assessment, most of these insurrectionary attempts, especially those following the *foco* strategy in which a small armed band voluntaristically tried to incite a revolution, had infinitesimal chances of success. These initiatives, undertaken quite indiscriminately across the region, were unrealistic from the outset. Therefore, most of them crumbled quickly in the face of state repression.

REFLEXIVE COUNTERDIFFUSION: HARSH SUPPRESSION OF GUERRILLA MOVEMENTS

It is noteworthy that in combating extremist insurgencies, conservative sectors shared the feasibility judgments of their radical-left enemies to a good extent: they also believed that revolutionary efforts had considerable chances of success. This commonality of perceptions across the ideological divide confirms that these views were neither the product of wishful thinking among the extreme left nor of deliberate scare tactics among the right. Instead, actors with antagonistic interests and ideologies relied on the same inferential heuristics, and therefore regarded the Cuban precedent as an indication that established regimes were surprisingly brittle and could be overthrown. Accordingly, these views reflected fundamental cognitive mechanisms rather than specific ideological goals or political interests.

Of course, however, their distinct political preferences then induced these ideological adversaries to act in opposite ways. Whereas the radical left sought to make the expected success of socialist revolution come true, the right and center tried to block this scary prospect. Armed uprisings therefore drew a repressive response. In fact, the very depth of conservative concerns motivated rather harsh countermeasures, even in democratic Venezuela (Wickham-Crowley 1992: 199–200). Because status quo defenders acted on the basis of problematic inferences as well, rather than rationally founded beliefs, they overshot by cracking down hard (for Argentina, e.g., see Salas 2003: 96–7, 102, 107, 127). As leftist radicals acted in precipitous ways by initiating armed challenges in unpropitious circumstances, so the right reacted in an exaggerated fashion, using sledgehammers to swat at mosquitoes.

This disproportionality is obvious, for instance, in the Peruvian case, which saw several insurgencies erupt in the same year, 1965. To combat these small guerrilla bands, which added up to fewer than 200 active fighters, the country's military insistently demanded napalm from the United States and allegedly killed up to 8,000 peasants in its counterinsurgency campaign (Rénique 2010: 326; Walter 2010: 70–1, 73–5; Gott 2008: 348; Brown 2017: 327, 333)![21] Bolivia's armed forces also displayed "unnecessary roughness": they simply mowed down a guerrilla grouping that had surrendered on the promise of fair, legal treatment extended by the country's leftist president, a general himself (Malloy and Gamarra 1988: 57; Gallardo Lozada 1972: 171, 174; Marchesi 2018: 105). These heavy-handed measures went far beyond the mandates of rational calculations.[22]

These excessive responses reflect the rash inferences derived via cognitive shortcuts, which led to the overestimation of the communist threat. The resulting fears in turn activated asymmetrical loss aversion. Whereas expectations of gains induced small numbers of radicals to push for revolution, prospects of losses led much larger numbers of conservatives to combat these efforts, and with disproportionate force. While challenges remained limited, they provoked determined and often brutal countermeasures. As argued in Chapter 3, loss aversion is crucial for explaining these excesses. Realistic calculations would have prompted more moderate actions, to avoid the collateral damage of brutality. For instance, the

---

[21] According to unconfirmed charges, during the mid-1960s the Colombian military used napalm in its anti-guerrilla struggle as well (Nieto Ortiz 2010: 207; Villamizar 2017: 265–6, 278).

[22] By contrast, Bolivia's President René Barrientos deliberately ordered the summary execution of Che Guevara in order to avoid the political trouble and conflict that he foresaw if the government put the world-famous revolutionary on trial (Brown 2017: 443). Thus, this murder resulted from some kind of cold-blooded rational assessment.

Peruvian military's demand for napalm created further complications in the country's relations with the United States, which were already tense due to other diplomatic conflicts (Walter 2010: chap. 3).

Status quo defenders' responses to guerrilla challenges were mediated by organizational structures. While these groupings shared fears of communist subversion, they calibrated their reactions in line with their organizational characteristics. Broad-based, internally pluralistic parties that had established mechanisms for open deliberation and collective decision making engaged in better information processing than more closed, hierarchical, uniformity-seeking institutions such as the military. Discussion and debate enabled mass parties to filter out the worst misperceptions and arrive at decisions that were closer to rational standards. Whereas these organizations managed to broaden their bounds of rationality, narrower limits prevailed inside tightly integrated institutions revolving around top-down principles, especially the armed forces. The effort to forge cohesion allowed cognitive shortcuts and loss aversion to hold sway and to reinforce perceptions of radical threat.

These interorganizational differences, which shaped the plans for coping with guerrilla challenges, prevailed even in a country like Peru during the mid-1960s, where the governing party and the armed forces were quite close in underlying ideological orientation, as the determined reformism of the military regime installed in 1968 confirms (Einaudi 1971: 18–31, 41; Villanueva 1972: chaps. 2–3; Jaquette 1975; Stepan 1978b: 135; North 1983: 248–51). The government of Fernando Belaúnde (1963–8), who headed the broad-based party Acción Popular, wanted to react to the armed uprisings of mid-1965 in cautious, limited ways. But the armed forces, driven by intense anticommunism (Peru. Ministerio de Guerra 1966: 5, 76–7, 80), pushed hard for a massive counterattack, threatened a coup to get their way,[23] and then acted with great "ruthlessness" (*FRUS 1964–1968*: 990; Rénique 2010: 326–7; Walter 2010: 70; Brown 2017: 326, 333; see also Mercado Jarrín 1974: 212–13).

Similarly, in Venezuela the military on several occasions pressured the reformist administrations headed by the pluralist Acción Democrática party to combat the welter of guerrilla groupings with greater energy (Miller 2016: 75, 85, 92, 114, 136, 144, 158–9, 168). With US help, the armed forces finally got their way in 1966–7, which enabled them to win a definitive victory. Overall, however, Venezuela's political parties with their broad-based support and political strength managed to consolidate civilian control over the armed forces. Based on their better information processing and internal debates, which kept the scary inferences derived from the Cuban precedent in check, they charted a fairly prudent course for countering the guerrilla threat. In particular, the government tried to target repression on combatants and

---

[23] As Chaplin (1968: 404, 406) highlights, however, the Peruvian military was not particularly coup-hungry (similar Tello 1983, vol. 2: 120–86).

thus prevent heavy civilian casualties. Moreover, it offered repentant fighters amnesties and readmitted the Communist Party to the electoral arena once this organization had repudiated armed struggle (Prada 1999: 92; Miller 2016: 151, 163–4, 180, 197).

Most importantly, Venezuela's governing parties enacted ample reform measures to retain mass support and thus deprive the insurgents of followers, as the next section shows. Due to this apt strategy, which reflected looser bounds of rationality, the guerrilla experience ended up corroborating trust in the incumbent parties and thus helped to consolidate democracy (Levine 1973: 47, 56, 61, 208; Wickham Crowley 1992: 196, 199). This outcome differed from other Latin American countries with weaker party systems and greater governability problems, where insurgencies – even after their defeat – left behind fears of a recurrence and nagging doubts in the resilience of democracy. These persistent concerns, which held considerable sway among the military, played a crucial role in the imposition of dictatorial rule in Peru in 1968 (Cotler 1978: 194, 205; Stepan 1978b: 135–6; Tello 1983, vol. 1: 123, 286–7, 327; Rénique 2010: 322–4, 327).

While well-organized parties arrived at a more sophisticated understanding of guerrilla challenges, many status quo defenders shared with Castro's disciples some of the facile inferences derived from the Cuban precedent – and therefore offered strong resistance to Castroites' isomorphic emulation efforts. Disproportionate loss aversion induced sociopolitical elites, the military, and many common citizens to advocate and support determined countermeasures to violent challenges. As these threatened sectors mobilized the coercive powers of institutionalized states, the small, ill-planned uprisings stood no chance. Left-wingers' schematic efforts faithfully to replicate the Cuban Revolution – in its officially codified version – ran afoul of countermeasures driven by the deterrent effects of the Cuban experience. For these reasons, isomorphic diffusion suffered uniform, decisive defeat at the hands of counterdiffusion.

Interestingly, the capacity of status quo defenders to contain the ill-planned Castro-style guerrilla struggles, confine rebels to marginal areas, and defeat most of these insurgencies quickly guaranteed the survival of liberal democratic regimes at that time. Due to the effectiveness of repression and the impact of preemptive political strategies, isomorphic efforts to emulate the Cuban Revolution did not gain mass support and turn into broad-based assaults on government power. Nowhere did the small *focos* lit by sparks from the Caribbean island turn into wildfires that threatened to burn down the whole house; instead, counterrevolutionary fire fighters soon succeeded in extinguishing or thoroughly containing these flames.

Because establishment forces managed to cope with the threat posed by attempts at isomorphic emulation, panic did not take hold and stimulate demands for fortifying the state via the installation of authoritarian rule. After all, liberal democracy proved its defensive prowess and resilience. As a result, the rash of rural guerrilla struggles did not directly prompt the overthrow of democracy in any Latin American country during the 1960s. Although there were some coup rumblings, pluralist regimes survived the immediate backlash provoked by Castro's success. While shaken in some cases, especially Peru, democracy did not fall prey to reactionary efforts designed to block direct replication. Only the delayed and limited adaptation of the guerrilla strategy via the move to urban terrorism, which went hand in hand with the radicalization of a wide range of sociopolitical forces, had that deleterious backlash effect during the subsequent decade, with the imposition of fierce dictatorships in Uruguay in 1973 and in Argentina in 1976.[24]

REASONED COUNTERDIFFUSION: PREEMPTIVE REFORM EFFORTS

While establishment forces were also affected by the cognitive inferences derived from the Cuban precedent and therefore combated isomorphic emulation efforts with great force, their firmer organizational structures enabled them to proceed with less tightly bounded rationality than the mostly haphazard guerrilla forces. Therefore, they designed a wider range of countermeasures that ended up going far beyond counterinsurgency. In particular, they complemented targeted repression with a more sophisticated strategy for forestalling further emulation efforts by left-wing radicals. Broad-based political parties in Latin America and the US government developed a comprehensive plan of ambitious reforms to preempt communist revolution in the region. Initially suggested by Brazil's centrist president Juscelino Kubitschek, this Alliance for Progress was announced with great fanfare and plentiful resource support by President Kennedy in 1961 as his political response to the Castro challenge (May 1968: 29–32; Taffet 2007: 26–7, 199–223; theoretical interpretation in Packenham 1973: chaps. 2–3).

During the subsequent years, centrist forces and moderate leftists across the region pursued wide-ranging reform programs. By trying to remedy Latin America's notorious social problems, they sought to address the unfulfilled needs and festering grievances that could create support for extremism. Land reform would satisfy peasants and keep them from joining or assisting rural guerrilla movements; education and health reform would enhance the life chances and employment opportunities of the urban poor and thus forestall radicalization; and support for democracy would keep institutional avenues open and give citizens political means for promoting their interests and causes in peaceful and constructive ways (Smith 1995: 214–23). With strong encouragement and plentiful subsidies from the regional hegemon, the

---

[24] Moreover, Brazil's authoritarian regime hardened greatly from 1968 onward in response to mass protests and to urban guerrilla movements that formed soon thereafter.

Alliance for Progress energetically pursued ample, deep-reaching reforms as an attractive alternative to Marxist revolution.

The Success of Preemptive Reforms in Venezuela and Colombia

In Latin America during the 1960s, however, this preemptive strategy had disappointing results, as discussed below. Democratic reformism achieved political success only where two broad-based, ideologically moderate parties that engaged in centripetal competition came to dominate the political and electoral arena, namely in Venezuela and Colombia (Levine 1973: 3, 5, 8, 25–9, 240–1, 255–6; Bejarano 2011; Miller 2016). The unusual strength and institutionalization of the Colombian and Venezuelan party systems allowed for reasonable governance and for substantial reform implementation, especially in Venezuela.[25] As political leaders had extensive programmatic or clientelistic linkages to important societal groups, they could control and commit their followers while leaving little room for antisystem mobilization (see Weitz 1986: 411; Dix 1990: 106–12).[26] Therefore, guerrilla movements – while strikingly persistent in both countries, especially in Colombia (see discussion below) – remained confined to marginal areas and did not pose direct threats to central government power.

In Venezuela, the center-left Acción Democrática (AD – Democratic Action) commanded ample mass support in urban and, especially, in rural areas. Having deradicalized after its eviction from power through a military coup in 1948, it advocated substantial but circumscribed social change, including education reform and land distribution to the peasantry (Kirby 1973). These measures, funded with the country's oil wealth and supported by the United States (Rabe 1999: 99–109; Miller 2016), benefited large sectors of the citizenry, reinforced popular allegiance to the governing party, and contributed to the consolidation of democracy (Wickham-Crowley 1992: 196, 199). At the same time, the center-right Comité de Organización Política Electoral Independiente (COPEI) gave voice to elite sectors, including business and the Catholic Church, which thus had a stake in the democratic system emerging from a pacted transition in 1958. As AD channeled mass demands and its developmental efforts bore some fruits, the political space for radicalism remained limited (Mercier Vega 1969: 106).

---

[25] On party (system) institutionalization in Colombia and Venezuela in comparative perspective, see Dix 1992 (491–93, 497, 500–3) and Mainwaring and Scully (1995: 6–18). On Colombia, see Dix (1990) and Archer (1995: 169–83), and on Venezuela, Kornblith and Levine (1995).

[26] While Colombia enacted less reform than Venezuela, little sociopolitical radicalism emerged during the time period under investigation. By contrast to Brazil, for instance, no peasant leagues demanded profound land reform, nor was there a labor party with strong populist and left-wing tendencies (see Chapters 5 and 6).

In fact, the governing party had especially firm support in the countryside. Because Acción Democrática controlled the country's main peasant confederation (Bejarano 2011: 162, 169), the rural *foco* strategy advocated in Che Guevara's famous manual (Guevara [[1961] 2007) did not find any broad backing among the rural population (Alexander 1964: 182–3, 190–1; Levine 1973: 53–4, 161–2). The Castro-inspired guerrilla movements that started fighting the state in the early 1960s and that received ample support from Communist Cuba therefore failed to undermine the new democracy's stability (Ellner 1988: 40, 46–50).[27] While it took the military years to defeat the rebels, this confined threat did not create serious doubts in civilian governance (Goldenberg 1971: 505–19). In fact, the struggle against the *guerrilleros* and the government's eventual victory stabilized the new democracy by strengthening the pro-regime consensus among the two main parties and the military (Alexander 1964: 116–17; Levine 1973: 47, 56, 61, 208). Thus, democratic reformism along the lines of the Alliance for Progress accomplished its ultimate purpose in Venezuela (Miller 2016; see already Alexander 1964: chaps. 23–24).

Paradoxically, however, while the strength of Venezuela's two main parties was crucial for ensuring governability and for marginalizing violent unrest, it also had a negative impact by perpetuating this unrest during the 1960s. In most Latin American countries, guerrilla movements formed in fairly haphazard ways as radicalized students and intellectuals were swept up by the ideological fervor and voluntaristic activism stimulated by the Cuban Revolution; consequently, insurgencies usually lacked organizational cohesion and political discipline, making it easy for professional militaries to defeat these ill-considered adventures. In Venezuela, however, the rebel movement starting in 1962 originated from a split inside Acción Democrática, whose youth wing – inspired by Castro's success – rejected the ideological moderation of the party leadership that came with governmental responsibility (Bejarano 2011: 166–7; Miller 2016: 66–9). Thus, the guerrilla forces recruited many members from an established organization, which gave it greater cohesion.

Moreover, in an unusual move for Latin America, Venezuela's Communist Party, another firm organization, for years embraced and supported armed struggle. Before the communist leadership backed off from violence in the mid-1960s (Miller 2016: 132, 138-9, 156), Venezuela's fighters therefore had more organizational grounding than insurgents in the rest of the region. Last not least, they also enjoyed disproportionate external support. Fidel Castro deliberately targeted resource-rich Venezuela and showered its guerrilla movements with a great deal of money, weapons, and even Cuban advisers (Miller 2016: 94, 100–1, 111, 133, 143, 157, 161–2, 168, 180, 182, 190, 216).

---

[27] The substantial, persistent support from Cuba, which during the 1960s saw resource-rich Venezuela as the primary target of its revolutionary export efforts, is documented recently in Miller (2016: 94, 100–1, 111, 133, 143, 157, 161–2, 168, 180, 182, 190, 216).

Despite many setbacks on the combat front that the Venezuelan military inflicted, rebels therefore persisted with a surprisingly protracted struggle.

Once again, however, Venezuela's new democracy proved its political aptitude: it employed a reformist strategy by opening up political space for left-wing radicals and thus drawing them away from the path of violence (Bejarano 2011: 160–3, 170–2, 175). From the mid-1960s onward, the government encouraged guerrilla fighters to demobilize by offering an amnesty (Miller 2016: 151, 163–4, 180, 197). Many extremists indeed moderated, joined a political party that abandoned revolutionary goals, and entered the electoral arena (Ellner 1988). This Movimiento al Socialismo (MAS – Movement toward Socialism) was the first grouping of the radical left in Latin America that underwent a thorough "renovation" (cf. Roberts 1998). Interestingly, the MAS moved to electoral participation in the early 1970s already, when left-wing extremism reached a high point in many other Latin American countries (as Chapter 5 shows). The new party won congressional representation, but did not manage to emerge from its small minority status nor to put strong competitive and radicalizing pressure on the political forces sustaining the reformist governments (Kornblith and Levine 1995: 49–51). As the leading center-left and center-right parties, AD and COPEI, long retained mass support, continued to dominate the electoral arena, and alternated in the presidential office, Venezuela's democracy escaped rather unscarred from the Cuba-inspired challenges that had emanated from the radical left throughout much of the 1960s.

Colombia also boasted two moderate parties with strong, country-wide popular support. These long-standing organizations managed to negotiate a restoration of oligarchical democracy after the horrific mass slaughter of *La Violencia*, a decade of party-fueled atrocities, which had culminated in a short-lived military dictatorship (Dix 1980; Hartlyn 1988: chaps. 3–4).[28] As the parties learned from these self-inflicted catastrophes and put a premium on negotiation and compromise (Wilde 1978), they institutionalized consociational mechanisms to guarantee sociopolitical stability for a transitional period of sixteen years (1958–74). This National Front foresaw alternation in the presidency, equal division of appointed positions, and a two-thirds supermajority for congressional decision-making.[29]

The price of this concern for preventing polarization and conflict, however, was a good deal of political immobilism.[30] Despite the desire to avert a Cuban-style revolution through preemptive reform (Hirschman 1973: 142, 156), it proved especially difficult to enact profound socioeconomic change to ameliorate poverty

---

[28] On the question of how democratic Colombia was during the National Front period, see Bejarano (2011: 219–23; see also Taylor 2009: 20–38).

[29] Dix 1967: 130–6, 164–8. For a thorough analysis of Colombia's pact-making and a systematic comparison with Venezuela, see Bejarano (2011: 98–128).

[30] The National Front did increase legislative productivity (Leal Buitrago 2011: 78–80, 84), however, and thus demonstrate a good deal of governability.

and inequality (Dix 1967: 150–8, 253). Land reform, though pushed both in the early and the late 1960s by the Liberal Party, remained limited (Havens, Flinn, and Lastarría-Cornhill 1980), and educational reform concentrated primarily on the expansion of coverage through the construction of elementary schools in underserved rural areas and the extension of secondary and university education (Arnove 1980). Yet while not very redistributive, these measures, sustained by considerable economic growth and by voluminous funding from the Alliance for Progress (Baskind, Lerdau, and Mesmer 2008: 139, 160), did benefit ample sectors of the population. Moreover, they provided additional patronage for the two parties to strengthen their clientelistic networks, the main linkages to large parts of the citizenry. As a result, throughout the 1960s and 1970s, Colombia's consociational regime sat firmly in the saddle.

Based on this political and organizational strength, the two main parties also managed to combat far-left challenges and to keep radical threats at bay, averting any risk to democratic survival (Ruhl 1981: 129–32, 142). With the institutionalization of bargaining and compromise, the two parties and their factions engaged in constant vetting of situational assessments and frequent deliberations about common strategies (Nieto Ortiz 2010, e.g. 158–61). As a result, the main actors had a good understanding of the power constellation and the problems and threats they were facing; while concerned about the danger emanating from left-wing extremists, especially after the Cuban Revolution, they never panicked, as, for instance, the testimony of a military leader suggests (Valencia Tovar 2013: 252–5, 261–3, 278–82, 288–9). In fact, according to this general, civilian politicians and the armed forces were internally divided on whether to combat this unrest with a "militarist" strategy of frontal combat or whether civic action could isolate the rebel leaders and persuade their poor supporters to lay down their arms (Valencia Tovar 2013: 259–64, 272–84). Eventually, the National Front combined both approaches and undertook a series of largely successful efforts to extinguish persistent pockets of violence. But the civilian and military leadership had learned from the long history of bloodletting that Colombia's distinctly weak state (Dix 1967: 171–9; Soifer 2015) could live without strictly enforcing its claim to the monopoly over legitimate coercion throughout all of its far-flung, rugged territory. As "the country was used to peasant guerrillas" (Valencia Tovar 2009: 155), the consociational regime adopted a satisficing approach to the problem of internal security.

As part of the new democracy's pacification efforts, the armed forces in 1964 attacked the peasant self-defense militias that maintained "independent republics" in some remote mountain areas of south-central Colombia, a remnant of the decade of violence (Villamizar 2017: 211–13).[31] In these desolate hideouts, communist cadres had won over and organized poor

---

[31] Even in their constitutive manifesto of 1966 (reprinted in Villamizar 2017: 777–79), the FARC revealed a strongly defensive posture.

people who had fiercely guarded their autonomy for many years, ranging from old liberal *guerrilleros* to bandits (Ugarriza and Pabón Ayala 2017: 45–50). Well-prepared military invasions, preceded by civic action programs to win cooperation from the civilian population (Nieto Ortiz 2010: 156, 168–70, 191–5; Valencia Tovar 2013: 254–5, 281–4), managed to take over the rebel territories (Maullin 1971: vi–vii, 46–7, 59–61). But these combat operations did not succeed in eliminating or capturing all the rebels. Instead, left-wing fighters melted away and fled to other remote areas (Osterling 1989: 280–1, 294–6). To withstand the state's assault, these communist groupings unified and formed the Fuerzas Armadas Revolucionarias de Colombia (FARC – Revolutionary Armed Forces of Colombia), which now sought to go beyond a purely defensive posture and proclaimed the ultimate goal of taking over the state.

Yet because this guerrilla army was not a spinoff of the Cuban Revolution, and because Colombia's mainstream Communist Party rejected the impatient approach embodied in Che Guevara's *foco* theory (Osterling 1989: 186–7; Villamizar 2017: 198–200, 243, 295), the FARC concentrated primarily on building a firm support base among the rural poor. Slowly and gradually, it tried to extend its territorial control, but did not initiate an all-out attempt to capture government power. As Hartlyn's (1988: 192) major study comments, "the FARC was a relatively small, cautious, rural-based and oriented movement in the late 1960s." In fact, constant military pressure kept these peasant rebels on the run and pushed them into distant regions (Ugarriza and Pabón Ayala 2017: 77, 81, 88, 91–4, 123–8). As a result, in the 1960 and 1970s this communist grouping did not endanger Colombia's consociational democracy.[32] While the FARC would later grow in the 1980s (Ugarriza and Pabón Ayala 2017: 163), it long failed to pose a serious threat to political stability and social order.[33] Economic growth, social distribution, and the clientelism and patronage dispensed by the two main parties helped to keep popular support for the FARC limited and to marginalize this guerrilla force. Consequently, conservative and centrist sectors did not perceive a mortal danger, and the military saw no reason to step in and grab command over the government.[34]

A more direct, unprecedented threat to the National Front regime arose from the Cuba-inspired and Maoist guerrilla forces that emerged anew in the early and mid-1960s.[35] A product of the enthusiasm unleashed by Castro's success

---

[32] Hartlyn 1988: 191–94; Wickham-Crowley 1992: 145–6, 201; Fajardo 2003: 17–18; Bejarano 2011: 164–5, 168–9.

[33] Goldenberg 1971: 382, 479–81; Rempe 1995: 313, 320–1; Gott 2008: 209–18, 227–36; Lyles 2016: 229–35; May, Schneider, and González Arana 2018: 93–99.

[34] Colombia's pacted regime also benefited from a long tradition of civilian predominance over the armed forces (Bejarano 2011: 139), but as Ruhl (1981: 132–4) shows, this additional factor was not decisive.

[35] Rempe 1995: 312, 323; Villamizar 2017: 189–260, 294–331. Fals Borda (1968: 52–4) empha-sizes the differences between these new, externally inspired guerrilla groupings and the old peasant self-defense forces that ended up bringing forth the FARC.

(Valencia Tovar 2009: 155–6, 234), the Ejército de Liberación Nacional (ELN – Army of National Liberation) was the typical student-based grouping of ultraradicals that proliferated in Latin America during the 1960s. Carried away by cognitive shortcuts that suggested good prospects for emulating the Cuban Revolution (cf. Osterling 1989: 307–11), the ELN launched its frontal assault against the state in the same ill-prepared and badly planned fashion as its regional counterparts (Ugarriza and Pabón Ayala 2017: 97–9, 102, 105). Consequently, the Colombian military, which targeted this acute danger with particular determination, managed to inflict grievous losses and quickly cripple this new fighting force. Intensive counterinsurgency campaigns that again combined brute firepower with intelligence operations and civic action programs allowed the military to kill or capture many rebel leaders and to dismantle much of their urban support network (Maullin 1971: 64; Valencia Tovar 2013: 309–11, 319–21; Villamizar 2017: 316–18). "Following a number of severe reverses in 1967, the ELN has disintegrated into rival, and sometimes warring, factions," RAND consultant Richard Maullin (1971: 18) reported.

Thus, for years the ELN made only minimal headway (Goldenberg 1971: 486–90), and by the early 1970s was almost completely defeated.[36] As experts on the conflict judge, "The theory of the insurrectional *foco* was extinguished in the midst of political contradictions and military attacks by the forces of order" (Ugarriza and Pabón Ayala 2017: 105; see 106–9). The Colombian state clearly succeeded in preventing a repetition of Castro's success on its territory. In the view of military expert Mark Ruhl (1981: 136; similar Ruhl 1980: 189, 193–6), "the army had reduced the guerrilla's ability to carry out major operations against the government. Actually, neither the ELN nor the FARC ever posed a serious danger to the National Front's survival because of the guerrillas' inability to generate popular support in rural Colombia" (similar Wickham-Crowley 1992: 154, 192, 201).[37]

Paradoxically, however, the strategic denial of ultra-left efforts to take national power and the marginalization of the guerrilla threat contributed to its persistence, which was exceptional for South America, though not unusual for violence-plagued Colombia with its weak state. As the armed forces managed to confine insurgents to peripheral areas of the far-flung nation separated by three Andean mountain chains, incumbent governments lacked the sense of urgency to extinguish the faint flame. For that reason, guerrilla movements continued to fester throughout the 1960s and 1970s, fueled by sociopolitical discontent at the elite domination and immobility of Colombia's civilian regime. Yet because these fighters did not endanger national-level stability, the consociational regime

---

[36] Ugarriza and Pabón Ayala 2017: 97–101, 109, 112, 116–21. The Maoist Ejército Popular de Liberación suffered the same fate (ibid. 130).

[37] Arrubla (1980: 210–12) stresses the weaknesses and divisions of the radical left, whose different groupings engaged in internal purges and even fought against each other (see also Villamizar 2017: 300–5, 309, 318–19, 324, 342–3).

survived. The armed forces, which gained free hand through state-of-siege legislation, succeeded in containing extremist threats and therefore saw no reason to overthrow democracy and take power.

Consequently, Colombia's party-based democracy managed to nip a potential coup move in the bud in 1965. At the beginning of the decade, a military grouping led by General Alberto Ruiz Novoa promoted an ambitious, wide-ranging strategy for combating left-wing guerrilla threats. Inspired in part by US counterinsurgency doctrines and by the reformist approach of the Alliance for Progress (Ruhl 1980: 200), this *Plan Lazo* sought to combine profound, deep-reaching social transformations with targeted counterinsurgency.[38] This bold plan, a precursor of the progressive project enacted by Peru's nationalist military regime after its 1968 coup, called for a serious attack on the socioeconomic and political privileges of Colombia's well-entrenched elites and for redistributive change to benefit the mass populace (Maullin 1971: 48–50; Nieto Ortiz 2010: 95–7, 154–64, 168–70). In a showdown in early 1965, establishment sectors, which had firm control over the two main parties, won; military factions concerned about the politicization and division of the armed forces forced Ruiz Novoa's dismissal.[39]

After all, at that time "the levels of political violence were declining, and no major political group was posing a social revolutionary threat to military class or professional interests," as specialist Mark Ruhl (1980: 193) highlights. In the absence of serious danger, an all-out effort involving the sacrifice of civilian elite interests seemed unnecessary; instead, Colombia's consociational regime could continue to muddle through. Indeed, with the formation of the National Front, the two main parties had just demonstrated their capacity to restore political stability and to guarantee governability, economic development, and moderate social distribution. Thus, whereas the novelty of the guerrilla threat in Peru's inchoate party system (cf. Mainwaring and Scully 1995: 17–20), which had difficulty maintaining political stability, induced the armed forces to take power in 1968, their colleagues in Colombia saw the reigning party cartel as a satisfactory bulwark against radical left-wingers, which always remained far from overthrowing the established order.[40]

---

[38] Valencia Tovar 2013: 272–78; Ugarriza and Pabón Ayala 2017: 71–75. Maullin (1971: viii–ix, 6, 52–8, 97–107) interprets this ambitious approach as part of the "new professionalism" (cf. Stepan 1973) that induced Latin American militaries during the 1960s to get deeply involved in civilian politics and that inspired the Brazilian military coup of 1964 (see Chapter 6). Valencia Tovar (2009: 90–92) corroborates this interpretation by embracing the concept.

[39] Maullin 1971: vii, 62; Ruhl 1980: 190–93; Nieto Ortiz 2010: 163–71; Valencia Tovar 2013: 276–77, 294–98. In subsequent years, the military's approach to guerrilla forces shifted more toward sheer repression (Maullin 1971: vii, 50–1, 63–4; Nieto Ortiz 2010: 211–12), which probably contributed to the persistence of armed challenges. By contrast, Venezuela's offers of amnesty and reintegration into civilian life brought lasting peace, as mentioned above.

[40] On the comparison between Colombia and Peru, see the interesting reflections by Ruhl (1980: 194–95, 201).

Colombia's consociational regime in fact maintained mass support through clientelistic linkages and a constant trickle of economic and social benefits (Taylor 2009: 69–81). Certainly, the institutionalization of compromise limited redistributive change such as land reform.[41] But economic growth, revenue-raising tax reforms, and ample funding from the Alliance for Progress (Baskind, Lerdau, and Mesmer 2008: 139, 158–60) allowed for sustained increases in the provision of social services such as education and health care (Taffet 2007: 149–74; Arnove 1980: 382, 389, 406; Baskind et al. 2008: 136–7, 145–9, 171). Moreover, National Front governments created popular mobilization programs that facilitated the cooptation of poorer groupings, enhanced party control over the citizenry, and limited political space for recruitment efforts by radical forces.[42] Last not least, intraparty competition gave some voice to critics of the consociational arrangements, including populists and communists, permitted the articulation of reformist proposals, and promoted the integration of new sociopolitical forces (Martz 1965: 324-5; Dix 1967: 145, 290; Hartlyn 1988: 85–90; Dix 1990: 111; Taylor 2009: 78–9; Bejarano 2011: 107, 164). Thus, "decision making through mutual adjustment" – Lindblom's (1965) characterization of democracy under bounded rationality – allowed Colombia's two-party system to preserve civilian rule despite a series of far-left challenges.

In sum, where fairly strong, broad-based political parties encompassed important mass sectors, enacted a modicum of reform, and distributed socioeconomic benefits during the turbulent 1960s, the strategy of the Alliance for Progress to support democratic governments in Latin America achieved some success. Preemptive change and the programmatic and clientelistic distribution of socioeconomic benefits kept popular support for Cuba-inspired guerrilla movements limited. The reasonable performance of civilian governance gave elite sectors, and especially the military, sufficient assurance that democracy could withstand externally inspired contention, including violent efforts to emulate the Cuban Revolution.

Arguably, the counterinsurgency strand of the Alliance for Progress also contributed to the survival of democracy in Venezuela and Colombia. Both countries cooperated closely with the United States (Lyles 2016: chaps. 5–6; on Colombia, see also Maullin 1971: 82–8), which emphasized the need to "win the hearts and minds" of the citizenry and in this way deprive guerrilla movements of popular support (Leal Buitrago 2010: 296–8; Nieto Ortiz 2010: 130–2). Therefore, the Venezuelan and Colombian armies largely avoided the

---

[41] Martz 1965: 332; Zamosc 1986: 35–6, 47–52; Randall 1992: 223–4, 232–4; Fajardo 2003: 10, 15–17. By foreseeing the expropriation of unproductive land, however, the agrarian reform helped to propel agricultural modernization and economic growth (De Janvry 1981: 131–5; Baskind, Lerdau, and Mesmer 2008: 207–10).

[42] Bagley and Edel 1980: 257–70. Where these mobilizational initiatives backfired and inadvertently stimulated radicalization, namely among the peasantry, the government responded with divide-and-rule efforts and targeted repression (ibid. 274–81).

widespread, massive repression that exacerbated polarization in the Southern Cone during the late 1960s and early 1970s and that pushed those countries into ever fiercer autocracy.[43] In fact, whereas the French-inspired counterrevolutionary doctrines embraced by Southern Cone militaries frontally questioned democracy (as Chapter 5 will examine), the US teachings employed in Venezuela and Colombia lacked this authoritarian bent. Contrary to widespread critical voices, cooperation with the United States and usage of the counterinsurgency strategy of the Alliance for Progress thus benefited the maintenance of democracy (Lyles 2016: 460–7).

Besides forestalling the success of guerrilla movements, the problem-solving capacity of development-oriented, reformist democracies and the popular support commanded by broad-based parties also kept Venezuela and Colombia from getting swept up in the massive groundswell of political radicalization that affected many other Latin American countries in the 1960s and 1970s (as Chapter 5 will analyze). Whereas Fidel Castro's triumph helped induce left-wingers across the region to turn more extremist and push impatiently for fundamental, revolutionary transformations, in Venezuela most of the Communist Party deradicalized (Ellner 1988). Learning from the failure of the guerrilla strategy, it foreswore extrainstitutional tactics and unconditionally entered the electoral arena, as mentioned above. And in Colombia, the grip that the two traditional parties maintained over the popular sectors prevented a strong left from emerging for decades.

Moreover, the very persistence of limited guerrilla attacks in marginal areas of Colombia served to discredit the legal left and hurt its prospects in the electoral arena (Archer 1995: 167, 196). The length of time during which rebels fought the democratic state in Venezuela had a similar deterrent effect and helped confine the party formed by former combatants in the early 1970s to small vote shares during the subsequent two decades (Ellner 1988: 108–10, 125, 133–5). Both countries therefore avoided the radical mobilization that other nations, especially in the Southern Cone, experienced. In line with the negative correlation mentioned in Chapter 3, a substantial guerrilla challenge tended to immunize countries against broader political radicalization. Scarred by efforts at the isomorphic emulation of Castro's success, Colombia and Venezuela were spared the more wide-ranging political repercussions of the Cuban Revolution, which ended up posing much greater risks to the survival of democracy.

The absence of pronounced, widespread challenges from the left stabilized the new democracies that had been forged via elite pacts in 1958 (Wilde 1978: 58–62; Levine 1978; Hartlyn 1988). As they had emerged from comparatively brutal military dictatorships, civilian politicians of all stripes had strong

---

[43] In Venezuela, the democratic government finally achieved victory over persistent albeit confined guerrilla movements through the formation of US-supported and US-trained mobile ranger battalions, which put the leftist fighters under relentless pressure with sustained, very targeted attacks (Miller 2016: 170, 173–76, 179, 187–8, 190–92, 200–1).

incentives to avoid an authoritarian relapse.[44] In turn, military institutions were aware of the negative repercussions of direct governmental responsibility, which politicized the armed forces, undermined their internal unity, and threatened hierarchical command (Bejarano 2011: 141–3, 148). While the military pushed civilian politicians to react more forcefully to acute threats, such as the Venezuelan guerrilla movements of the early 1960s (Miller 2016: 75, 85, 92, 114, 136, 144, 158–9, 168), they undertook no serious moves toward taking over government power.[45] For these reasons, Colombia and Venezuela avoided the right-wing backlash that tore apart many other Latin American democracies in the 1960s and 1970s. The authoritarian reverse wave that engulfed the Southern Cone and the Central Andes therefore left South America's Caribbean coast untouched.

The Blockage of Preemptive Reforms in Peru and Bolivia

While quite successful in Venezuela and Colombia, the strategy of preventative problem alleviation faced enormous obstacles in many other Latin American countries. Most fundamentally, as the very depth of inequality suggested, sociopolitical elites were firmly entrenched in the region, and reluctant suddenly to give up many of their privileges. In a goal conflict that plagued the wide-ranging reform effort, democracy itself posed obstacles to socioeconomic change: liberal safeguards and institutional checks and balances dispersed political power and offered veto opportunities to the conservative opposition. Moreover, electoral competition sometimes induced partisan forces that in principle shared the government's policy goals to help block change so as not to allow their political rivals to gain credit for changes that these opposition parties themselves hoped to enact.

Both of these stumbling blocks played an especially deleterious role during the mid-1960s in Peru, where fierce electoral competition pitted two ideologically similar parties against each other, namely the eternal opposition party Alianza Popular Revolucionaria Americana (APRA – American Popular Revolutionary Alliance) against the governing Acción Popular (AP – Popular Action). Because APRA did not want AP to enact a program of change very similar to its own long-standing proposals, centrist president Fernando Belaúnde Terry (1963–8) saw his progressive reform efforts hindered and undermined for years.[46] While advocates of

---

[44] Arrubla (1980: 208–9) highlights the great fear of a renewed military takeover among Colombia's party elites.

[45] Venezuela did experience some locally confined military rebellions, however, including two left-wing, nationalist uprisings, which, however, had an unclear, confused ideological orientation (Machillanda Pinto 1988: 88–92), and were quickly suppressed. But some of these left-leaning military personnel then joined the guerrilla forces, contributing to their remarkable resilience in the face of governmental counterattacks.

[46] Reh 1970: 14, 27–8, 35–7; Einaudi 1971: 21, 25, 29, 33; Hilliker 1971; Harding 1975: 230–5; Kuczynski 1977: 26–7, 39–41, 62, 66, 70, 174–75, 278–83; Albertus 2015: 199, 206–7.

sociopolitical change urged the chief executive to employ autocratic means, for instance by closing Congress and pushing through reforms by decree (interview with Ochoa 1996; Kuczynski 1977: 27, 282; Cotler 1978: 198; Rénique 2006: 94), Belaúnde insisted on maintaining pluralist democracy. In Peru, therefore, the Alliance for Progress strategy foundered on the inherent tension between ambitious reform goals and the checks and balances of liberal democracy. Fierce party competition and rivalry over reform leadership (Hilliker 1971: 139–40, 155–6) created a paradoxical blockage.[47]

The failure to redress the country's profound socioeconomic deficits seemed to turn especially worrisome when Cuba-inspired guerrilla movements erupted in the mid-1960s.[48] Although the armed forces suppressed these ill-prepared rebellions quickly (and brutally: Monteforte Toledo 1973: 44–5; Walter 2010: 70–1), they feared a recurrence or, eventually, a massive popular uprising (Astiz and García 1972: 677–8; Nunn 1979: 394–5; Walter 2010: 87, 109–10, 113). No wonder that the military in 1968 evicted the ineffectual Belaúnde in order to propel profound socioeconomic change in an unencumbered fashion (Cotler 1978: 199; McClintock 1994: 301–3; Albertus 2015: 200–2, 224). Thus, the armed forces did what their civilian predecessor had refused to do,[49] namely abolish democracy to impose drastic reform.[50]

Because in the late 1960s and early 1970s the military did not face any active insurgency,[51] they replaced the brutal repression of the mid-1960s with the

---

The Peruvian military had direct experience with this paralysis, because later dictator Francisco Morales-Bermúdez (1975–80) served as finance minister under Belaúnde in 1968 and bitterly complained about the government's failure to push through necessary reforms (see his interview with Prieto Celi 1996: 106–10).

[47] Peruvian guerrilla leader Luis de la Puente (1964a: 7) then invoked the failure of Belaúnde's reform strategy to justify his own call for violent revolution.

[48] Einaudi 1971: 25–6, 41; Goldenberg 1971: 461–7; Walter 2010: 68–79; see also Pion-Berlin 1988: 417, 420, 424.

[49] After the election-driven coup of 1962, there had already been currents inside the military that sought longer-term rule to promote development and thus forestall leftist radicalism, for instance through an agrarian reform (Einaudi 1971: 32, 37; Cotler 1978: 195–96; Prieto Celi 1996: 94, 127; Brown 2017: 311–12). But the advocates of this preemptive strategy found limited support because before the eruption of guerrilla war in the mid-1960s, the communist threat did not yet have high salience (cf. Astiz and García 1972: 677–78). Moreover, the US government was committed to the prodemocratic principles enshrined in the Alliance for Progress and therefore condemned the coup and pushed for new elections (Rabe 1999: 116, 119–20; Walter 2010: 16–23).

[50] The military regime justified its 1968 takeover in these terms (Peru. Junta Revolucionaria [1968] 1983: 284–5). See also interviews with numerous leading generals in Tello (1983, vol. 1: 39, 289; and Tello 1983, vol. 2: 66–7, 120, 246); comments by later military ruler Francisco Morales-Bermúdez (in Prieto Celi 1996: 100–1, 112–14, 131); and Mercado Jarrín (1974: 194, 198). See also Reh (1970: 9–14) and Stepan (1978b: chap. 4).

[51] Moreover, Peru did not experience the broad political radicalization that affected other Latin American countries, especially in the Southern Cone, as Chapter 5 highlights. Because the established order faced no active challenges from the bottom up, the military commanded the latitude to impose profound change from the top down.

strategy of preemptive change that President Belaúnde had not managed to push through. Based on their autocratic power concentration, they sought to revamp Peru's socioeconomic and political structures and resolve the long-standing problems that, so they feared, revolutionary radicals could in the future exploit for their subversive goals. In the generals' eyes, the absence of an active guerrilla challenge offered the breathing space to remedy their country's serious economic and social ills and thus vaccinate the nation against any later infection by the communist virus. As the military did not face acute danger from below – that is, from political groupings in society – they took over the state and imposed a "revolution from above" (Trimberger 1978), which ultimately had counterrevolutionary goals.

The way in which the Alliance for Progress strategy had failed in Peru thus accounts for the unusually progressive but profoundly anticommunist course of the subsequent authoritarian regime. This reformist dictatorship decreed a number of ambitious transformations, including a wide-ranging land reform (overviews in Lowenthal 1975; Chaplin 1976; Lowenthal and McClintock 1983; also see recently Albertus 2015). In this way, it sought to trace a "third way" of development, distant from capitalism, yet averse to Marxism, as military president Juan Velasco Alvarado (1968–75) frequently proclaimed.[52] After all, as Alfred Stepan (1978b: 136) found out through his ample contacts in the Peruvian military, "officers [worried] that, should a revolution be successful, the military, as the coercive force of the oligarchy, could suffer institutional dissolution and even the firing squad. Such had been the fate of the Cuban regular army" (similar Tello 1983, vol. 1: 318, 321). To forestall this scary prospect, President Velasco decreed profound reforms from the top down to prevent a revolutionary explosion from the bottom up.

In Bolivia, the contradiction between the two priorities of the Alliance for Progress, democracy and socioeconomic reform, was even more pronounced. The 1952 revolution had empowered a variety of sectors to push for ambitious pent-up goals but had aggravated the difficulty of establishing strong state institutions that commanded the concentrated power to enact a coherent development program (excellent analysis in Malloy and Gamarra 1988: 106–13, 210–14). The ever more faction-ridden movement-party that had led the revolution, the Movimiento Nacionalista Revolucionario (MNR – Nationalist Revolutionary Movement), failed to overcome the tremendous dispersal of power in this deeply fragmented polity, the prototype of a "praetorian society" à la Huntington (1968: chap. 4). As Bolivia's strikingly weak state faced multiple potent veto groups, many of which were armed and

---

[52] For Velasco's outspoken opposition to Marxism and communism, see Walter (2010: 163, 206, 211, 224, 229, 237, 291) and Tello (1983, vol. 2: 186); see also Stepan 1978b: 142. General Edgardo Mercado Jarrín (1974: 220–1), an important minister in Velasco's regime, also highlighted the regime's distance from Marxism, as did a number of leading generals interviewed by Tello (1983, vol. 1: 100, 347; vol. 2: 24, 257).

rather militant, democracy hindered the achievement of Alliance for Progress goals.

As a result of this fragmentation of power, President Víctor Paz Estenssoro (1960-4) did not manage to impose his economic development project, although with US support he employed ever more repressive and authoritarian means (Field 2014). A powerful, intransigent left that comprised many currents of Marxism (Malloy and Gamarra 1988: 59–60; Lora 1982: 172, 180, 198–9) and that was further radicalized and supported by the Cuban Revolution (Field 2014: 26, 68–79, 146, 160) defied the president with all means, including a good deal of open violence (Dunkerley 1984: 109–11, 118–19). Government officials and US diplomats feared that these extremists might well end up taking power and turning Bolivia into a second Cuba (*FRUS 1964–1968*: 341, 343; Field 2014: 14–15, 18–19, 36, 48, 57, 78–9, 103–4, 132–3, 141, 193). As later in Peru, the armed forces, which postrevolutionary administrations rebuilt to gain greater control over organized coercion (Corbett 1972: 404–8), soon sought to break resistance to the reform strategy. Therefore, General René Barrientos in 1964 overthrew Paz (Brill 1967: 18–47; Dunkerley 1984: 122; Klein 1992: 244–5). The new president then crushed extreme-left resistance with brutal force in order to impose the development strategy elaborated by Paz with US guidance.[53] Similar to Peru, and later inspired by Peru's nationalist military dictatorship (Dunkerley 1984: 157, 162–3), this authoritarian regime depicted itself as the executor of the socioeconomic strategy that democracy had kept its civilian predecessor from pursuing successfully.

In sum, democracy itself hindered the reform efforts undertaken under the Alliance for Progress in Peru and Bolivia. To enact the changes that they regarded as necessary for guaranteeing sociopolitical stability and foreclosing radical challenges emanating from the Cuban Revolution, military generals therefore overthrew democratic governments. After cutting the Gordian knot through the imposition of autocracy, they pursued a fairly progressive, but staunchly anticommunist course.

Political Failures of Preemptive Reforms: Unintended Radicalization

In several Latin American countries, democratic governments did manage to enact socioeconomic and political reforms; but ironically, these changes did not have the pacifying effect intended by the Alliance for Progress.[54] While the alleviation of grave problems often has a moderating impact in the long run,

[53] *FRUS 1964-1968*: 347, 349, 354–5, 358; Malloy 1971: 138–46; Dunkerley 1984: 121–6; Malloy and Gamarra 1988: 1–2, 9, 43–4, 107; Diez de Medina 1972: 55, 63, 69, 285–6.
[54] In Brazil, for instance, US policy makers deliberately sought to "direct" aid that had an "immediate impact" "to the centers of greatest discontent in the northeast" (*FRUS 1961–1963*: 455) – the poorest region of the country, where the radical peasant leagues led by Cuba-inspired and Cuba-supported Francisco Julião (Sales 2007: 35–54) were agitating for land redistribution.

reform initiatives frequently stir up political conflict and polarization in the short run, as Alexis de Tocqueville ([1856] 1978: 179–82, 185–7) famously highlighted. The effort finally to remedy long-standing problems raises great hopes and can unleash an explosion of pent-up demands. This risk of unintentional radicalization exists especially if these changes are launched with overambitious rhetoric, such as President Kennedy's appeal to "revolutionary ideas and efforts" (reprinted in Taffet 2007: 204) in the initial announcement of the Alliance for Progress in 1961 and the "revolution in liberty" proclaimed by the Eduardo Frei Montalva government (1964–70) in Chile (Fleet 1985: 80). Facing such a major reform project, the forces privileged by the status quo dig in their heels out of asymmetrical loss aversion and fiercely resist the sudden questioning of well-entrenched structures. For that reason, in part, the changes actually implemented fall short of the high-flying expectations raised by the government's bold pronouncements, as it happened in Chile (Baskind, Lerdau, and Mesmer 2008: 64–7, 83–4, 101). Because both sides of the reform divide mobilize, escalation results and politics becomes acrimonious and contentious.

The Alliance for Progress, which rested on the benign assumptions of US liberalism and pluralism (Packenham 1973: 69–74), underestimated the potential for this kind of transitional polarization and conflict and was unprepared for its political repercussions.[55] The depth of Latin America's socioeconomic problems, especially social inequality and mass poverty, obstructed negotiation and compromise. In the short run, therefore, the reform strategy had unanticipated consequences that were diametrically opposite to its proclaimed goals: rather than producing moderation, it provoked conflict. In particular, reforms failed to take the wind out of the sail of the left, especially its more radical sectors; instead, the very push for changes seemed to give additional impetus to a brewing storm of extremism.

In a striking example of this troublesome dynamic, stiff competition in Chile's programmatic party system led to the outbidding of a reformist president on the left flank (Baskind, Lerdau, and Mesmer 2008: 25, 30, 54–6, 63–6, 71, 102). This escalation of promises unleashed the very radicalization that the Alliance for Progress meant to avoid. As Christian Democrat Eduardo Frei promoted a comprehensive reform program, Chile's powerful, ideologically oriented left demanded a real, Marxist revolution. In their view, the centrist government's land reform, education and health reform, and partial nationalization of copper (the country's main export) were much too limited

---

[55] After it initially highlighted the goal of "broadly-based political stability," an early evaluation (*FRUS 1961–1963*: 83) mentioned the risk that "pressure for Alliance for Progress reforms may actually feed extremist strength since propertied groups are not ready to give way without a struggle." But this report immediately added that "despite its immediate effect in stirring up political discords, the Alliance for Progress may carry with it means to resolve the conflict" (ibid. 83).

and meager. Especially the increasingly radicalized Socialist Party pushed for much quicker and more profound change (Valenzuela 1978: 37–9; Arrate and Rojas 2003, vol. 1: 387–92, 424–8).

Partisan competition also drove an upsurge in political mobilization. As the Christian Democrats tried to outflank the left by activating hitherto quiescent sectors, especially among the urban and rural poor, the left marshaled its powerful organizational apparatus, which had its stronghold in the militant labor movement. Street protests therefore proliferated, turning increasingly contentious and sometimes even violent in this hothouse atmosphere (Valenzuela 1978: 27–33; Garretón 1983: 33–5). As a result, despite the economic and social progress it achieved and its positive long-term consequences for Chile's modernization (Baskind, Lerdau, and Mesmer 2008: 31–3), the Alliance for Progress suffered political failure. Instead of bringing social satisfaction and political tranquility, and instead of strengthening the centrist parties, the determined push for reforms stimulated division, escalation, and conflict. Worst of all from the perspective of its proponents, the US-supported reform drive culminated in the electoral victory of the Marxist left, which promised a true "march to socialism."

Despite the absence of equally powerful and cohesive left-wing parties, similar scenarios of radicalization seemed to play out in Brazil under President João Goulart (1961–4)[56] and, to some extent, in Argentina under President Arturo Frondizi (1959–62). Both leaders promoted economic development, and Goulart in particular tried to advance a range of important social measures and "basic reforms" as well. For this purpose, the Brazilian president supported the push for land reform in the impoverished northeast and mobilized a number of urban sectors (Skidmore 1967: 234–48; Ferreira and Gomes 2014: 161–227). Certainly, by contrast to Chile's Socialist Party, there was no major party advocating Marxist revolution in Brazil and Argentina. Instead, the strongest political forces, especially Argentine Peronism, were amorphous populist movements with rather ill-defined political goals and unclear ideologies. But this fluidity did little to mitigate conservative concerns, which focused on the clandestine approach that communist subversion seemed to employ. After all, Cuba's Castro had led a welter of movements to power which only later morphed into a communist regime. Because fluidity opened the door for a wide range of possibilities, conservatives feared that with their vanguard organization and iron determination, communists would be in an excellent

---

[56] In fact, during his first year and a half in office, Goulart also faced fairly tight limits arising from democratic institutions. After the unexpected resignation of President Jânio Quadros (1961), powerful military sectors had feared then vice president Goulart's leftist tendencies, and had therefore conditioned his succession to the chief executive office on the imposition of a "parliamentary" (in fact, semipresidential) system of government, which seriously restricted Goulart's formal attributions. President Goulart then used his social reform proposals in part to win mass support for a referendum that eliminated these constraints and restored full presidentialism in January 1963.

position to take advantage of this openness and manage to grab power (as regards Argentine Peronism, see Cavarozzi 1983: 90–1).

In fact, Brazil's Goulart responded to right-wing resistance against his reform program by radicalizing his push for change (Goldenberg 1971: 429–40). For this purpose, he took determined steps toward mass mobilization (Skidmore 1967: 253–6), which, in turn, seemed to threaten established privileges and institutional hierarchies, even inside the military (Stepan 1978a: 130–2; see also Stepan 1971: 158–65). Consequently, democratic reformism ended up exacerbating conflict in an uncontrollable fashion, pushing Brazil into a political crisis that ran counter to the goals of the Alliance for Progress. And in the Argentine case, the powerful Peronist movement was waiting in the wings (Halperin Donghi 2010: 130), ready to take over once the milder reforms undertaken by politically constrained President Frondizi would predictably fail. Thus, in both of these countries the political strategy of the Alliance for Progress seemed to prove incapable of enhancing sociopolitical stability and thus immunizing these nations from the perceived threat of communism.

A similar dynamic, which brought even more dramatic radicalization, played out in postrevolutionary Bolivia after the military president who had overthrown democracy to impose the Alliance for Progress development strategy, René Barrientos, died in an accident (1969). Because the next general lacked his predecessor's charisma, he sought to legitimate his precarious rule by reviving popular mobilization for social causes and by charting a nationalist course similar to and inspired partly by his Peruvian counterpart, military president Juan Velasco Alvarado (1968–75).[57] Under his left-wing successor, General Juan José Torres, the resulting effervescence led to the proclamation of a "socialist republic." This radical experiment culminated in the convocation of a popular assembly in 1971, reminiscent of the soviets that had arisen in Russia during the revolutionary year of 1917 and that had paved the way for the takeover of Bolshevism (Zavaleta Mercado 1974: 104, 187–8, 231; Dunkerley 1984: 185–97; Derpic 2012: vi, 1, 3–5, 27, 53). Important currents in this amorphous body indeed advocated "direct action" designed to conquer national power via a mass insurrection (Gallardo Lozada 1972: 322–4; Whitehead 1972: 89–90; Lora 1982: 201, 204–7). Thus, Bolivia's populist revolution of 1952, which had long charted a reformist, noncommunist course and which had therefore received support from the United States, finally seemed to turn into a true Marxist effort to overturn the socioeconomic and political system.[58] Once again, long-standing preemptive efforts were about to produce the very outcome that they had originally been designed to avert. Predictably, this radicalization instilled enormous fear

[57] *FRUS* 1969–1976, vol. E–10, doc. 88; Malloy 1971: 152; Dunkerley 1984: 157, 162–3; Corbett 1972: 417–20, 426, 428; Malloy and Gamarra 1988: 45–6, 49.

[58] From a left-wing perspective, Zavaleta Mercado (1974: 182–4, 207–12) highlights the limitations of these revolutionary efforts – but the right and center certainly feared a total loss of control.

among Bolivia's middle sectors, elite, large parts of the military, and US and Brazilian government officials.[59]

Consequently, a coup led by Colonel Hugo Banzer soon ended the experiment in radicalism and installed a reactionary authoritarian regime (Corbett 1972: 423–5; Dunkerley 1984: chap. 6; Klein 1992: 254). This autocracy, modeled after and supported by the dictatorship in neighboring Brazil (Gallardo Lozada 1972: 401–3, 411–12; Klein 1992: 256–8; Harmer 2011: 166–8), tried to create a bureaucratic-authoritarian regime by enlisting civilian technocrats and by erecting the institutional trappings of a developmentalist state (Malloy and Gamarra 1988: 63–4, 68, 80, 91–4, 108–9). But underneath this formal façade, Banzer mostly relied on large-scale clientelism and patronage politics in trying to consolidate his ever-precarious rule over Bolivia's fractious, uninstitutionalized polity (Malloy and Gamarra 1988: 80–3, 92, 110–13, 117–19, 214–15). In line with this study's central argument about the reactionary nature of these dictatorships, the very depth of the preceding threat enabled President Banzer to hang on for seven years, an unusually long time in a country plagued by endemic political instability (Dunkerley 1984: 201; Malloy and Gamarra 1988: 213–14).

Similarly, in Argentina the democracy restored in 1973 experienced an effervescence of mobilization and, in particular, a proliferation of political violence. Whereas in the early to mid-1960s an important current in the military had regarded Peronism as a bulwark against communist extremism, the striking radicalization of Peronist groupings during the 1966–73 military regime, which took hold especially among the movement's youth wing (Ollier 1998: 110–16), changed the balance of forces. Urged on by exiled leader Juan Perón, who used the youthful radicals for engineering his return to power (Gillespie 1982: 46, 70, 103–4, 122), growing numbers of militants swelled the ranks of the *Montoneros*, the largest of several urban guerrilla movements (Gillespie 1982; Moyano 1995). Typically, however, the sorcerer lost control over his apprentices. When returning to the presidency in 1973, the old *caudillo* tried to disavow violence and rein in the *Montoneros* – but to no avail. After Perón's death in 1974 and the succession of his politically inexperienced wife, chaos spread and violence skyrocketed. Based on "simplistic" assumptions (Moyano 1995: 102, 132) and overly influenced, even "seduced" by foreign precedents, most prominently the Cuban Revolution,[60] guerrilla groupings acted "devoid of apparent political rationality" (Moyano 1995: 2; see also 8). These extremist sects, whose quest for unity and conformity turned them into hothouses for groupthink (cf. Moyano 1995: 75–6, 102, 132; Ollier 1998: 189,

---

[59] *FRUS* 1969–1976, vol. E-10, docs. 93, 102, 104, 109, 115; Gallardo Lozada 1972: 323–4; Dunkerley 1984: 192–97; Malloy and Gamarra 1988: 64–9, 75–77, 79, 81, 213; Harmer 2011: 125–6; Gaspari 2003: 347.

[60] Moyano 1995: 118, 133–4. On the Montoneros' "Guevarist" orientation, see also Gillespie 1982: 48, 50, 58, 60, 67, 78–79, 83, 106–7. On the multitude of Argentine and Latin American guerrilla movements operating in Buenos Aires under the Peronist governments, see recently Marchesi (2018: chap. 4).

194, 203–11), fell prey to the illusion that they could dialectically trigger the downfall of the established sociopolitical order (Reato 2012: 187–9).

In sum, the preemptive reform strategy, a fairly sophisticated effort at counterdiffusion, in most cases had disappointing outcomes. While democracy itself hindered the enactment of change in Peru and Bolivia, in several other countries the reform drive failed to calm radicalism, which the Cuban Revolution inspired across Latin America (as Chapter 5 documents). In Chile, Brazil, and Argentina, democratic governments did promulgate and implement more or less ambitious measures, but these reforms did not have the pacifying impact intended by their advocates. On the contrary, party competition stimulated growing radicalization and fierce conflict. Rather than preempting demands for truly profound, contentious transformations, the Alliance for Progress provoked even stronger calls for revolution. Status quo defenders seemed to face the scary scenario outlined by Alexis de Tocqueville ([1856] 1978: 185–7), namely that governmental efforts to address long-standing problems through controlled change can paradoxically open the door for a major, cataclysmic revolution. In the mid- to late 1960s, more and more Latin American elites arrived at the terrifying conclusion that they were confronting the same nightmare. These threat perceptions set the stage for ever more insistent efforts to find protection through the imposition of authoritarian rule, as Chapter 5 explains.

CONCLUSION

This chapter has examined the direct repercussions of Castro's Revolution, which had a profound effect on boundedly rational actors across the ideological spectrum. The availability heuristic drew overwhelming attention to the Cuban precedent, and the representativeness heuristic induced people to generalize its presumed lessons and believe in its easy replicability across the region. While much of the Latin American left engaged in mobilizational activism on behalf of radical projects, the most extremist groupings initiated isomorphic imitation attempts by starting guerrilla struggles in most countries south of the Rio Grande. Predictably, loss aversion motivated established governments, often pushed by their militaries, to eradicate these ill-planned insurgencies with determined, often brutal force. Out of fear driven by their own overestimation of the Cuban precedent, they overshot and cracked down unnecessarily hard. Thus, attempts to spread communist revolution provoked determined efforts at counterrevolution, which uniformly defeated the violent assaults spearheaded by Castro-inspired extremists.

Interestingly, however, a wide range of political forces went beyond this reflexive counterdiffusion and adopted a more sophisticated containment strategy as well. In particular, broad-based parties, which have looser bounds of rationality, sought to remedy the socioeconomic and political problems that could provoke radicalization and thus allow revolutionaries to garner popular backing. To prevent the spread of the Cuban Revolution, the United States under President Kennedy supported this preemptive reform strategy via the ambitious Alliance for Progress. But as discussed in the preceding sections, this reasoned response rarely succeeded. Instead, the inherent tension between liberal democracy and determined change and the time inconsistency often plaguing thorough reforms (short-term trouble versus long-term benefit) foiled the Alliance for Progress in most of Latin America. Therefore, tendencies toward radicalism persisted and even gathered further steam. How would conservative sectors respond to this increasing threat? Chapter 5 investigates the broader repercussions emanating from the Cuban Revolution, which pointed in a much more reactionary and autocratic direction.

5

Waves of Radicalization and Reaction

The preceding Chapter 4 showed that the striking impact of the Cuban Revolution, mediated by cognitive heuristics, spurred an interactive double movement of radical diffusion and status quo-oriented counterdiffusion. Castro's stunning success stimulated a host of isomorphic imitation attempts via guerrilla movements that closely followed Che Guevara's rural *foco* approach. Yet loss aversion induced a wide range of establishment sectors to use full force and repress these unrealistic emulation efforts, which erupted fairly indiscriminately across most of Latin America. At the same time, incumbent governments responded to the challenge arising from the Cuban Revolution in a less reflexive and more deliberate way. They tried to enact socioeconomic and political reforms designed to alleviate the long-standing, serious problems that radicals could take advantage of to win mass support for profound transformations. Driven by the same determination to forestall a "second Cuba," the United States, whose decision makers were affected by cognitive shortcuts as well, strongly encouraged and generously backed this preventative approach through the Alliance for Progress.

As the last sections of Chapter 4 demonstrated, however, this carefully designed strategy for averting revolutionary contagion did not often achieve success. In some Latin American countries liberal checks and balances helped to block reform, while in others democracy's competitive dynamic fueled precisely the polarization and radicalization that the Alliance for Progress intended to avoid. Rather than being contained, leftism advanced and spread, especially in regionally important countries such as Brazil in the early 1960s, and in Argentina in the late 1960s and early 1970s. This Cuba-inspired radicalization went farthest in Chile, which turned into a globally salient model as the first country on earth where a coalition led by two openly Marxist parties won the presidency through free, democratic elections in 1970.

The present chapter traces the broader groundswell of radicalization that large parts of the Latin American left, as well as part of the center such as Chile's Christian Democracy, experienced after the Cuban Revolution (comprehensive documentation in Adler 1970). By fomenting the competitive dynamic fueled by democratic reformism, Castro's surprising success helped to exert a powerful ideational impact. Whereas only a few extremists jumped to the conclusion that the isomorphic replication of the communist power grab via guerrilla movements was feasible and promising, a much wider swath of leftists, populists, and centrists heuristically inferred from the dramatic Caribbean revolution that established sociopolitical structures were brittle and precarious. Consequently, they came to believe that the room for political agency and the possibilities for effecting thoroughgoing transformations were much larger than observers of all stripes had long believed. The idea spread that a new society was possible! Many progressives of variegated stripes therefore mobilized to push for profound change (Castañeda 1993: 48–9, 67–81; Wright 2001: 39–56).

Predictably, however, this groundswell of radicalization reinforced the fears of status quo-oriented sectors (see recently Brands 2010: 27–8, 40, 48–9, 55, 66, 72, 75, 107–8). The very strength of the transformational impulse activated intense loss aversion among conservative elites such as landowners, businesspeople, part of the clergy, and – most consequentially – much of the military. The fact that revolutionary Cuba inspired and supported this broader radicalization, as glaringly proven by Fidel Castro's unprecedented visit of twenty-five days to Salvador Allende's Chile, further aggravated these fears, which US foreign policy makers shared as well. In the eyes of establishment sectors, radicalism, which could sooner or later pave the way for a well-organized, dedicated Marxist vanguard to take power, seemed to be advancing relentlessly, like a massive stream fed by a host of tributaries, yet propelled mainly by one scary force, international communism.

Because preemptive reform had failed to forestall this radicalization in good parts of South America and had instead exacerbated it in several countries, most clearly in the Southern Cone, liberal democracy came to look weak and vulnerable. After all, competitive civilian rule had proven incapable of coping with the increasing danger. In fact, pluralist liberalism was paradoxically guaranteeing freedom of maneuver to radical leftists, seen as the worst enemies of liberty. What perverse, self-defeating strategy of defense was that?

Consequently, more and more status quo defenders embraced the idea that the most effective, if not the only option for combating the perceived threat of communism was the installation of authoritarian regimes. The strong hand of autocracy seemed required for stemming the rising tide of left-wing extremism (cf. Mainwaring and Pérez-Liñán 2013: 36–9, 77–80, 104–14). Establishment sectors therefore started to advocate a drastic regime change, which in the eyes of the most reactionary groupings had to go beyond a simple interruption and quick restart of democracy. Instead, a more thorough transformation might be necessary for preventing a reemergence of radicalism. To fortify the state for this ambitious task, the new autocracies differed from the traditional, personalistic type of dictatorship that had fallen in Cuba (and that was later to fall in Nicaragua, see Booth 1998). Instead, these authoritarian regimes installed institutional leadership by resting on the armed forces as an organization. Moreover, they promoted ambitious development projects to overcome the socioeconomic problems that left-wingers could exploit.[1]

This new model of "re-foundational" autocracy (Garretón 1983: chap. 3; see also Stepan 1978b) gradually emerged after the 1964 coup in Brazil. The lusophone dictatorship then inspired and actively supported imitation efforts across the region (Gaspari 2003: 346–64). Many Latin American countries, especially Argentina (1966 and 1976), Chile (1973), Uruguay (1973), and – in a more progressive variant – Peru (1968), instituted anticommunist bureaucratic-authoritarian regimes as well. In underdeveloped Bolivia with its institutionally weak polity, however, which resembled a "praetorian society" à la Huntington (1968), implementation of this new regime model fell far short of the Brazilian precedent and remained closer to a personalistic dictatorship (Malloy and Gamarra 1988: 91–2). In sum, most of the new autocracies were quite similar in structure, based on rule by the military as an institution, and they shared anticommunist goals and a determined development orientation.[2] Even the intensely nationalist, initially left-leaning dictatorship in Peru rested on these foundations (Nunn 1979: 393) and tried hard to boost the technical capacities of the state for developmental purposes.[3] Its fundamental goal was to impose thorough, wide-ranging reforms from the top down precisely in order to avert a truly revolutionary explosion from the bottom up (Stepan 1978b: 120–3, 129–31, 135–6).

These authoritarian regimes differed, however, in specific ideological orientation, depending on the way in which the preemptive strategy of democratic reformism had failed. Where the Alliance for Progress had backfired and led to the unintended consequence of fueling radicalization, as in Brazil, Chile, Argentina, and Uruguay, highly repressive, antimobilizational conservatism prevailed. By contrast, where democracy had obstructed reforms, as in Peru, the new military regime took it upon itself to decree profound

---

[1] The military regimes established in the 1960s, such as Brazil (1964), Argentina (1966), and Peru (1968), relied primarily on a state interventionist approach, whereas the dictatorships imposed in the 1970s, namely Chile (1973), Uruguay (1973), and Argentina (1976), employed a neoliberal strategy.

[2] As Linz (1973) emphasized, even in the long-lasting Brazilian case these dictatorships did not achieve firm institutionalization, with stable, broadly recognized rules for transferring and exercising government power. But their foundational core was the military as an institution, not an individual leader sustained by personalistic loyalties. Even Augusto Pinochet in Chile, who quickly established his predominance and then perpetuated himself in power, based this preeminence on the institutional hierarchy of the army and the institutional structures of his 1980 constitution. Accordingly, he relinquished power after losing the constitutionally mandated plebiscite of 1988. Due to this institutional core, the patrimonial, even Sultanistic label sometimes applied to the Chilean dictatorship (Remmer 1991: 141–2) is problematic (similar criticism in Huneeus 2007: 76–8).

[3] See interview with later military ruler Francisco Morales Bermúdez in Prieto Celi (1996: 114–18, 123–5, 131–2, 153, 159).

socioeconomic change by autocratic fiat.[4] While this more progressive version of anticommunist dictatorship shared the nondemocratic institutional setup of the reactionary variant, it hoped for societal receptivity and support for its reform program,[5] and therefore proceeded in a much less repressive way. But this interesting experiment ran afoul of its inherent tensions, failed to find strong societal sustenance, and did not achieve political success (Lowenthal 1975; Stepan 1978b: 290–7, 301–16; Lowenthal and McClintock 1983). Consequently, a moderate military faction removed the progressive wing in a 1975 coup and steered the Peruvian dictatorship more in the direction of the exclusionary, conservative autocracies prevailing in the Southern Cone.

Theoretically speaking, the installation of institutional, development-oriented dictatorship across Latin America reflected bounded rationality on both sides of the ideological divide. As the amazing groundswell of radicalization shows, many leftists were "carried away" by the optimistic inferences that cognitive heuristics made them draw from Castro's success; consequently, they clearly overestimated the ease of effecting profound change. The left's high hopes, the resulting push for overambitious transformations, and the exalted, revolutionary rhetoric with which these changes were often promoted, in turn instilled deep fear among status quo defenders, who saw the established order as precarious as well, sharing the fundamental inference that left-wingers derived from the Cuban Revolution. The resulting threat perceptions prompted asymmetrical loss aversion among conservatives, who – feeling pressed against the wall by rising extremism – were determined to fight back with all means, including brutal coercion and autocratic imposition. In the world of bounded rationality, exuberant left-wing diffusion once again provoked fierce right-wing counterdiffusion.

Establishment sectors depicted this reactionary response as mere defense against the exaggerated activism of the left, that is, an instrumentally rational way of safeguarding their core interests. But in fact, there was a good deal of cognitive distortion driving the right and center's threat perceptions. Many leftists were more noisy than powerful (see, e.g., Quiroga Zamora 2001: 104–5, 111–12); even calls for armed struggle were rarely followed by serious preparations; and in the rare case where workers' militias did form, they were no match for Latin America's professionalized armies (see, e.g., Whelan 1989: 516, 573–4; Haslam 2005: 208–9).[6] Moreover, leftists had neither the coordination nor the systematic plan that rightists suspected; instead, division

---

[4] On the distinctive ideological orientation and ambitious reform approach of Peru's military regime, see also Philip (1976: 36–9).

[5] Radical peasant organizer Hugo Blanco (1972: 145, 150) indeed reports that these reform measures caused "confusion among the left" and that "a great part of the left has capitulated contemptibly before [what in his eyes was] this bourgeois government."

[6] Here again, Bolivia constitutes an exception, as the country's military for many years had the hardest time imposing state authority on militant armed miners (for these struggles, see Field 2014; Malloy and Gamarra 1988; Dunkerley 1984: chap. 4).

and infighting were rife.[7] Therefore, realistic assessments would have shown that the effective danger of a Marxist revolution was limited, usually very limited. But the unexpected success that communists had achieved in Cuba induced conservatives to overestimate the probabilities of emulative takeovers across the region. Cognitive heuristics stimulated thinking in worst-case scenarios.

The distorted views and the correspondingly ill-considered actions of both sides, another round in the interactive dynamic of diffusion and counterdiffusion highlighted in this book, had tragic consequences. Above all, exaggerated threat perceptions led military coup makers to crack down with vastly excessive force and to employ atrocious means of repression, including mass torture, assassinations, and forced disappearances, even after their rule was effectively consolidated (see for Chile, Hurtado 1990). As political scientist Carlos Huneeus (2007: 46; see also 32) explains for the Chilean case, "the use of violence to seize power was not inevitable," but arose from an overestimation of the danger posed by the radical left. The tragic overreactions that occurred in country after country clearly overshot the defensive measures that any rational calculation would have suggested. Due to "a sense of crisis, loss, and the fear of new losses" that was exacerbated by cognitive-psychological distortions (Pereira 2003: 43), reaction crushed revolution with "unnecessary" brutality.

Despite the enormous costs of these crackdowns, however, the spiral of deviations from standard rationality advanced yet one step further. Under the spell of revolutionary illusions, the most radical sectors of the left sought to drive this interactive dynamic all the way to their end goal. In provoking military coups, they hoped that naked state repression would finally prompt the explosion of a popular insurgency and in this way usher in the socialist transformation, as Che Guevara himself had preached (Brown 2017: 203, 256–7). But this additional turn in the dialectic of revolution and reaction clearly failed to materialize. The fierceness of military repression in itself deterred and forestalled any revolutionary upsurge. Moreover, while the new dictatorships imposed terrible costs on radicals and left-wingers in general, they also brought relief from polarization and turmoil for the large mass of the citizenry; in the aggregate, these relative gains seemed to predominate, inducing a majority of the citizenry to endorse or acquiesce in military takeovers and dictatorial rule.[8] Deprived of mass support, the remaining leftist stirrings fell prey to the tremendous institutional strength of reactionary autocracies and their unscrupulous determination to employ brutal force. For these reasons, right-wing reaction decisively defeated left-wing revolution and managed to forestall another swing in the ideological pendulum.

---

[7] For Brazil, e.g., see Moraes 2011: 47, 58–63, 67, 90, 173–82, 214, 217, 222–5, 228, 275–7, 285, 288–91, 327; Ferreira and Gomes 2014: 157, 192–3, 205, 280–1, 321–2.

[8] See in general Brands 2010: 111, 116, 120. See on specific countries Soares 1979: 450–2; Cohen 1989: 41–6; Potash 1996: 508; Novaro and Palermo 2003: 23–33; Motta 2014: 11–13.

The present chapter substantiates these arguments by discussing the widespread radicalization of the 1960s and early 1970s that affected a number of Latin American countries. Attention then turns to the resulting fears of status quo defenders and their eventual call for the clenched fist of autocratic rulers. To examine the imposition of institutional, developmentalist dictatorship in some depth, Chapter 6 then focuses on the case of Brazil, which turned into a model for the rest of the region. Analyses of Chile and Argentina follow.

THE GROUNDSWELL OF RADICALIZATION UNLEASHED BY THE CUBAN REVOLUTION

As the preceding Chapter 4 showed, in several Latin American countries democratic competition spurred political and programmatic polarization and helped to fuel the radicalization of broader segments of the left. This radicalization was so powerful that it also affected a number of centrist sectors, and even some originally right-wing groupings, especially those of a Catholic background (e.g., Ollier 1998: 87, 100–1; Langland 2013: 70–1). Underlying this political dynamic was the powerful ideational impact of the Cuban Revolution, which seemed to suggest the feasibility of profound, comprehensive sociopolitical change. The heuristics of availability and representativeness inspired not only the few radicals who sought to emulate Castro's success directly by initiating a host of guerrilla struggles. In addition, much broader political sectors drew problematic, overoptimistic inferences from the stunning events on the Caribbean island.

Above all, as documented below, a wide range of forces and groupings jumped to the conclusion that established socioeconomic and political structures were much more precarious than had long been assumed, that seemingly entrenched elites could be dislodged with surprising ease, and that a majority of the population would support these ambitious efforts. Essentially, many observers drew distinctly voluntaristic lessons from the Cuban Revolution (Wright 2001: 39–45): they came to believe that entrenched structures were much less constraining than they appeared and that determined agency could make a big difference. While Latin America had long suffered from economic backwardness and dependency, widespread poverty and egregious social inequality, and political oppression and instability, suddenly it seemed that for those who tried hard enough to push for change, great improvements lay just around the corner.

In Latin America, the Cuban Revolution provided the main impulse for this revaluation of the prospects of transformative collective action, which affected a wide range of political sectors. After all, the availability heuristic draws disproportionate attention especially to experiences inside the same region (see in general Weyland 2007: 47–9), and given the commonalities prevailing among Latin American countries, the representativeness heuristic suggested the applicability of lessons derived from this intraregional success. Mechanisms of bounded rationality thus help explain why Castro's feat found such enormous resonance in Latin America during the 1960s.

While having less direct impact, extraregional experiences reinforced the voluntaristic beliefs inspired by the Cuban Revolution in important ways. The French defeats in Indochina and Algeria showed what developing countries could accomplish with sufficient willpower; the growing difficulties that the United States faced in Vietnam, a "third-rate peasant nation" in the words of Henry Kissinger, boosted this belief and provoked an eagerness in Latin America to challenge the regional hegemon and its local allies. In turn, the civil rights movement in the United States and the student protests gathering steam across the globe were widely seen as proof that bottom-up challenges against established elites had good chances of success. All across the world, activism seemed to pay surprising dividends.[9]

The Cuban Revolution and these extraregional experiences seemed to place a premium on political ambition. Status quo defenders' emphasis on the obstacles to change (cf. Hirschman 1991: chap. 3) increasingly fell on deaf ears. Thoroughgoing reform seemed unavoidable and revolution possible. The powerful wind of change blew in the face of conservative sectors, which had to confront a strong "mobilization of bias" (Schattschneider 1975: 30) when trying to defend the established system. As in Bob Dylan's words, "there was . . . revolution in the air," such progressive hopes found strong resonance in Latin America. In the words of a Brazilian student activist (interview with Van der Weid 2008), the perception prevailed "that the world was heading toward a revolutionary movement." Even centrist sectors couched their reform efforts in overambitious terms. For instance, Chile's Christian Democratic President Eduardo Frei Montalva (1964–70), a solid centrist, labeled his ambitious reform program a "revolution in liberty."[10] Who now reads political documents from the 1960s and early 1970s is amazed at the multitude of profound changes that a broad range of political groupings suddenly regarded as feasible.

This bout of voluntarism found special receptivity among the political left, which in its fundamental ideological orientation embraces the possibility and desirability of change. Under the influence of the Cuban Revolution and the extraregional "struggles," many left-wingers now updated their probability assessments and came to see much higher chances for achieving their goals.

---

[9] See interviews with Chilean leftists in Arancibia 2006: 170, 299–300, 336, and testimony by Brazilian leftists in Palmeira 2008, Sirkis [1979] 2008a, 2008b, and interview with Sirkis 2008.

[10] Similarly, under the impact of the Cuban Revolution, Liberal Party politician Alfonso López Michelsen in Colombia, a moderate reformist at the time, changed the name of his Movimiento de Recuperación Liberal in 1960 to Movimiento Revolucionario Liberal (Villamizar 2017: 196–7).

While traditional communists retained their structural determinism, and therefore urged continuing caution, other currents of socialism got carried away by the inferential tailwind that the availability and representativeness heuristics derived from Castro's success. Accordingly, these sectors now pushed hard for more transformations, more profound transformations, and quicker transformations. They turned more ambitious, impatient, and intransigent. Negotiation and compromise came to look like betrayal; instead, resistance had to be broken, if necessary with violence.[11]

Certainly, this powerful urge for change was understandable. After all, Latin America had long been suffering from severe problems such as injustice and misery, for which left-wing recipes claimed to offer solutions. But of course, the need for change does not in any way guarantee its feasibility. From a rational perspective, it is decisive to assess the probability of change, which depends on the prevailing constellation of power. It is this crucial step that cognitive heuristics turned into a simple leap of faith. Impressed by Castro's apparent success, many left-wingers assumed that similar changes were feasible across the region. Inferential shortcuts thus inspired sudden hopes that long-standing problems could finally be overcome, and these logically problematic expectations then spurred an outburst of radical reform efforts.

These voluntaristic tendencies affected a wide range of progressive forces, even outside the left. In fact, radicalization found special receptivity among populist movements, which in many Latin American countries has long commanded much broader support than leftism, especially among the popular sectors (Castañeda 1993: 48–9). Because populism lacks clear, firm ideological and programmatic definitions, it proved highly susceptible to the cognitive inferences derived from the Cuban Revolution. Argentine Peronism, for instance, which in ideological terms is a complete hodgepodge ranging from the radical right to the radical left, faced a strong pull to the left in the 1960s and early 1970s, especially among its youth wing. While Juan Perón had founded the movement in the 1940s precisely as an antidote to revolution (Waisman 1987: chaps. 6–7), many of its activists now came to call for revolution, however ill-defined; in fact, the aging *caudillo* fueled this fervor to engineer his triumphant return from exile (Gillespie 1982: 46, 70, 103–4, 122). From the late 1960s onward, more and more Peronist cadres embraced armed struggle and formed the *Montoneros*,[12] which engaged in increasingly brutal urban guerrilla warfare.

---

[11] For Brazil, e.g., see Moraes 2011: 17, 27–8, 31, 63, 73, 84–5, 89, 95, 127, 134–5, 203–4, 219–20, 223–4, 232, 297, 340; for Peru, see Rénique 2010: 317–23).

[12] Interestingly, the *Montoneros* reflected the tremendous ideological heterogeneity of the Peronist movement: several of their top leaders had a personal background in the extreme nationalist right! What held them together was less ideology than the penchant for violent action (Gillespie 1982: 47–52). Given the guerrilla's ideological heterogeneity, the military regime of 1966–73 was initially confused, as short-term dictator Alejandro Lanusse explains in his memoirs

Brazil's populist movement, orphaned after the suicide of its original leader Getúlio Vargas in 1954, was even more heterogeneous and fluid than Peronism. Stimulated by the Cuban Revolution, several old and new currents therefore underwent significant radicalization during the early 1960s (Skidmore 1967: 278–83; Langland 2013: 68–81). As a former activist highlights, "the Cuban slogans [e.g., 'the duty of the revolutionary is to make the revolution'] hammered (!) the heads of the New Left militants" (Reis 2006: 23). Accordingly, the peasant leagues led by Francisco Julião in Brazil's impoverished northeast declared Castro's transformation as their model (Moraes 2011: 84–97, 134, 203, 223–4, 232; see also Ridenti 1993: 63). Consequently, they wanted to prepare for violent revolutionary struggle, claimed to command 100,000 armed peasants (Ridenti 1993: 219; Rollemberg 2001: 25), and actually created training camps for guerrilla fighters, which the military forcibly closed in 1962, however.[13] Furthermore, radical unions escaped from the strictures of Brazil's state corporatist system of interest representation by forming an overarching "general commando," which – headed by communists – pushed for drastic political change.

Similarly, Catholic youth movements fell under the spell of Castro's success such that a leader commented in retrospect, "we were all Cuban revolutionaries" (Herbert de Souza cited in Sales 2007: 30). Even lower-ranking military personnel unionized and defied the generals with far-reaching demands (Stepan 1971: 158–65; Ridenti 1993: 206–11). This challenge to hierarchy, a constitutive principle of the armed forces, was unprecedented – and would soon prove a costly mistake. Riding on and reinforcing this wave of mobilization, President João Goulart (1961–64) with ever greater urgency advocated "basic reforms," such as land redistribution; moreover, he confronted the conservative opposition with demands for increased presidential powers, and his supporters threatened simply to impose profound change against resistance. Similar to Argentina, Brazil thus experienced a dramatic upsurge of demands for ambitious transformations.

As Cuba-inspired radicalization affected populist movements, it had a particularly strong impact on the left, especially the new groupings sprouting up outside the Communist Party; the Moscow-linked comrades, by contrast, mostly clung to their deterministic stage theory and therefore dismissed efforts to achieve immediate socialist revolution as adventurism. This stodgy prudence drew dismissive rejection from the wide range of less dogmatic leftists, who often fell for the new forms of mobilizational activism. Sectors inspired by the progressive turn of the Catholic Church proved particularly passionate in their militancy, sometimes going so far as to condone political violence (for Brazil,

---

(Lanusse 1977: 134–5; Lanusse 1994: 247–9). The authoritarian government did not know how best to respond to this challenge.

[13] Julião 1982: 101–3, 112,122–3, 171–2; Azevêdo 1982: 93–5; Gaspari 2002: 178–9; Sales 2007: 35–54.

see Ridenti 1993: 25–9; Sales 2007: 15–34). But even established political forces were swept away by the groundswell of radicalization that the Cuban Revolution unleashed all across the region.

As a prime example, the Socialist Party of Chile, for decades a paragon of democratic responsibility, caught the fever of extremist voluntarism.[14] After it had long pursued its transformational goals through liberal institutions, the Cuban Revolution stimulated it to proclaim in 1967 the programmatic acceptance of "armed struggle" (Arrate and Rojas 2003, vol. 1: 425–6; see also Walker 1990: 137–8, 143, 146, 153–4). Such overheated rhetoric[15] helped to foment street violence, and under the Salvador Allende government (1970–3) contributed to the formation of worker militias, which engaged in illegal factory takeovers (see, e.g., Haslam 2005: chaps. 2, 7). That this extremism could flourish in a long-standing democracy shocked right-wingers (Jarpa 2002: 113–17, 161–2, 183, 189; interview with Jarpa 2007) and caused increasing concerns among centrist sectors as well,[16] as Christian Democratic leaders Eduardo Frei Montalva, Renán Fuentealba, and Patricio Aylwin stressed.[17] The military was especially worried about the rise of armed formations on the radical left, which threatened to undermine its cherished monopoly over organized coercion (Sigmund 1977: 226–7, 240, 256, 258, 288–9).

As a minoritarian, but especially consequential aspect of this massive radicalization, Argentina, Brazil, and Uruguay saw urban guerrilla movements emerge (Wright 2001: 93–109; Marchesi 2018: chaps. 1, 4). This leftist terrorism was fed mainly by student radicalism, which in turn had received a strong impulse from the Cuban Revolution. The eagerness to employ political violence was further inflamed by the influential guerrilla manual of Régis Debray (1967), who drew distinctly voluntaristic lessons from the Cuban success.[18] In Argentina and Brazil, the repressive countermeasures undertaken by military regimes added further fuel

---

[14] Arrate and Rojas 2003, vol. 1: 333–42, 393–9, 425–8; Faúndez 1988: 164–70, 173; Quiroga Zamora 2001: 16–23, 29; Schnake 2004: 133, 137–9, 153, 174–5; Núñez 2013: 80, 83–5, 114–15; see interviews with politicians from across the ideological divide in Arancibia 2006: 169–72, 257–60, 299–300, 305, 334–5, 372, 417–18, 424–5, 449, 460.

[15] In his interview with Patricia Arancibia (2006: 173), Carlos Altamirano, the most outstanding leader of the radical wing of Chile's Socialist Party in the early 1970s, highlights that there actually were not many armed leftists in the country under the Allende government – but that the radical left engaged in a rhetoric (*un lenguaje*) as if it commanded thousands of fighters. In retrospect, Schnake (2004: 174, 180, 183, 199) also marvels at these rhetorical excesses. Historian Peter Winn (2010: 244–7, 251–3) highlights the wide gap between violent rhetoric and nonviolent practice as well.

[16] One reason for this shock was that Chile's relatively small political elite had been crisscrossed by a web of personal connections and long-standing friendships – which was unexpectedly strained by the polarization and hostility of the late 1960s and 1970s (interview with Molina 2007).

[17] See, respectively, Frei Montalva 1974: 20, 23, 25; Fuentealba quoted in Valenzuela 1978: 89–92; interview with Aylwin in Serrano and Cavallo 2006: 238–9, 247–8; see also Arriagada 1974, espec. 298–307.

[18] Author interview with Sirkis 2008; see also Marambio 2007: 57–8.

to the fire, which Perón deliberately fanned to plot his own return to power (Gillespie 1982). But even a long-standing democracy could fall prey to this explosion of violence, as the tragic case of Uruguay shows (Rey Tristán 2005). Following Che Guevara's earlier advice (Brown 2017: 203, 256–7), urban guerrillas tried to destroy liberal democracy in the perverse hope that a dictatorship with its naked repression would facilitate their recruitment efforts and sooner or later trigger a mass insurrection (Shapiro 1972: 102; Rey Tristán 2005: 159). This "dialectical" calculation (Kaufman 1979: 36) demonstrates the twisted rationality of extreme leftists inspired by the Cuban Revolution: they proceeded in a goal-oriented way, but their assessments of probabilities and risks were seriously distorted by simplistic inferences drawn from the Cuban case, namely the belief that bold and risky popular activism was not that difficult to stimulate.

In sum, the dramatic precedent of Communist Cuba fired up many left-wingers, populists, and even centrists, and inspired a variety of profoundly reformist and revolutionary efforts across Latin America. Processed with the heuristics of availability and representativeness, Castro's success fueled high hopes and triggered a striking wave of radicalism. Yet the distorted inferences that spurred these extremist efforts set up their protagonists for failure after failure, sooner or later. After all, status quo-oriented sectors were deeply impressed by the Cuban precedent as well, but due to their very different interests and goals, they offered increasingly fierce resistance against any efforts to proceed toward the replication of Castro's feats.

COUNTERDIFFUSION: THE REACTION OF RIGHTIST AND CENTRIST FORCES

Fears of Communism

The massive radicalization of leftist, populist, and even some centrist political forces aroused enormous fears among conservative sectors. Urgent demands for profound transformation jeopardized the core interests of business elites, traditional clerics, rightist politicians, and most of the military. The extremist challenge therefore activated loss aversion and provided a strong impetus for defensive measures. Elite sectors that commanded disproportionate resources and power capabilities due to their privileged position were determined to dig in their heels.[19] And because people attach far greater subjective weight to losses than to objectively equivalent gains, they found a great deal of support: the Latin Americans who opposed a profound transformation, not to speak of communism, always outnumbered those who pushed for dramatic change. Even Chile's Salvador Allende, though sustained by two long-standing, unusually strong left-wing parties, never won a majority in

---

[19] These fears are amply reflected in the massive analysis of the Chilean case by Whelan (1989: e.g. 300–1, 310–11), who drew on close access to the principal actors and many supporters of the Pinochet regime.

democratic elections (Silva Solar 1979: 319; Tapia Videla 1979: 28). Indeed, 53.1 percent of survey respondents "reject[ed] socialism" in 1973 (data in Bermeo 2003: 173). Similarly, polls show that most Brazilians opposed communism in the early 1960s.[20] Moreover, as the threat seemed to grow over time, the camp of status quo defenders increased further in size, and they deepened their intransigence.

Therefore, contrary to class approaches,[21] the struggle over change in Latin America during the 1960s and early 1970s did not pit the small upper class against the large numbers of workers and the popular sectors more broadly. Instead, resistance to radicalism extended far down in the social pyramid, comprising not only good parts of the middle class, but also many workers, farmers, and peasants. In Argentina, for instance, the Peronist labor movement had a strong right wing, which soon turned against the Peronist *Montoneros* guerrilla and joined the fight against extremism, even via anticommunist death squads (Novaro and Palermo 2003: 80–2). And in Chile, traditional social and religious values, conservative and liberal political concerns, and, later, the experience of hyperinflation, shortages, and constant turmoil under the Allende government kept many poorer people in the countryside and in the cities from backing leftist radicalism (see, e.g., Silva Solar 1979: 319–20; Fleet 1985: 136, 138, 149–50, 152).[22] Like rational choice, class approaches, which depict collective segments of society as rational actors, run afoul of the realities of bounded rationality, especially people's intense aversion to losses.

Interestingly, the widespread, usually rapid defeat of rural guerrilla movements that directly tried to imitate the Cuban Revolution did not extirpate the danger of communism in the eyes of status quo defenders. From their perspective, armed insurgencies were only the tip of the iceberg, initiated by the extremist fringe that was emerging with the much broader process of radicalization; the failure of the greatest hotheads did not guarantee that the danger posed by the vaster range of leftists and populists had receded.

After all, according to the doctrine of revolutionary war embraced by Latin American militaries and disseminated to society, the turn toward guerrilla warfare occurs in the third of the five stages in which communist subversion advances.[23] Consequently, the repression of insurgent movements does not eradicate all the dangerous preparatory work and the far-reaching infiltration that radicals and communists succeeded in undertaking during the earlier stages

---

[20] In March 1964, for instance, 76 percent of survey respondents opposed the legalization of the Communist Party (Lavareda 1991: 159). And in mid–1963, only 19 percent identified with the left overall (Lavareda 1991: 156). Moreover, in a June 1964 survey in Guanabara state, which comprised the city of Rio de Janeiro, 63 percent of respondents regarded it as "a bad measure" if communists were amnestied (Tendências – Eleições Presidenciais 1994: 15).

[21] See Kay 1975 and especially Stallings 1978 for Chile, and in general Rueschemeyer, Stephens, and Stephens 1992 and Acemoglu and Robinson 2005.

[22] For Brazil, see Soares 1979: 450–2.

[23] Fragoso 1959: 22; Carvalho 1964: 86–94; Oliveira 1964: 32, 36–41, 45; Brasil 1964: 20–1; D'Araujo, Dillon Soares, and Castro 1994: 78–9.

(cf. Peru. Ministerio de Guerra 1966: 39, 77, 79). Based on this remaining foundation, new insurrections could well erupt, sooner or later. Thus, even if the forces of order won some early battles in the monumental fight against communism, the suppression of *guerrilleros* did by no means seal victory in the revolutionary war. Although the tip was chopped off, the dangerous iceberg kept lurking and jeopardizing the ship of the state.

These intense fears were expressed by the Peruvian military in 1966, for instance. After the armed forces had defeated several guerrilla bands operating in the Andes, the Ministry of War commented, "this does not mean that the 'revolutionary' war in Peru is finished; the 'virus' of subversion is latent and has surreptitiously penetrated the universities and the high schools, the unions and the offices, the clubs and the private homes. The enemy is all over the place and the citizenry needs to understand that."[24] In a similar vein, conservatives in Uruguay were worried less about the violent *Tupamaros* than about the 18 percent of the vote that a Broad Front of leftist forces (Frente Amplio), which had connections to this urban guerrilla movement (Rey Tristán 2005: 345–69), suddenly won in the 1971 elections. That almost a third of voters in the capital Montevideo, where the Frente Amplio commanded particular strength, "were disloyal to the established order . . . was a situation potentially much more dangerous than anything a relatively small guerrilla band alone could create" (González 1991: 40).

Moreover, Latin American radicalism continued to count on external inspiration and support. After all, the variegated US efforts to suffocate the Castro regime in Cuba or foster its removal by counterrevolutionaries had uniformly failed (Brown 2017: part 1). Relentless US pressure had actually backfired by driving the Cuban revolutionaries ever more firmly into the arms of the Soviets, the West's global rival in the Cold War. The Caribbean island turned into an outpost of communism's motherland, which in the eyes of status quo defenders – both in the United States and in Latin America – was the main promoter of radical change at the global level. In fact, with the spread of radicalism in the southern subcontinent, Communist Russia and Cuba seemed to gain ever more footholds inside the region, for instance with the Soviet-style "popular assembly" in Bolivia (1971) and especially the victory of Marxist Salvador Allende in Chile.[25] From the US perspective, this stunning election outcome in the Southern Cone seemed to expose the core of Latin America to a two-sided attack, from Communist Cuba in the north and radical-socialist Chile in the south (Fagen 1975: 297).

[24] Peru. Ministerio de Guerra 1966: 80; see also 76–82, and Nunn 1979: 391, 394–5. These concerns were not completely unfounded, however: in line with Che Guevara's Bolivian guerrilla project, there were efforts to restart armed insurrection in Peru in 1966–67 (Lust 2015: 233–5).

[25] On the radicalism of both of these leftist experiences, see Zavaleta Mercado (1974). Allende repeatedly stressed his commitment to Marxism in his conversations with Régis Debray (1971: 62, 67, 81, 118). On US fears about the Soviet Union gaining a foothold in Bolivia, see *FRUS 1969–1976*, vol. E-10, docs. 102, 104.

Conservatives in Latin America, most consequentially the military officers running Brazil, shared this perception of heightened threat. Fearing spillover from Allende's "march to socialism," they supported the opposition in Chile, especially inside the armed forces (Harmer 2011: 227–9, 273), and combated leftism in Bolivia as well.[26] Thus, fear of Latin American radicalism gripped not only the "hegemonic" US, but also rising regional power Brazil and even Argentina (Malloy and Gamarra 1988: 142, 144–5). In sum, "The *Espoir* [hope] of the Left was reflected in the inverted mirror of the *Grande Peur* [great fear][27] of the more conservative groups of society," as well as their foreign friends and allies (Perelli 1993: 30).

Loss Aversion and the Quest for Protection

In the world of bounded rationality, where asymmetrical loss aversion distorts the valuation of benefits and costs, all these concerns about radicalism bred a fierce determination among domestic and foreign status quo defenders to fight back with all means. Broad sectors on the right, sooner or later joined by centrist forces, responded with great energy to overheated leftism and populism. The underlying reason was that they drew the same cognitive inferences from the Cuban precedent that inspired the groundswell of radicalism. They shared the belief that incumbent regimes in societies plagued by serious problems were precarious and could eventually fall to radical challenges. But of course, in light of their divergent interests, these shared perceptions prompted the decision to act in diametrically opposite ways: conservatives sought to prevent any replication of leftist success at all cost. Consequently, as the left mobilized for winning power, through electoral or violent means, the right, with substantial support from the center, prepared to counteract this threat; it betrayed its deep fears by mobilizing all its resources, advocating drastic solutions, and even endorsing the use of brute force and autocratic imposition.

In more and more countries of the region, this frequently panicked quest for a reliable safeguard against radicalism ended up producing support, or at least acquiescence in dictatorial rule. After all, political liberalism and democracy had paved the way for the rise of left-wing extremism. In fact, democracy seemed to face an inherent handicap in responding to this threat: it provided institutional protection even for those sectors that – in the eyes of conservatives – tried to destroy it via the imposition of communism. As the doctrine of revolutionary war emphasized, liberal democracy therefore suffered from a potentially fatal contradiction (Martins Filho n.d.: 13–14, 19–22; Lyles 2016: 309–10, 364). To combat its enemies effectively, the state needed to foreclose Marxist infiltration

---

[26] Dunkerley 1984: 183, 197–8, 201; Malloy and Gamarra 1988: 63–4, 68, 80, 91–4; Harmer 2011: 125–6, 166–8; Gaspari 2003: 346–8.

[27] This is an allusion to the French Revolution of 1789, when scary rumors and conspiracy theories drove many people into revolutionary action, as Lefebvre's (1979) seminal study highlighted.

by temporarily limiting liberal freedoms, by dismantling radical organizations, and by extracting intelligence from dangerous activists, especially armed fighters, if need be with rather unpleasant means. As French military thinkers on counterinsurgency, informed by their experiences in Algeria, had reasoned, it was better to put the thumbscrews on a few "terrorists" rather than have the citizenry suffer the damage caused by their bloody attacks.[28] Thus, widely shared threat perceptions brought forth support for authoritarian rule as the lesser evil, varying in strength and fierceness with the acuteness of the extremist threat that a country seemed to face (seminal: O'Donnell 1978: 6–9, 19).[29]

Through its powerful deterrent effects, leftist radicalism provided the fundamental motive for the wave of military coups that rippled through Latin America from the early 1960s onward, reversing the prodemocratic trend of the late 1950s (Wright 2001: chap. 9; Brown 2012). While some hardliners took advantage of the communist threat to pursue their political self-interests or ideological goals, ample evidence suggests that many coup makers and their backers were genuinely convinced of the grave danger confronting their countries. Given the unexpected success of Castro's small group of fighters, the Cuban leader's quick metamorphosis from democratic nationalist to committed Marxist, his alliance with the Soviet Union, and the clandestine, subversive strategy of many groupings that tried to emulate the Cuban example, right-wing sectors took any far-left stirrings as indications of serious trouble. In their eyes, from Lenin onward, communists with their tight organization and ideological zeal had demonstrated an uncanny ability to thrive on turmoil and grab power, never to relinquish it again. Therefore, any potential danger from the far left needed to be rooted out completely (Stepan 1971: 153–8, 173–4; Pion-Berlin 1989).

Evidence for these intense fears is abundant and there is no good reason to doubt their authenticity. For instance, General Octávio Costa, a high-ranking official in Brazil's bureaucratic-authoritarian regime (1964–85), emphasized how much the armed forces in the early 1960s worried about "the insurrectionary war, the revolutionary war," which "was already beginning" with the mobilization for land reform. "This priority given to counter-revolution . . . turned obsessive during the Goulart government [ousted in the 1964 coup], because the perturbation of order in the cities and the rural areas configured, in the perception of the military, the steps of a revolution on the march" (interview in D'Araujo, Dillon Soares, and Castro 1994: 77–9). These threat perceptions arose from the

---

[28] Mazzei 2002: 127–8; Lyles 2016: 365; in more general terms, Fragoso 1959: 23.

[29] As Remmer and Merkx (1982: 8–16) show, differential threat levels do not completely explain the fierceness of the subsequent backlash and the characteristics of the resulting autocracies; of course, other factors matter as well. For instance, the solidity and intensity of Peronist commitments among the citizenry induced dictator Onganía to close the electoral arena in Argentina despite low prior threat of radicalization; by contrast, due to the malleability of Brazil's party system, the governing generals continued to permit legislative elections, although in their eyes, the democratic Goulart government had posed a medium-high threat.

Cuban Revolution: "There was a process of socialization on the march. Cuba exported subversion. Cuba was the precedent for the [radical-left] theory of the [guerrilla] *foco*, the creation of liberated areas that would spread all over Brazil," as General Costa explained (in D'Araujo, Dillon Soares, and Castro 1994: 95). In a very similar fashion, the Peruvian military – despite its reformist orientation and calls for a "social-democratic revolution" (Peru. Ministerio de Guerra 1966: 80) – was intensely fearful that the subversive efforts inspired and supported by Cuba[30] were part of a "revolutionary war" threatening the country (Peru. Ministerio de Guerra 1966: 76–82).[31]

How the depth of this fear helped undermine democracy is exemplified by the Uruguayan case. Juan Bordaberry from the Colorado Party, who in a 1973 self-coup destroyed the decades-old democracy, won the 1971 presidential election with a "campaign [that] was largely a negative one, asking his countrymen to vote against communism rather than for any program of reform and change. A typical Colorado billboard poster read:

Were you afraid in the past? Are you afraid now? How long have you been afraid? Think before you vote, because if you don't you will be afraid for the rest of your life. (reproduced in Shapiro 1972: 103)

Some scholars dismiss these exaggerated, unrealistic concerns as ideological façades for selfish motives or class interests (e.g., McSherry 2005: 24–9; cf. Bandeira 1983: 127, 130, 153–4). Such manipulation certainly played a role as reactionary sectors sought to win broader support and therefore deliberately spread fear (e.g., Dulles' interview with Brancante 1965). But a wealth of documentation shows that many right-wingers saw the radical left as a real danger and acted in a sincere fashion out of genuine concern (see recently Brands 2010: 127). For instance, all twelve generals interviewed by scholars about the motives of Brazil's 1964 coup highlighted communism;[32] some called the military takeover a countercoup – a reaction to radical-left challenges.[33] In the same vein, Brazil's military journal in the early 1960s published numerous articles about the danger of a "revolutionary war."[34]

---

[30] The Cuban connection is strongly emphasized in Peru. Ministerio de Guerra 1966: 12, 15, 24, 27–8, 42, 46–7, 54, 76–7.

[31] Similarly, General Edgardo Mercado Jarrín (1974: 202–3, 215), a leading member of the reformist military regime (1968–75), thought in terms of "the counterinsurgency war" and claimed that radical "subversion" served "foreign interests."

[32] Interviews in D'Araujo, Dillon Soares, and Castro 1994: 11, 40, 46, 60, 91, 95, 126–7, 142–3, 155, 161, 175, 190, 206–7, 214–15, 230–1; see also former military president Ernesto Geisel in D'Araujo and Castro 1997: 162, 168; and Muricy 1993: 442–5, 456–67, 460, 482, 505–6, 514–15, 525. Brazil's first military president Humberto Castello Branco shared the intense concerns about communism (Dulles 1978: 241, 250, 253–8, 266–7, 270–1, 313–16, 323–5, 334, 339, 353, 371, 376–9).

[33] D'Araujo, Dillon Soares, and Castro 1994: 206–7, 224; see also Muricy 1993: 479, 485, 507; see Chirio 2003: 73–4, 79.

[34] Estudo de Situação 1963; Ferreira 1963; Martins 1963; Oliveira 1964.

The Cuban Revolution also made a profound impression on Peru's leading military academy, which quickly refocused on "the internal enemy" and prepared for "revolutionary war."[35] In 1959 already, the director, General Marcial Romero Pardo, warned against the "constant danger of the Communist threat" (cited in Villanueva 1972: 126). The eruption of several guerrilla movements further aggravated these threat perceptions.[36] Similarly, the Cuban Revolution scared Argentine officers (Cousins 2008: 70), who from the early 1960s onward worried about the danger of "Communist revolutionary war," as General Osiris Villegas expounded in a major book (Villegas 1962; see Mazzei 2002: 132–3).[37] Interestingly, Villegas soon turned into the "chief ideological architect" of the military regime that grabbed power in 1966 (Pion-Berlin 1988: 390). Demonstrating the persistent intensity of these fears, a long-standing leader of the Chilean right started a confidential author interview (Santiago, July 2007) about the democratic transition of the 1980s (!) by producing the "Resolution of Chillán" (1967), in which the radicalized Socialist Party had committed to armed struggle. In his view, this imprudent proclamation had unleashed the polarization leading to the 1973 coup and the long-lasting authoritarian regime.

As this wealth of evidence suggests, the threat perceptions of many rightists rested on genuine conviction. From an objective standpoint, these fears were exaggerated and sometimes resembled paranoia. The institutional solidity of the state and the military's professional strength guaranteed effective immunity from communist subversion.[38] Most Cuba-inspired and supported guerrilla movements quickly ended in failure, and the broader process of political radicalization encountered potent obstacles and prompted powerful resistance as well. Yet under the shock of the Cuban Revolution, status quo defenders discounted these realities. Conservative panic was driven by deviations from full rationality, especially the heuristics of availability and representativeness.[39] These cognitive shortcuts ironically made right-wingers jump to similar conclusions as left-wingers concerning the ease of communist revolution.

---

[35] As Nunn (1979) documents, the Peruvian military had for decades held a developmentalist orientation and emphasized its domestic political and "civilizational" role. Interestingly, these orientations resulted in part from a series of teaching missions by the French military (1896–1940: Nunn 1979: 414–15).

[36] Peru. Ministerio de Guerra 1966: 76–82; Prieto Celi 1996: 101, 131.

[37] Concerns about "revolutionary war" also ran high among the Colombian military (Velásquez Rivera 2012).

[38] The exception is Nicaragua's Sultanistic regime (Wickham-Crowley 1992: 269–71).

[39] My interpretation thus agrees with Brands' (2010: 127) powerful argument about "the essential sincerity" of right-wing threat perceptions, but disagrees with part of his claim that the resulting counterrevolutionary measures "were the logical – if exaggerated – response to the leftist radicalism of the period." Instead of being "logical," that is, essentially rational, the conservative response was deeply shaped by cognitive deviations from full rationality, and these deviations account for the "outrageously disproportionate" (Brands 2010: 127) nature of the reactionary response.

Shared by both poles of the ideological spectrum, these inferences did not arise from right-wing manipulation. Of course, what gave leftists hope made rightists shudder with dread – and spurred a fierce determination to crush left-wingers' hopes with all means.

As an example of this backlash effect, even before the coup of 1973, the Chilean military cracked down really hard on the attempts of radical leftists to recruit support inside the armed forces, which the military leadership saw as subversion of hierarchy and discipline. Therefore, they arrested a large number of personnel involved in these organizational efforts and applied torture – even under the democratic regime existing at that time. As historian Jonathan Haslam (2005: 201) explains, this remarkably fierce response was "a product of fear, albeit exaggerated out of all proportion." In line with the main argument of this study, cognitive shortcuts fueled this overreaction.

In a similar vein, Brazil's military regime imposed full despotism in 1968, when an incendiary speech by a leftist congressional deputy and large-scale street demonstrations inspired by the Cuban Revolution and by subsequent radical challenges in Latin America instilled pervasive fear of "subversion" among regime insiders.[40] When the National Security Council met to institute a harsh dictatorship, many generals and ministers expressed their concern about "the subversion that is on the march" (Conselho de Segurança Nacional 1968: 7, 9, 14–15, 19–21, 23). These acute threat perceptions triggered loss aversion, which made a particularly frank government minister "ignore all the scruples of conscience" and explicitly endorse the formal imposition of dictatorial rule (Conselho de Segurança Nacional 1968: 13). Most other generals and politicians agreed, ushering in years of brutal repression. Interestingly, even the CIA marveled at "the military's excessive preoccupation with subversion, real or imaginary" (document reprinted in Rocha 2016). Once again, cognitive mechanisms caused significant distortions and precluded a rational perspective.

Ample groupings among the moderate right and the center came to back, accept, or acquiesce in these counterrevolutionary efforts because they also developed exaggerated fears of the radical left. They overrated the danger of communism, which rarely had a realistic chance of taking over a country. Excessive threat perceptions derived via cognitive heuristics activated loss aversion, which made them consent to heavy-dosage medicine, including the bitter pill of military dictatorship (Serrano and Cavallo 2006: 247–8; Fleet 1985: 149–79).

Intense loss aversion had its most tragic repercussions in the excess of repression that the institutional autocracies unleashed against their enemies, especially the urban guerrilla movements proliferating in the Southern Cone from the late 1960s onward. The police and military responded to leftist

---

[40] Former student activist and urban *guerrillero* Sirkis recognized this backlash dynamic (interview 2008) and commented that, "politically speaking, [the student protest of] 1968 was a disaster in Latin America" by prompting reactionary crackdowns.

violence with brutal crackdowns, and clandestine right-wing death squads, active especially in Argentina, employed even greater cruelty. This tendency toward "overkill" (cf. Pion-Berlin and Lopez 1991: 68) persisted even after radical organizations had suffered strategic defeats and managed to engage only in sporadic terrorism (Novaro and Palermo 2003: 75–9, 83–4, 88–93). Determined to root out the subversive threat completely, reactionaries were unconcerned about vastly overshooting their target by torturing, killing, and "disappearing" countless people, even those not involved in terrorist acts.

This fear-driven overreaction had its biggest political impact in Uruguay, where right-wingers pushed for an authoritarian (self-)coup in 1973 and took open dictatorial power in 1976 – although the violent Tupamaros had already been defeated in 1972 (Kaufman 1979: 11, 13, 35–6; González 1991: 40–3). But frightened conservatives were convinced that the iron fist of anticommunist autocracy was required for eradicating the broad radicalization that had given rise to the urban guerrilla movement and that continued to find its political expression in the Broad Front, scarily successful in the elections of 1971 (González 1991: 40). For this purpose, the dictators in Montevideo instituted a reign of terror, employing massive torture. While the career interests of repressive agents and the political goals of hardliners played a role in this paroxysm of repression, these forces only secured the necessary backing for their misdeeds because much broader segments of status quo defenders were under the spell of the heuristically inferred communist threat and the resulting loss aversion.[41]

Scholars commonly bemoan these "unnecessary" overreactions, which they depict as a "relentless witch hunt against a relatively compliant citizenry" (cf. Pion-Berlin and Lopez 1991: 68). These criticisms provide indirect evidence for the costly deviations from standard rationality postulated by the central argument of this book (e.g., Sigmund 1977: 256, 258; Pion-Berlin 1988: 385; Haslam 2005: 201; Winn 2010: 267–8; Harmer 2011: 232, 244–6, 254, 271). In their monumental study of Argentina's last military regime, for instance, Novaro and Palermo (2003: 73) highlight "the inverse [negatively correlated to diminishing guerrilla violence] and absolutely disproportionate advance of legal and illegal repression." Considering specific aspects of the authoritarian crackdown, these authors comment that, "in many cases torture sessions were extended over time, independent of the search for information, until the total dehumanization of the kidnapped person" (Novaro and Palermo 2003: 112). Similarly, Moyano (1995: 93) argues that the police and military could have defeated the guerrillas with regular means, "making the dirty war [of mass

---

[41] Seeing himself as the defender of Chile in a war against the radical left, dictator Augusto Pinochet never grasped the human rights issue that the military regime's atrocities raised; as a close confidant highlighted (interview with Rodríguez 2007), Pinochet could not understand that his regime had committed any crime (*delito*).

torture, forced disappearances, and illegal killings] unnecessary . . . The 'war' was directed not against the guerrillas but against society at large . . . The guerrillas' behavior alone cannot account for the ferocity unleashed in 1976."

Conclusion

As this chapter shows, the authoritarian wave of the 1960s and 1970s resulted from the deterrent effect of the leftist extremism sparked by the Cuban Revolution. As radicalization advanced, as revolution seemed to beckon, and as calls for armed struggle spread, military coups proliferated that sought to eliminate or forestall these threats through the institution of repressive dictatorships. Left-wing diffusion thus bred right-wing counterdiffusion; overambitious progressive efforts spurred an overly fearful reactionary backlash. Typically, this defensive response had disproportionate severity: due to the distortions of bounded rationality, the countermeasures overshot the target with excessive strength and unusual cruelty. Because the left pushed hard for profound change, the right responded with massive knockout blows delivered especially by autocratic rulers and their brutal henchmen.

Chapter 6 analyzes how this interactive dynamic of left-wing diffusion and right-wing counterdiffusion unfolded in three high-profile cases, namely Brazil, Argentina, and Chile. While the impact of the Cuban Revolution gave rise to different types of challenges at different times, the specter of Castroite socialism helped to provoke similar reactions, namely military interventions that instituted autocracies with long-term projects guided by ambitious political and developmental goals. Across the region, the voluntaristic hopes of major improvements inspired by Cuba's "success" were brutally squashed, ushering in lengthy stretches of repressive authoritarian rule.

6

The Imposition of Institutional Authoritarianism

Brazil, Argentina, Chile

After the last chapter highlighted the interactive dynamic of radicalization and reaction that engulfed Latin America during the 1960s and 1970s, the present chapter analyzes the installation of autocracy by examining the emblematic cases of Brazil, Argentina, and Chile in some depth. Status quo defenders in these countries faced a variety of perceived threats that had different degrees of magnitude and severity – but the strong anticommunist fears that cognitive heuristics derived from the striking precedent of the Cuban Revolution prompted similar autocratic responses. Amorphous populist forces posed limited challenges to the existing sociopolitical order in Brazil and Argentina, whereas true Marxist parties pursued revolutionary goals in Chile. The advocates of radical change did not advance much beyond proclamations and projects in Brazil, while managing to enact and enforce a host of profound transformations in Chile. Yet despite these substantial differences in actual danger, conservative elites and even a number of centrist sectors sooner or later reacted in the same way, namely via the forceful displacement of left-wing forces and the installation of military dictatorship. The specter of "another Cuba," which triggered particularly intense loss aversion, underlay these strikingly similar countermoves.

Conservatives had the most reason for concern in Chile. After all, the country boasted a powerful left, led by well-organized socialist and communist parties of substantial size, which had come close to winning the presidency already in 1958. Under the influence of the Cuban Revolution, the socialists underwent a profound radicalization during the 1960s, started to push for an immediate socialist transformation, and even pronounced their adherence to armed struggle. After the leftist coalition won the 1970 election, the government of Salvador Allende (1970–3) indeed initiated a determined march toward socialism. Above all, the new administration expropriated large swaths of land and numerous domestic and foreign businesses, often in ways that mainstream sectors found legally questionable. As established elites suffered serious costs and as cognitive heuristics exacerbated the fears of sliding into full-scale communism, asymmetrical loss aversion prompted the brutal coup of September 1973 and the subsequent outburst of harsh repression.

In Brazil and Argentina, by contrast, populism had long encapsulated large parts of the working class and other popular sectors, keeping left-wing forces weak and relatively moderate. Brazil's Communist Party, for instance, prepared for a bourgeois – not socialist – revolution in line with orthodox stage theories and dismissed the radicalization stimulated by the Cuban Revolution as irresponsible adventurism. But Castro's feats inspired a "new left" that started to push for profound transformations, especially sweeping land reforms. These demands in turn fired up a wide range of populist forces, giving rise to a broad yet heterogeneous, weakly organized, and divided groundswell of mobilizations for thorough change. This exuberant popular energy and strong transformational impetus, which lacked clear goals and well-defined projects, was particularly scary for establishment sectors. Future developments seemed so unpredictable and open-ended. Would the push for change really end with a few social reforms, or would it get out of hand and pave the way for communist radicals to hijack these impulses, as in conservative eyes had happened in Cuba? To forestall these risks in the early years after Castro's unexpected embrace of socialism, status quo defenders "pulled the emergency brake" through the military coup of 1964.

The Argentine case was even more complex because the role and impact of Peronism was difficult to figure out. Initially, establishment sectors, including important segments of the country's faction-ridden military, saw this populist mass movement as a bulwark against the radicalization emanating from the Cuban Revolution. But exiled leader Juan Perón, deposed in a 1955 coup, came to promote extremism to obstruct governability and thus force his readmission to Argentine politics. Youth groupings from inside and outside the Peronist movement proved receptive to these appeals; after all, they felt inspired by Castro's success and the broader transformational fervor of the 1960s. As anticommunist sectors imposed a military regime in 1966, growing numbers of young radicals, egged on by the old populist, responded to the repressive closure of the electoral arena by moving toward armed struggle, especially via urban guerrilla attacks. After the 1966 dictatorship ran afoul of popular protests, and after redemocratization in 1973 had failed to dissuade extremists from employing political violence, the armed forces combated the growing chaos with a brutal crackdown in 1976 which ushered in more than seven years of military rule and a paroxysm of state terror.

In sum, the radicalization stimulated by the Cuban Revolution took different forms and pathways in Brazil, Argentina, and Chile. But because cognitive shortcuts made status quo defenders sooner or later see these challenges as country-specific manifestations of the same fundamental threat, namely communism, they reacted in rather uniform ways through the imposition of institutionalized autocracy pursuing ambitious development projects. As perceptions of danger were fueled by the outstanding precedent of Castro's profound socialist transformation, establishment sectors settled on a common response and thus propelled a wave of military dictatorship. The present chapter discusses the three most prominent cases of this authoritarian riptide in temporal order, moving from Brazil to Argentina, and then Chile.

FEARS OF COMMUNISM AND THE INSTALLATION OF INSTITUTIONAL AUTHORITARIANISM IN BRAZIL

The cognitive mechanisms that fueled the widespread perceptions of the communist threat and thus helped drive the Latin American coup wave of the 1960s and 1970s played out very clearly in the prototypical case of Brazil. The events leading up to the military coup of 1964 show the impact emanating from the surprising success of the Cuban Revolution, as mediated by inferential shortcuts. Moreover, particularly rich source materials allow this study to trace how Castro's feats galvanized the anticommunist preoccupations that had already prevailed among conservative politicians and inside the military, and that had acquired greater intensity with the increase in Soviet power and activism during the Cold War. In this context, the imposition of communism on the Caribbean island sounded alarm bells and made growing domestic radicalization look much more dangerous, namely as the preparatory steps for another radical takeover. What had caused concern before, now – due to the Cuban Revolution – aroused acute fear and sometimes panic. Typically, as important sectors, especially in the armed forces, foresaw increasing risks of enormous costs, the powerful mechanism of asymmetrical loss aversion set in, inducing status quo defenders to combat the perceived threat with all means.

Another reason to examine the rise of the Brazilian dictatorship is that the regime emerging after the overthrow of democracy in 1964 turned into the regional model of a security-obsessed, yet developmentally oriented, institutional military regime. During the Latin American coup wave, a process of horizontal diffusion unfolded inside the broader dynamic of counterdiffusion. To avoid contagion by the virus of communism that the Cuban Revolution unleashed in the western hemisphere, conservatives in the region looked for a powerful vaccine and found it in the institutional autocracy established in the lusophone giant. As Chapter 7 explains, Brazil's developmentalist authoritarianism came to be regarded as especially strong and resilient to radical challenges. In the eyes of status quo defenders, it could provide reliable protection against infection by communism. This new autocratic model therefore spread as a means to forestall the spread of the Cuban Revolution. Given its theoretical and substantive significance, the Brazilian case therefore deserves special consideration.

Brazil's armed forces had been committed to anticommunism at least since the times of dictator Getúlio Vargas (1930–45), who had used a Marxist uprising of 1935 to justify his authoritarian self-coup of 1937. In subsequent decades, the military deliberately commemorated this outburst of left-wing violence to keep the trauma alive.[1] In this way, the armed forces cemented hostility against the radical left.[2] No wonder that President Eurico Dutra (1946–51), a former general, outlawed the Communist Party at the very beginning of the Cold War (French 1992: 221, 225–6, 259–61). Because Brazilian elites were convinced of the geostrategic importance of their country, they saw it as a prime target for Soviet efforts to spread the Marxist gospel to the Americas. These fears intensified during the 1950s, when leftist revolutionary efforts and anticolonial struggles seemed to be advancing across the world (Martins 1963). In light of this growing danger, the new military teachings in France, which had to confront several of these insurgencies – in Indochina and the Maghreb – started to find great resonance in Brazilian military circles toward the end of the 1950s.[3] The French doctrine about "the revolutionary war" and about the most effective ways to win this dangerous contest was eagerly absorbed by Brazilian officers, especially in the leading military academy (Escola Superior de Guerra – ESG), as the translation and analysis of the ample French oeuvre shows.[4]

These teachings, which later guided the armed forces during the military dictatorship of 1964 to 1985,[5] emphasized that extremists initiated violent attacks, especially open warfare, only at the intermediate stages of a revolutionary war, after they had already laid the preconditions for insurrectionary success. Most critical were the early, preparatory stages, when clandestine radicals tried to spread their pernicious ideology and win support in insidious ways, taking advantage of the freedom guaranteed by political liberalism and democracy.[6] The doctrine of revolutionary war thus implied

---

[1] Motta 2002. Strikingly, in early 1963, when fears about communist penetration intensified inside the armed forces, the main military journal republished a long "prayer" pronounced by a general in 1937 in honor of those fallen during the suppression of the communist uprising of 1935 (Cavalcanti 1963). For an interesting discussion about how threat perceptions can become self-perpetuating, see Stein (2013: 381).

[2] D'Araujo, Soares, and Castro 1994: 11–12, 76–7, 126, 227–8; D'Araujo and Castro 1997: 101, 141; Farias 1998: 129–32.

[3] For boundedly rational actors, French teachings were much more convincing in the late 1950s and early 1960s than US counterinsurgency doctrines, because the former were derived from immediate experiences that the French had encountered directly in their anticolonial wars in Indochina and North Africa (Lyles 2016: 311, 343). By contrast, before the Vietnam War, the United States had not yet confronted a "revolutionary war" (Martins 2008: 41).

[4] Fragoso 1959: 5, 51–60; Oliveira 1964: 30, 36; D'Araujo, Dillon Soares, and Castro 1994: 77–9, 95. See also the wealth of military writings on "the revolutionary war" cited in Brasil (1964: 52–4), a pamphlet published under a pseudonym that the dean of the contemporary history of Brazil, Thomas Skidmore (1988: 314, n. 3), regards as a faithful expression of the thinking prevalent among military hard-liners.

[5] A wealth of documents proves this impact, e.g., Brazil. Ministério da Aeronáutica 1973; see also Selcher 1977; Araujo 2012: 50–4; Martins 2012: 522, 530–5. Demonstrating the formative impact of these teachings, Brazilian military doctrine has maintained a focus on "revolutionary war" to the present day (V. Pereira 2018: 40, 46, n.16).

[6] Fragoso 1959: 22; Estudo de Situação 1963; Carvalho 1964: 86–94; Oliveira 1964: 32, 36–41, 45; Brasil 1964: 20–1; cf. Brazil. Ministério da Aeronáutica 1973: 21–3.

that the traditional military focus on armed combat came too late; instead, efforts to protect national security had to start much earlier, by preventing procommunist groupings from proselytizing in the first place. Of course, the big problem was deficient information: because extremists deliberately hid their true goals, communists strategically clothed themselves in the mantle of democratic nationalism and social reformism. How, then, to identify dangerous radicals and distinguish them from honest reformers?

This problem became especially acute and acquired great salience with the Cuban Revolution,[7] which powerfully stimulated left-wing enthusiasm, mobilization, and emulation efforts in Brazil.[8] After all, Fidel Castro himself turned from democratic nationalist and social reformer to radical Marxist and openly allied with Soviet communism – a "betrayal" of his initial promises that Brazil's military conservatives highlighted in a crucial document.[9] The theoretical possibilities outlined by French writings, namely that reformists would morph into revolutionaries or reveal their true identity as Marxists, now had a stunning intraregional precedent! As the expanding wave of "revolutionary wars" (Fragoso 1959: 11; Muricy 1964: 7–9) seemed to have reached the shores of Latin America, the potential danger arising from radical leftism suddenly assumed much more serious dimensions in the eyes of status quo-oriented sectors, especially in the armed forces.

Consequently, more and more military officers, who also reached out to civilian conservatives (Martins Filho n.d.: 19–22),[10] now became convinced that Brazil was already in the early, preparatory stages of revolutionary war; if unchecked, this subversion could easily lead to a similar outcome as in Cuba.[11] Left-wing organizing, which turned more ambitious from the late 1950s onward, was now interpreted as the systematic groundwork that extremists were laying for a later push toward a profound overhaul of the socioeconomic and political order (Ferreira 1963: 30–2). Conservatives were particularly concerned about the formation of a radical labor peak organization (Comando Geral dos Trabalhadores – CGT: Delgado 1986) and the emergence of numerous peasant leagues demanding land redistribution, especially in the poor northeast (Azevêdo 1982). Thus, the Cuban precedent, combined with Castro's active efforts to

---

[7] Carvalho 1964: 85; Tavares 1964: 114; D'Araujo, Dillon Soares, and Castro 1994: 79, 95; Skidmore 1988: 4.

[8] Moraes 2011: 17, 27–8, 31, 63, 73, 84–5, 89, 95, 127, 134–5, 203–4, 219–20, 223–4, 232, 297, 340.

[9] Documento Leex 1963: 347; Vaz 1964: 38–9; see also Stepan 1973: 50, 56 n.14; *FRUS 1964–1968*: 411.

[10] Civilian reactionaries, such as Rio de Janeiro's opposition governor Carlos Lacerda (see Dulles 1996: 38–41, 103), shared the threat perceptions. Bilac Pinto, a leader of the conservative opposition party União Democrática Nacional (UDN), gave speeches in Congress and published newspaper articles warning about "the revolutionary war," in terms that closely followed military thinking (Pinto 1964). For similar statements by Lacerda, see US State Department 1964, document A–871: 2.

[11] See, e.g., Dulles 1978: 255–9, 265, 273, 282, 304, 313, 325, 377.

spread his revolutionary gospel to Brazil (Almeida 1990: 56–7; Rollemberg 2001; Sales 2007: 42, 48–52), made a limited problem appear like a big, potentially uncontrollable threat. Fear spread.[12]

The doctrine of revolutionary war emphasized a fundamental conundrum that military circles were facing: by the time that left-wingers initiated the open battle for power, they had already established such firm support bases that their ultimate victory was already very likely. The decisive phase for determining the eventual outcome concerned the preparatory efforts of infiltration, support building, and subversion – but the political struggle over ideas and organizations lay outside the traditional purview of the armed forces (Brasil 1964: 20–1; Oliveira 1964: 45). The "logical" solution to this puzzle was a massive "military role expansion" (Stepan 1973): The armed forces had to get deeply involved in politics. In particular, the military had to create an internal intelligence apparatus that would identify and hunt down extremists before their clandestine subversion could come to fruition (Brasil 1964: 23–4; cf. Burnier 2005: 66–8).[13] Moreover, the armed forces needed to take responsibility for domestic development and help overcome the problems that radicals sought to exploit for winning support. For these purpose, the military needed ample influence over the government; in case of serious threat, they simply had to take over the reins of the state.

By creating the specter of a clear and present danger and by turning the theoretical debates about revolutionary war into concrete, acute fears, the Cuban Revolution thus induced the armed forces to extend their field of operation from the battlefield to politics. Indeed, officers eagerly disseminated the doctrine of revolutionary war inside the military (Muricy 1993: 461–4, 473–4, 518). They also reached out to civilian conservatives and businesspeople, who came to espouse the military's views on the revolutionary risks facing Brazil.[14] Moreover, these threat perceptions prompted doubts in the defensive capacity of democracy. After all, liberal guarantees of freedom opened the door for the enemies of liberty, including antidemocratic communists.[15] Military sectors therefore came to worry about Marxist infiltration in all areas of society, the university, the state, and even inside the armed forces (Carvalho 1964: 91–100). Could democracy withstand this creeping penetration and pernicious subversion – or would it crumble under an eventual mass assault or be overturned from inside the government?

---

[12] Assunção (2005: 2) argues that fear was the cornerstone of the thinking of General Golbery do Couto e Silva, who turned into the intellectual mastermind of the post-1964 military regime.

[13] General Edgardo Mercado Jarrín (1974: 215–20), an important minister in Peru's reformist military regime, also emphasized the crucial importance of "intelligence in the counterinsurgency war" (see also Tello 1983, vol. 1: 121–3, 291; vol. 2: 246–7). On the need for the military to get more involved in politics, see Mercado Jarrín (1974: 212–15).

[14] Muricy 1993: 435; Pinto 1964; Dulles 1996: 190–4, 201, 203.

[15] Fragoso 1959: 22–3, 40; cf. Brasil. Ministério da Aeronáutica 1973: 21–3; see also Martins Filho 2008: 44.

The latter possibility looked increasingly likely after left-leaning populist João Goulart ascended to the presidency in 1961 and turned more radical with his mobilizational efforts and his ambitious social reform program. As former labor minister and then vice president, this politician had long-standing connections to the ever more contentious unionists and to other left-wingers, including Brazil's substantial groupings of communists. Conservative sectors led by the military leadership had therefore tried to block his ascent to the chief executive office after President Jânio Quadros' unexpected resignation. As a compromise, before Goulart's installation, his presidential powers were severely clipped via the institution of a semipresidential system (Skidmore 1967: 211–15; Labaki 1986: 102–33). In his struggle for restoring full presidential attributions, Goulart mobilized mass support for "basic reforms" and endorsed ever farther-going demands for change, such as large-scale land redistribution. In this effort, the president drew support from a wide range of popular groupings radicalized by the Cuban Revolution; he in turn backed these sectors and stimulated their forceful demand making.

Predictably, the theories about revolutionary war and the dramatic precedent of Cuba (Pinto 1964: 136, 141, 146–7, 150) made status quo-oriented sectors fear that Goulart's efforts would pave the way for radicals and communists to win ever greater influence and soon take control, either by using the left-populist president as an instrument or by eventually pushing him aside.[16] As radical sectors proceeded toward open contention and some leftists, such as a Cuban-supported wing of the peasant leagues agitating for land redistribution in the northeast, even prepared guerrilla movements (Sales 2007: 35–54; Moraes 2011: 84–97, 223–4; Dezemone 2016: 145), military officers concluded that Brazil was reaching the dangerous turning point in the revolutionary war. Extremists seemed to command enough strength and support that they were getting ready for violent assaults on power.[17] Shaped by cognitive shortcuts, these concerns about the dangers of communism were quite exaggerated.[18] They did not consider the organizational weakness and fragmentation of change-oriented sectors and the rivalries among their leaders[19] which made any coordinated attack on the established order exceedingly unlikely. But after the recent precedent of the Cuban Revolution, these excessive fears found increasing resonance.

---

[16] Ironically, shortly after assuming the presidency, Goulart himself impressed upon the US ambassador the communist danger facing Brazil and highlighted the inspiration provided by Fidel Castro; his goal seems to have been the desire to obtain "continued large-scale US assistance" (*FRUS 1961–1963*: 449).

[17] Muricy 1964: 9, 14–15, 17; Tavares 1964: 119–21; see also Muricy 1993: 435, 465, 474; Pinto 1964: 53, 65–78; Dulles 1978: 306, 314–15, 321–6.

[18] With wild exaggeration, Pinto (1964: 166–7), for instance, claims that communists "had a vast set of guerrillas organized" in Brazil during the early 1960s.

[19] Moraes 2011: 47, 58–63, 67, 90, 173–82, 214, 217, 222–5, 228, 275–7, 285, 288–91, 327; Ferreira and Gomes 2014: 157, 192–3, 205, 280–1, 321–2.

Due to the mechanisms of bounded rationality, the Cuban precedent thus helped to fuel a deepening polarization of Brazilian politics. Swept up in the radical wave unleashed by Castro's success, left-wingers failed to grasp the "correlation of forces" (Moraes 2011: 253, 256, 319; Falcão 2013: 309) and clearly overestimated their own strength.[20] Therefore, they acted in "politically dumb" ways (interview with former communist leader José Salles in Sereza 2016), turned ever more radical, and strongly pushed for a thorough transformation. After center-right forces had long offered concessions and accepted negotiated reforms, leftist intransigence made them harden their position as well.[21] By late 1963, the left's growing radicalism instilled increasing fear of "drifting toward . . . 'another Cuba' at the other side of the ideological spectrum."[22] These threat perceptions triggered loss aversion and induced even centrist congress members to resist Goulart's reform efforts. Consequently, conflict between the main branches of government deepened.

When the president sought to break the deadlock through a state of emergency or the convocation of a constituent assembly, opposition politicians and military officers came to fear that he planned to perpetuate himself in power, impose left-wing authoritarianism, and thus enable radicals to push through their revolutionary goals.[23] Growing numbers of conservatives therefore plotted armed resistance in case Goulart moved against the legislature or attempted a self-coup, as his brother-in-law, radical populist leader Leonel Brizola advocated.[24] In their own eyes, these conspirators merely intended to defend democracy, especially the liberal separation of powers and the independence of all branches of government (Dulles 1978: 321–6; Ferreira and Gomes 2014: 293–4). Of course, these defensive efforts would also block the profound socioeconomic transformations sought by the Goulart government, which commanded considerable support among the mass citizenry (Motta 2014: 5–7, 11).

Brazil's political system was sliding into dangerous polarization, exacerbated by President Goulart's determined turn to the left in March 1964 (Ferreira and Gomes 2014: 273–5, 279, 291). Communist Party leader Luis Carlos Prestes went so far as to declare "that Goulart or Brizola could play, in Brazil, the same role of Fidel Castro in Cuba."[25] In response, status quo defenders' concerns about communism

---

[20] Moraes 2011: 191–205, 355; Ferreira and Gomes 2014: 223, 256–7.

[21] Ferreira and Gomes 2014: 196–7, 202–3, 214–17, 235, 239, 257.

[22] Reported by Walters 1978: 377–8; see also Ferreira and Gomes 2014: 185, 257, 347; Dezemone 2016: 135, 153, n.7.

[23] Castello Branco 1964; Carvalho 1964: 102; Dulles 1996: 166–9, 210, 216, 221–2; US State Department 1964, document A–871: 1–4.

[24] Bandeira 1983: 131, 159; see also Leacock 1990: 174; Moraes 2011: 278, 339; and Ferreira and Gomes 2014: 217–18, 271–2, 279–82, 285, 288–90; see on these fears: Muricy 1964: 14, 19, 21–3, 35–6; US State Department 1964, document A–871: 1–4; Silva 2014: 160, 165, 167, 171, 224–7, 258.

[25] Ferreira and Gomes 2014: 257; see also Moraes 2011: 135. Allegedly, Brizola himself "said he would like to be the Fidel Castro of Brazil," as US diplomats reported (*FRUS 1964–1968*: 400).

and the determination to combat it intensified as well,[26] and these concerns found majority support among the population. For instance, 54 percent of survey respondents from São Paulo in early 1964 saw "communism growing in Brazil" (Dias 2014: 5), and 81 percent among those viewed communism's growth as a danger (Motta 2016: 7; Motta 2014: 8–10). Consequently, 80 percent in a subsequent poll wanted to keep the Communist Party outlawed (Sugimoto 2003: 3). Thus, as hopes of emulating the Caribbean precedent fired up the left, fears of revolution scared the right, spread to ever broader segments of the center, and reinforced their loss aversion. A variety of status quo-oriented groupings therefore mobilized to forestall this frightening prospect with all means.

Yet the fate of President Goulart, who long maintained fairly high public approval ratings (Motta 2014: 5–6), was sealed only when he seemed to undermine the military institution as such – which therefore took the lead in his ouster (Skidmore 1967: 296; Skidmore 1988: 17, 27). Specifically, Goulart's backing for lower ranks inside the military who challenged their superiors[27] was the "point of no return" by inducing the strong legalist segment of the military [28] to support the president's overthrow.[29] With this subversion of discipline and hierarchy,[30] Goulart jeopardized the institutional integrity of the armed forces, the constitutionally appointed guarantor of national security.[31] If this last bulwark were undermined,[32] communist victory in the revolutionary war would be hard to avoid, as many generals worried.[33] In their eyes, the sapping

The US Embassy also feared that Miguel Arraes, a left-nationalist leader in Brazil's northeast, "would 'Cubanize' Brazil if he came to power" (Fico 2008: 78).

[26] US State Department 1964, document A-1116: 7, 13–14; Leacock 1990: 192–7; Motta 2016: 5–10.

[27] Testimony in Cavalheiro 2011; see also Moraes 2011: 99–115.

[28] Cf. Tavares 1964: 113–14; D'Araujo, Soares, and Castro 1994: 41, 47, 85, 102–3, 125, 131, 142; D'Araujo and Castro 1997: 151, 153, 171; Muricy 1993: 479, 500, 514–15; on Brazilian generals' long reluctance to support a coup, see also Walters (1978: 378, 384, 390).

[29] D'Araujo, Soares, and Castro 1994: 12–14, 41–3, 46, 50, 92, 107, 142–3, 161, 198, 207–8, 214, 229; D'Araujo and Castro 1997: 148, 159; FRUS 1964–1968: 433; Stepan 1978a: 129–32; see military documents reprinted in Pinto 1964: 203, 208–15. Similarly, as highlighted below, the crucial trigger of the Chilean military's decision to overthrow President Salvador Allende in 1973 was the emergence of radical leftist worker militias and armed movements, which threatened the military's monopoly over organized coercion (Sigmund 1977: 226–7, 250, 256, 258, 288–9; Valenzuela 1978: 98–103; see also Haslam 2005: 181, 188).

[30] Left-leaning officers despaired that Goulart and his civilian supporters had no understanding of the essential significance that the military attached to internal discipline and hierarchy. In their view, the president supported the mobilizational efforts of lower ranks without anticipating the severe consequences (Moraes 2011: 274, 301, 305, 309–11, 334).

[31] Gaspari 2002: 56, 91–2; Ferreira and Gomes 2014: 179–81, 315–32, 337, 343, 351–3; see in general Linz 1978: 60.

[32] On March 20, 1964, US diplomats called "the armed forces of Brazil . . . the only substantial bulwark against the threat of communist takeover" (US State Department 1964, document 1124: 12).

[33] Denys 1967: 11; Muricy 1964: 12–13, 23; Silva 2014: 196, 262, 266, 270–1, 284, 336–7. As former communist leader José Salles (interviewed in Sereza 2016) stresses with some self-

of military unity foreshadowed the destruction of the institution and its replacement by a Cuban-style militia.[34] Even worse, these attacks on the armed forces could culminate in the kind of disaster exemplified by the mass execution of "old regime" officers after Castro's takeover (Gaspari 2002: 177; cf. Dulles 1978: 252). Thus, once again, the Cuban precedent projected a worst-case scenario for Brazil.

In March 1964, an overwhelming majority of military personnel therefore came to believe that the revolutionary war engulfing Brazil was about to move into its acute stages and that it was high time to put an end to this nightmare.[35] Because legalist currents had no history of conspiracies, they commanded the legitimacy to rally support for President Goulart's ouster (Dulles' interview with Golbery do Couto e Silva 1965). In their perception, they were not proactively grabbing power, but merely seeking to preempt a radical-left takeover.[36] As Silva (2014; similar Mendonça 2007: 168–9, 180–1) argues, they saw themselves as making a countercoup, not a coup – a "democratic counter-revolution," in a general's words (Tavares 1964: 105; cf. Dulles 1978: 319). In their own understanding, the conspirators did not pursue a gain, but desperately tried to avert a huge loss. In line with the asymmetry documented by cognitive psychology, this negative motivation induced a large majority of officers to support the defensive move of maintaining military discipline and broader sociopolitical stability, and to evict a chief executive who had begun to undermine these conservative priorities.[37]

Interestingly, the military leaders who ended up overthrowing President Goulart clearly overestimated the threat they were facing. Because they overrated the strength of the left, both inside the armed forces and in society at large, they expected the coup attempt to usher in one to three months of serious fighting.[38] But in fact, resistance collapsed instantaneously, and the new power holders consolidated their stranglehold over the country within a couple of days. This easy victory was especially remarkable because the coup came earlier than planned, triggered by the impetuous, precipitant move of one conspirator, General Olympio Mourão.[39] The absence of armed opposition should have cast doubt on the earlier threat perceptions that Brazil was reaching

critical exaggeration, after the challenges to military hierarchy and discipline, "there was no leftist officer in the Navy who would not have been in favor of a coup."

[34] Documento Leex 1963: 349; Costa 1964: 74; Dulles 1978: 323.
[35] Brasil 1964: 25–52; Costa 1964: 63, 72–3; D'Araujo, Dillon Soares, and Castro 1994: 38, 78–9; see also US State Department 1964, document A-1211: 8.
[36] Castello Branco 1964; Carvalho 1964: 84, 102; Muricy 1964: 20–3, 35–6; Dulles 1978: 321–6, 329–30, 341.
[37] D'Araujo, Dillon Soares, and Castro 1994: 38, 59–60, 131, 143, 155, 159, 191, 199, 206–7, 216–18, 222, 224, 228–32.
[38] Dulles' interview with Reis 1965; see also Muricy 1964: 27, 37; Muricy 1993: 513–14, 518, 542; Gaspari 2002: 133–4.
[39] Dulles' interview with Kruel 1975: 4–5, and with Walters 1975: 9; D'Araujo, Soares, and Castro 1994: 158, 160, 179, 220; see also Ferreira and Gomes 2014: 335–6; Smith 2015: 270.

the operational stages of the "revolutionary war," when well-entrenched radical forces have garnered strong support and get ready for violent challenges to the established order. While extremists produced a great deal of noisy rhetoric and engaged in constant activism, they were in fact fragmented and operated without clear plans, not to speak of a coordinated strategy (Moraes 2011: 356–8; US State Department 1963, document A–61: 3–4). Indeed, post-coup investigations into earlier radical initiatives found much less organizational strength than expected (Leacock 1990: 252). For instance, the "groups of eleven" promoted by populist leader Leonel Brizola,[40] whose incendiary rhetoric did much to stoke fears among the armed forces,[41] were far from constituting effective popular militias on the Cuban model (Dulles' interview with Martinelli 1966; Gabeira [1979] 1996: 14; Ridenti 2007: 27; Moraes 2011: 325).

In sum, cognitive shortcuts aggravated threat perceptions galvanized by the Cuban Revolution, and loss aversion then prompted a widespread, strong determination to block the feared slide into communism. As military specialist David Pion-Berlin (1988: 385) highlights, "the Brazilian military let its exaggerated fears of leftist activity get the better of it, provoking a long period of unrestrained, disproportionate, and unnecessary state terror." Mechanisms of bounded rationality are important for explaining the surprisingly uniform reaction of status quo defenders, especially the military, to left-wing challenges. The ouster of populist President Goulart, seen as facilitator of the advancing preparations for a revolutionary war, therefore found strong support among sociopolitical elites, middle sectors, and broad segments of the citizenry.[42] Thus, the negative goal to defeat leftist radicalism elicited a great deal of backing.[43]

---

[40] Moraes 2011: 149–54; Ferreira and Gomes 2014: 205–10.

[41] Brasil 1964: 16–17, 49–50; Tavares 1964: 122; see also Leacock 1990: 146–7, 150–1; Moraes 2011: 318.

[42] In a May 1964 survey conducted in São Paulo, 54 percent of respondents regarded the ouster of President Goulart as a "beneficial measure" for the country, while only 20 percent condemned it as deleterious. Moreover, in a June 1964 survey conducted in the state of Guanabara (essentially the city of Rio de Janeiro), for instance, 62 percent of respondents "would accept" that if new dictator Humberto Castello Branco "achieved good governance," he "could continue to govern after 1965, even without elections" (Tendências – Eleições Presidenciais 1994: 14 and 12, respectively; see also Motta 2016: 8–9; Motta 2014: 11–21). On the ample demonstrations of support for the coup by the mass citizenry, see Ferreira and Gomes (2014: 14).

[43] In a poll held in São Paulo in May 1964, 25 percent of respondents listed as the most urgent problem "the purge of Communism," the second priority after inflation, mentioned by 29 percent (Sugimoto 2003: 3). Accordingly, 74 percent approved the removal of communist deputies from the legislature, and 72 percent "the imprisonment of trade union leaders linked to the Communists" (Sugimoto 2003: 3; Motta 2016: 9). Moreover, in March of 1964, 76 percent of respondents in Brazil's eight major cities opposed the legalization of the Communist Party (Bermeo 2003: 90–1).

Specifically, all of the coup makers feared communism, tried hard to end the revolutionary war that in their eyes was about to engulf the country, and were dead set on preventing Brazil from turning into a second Cuba, a prospect that many saw as imminent.[44] But while they shared the diagnosis of the disease threatening the country, they disagreed on the dosage of the medicine that was required for extirpating the communist virus. Legalist sectors led by the new president, Marshal Humberto Castello Branco (1964–7), believed that the purging of the government and the suppression of radical organizations would effectively stop the revolutionary war. Therefore, democracy could and should resume soon.[45] This plan was premised on the assumption of the underlying health of Brazil's body politic, which would quickly recover after the country's infection with radicalism had been contained with the antibiotics of temporary repression.

A strong, determined sector in the armed forces, however, saw the danger of radicalism more deeply rooted. Particularly fearful (Gaspari 2002: 133), these hard-liners attributed continuing subversive capabilities to communists, who could take advantage of the enormous inequalities and socioeconomic deficits plaguing Brazil. As the Cuban case had demonstrated, extremists could easily take over a country; and as Castro's continuing efforts to export his revolution showed, they stood ready to exploit any weakness. In the eyes of military officers who were impressed by the determination and savvy of their communist enemies, the 1964 coup merely meant that the forces of order had temporarily won out in one stage of the revolutionary war, when radicals had made a premature end run for power. But the sporadic insurrectionary efforts that erupted in Brazil after the military takeover (Rollemberg 2001: 27–64; Gaspari 2002: 180–207; Ridenti 2007: 30–7) seemed to suggest that the danger had not yet passed. In particular, President Goulart's ouster and the targeted repression employed thereafter had not rooted out the long-standing infiltration and support building that extremists had achieved during the earlier, clandestine stages of the revolutionary war.[46] Accordingly, a much more comprehensive and thoroughgoing process of political-ideological cleansing was required[47] that would, for instance, retake control of the education

---

[44] Burnier 2005: 62, 69; D'Araujo, Dillon Soares, and Castro 1994: 40, 46, 60, 91, 95, 126–7, 142–3, 155, 161, 175, 190, 200, 206–7, 216–17, 227–31.

[45] D'Araujo and Castro 1997: 166–8, 173, 180, 199–200; see also Pereira 1998: 56–7. Interestingly, the first military president, Humberto Castello Branco, saw the long-standing yet ossified authoritarian regimes of Portugal and Spain as deterrents to avoid (D'Araujo, Dillon Soares, and Castro 1994: 217, 225).

[46] Burnier 2005: 69–70; D'Araujo, Dillon Soares, and Castro 1994: 234; see *FRUS 1964–1968*: 466, 469, 485.

[47] These purges involved a multitude of "police-military investigations," which were published in hundreds of volumes comprising thousands of pages. For a listing, see Os Inquéritos Policiais-Militares e a Ditadura Militar no Brasil (1964–1985) n.d.

system and replace critical, subversive messages with system-stabilizing teachings.[48]

Even more fundamentally, these hard-line sectors were determined to forestall a reemergence of radicalism in the future by making a major, state-directed push to alleviate the grave development problems that – in their eyes – extremists used as a pretext for stirring up contention. Interestingly, these reactionaries realized that "subversion" was not merely the product of external, Cuban and Soviet conspirators; instead, it fed on serious structural deficits that kept large numbers of Brazilians poor and in unfair conditions. Therefore, economic development and social reform were imperative. In many ways, these currents inside the military wanted to resume the strategy of preemptive reform, though with a more conservative orientation – focused more on economic growth than on social redistribution. Moreover, they intended to steer and control these developmentalist efforts from the top down in order to avoid any bottom-up mobilization, ideological polarization, and political conflict. Thus, the heavy hand of autocracy would prevent the "contradiction" afflicting the Alliance for Progress by imposing moderation even in the short run. Due to authoritarian guidance and control, reform would not unleash radicalization, but bolster sociopolitical stability.

Of course, this strategy of conservative modernization, combined with the thorough eradication of leftism, would take considerable time. To guarantee its systematic pursuit, the armed forces therefore could not relinquish power nearly as quickly as legalist sectors wanted. Instead, to achieve the ambitious goal of transforming Brazil and thus protecting it forever from radicalism, the dictatorship had to assume lasting responsibility. A rapid restart of democracy would simply bring the traditional "political class" back to power, who had failed to resolve the country's development issues and had proven incapable of stopping the slide into radicalism, if not opportunistically acquiescing in it. To forestall a simple recurrence of this cycle, a new leadership group committed to national security and accelerated development had to take over, namely military officers schooled in the doctrine of revolutionary war and civilian experts who could competently resolve economic and social problems (Stepan 1971: 173, 179–87; Stepan 1973).

Because due to loss aversion the coup makers of 1964 had rallied around the negative goal of stopping the feared advance of radicalism, they did not take power with a clear "positive" plan. In this fluid situation, the fundamental asymmetry in the valuation of gains versus losses played into hard-liners' hands. Their continuing concerns ended up weighing more heavily than the more benign views of the soft-liners. As right-wingers saw persistent threats, they pressed hard for more comprehensive repression. These measures in turn drove away centrist sectors that had initially supported the military takeover,

---

[48] D'Araujo, Dillon Soares, and Castro 1994: 19–20, 89–90, 95, 115–16, 131–2, 164, 232–4.

thus depriving soft-liners of political allies (Stepan 1971: 219–28; Skidmore 1988: 19–20, 45–50).

Moreover, the extended crackdown exacerbated the radicalization of opposition forces, especially among young intellectuals who were inspired by the Cuban Revolution and who got soon caught up in the global wave of student protests culminating in the mythical year of 1968. Of course, this polarization "corroborated" the fears of military hard-liners, who had long regarded the education system as a crucial arena in the preparatory stages of the revolutionary war. As public manifestations spearheaded by radical students proliferated and garnered increasing mass support, hard-liners reacted to this contentious challenge by turning the military regime into a full-scale dictatorship (Skidmore 1988: 73–84; Pereira 1998: 58–60; Ridenti 2007: 37–8; Langland 2013: 161–79). When the most extremist students responded with urban guerrilla warfare, the autocracy ruthlessly bared its teeth and installed a system of mass terror, with cruel torture and targeted killings (Skidmore 1988: 84–9, 101–4, 117–35; Sales 2007: 55–105).

At the same time that an initially moderate, military-civilian regime morphed into naked repressive despotism, the authoritarian leadership pursued ever more ambitious development plans. After Goulart's overthrow had ushered in a stringent economic stabilization program to resolve the grave economic problems erupting in the early 1960s, the dictatorship decided to adopt a more proactive project. The more hard-line president who took over from Marshal Castello Branco in 1967 therefore started to push for accelerated economic growth (Skidmore 1988: 68–71). His successors promoted some social initiatives as well, especially through a regime-supportive literacy program and the creation of a rural social security system. As industrialization advanced, the state took an increasingly prominent role in the economy, especially by supporting and partially carrying out an ambitious effort to build capital goods and basic industries in the 1970s (Bresser Pereira 1985: 234–6).

Due to the institutionalized nature of the armed forces, the autocracy did not see the emergence of one general as the predominant personal leader, as it used to happen in the prototypical Latin American dictatorship of earlier times. Instead, the military somewhat haphazardly achieved a series of fairly regular turnovers in the chief executive position (Skidmore 1988: 51–3, 93–101, 149–51). Moreover, the Brazilian autocracy avoided the boundless cronyism of many unaccountable regimes, filled top operational positions in a meritocratic way, and thus recruited a great deal of talent (Bresser Pereira 1985: 214–15). The institutional nature of the autocracy, its strong developmentalist orientation, and the "miraculous" performance it achieved until the mid-1970s turned the Brazilian regime into a model for the rest of the region. This new type of "bureaucratic authoritarianism" (O'Donnell 1979) seemed to guarantee the stability required for defeating acute radical threats, for revamping economy and society, and for immunizing them against future communist infiltration. In the eyes of status quo defenders across the Americas, including the United States, Brazil had come up with a promising recipe for protecting the body politic against the extremist virus that the Cuban Revolution had made so virulent in Latin America. Chapter 7 will next examine the demonstration effects that emanated from this new model and the horizontal diffusion processes it helped set in motion.

RISING RADICALISM AND DEEPENING DICTATORSHIP IN ARGENTINA

The political repercussions of increasing radicalism, especially the impetus it gave to the imposition of ever fiercer autocracy, are particularly obvious in Argentina. Under the impact of the Cuban Revolution, popular and progressive movements pursued more profound transformations and spawned growing currents that advocated and employed political violence. As left-wing extremism expanded over the course of the 1960s and early 1970s, status quo-oriented sectors perceived increasingly grave threats. Intensifying fear among the citizenry and inside the armed forces prompted several military interventions. Each one of the resulting dictatorships was more brutal and more ambitious in its reactionary project than the preceding one. Specifically, these autocracies cracked down ever harder on their proclaimed enemies, sought with growing determination to root out the sources of radicalism, and tried to revamp the country's development model and political system (Pion-Berlin 1997: 49–63; Novaro 2006: 36–82; Brown 2011: chap. 9). In line with the theoretical approach of this book, intensifying loss aversion drove this increasingly profound and comprehensive backlash.

After six decades of relative political stability under initially oligarchic but gradually democratizing rule, mass mobilization revolving around personalistic leadership helped to provoke the military coup of 1930. The subsequent restoration of oligarchic, conservative domination allowed Juan Perón to appeal to a broad range of excluded sectors and whip up mass support for his own quest for overwhelming leadership. Based on widespread plebiscitarian acclamation, Perón created a prototypical populist movement that swept the electoral arena based on impressive majoritarian backing, yet also systematic attacks on the opposition. As conflicts with established sociopolitical forces, especially business sectors, the Catholic Church, and currents in the military, grew, the populist leader eventually fell to a coup in 1955 (Waldmann 1974: 262–7). Because the conservative generals feared a return of Peronist demagoguery, they proscribed this populist movement when allowing for new elections. Accordingly, the approximately 30 percent of hard-core Peronists among the citizenry were deprived of their preferred electoral option. The restricted democracy of the late 1950s and 1960s therefore suffered from a congenital legitimacy deficit; the governments that

emerged from the truncated electoral contests lacked political strength
(O'Donnell 1979: 183–7). Concerned about low governability and worried
about a groundswell of support for readmitting the Peronists to the electoral
arena, the armed forces cut short the presidential term of Arturo Frondizi
(1958–62).

A crucial reason for the 1962 coup was the fear of communism raised by the
Cuban Revolution (Rouquié 1985: 156–9, 169–70, 175, 183, 193; Cousins
2008: 70). Despite the geographical distance, Argentina was one of the first
countries in the region to experience emulative guerrilla movements, which
erupted in 1959, and then again in 1963 to 1965 and in the late 1960s.[49]
While these ill-prepared efforts suffered quick suppression (Brown 2017:
380–2, 388–91, 397–8), their very emergence activated the long-standing
worries about left-wing extremism that had deep roots in Argentina's
conservative armed forces. Interestingly, the country's military had been the
first in Latin America to absorb the French doctrines of "the revolutionary war"
derived from the experiences of Vietnam and Algeria. In the late 1950s and early
1960s, French instructors who had participated in these counterinsurgency
efforts taught at Argentina's military academies.[50] After the Cuban
Revolution, the armed forces published an enormous number of articles about
the danger of "the revolutionary war" in their professional journals, quite a few
written by French experts (Rouquié 1985: 158–9). General Osiris Villegas, later
the principal ideologue of the ambitious dictatorship installed in 1966, wrote
a major book on this very topic in 1962.[51] At that time, even high school
students in the military lyceum "educated themselves in the conceptions of
counterrevolutionary war," as a later left-wing guerrilla fighter reports
(interviewed in Campos 2013: 84).

For these reasons, there was considerable concern among the armed forces
about the threat posed by communism (documents in Cavarozzi 1983: 87–8; see
also Salas 2003: 69–72). Some officers even believed that President Frondizi,
a very moderate center-leftist, harbored communist tendencies or, at least, was
too tolerant of radical left-wingers.[52] But these clearly exaggerated concerns did
not find overwhelming support inside the military, not to speak of civilian

---

[49] Moyano 1995: 21–4; De Riz 2010: 24, 35; Díaz Bessone 1986: 82–92.
[50] Pion-Berlin 1988: 423; Perelli 1993: 28, 33, 46–7, n. 48; Mazzei 2002; Novaro and Palermo
2003: 83–4; Guerrero Velázquez 2011; Ranaletti 2011; Rock 1993: 195–8; Reato 2012: 76–84,
97; Lyles 2016: 419–22.
[51] Villegas (1962); similar Díaz Bessone (1986). Interestingly, Villegas' treatise highlighted exactly
the same themes as the literature on the "revolutionary war" produced in Brazil, for instance the
five stages of its advance, the weaknesses that democracy faced in combating it, etc. These
striking parallels show how faithfully Latin American officers absorbed these French teachings,
and how little they adapted them to the specific characteristics of their own countries.
Surprisingly, for instance, Villegas (1962) does not examine the role of Peronism – a crucial
oversight, considering the tremendous importance of this movement for Argentine politics.
[52] *FRUS 1961–1963*: 386; Rouquié 1985: 170–1, 176–7, 180, 220; Salas 2003: 103, 105, 108;
Brown 2017: 236.

politicians, who held only limited threat perceptions in the early 1960s.[53] After all, any sparks flying from Cuba would not find much tinder to set the Pampas on fire. Argentina had for decades lacked a significant political left. Its Socialist Party had charted a comparatively moderate course and had withered away with the rise of Peronist populism in the 1940s. Perón, in turn, whose initial inspiration emanated from Mussolini's fascism (Finchelstein 2014: chap. 4), had deliberately formed his populist mass movement as a counterrevolutionary, anti-Marxist force; one of the main goals of his developmentalist, nationalist regime (1946–55) had been to immunize Argentina against the allures of international communism (Germani 1978: chap. 6; Waisman 1987).

On the other hand, however, continuing populist mass mobilization and the exiled Perón's desire to return to Argentina and restore his erstwhile political hegemony posed their own risks for sociopolitical elites, including the military, which feared political marginalization and revenge for the coup of 1955. The political significance and role of Peronism therefore provoked serious disagreements among the country's armed forces, which had long been unusually divided. After the coup of 1962, these internal conflicts deepened (Potash 1996: 2–10, 21, 25–7). The more reactionary *Colorado* wing wanted to establish a lasting dictatorship and eradicate Peronism as an uncontrollable mass movement that could open the door for left-wing radicalism (see, e.g., Cavarozzi 1983: 90–1). The grouping of *Azules*, by contrast, hoped to channel part of the Peronist vote toward more acceptable political forces, prevent this populist movement from recovering electoral hegemony, and thus tame it through electoral engineering.[54] Because in 1962–3, Peronism itself was not infected by the virus of communism (cf. Cavarozzi 1983: 91),[55] the latter position prevailed and the interim government soon called new elections, while again prohibiting the Peronists from running candidates.

Yet this "impossible game" (O'Donnell 1979: chap. 4) induced Peronist voters to widespread ballot spoiling and gave new President Arturo Illia (1963–6) a cripplingly weak electoral mandate with little more than 25 percent of the popular vote (O'Donnell 1979: 191–2; Potash 1996: 116–17). Lacking the energy and charisma to fill this power vacuum and to erode the political strength of Peronism, the chief executive of this precarious democracy fell to another coup in 1966, which was triggered by the determination to prevent Peronist-supported candidates from sweeping the elections originally scheduled for 1967 (*FRUS 1964–1968*: 294, 317, 325; Rouquié 1985: 247–8). As civilian politicians had failed to resolve the

---

[53] As a result, military efforts to incorporate the doctrine of the "revolutionary war" into new national defense laws failed in Congress in 1960 and 1961 (Summo and Pontoriero 2012: 295–300).

[54] Rouquié 1985: 213; Potash 1996: 46–50, 79–82; Halperin Donghi 2010: 136–38.

[55] Even the United States, however, was concerned about indications that "communism" was beginning to make advances inside Peronism (*FRUS 1961–1963*: 389–90).

problem posed by Peronism's fervent mass base, the armed forces now took it upon themselves to promote an ambitious development program whose economic and social benefits would draw support away from the exiled Perón. With this strategy, new dictator Juan Carlos Onganía also sought to immunize his country against the risk of communist subversion that the military continued to see.[56] Accordingly, the regime claimed in its founding document that Argentina had been exposed to "a subtle and aggressive Marxist penetration in all spheres of national life," in "a climate that is favorable to extremist upsurges and that puts the Nation at risk of falling before the collectivist danger."[57]

Given these – clearly exaggerated – threat perceptions, the military regarded deep-reaching and comprehensive countermeasures as necessary, which needed to go far beyond repressive efforts by revamping Argentina's socioeconomic and political structures (Guglialmelli 1967). Only in these ways could extremists be prevented from preparing the "revolutionary war" that the regime's chief strategist feared (Villegas 1962: 48, 57–8, 200). Because the major transformation envisioned by Onganía foresaw a sequence of steps, the new regime wanted to stay in power for quite a while. With this ambitious project and extensive timetable, Argentina's autocracy took a great deal of inspiration from the developmentalist dictatorship emerging in Brazil.[58] Specifically, Onganía intended to recharge economic growth, gradually boost popular wellbeing, and then restructure the political party system.[59] Only after the beneficiaries of this accelerated development would abandon Peronism and come to support political forces that shunned demagoguery could the electoral game resume – far in the future.

After a painful round of initial adjustment, the Onganía regime indeed succeeded in stimulating economic growth during the late 1960s. But its efforts to distribute the fruits of this growth more broadly remained limited (De Riz 2010: 61–2). Moreover, the regime leadership suffered from dangerous political isolation, even inside the armed forces, which the dictator deliberately kept distant from governing responsibilities. Growing social discontent erupted in a massive, spontaneous uprising in the industrial city of Córdoba in 1969, which shook the dictatorship to its core, exacerbated the long-standing divisions inside the military (Potash 1996: 246–56; Gomes n.d.: 15–20), and soon led to Onganía's ouster. As a result, the ambitious goal to redirect Argentina's socioeconomic and political development and thus undermine the strength of Peronism, whose mobilizational dynamism powerful elite sectors

---

[56] Cousins 2008; De Riz 2010: 35, 37, 40, 51; Halperin Donghi 2010: 154–6; Rock 1993: 199–200, 203, 213–40.

[57] Acta de la Revolución Argentina 1966; see also Potash 1996: 177; and Botana, Braun, and Floria 1973: 252, 478, 482.

[58] *FRUS 1964–1968*: 302; De Riz 2010: 37–8; see also Rouquié 1985: 232–4; Brown 2017: 397.

[59] Onganía 1967; Botana, Braun, and Floria 1973: 15–17; O'Donnell 1982: 95–103; De Riz 2010: 42–61; Rouquié 1985: 264–83.

continued to see with concern, suffered a quick abortion. The autocracy's subsequent demise contrasts with the fate of Brazil's developmentalist regime, which during the same years managed to consolidate its hold on power and which expanded and intensified its repression. Argentina seemed to escape a harsh dictatorship – but not for long.

One of the root causes of the sociopolitical discontent that blew up in Onganía's face was the massive radicalization of Latin American politics during the 1960s, which affected Argentina as well (De Riz 2010: 67–9, 75–8). While Peronism for years had indeed provided a bulwark against the spread of extremism, it was, ironically, military intervention in politics, especially the imposition of autocratic rule in 1966, that opened the floodgates for radicalization (Ollier 1998: 111, 132). As democratic channels were closed, opposition movements of all stripes, including Peronism, felt compelled to resort to other means, such as street protest, contention, and violence. In fact, from his exile Perón himself systematically stimulated radicalization in order to undermine the military regime and thus prepare his own return to power. While in actuality a staunch anticommunist, the old manipulator courted left-wing extremists and opportunistically advocated the use of violence.[60] The Peronist movement, including its ever more radical currents, won growing support from middle-class sectors that, in the face of military repression, lacked alternative avenues for voicing their demands. Left-wing extremists, in turn, sought to take over this populist mass movement because it had its core constituency among the working class, the supposed protagonist of the eventual socialist revolution (Langieri 2013: 174–5). As a result, Peronism developed a powerful left wing that spawned increasing violence and gave rise to the *Montonero* guerrilla movement (Gillespie 1982; Ollier 1998). Fed by resurgent Marxism and radicalized Catholicism, a welter of other militarist groupings emerged as well (Moyano 1995; Ollier 1998; Campos 2013: 77–9, 83–9).

Under the influence of the Cuban Revolution and the guerrilla doctrines codified first by Che Guevara, then Régis Debray, Argentine guerrilla movements had initially followed the rural *foco* strategy (Brown 2017: 380–2, 388–91). Yet because its open landscapes and the concentration of the population in urban areas made Argentina particularly ill-suited for the simple imitation of the Cuban model, leftist fighters in the late 1960s adapted this model (Gillespie 1982: 76–9; Brown 2017: 246, 404–8), moved to the cities, and spearheaded a growing number of bank robberies, kidnappings, and other attacks.[61] Guided by the political goal of discrediting the established order, the

---

[60] In turn, Peronist left-wingers who had fallen under the influence of the Cuban Revolution, especially John William Cooke, "tried to Cubanize Perón," as a former militant reported (cited in Langieri 2013: 174; see also Brown 2017: 384–7).

[61] The same sequence of a Cuba-inspired rural approach, which quickly failed and then led the surviving *guerrilleros* to move to the cities, played out in Chile (Marambio 2007: 61).

urban *guerrilleros* initially targeted their actions carefully and avoided indiscriminate bloodshed. As they faced an unsuccessful, illegitimate military regime in the early 1970s, they won a great deal of public sympathy and support.[62] The armed forces, in turn, lacked the popular and elite backing to crack down hard and unleash the level of repression that the extirpation of the guerrilla movements would have required.[63] Facing these constraints, the military leadership and many civilians wagered that only Peronism's return to power could pacify the country (Ollier 1998: 143–8; De Riz 2010: 77, 96). Once democracy was restored and avenues for peaceful change reopened, there seemed to be no good reason to keep employing violence. And as Perón had actively fomented radicalization and had thus helped to conjure up the storm (Ollier 1998: 132–6, 141–2), he would certainly want to calm it after his return from exile – as the last military ruler, Alejandro Lanusse (1977: 230–1, 273, 294–5) hoped.

Tail between the legs,[64] the armed forces therefore relinquished power in 1973. After his triumphant return from exile, the aging Perón, quickly reelected to the presidency, indeed tried to combat radicalism, especially inside his own movement (Moyano 1995: 36–8). But the sorcerer failed to tame the violent impulses that he himself had helped to stir up. Because the scheming populist charted a distinctly nonrevolutionary course, the extremist wing of Peronism felt betrayed and redoubled its attacks on the established order. In particular, the expanding guerrilla forces turned more militaristic and resorted to indiscriminate violence (Moyano 1995: 8, 50, 57, 60, 75, 90–1), which undermined their public support (Bermeo 2003: 201–2). As the citizenry became ever more apprehensive, the police intensified their repressive efforts, and clandestine death squads, fed by reactionary and fascist currents in Peronism (Finchelstein 2014: 112–21), started operating. After Perón died in 1974 and his politically inexperienced wife succeeded him, the government lost control and violence from all sides increased further. In despair, Isabelita Perón in 1975 empowered the military to "eliminate" the guerrilla movements, as officers involved in the repression stress.[65]

---

[62] Gillespie 1982: 96–9, 110–11, 115, 119; Moyano 1995: 96–8; De Riz 2010: 77, 102.

[63] Gillespie 1982: 113–15. Traditionally, the Argentine military was reluctant to participate in counterinsurgency campaigns (Astiz 1969: 874).

[64] Lanusse (1977: 262, 281, 298–303) admits the "errors" he made during this exit strategy and engages in considerable "self-criticism."

[65] Reato 2012: 28–9, 137–44,149–50,155–6, 291–7; Díaz Bessone 1986; 245–55; see also De Riz 2010: 164, 170, 176; Rock 1993: 224. In a long interview (Reato 2012: 28–9, 141–2, 149, 155–6, 205), former dictator Jorge Videla, president from 1976 to 1981, repeatedly invokes this authorization of an all-out attack on the guerrilla forces to argue that the military coup of 1976 was unnecessary and may have been a mistake; the tottering democracy had already conceded the armed forces free rein to destroy their enemies with all means.

Given the failure of the Onganía regime, the armed forces were reluctant to overthrow the tottering government.[66] But due to the new president's utter ineptitude, the meltdown of political authority, and the spiraling violence (Wynia 1978: 221–7), they finally saw no alternative. Governing as an institution, they instituted a dictatorship in March 1976 that proclaimed a "process of national reorganization" – a euphemistic name for the all-out attempt to impose a total transformation of Argentina's socioeconomic and political development (Novaro and Palermo 2003: 33–50; Quiroga 2004: 63–7). Because the military saw their country sinking into chaos, assailed by left-wing subversion (Pion-Berlin 1988: 395–9) and right-wing paramilitarism,[67] they intended to effect even more profound and comprehensive changes than General Onganía had tried a decade before.

Specifically, the new dictatorship embarked on drastic economic liberalization in order to destroy radical leftism and Peronist populism, which had a strong social base in the union movement. Stiff market competition should discipline the economy, disaggregate society, undermine the capacity for collective action, and thus forestall sociopolitical contention. To impede conflict, the autocracy prohibited political parties, closed down public debate, and assigned all administrative tasks to military officers and civilian technocrats (Novaro and Palermo 2003: part III). And it combated its enemies on the radical left with an unprecedented storm of repression, which caused at least 13,000 deaths and forced disappearances, subjected scores of people to cruel torture, and induced innumerable Argentines to flee into exile. This cruel crackdown was driven by asymmetrical loss aversion: "Perceiving a full-blown crisis, and fearing disastrous losses, the military set about developing an entirely new institutional matrix [of state terror] . . . : the ghoulish machinery of [forced] 'disappearance'" (Pereira 2003: 42; see ibid. 43).

The depth of this transformative project, especially the scope and brutality of the repression, reflected the profound fears driving the coup makers, their many henchmen, and the millions of citizens endorsing their actions (Pion-Berlin 1988: 385, 397–8). Notably, the overthrow of democracy found majority support,[68] which extended even to the forceful repression of the guerrilla forces, as the available evidence suggests (Moyano 1995: 96, 98, 152). In the eyes of these numerous backers of harsh autocracy, the country had been rudderless under the democracy restored in 1973; spiraling violence from all sides had threatened to cause chaos. Given these serious problems, the military and their civilian supporters, ranging from established elites to many common

---

[66] *FRUS 1969–1976*, vol. 11, part 2, chap. 1: 53, 85–6, 88, 97; see also Bermeo 2003: 216.

[67] As Bermeo (2003: 218) stresses, "the emergence of right-wing paramilitary groups was a grave blow to the military as an institution, for it meant that its 'monopoly of force' had been lost to two opposing groups" [emphasis in the original].

[68] O'Donnell 1983; Novaro and Palermo 2003: 23–5, 30–3; Brands 2010: 111, 116, 120; Schmidli 2013: 8; Finchelstein 2014: 124–5.

citizens, saw an urgent need for major surgery. The architects of the autocracy therefore set themselves the ambitious task of fundamentally redirecting the country's development. They wanted to break with the past, put Argentina on a different structural and institutional foundation, and in these ways forestall any resurgence of radicalism in the future. Perceptions of grave threats thus brought forth a massive reaction and gave rise to a reconstruction project of monumental proportions and a fierce determination to crush any resistance to these ambitious goals with all means.

The sequence of military coups and authoritarian regimes in Argentina thus demonstrates the backlash mechanism highlighted in this study, especially the interaction of diffusion and counterdiffusion. As growing radicalization inspired by the Cuban precedent and other contentious experiences of the 1960s fueled perceptions of ever greater threats among conservative groupings, asymmetrical loss aversion motivated increasingly forceful and deep-reaching countermeasures. The more Argentina seemed susceptible to the advancing wave of extremism set in motion by Fidel Castro's success, the stronger was the resolve of status quo-oriented sectors to forestall this scary prospect. When some of these sectors still saw Peronism as an alternative to and even a bulwark against communism (cf. Lanusse 1994: 108, 135–8), the efforts to weaken support for this populist movement remained relatively mild, and repression narrowly targeted the sporadic guerrilla movements. Yet when the proclivity to use violence spread and infected Peronism as well, repression expanded and intensified, and the attempts to impose socioeconomic and political change assumed increasing magnitude, until they culminated in the project to re-found the country from 1976 onward.

In sum, as the perceived challenges grew, so did the response, spearheaded by the political force that commanded the *ultima ratio* of power, namely the military. Diffusion efforts from the left prompted intensifying counterdiffusion by the right, increasingly supported by centrist sectors. Due to the disproportionate strength of loss aversion, counterdiffusion proved much more powerful; therefore, the revolutionary efforts of the left suffered a crushing defeat in Argentina, as in the rest of Latin America.

While this escalation of extremist challenges and reactionary countermeasures is understandable in the world of bounded rationality, it clearly diverged from fully rational behavior. Both the ambitions of radicals and the threat perceptions of conservatives, which interacted to propel this spiral, had tenuous bases in political reality. Leftists' initiatives were wildly unrealistic, and right-wingers' fears were exaggerated.

As regards leftist challengers, socialists and communists lacked organizational bases in Argentine society and found the partisan arena occupied by established groupings with firm roots among the citizenry, especially the massive Peronist movement; there was little room to gain a foothold. The left-wingers who therefore chose the violent route found prospects of success poor as well. The strategy of creating rural *focos* was unpromising in a heavily urbanized country with ample plains and few forests to hide in (Moyano 1995: 51); and no urban guerrilla movement has ever succeeded in taking power in the history of revolution.[69] The "absolute ignorance" and the "over-ambition, amateurism, and adventurism" (Gillespie 1982: 83 and 90, respectively) with which the *Montoneros* proceeded did not help. Moreover, the militaristic approach that, in line with Guevara and Debray's teachings, the guerrilla movements soon adopted was especially ill-advised:[70] it antagonized the bulk of the population and thus pushed the *guerrilleros* into isolation, leaving them exposed to the forces of repression.

For these reasons, the radical left, which suffered from tremendous internal divisions (Langieri 2013: 165–76), never had a chance of winning power in Argentina – but for years it held the illusion of impending victory (Novaro and Palermo 2003: 74–9). The very strategy of choosing violence, for lack of political-electoral prowess, was predictably self-defeating. Academic observers uniformly regard this militaristic approach as a fundamental mistake (Gillespie 1982; Moyano 1995; Brown 2017: chap. 13). The failure of the Argentine left becomes obvious in a comparison with Brazil, where radicals seemed to have won a breakthrough with President Goulart's determined embrace of "basic reforms" in early 1964. The contrast with Chile, where a Marxist-led government held power for three years and advanced a long way on its "march to socialism," is especially stark.

As the left lacked a realistic chance of imposing its transformational designs on Argentina, the fears of the right were, from a rational perspective, exaggerated as well. From the Cuban Revolution onward, segments in the military saw an acute communist threat, even inside the Frondizi government – yet without any real foundation.[71] Due to the scary Caribbean precedent, the heuristics of availability and representativeness blew threat perceptions completely out of proportion. The leading expert on Argentina's armed forces, Alain Rouquié, highlights the resulting "deformations," "extravagant denunciations," and "apocalyptic predictions." In his view, "the creepy obsession with an omnipresent and all-powerful Perón-Communism led to a dangerous self-intoxication of the cadres of the military" already in the early 1960s (Rouquié 1985: 156–7).

In subsequent years, the advance of radicalism and the proliferation of violence did increase the danger facing status quo-oriented sectors. But their worries shot up as well, again in disproportionate ways: fear continued to be much higher than actual risk; many people overestimated the probability of suffering losses. As the dean of Argentine historiography, Tulio Halperin Donghi (2010: 154), marvels, the military "leaders believed with so solid a faith in the presence of urgent threats against the social order, which the

---

[69] I owe this observation to my departmental colleague Raúl Madrid.
[70] Moyano 1995: 8, 50, 57, 60, 75, 90–1, 95; see also Gillespie 1982.
[71] Rouquié 1985: 156–9, 169–71, 175–7, 180, 183, 220.

[neutral] observer found difficult to discover."[72] Social scientist Liliana de Riz (2010: 185) also stresses the problematic repercussions of "the fear of an international Marxist conspiracy – even when little or no evidence justified that concern."[73]

This excess of fear had tragic consequences. It prompted intense loss aversion, which then stimulated exaggerated, inordinately severe countermeasures. Above all, exaggerated fear drove the depth and cruelty of repression that the police, military, and informal death squads inflicted on radical leftists and suspected extremists – before (Novaro and Palermo 2003: 69–70; Finchelstein 2014: 112–21) and after the coup of March 1976. In fact, although the guerrilla movements suffered a strategic defeat by late 1976,[74] large-scale repression continued at a clearly disproportionate scale, as the data collected by Moyano (1995: 94) show. "This policy of overkill" clearly diverged from any "rational calculation," as military expert David Pion-Berlin (1988: 385) argues. The paroxysm of state terror was unnecessary from the standpoint of hard-nosed cost-benefit assessments and exposed the perpetrators to the risk of later retribution, as indeed came to haunt many of them in subsequent decades.[75]

THE OVERTHROW OF A MARXIST GOVERNMENT AND IMPOSITION OF HARSH AUTOCRACY IN CHILE

Compared to Brazil and Argentina, threats to the socioeconomic and political order were much more severe in Chile before the brutal coup of 1973.[76] Brazil in the early 1960s and Argentina in the mid-1970s featured populist governments that advocated progressive measures (especially in the case of Goulart), but that had not yet enacted many ambitious reforms; consequently, the actual losses imposed on establishment sectors were limited. In Chile, by contrast, "a Marxist dominated coalition" (Remmer and Merkx 1982: 12; see also Haslam 2005: 6), the Popular Unity (Unidad Popular – UP) led by the comparatively moderate Communist Party and the radicalized Socialist Party (see Chapter 5), won government power. Although Salvador Allende received

---

[72] In 1965, for instance, the CIA discounted threats from the radical left (*FRUS 1964–1968*: 294–5) that in 1966 helped induce the Argentine military to grab power in a coup.

[73] Similarly, Moyano (1995: 64) highlights the "misconceptions" held by the military and the economic elite, which "assumed that the ties between guerrilla and popular organizations were closer than they really were."

[74] See Moyano 1995: 90; Novaro and Palermo 2003: 76–7.

[75] Strikingly, former dictator Jorge Videla emphasizes in a long interview (Reato 2012: 155–7) that from a strictly military standpoint, the coup of 1976 was a mistake because the tottering democracy had already given the armed forces free hand for combating terrorism; by contrast, the overthrow of democracy weakened the legitimacy of the counterinsurgency effort and ended up leading to the imprisonment of its protagonists.

[76] O'Donnell 1978: 6–9, 19; O'Donnell 1982: 54–5, 58–9, 72–3, 94.

little more than one-third of the presidential vote and the UP held a minority of seats in Congress, the left now pushed ahead with the goal to "overthrow ... the bourgeois state" (Allende in Debray 1971: 82). Obviously, pursuing a deep-reaching transformation on such a narrow political base constituted a very difficult and risky project (Landsberger and Linz 1979: 409, 423, 434; Tomić 1979: 221–2, 228–9). In its ambitious march toward socialism, the UP administration enacted a host of deep-reaching redistributive reforms which created substantial costs for elites and which literally threatened some of these sectors, especially large landowners on traditional estates, with extinction. After "Allende's election set off a panic" on the right and "fear gripped many ... elite families" (Baldez 2002: 54–5), the UP's determined socialist transformations confirmed and exacerbated these serious and acute concerns.

After all, the Allende administration greatly expanded and sped up the land reform enacted under the preceding government of Eduardo Frei from the (then) center-left Christian Democratic Party (1964–70). In fact, the socialist-communist coalition government quickly lost control over the implementation of agrarian redistribution, which prospective beneficiaries and their radical leftist supporters increasingly took into their own hands. "Thousands of peasants took direct action and seized hundreds of rural properties," as a favorable commentator highlights (Kay 1975: 5). Illegal takeovers of land proliferated, accompanied by a good deal of heated, extremist rhetoric and more and more outbreaks of violence.[77] Consequently, uncertainty spread, exacerbating threat perceptions among landowners and among a much wider range of upper and middle sectors (Whelan 1989:[78] 306–8, 343; Arrate and Rojas 2003, vol. 2: 71): where would this revolutionary transformation stop?

The expropriation of factories and mines that the Allende government pursued with considerable zeal exacerbated sociopolitical polarization as well. While a widely popular initial step, namely the complete nationalization of Chile's main natural resource, copper, had found unanimous backing in Congress (Valenzuela 1978: 52), other takeovers were more controversial. Therefore, the government sought to evade the opposition-controlled legislature by enacting numerous expropriations via legal loopholes, rather than by trying to pass new laws (Velasco Letelier 1976: 714–24). In particular, a fleeting Socialist Republic in 1932 had left long-forgotten, never-used rules on the books that allowed for takeovers under special conditions, mostly meant as temporary measures. But the Allende administration

---

[77] Sigmund 1977: 136, 139–40, 182; Tapia Videla 1979: 34, 42–3; Landsberger and Linz 1979: 420–1; Winn 2010: 246–53. Quiroga Zamora (2001: 260–70) reprints interesting documentation on a radical's systematic efforts to provide Allende supporters with training in the use of arms.

[78] Whelan based his detailed, comprehensive account on unprecedented, often confidential access to right-wing (and other) sectors, including generals who later played a central role in the Pinochet regime. Therefore, his book constitutes a valuable source on the exaggerated threat perceptions of Allende's adversaries and enemies. For this purpose, I draw on this biased volume.

interpreted these special conditions rather broadly and enacted takeovers as if they were permanent. The Popular Unity also took advantage of labor disputes – which "in some cases the government actually encouraged," as a sympathetic observer mentions (Kay 1975: 5) – in order to intervene in businesses and effectively expropriate them as well.[79] This resolute push for state takeovers, especially the bypassing of Congress and the disregard for legal certainty, spurred growing concerns among private business, the conservative National Party, and increasingly the centrist and center-left Christian Democrats as well (Arriagada 1974: 137, 140–9, 180–4; Tapia Valdés 1979: 301–3; Tapia Videla 1979: 46–7; Huneeus 1981: 264–5; see also Whelan 1989: 342, 394).

To tame this nationalization drive, forestall state domination, control the executive's hyperactivism, and reassert congressional prerogatives, the centrist opposition tried to delimit the area of public ownership via a constitutional amendment in early 1972, which sought to require legislative approval for further expropriations.[80] But conservative groupings distrusted the president and feared his proclaimed march to socialism (Valenzuela 1978: 73–7; Tapia Valdés 1979: 310–11), and radical leftists rejected legal hindrances to their ambitious program (Tapia Videla 1979: 55). The failure to reach agreement triggered a serious constitutional conflict between Allende and the Congress, which dragged on and drew in the judiciary as well.[81] As both sides used all the available institutional mechanisms for instrumental purposes, this festering conflict did much to undermine democratic legitimacy (Valenzuela 1978: 84, 90, 93, 124–5, n. 52).

Despite this institutional stalemate, the Popular Unity coalition continued with its expropriation drive, pushed by the most radical sectors inside the Socialist Party, which tried with all means to speed up the advance of revolution (Landsberger and Linz 1979: 413–14, 435). Eventually, as in the countryside, illegal takeovers of enterprises became more frequent (Tapia Valdés 1979: 302). A failed coup in June 1973, in particular, triggered a large number of factory occupations: "Some 30,000 small and medium-sized enterprises were rapidly snatched up by the left" (Haslam 2005: 181), as extremists sought to mobilize armed workers to defend their revolutionary efforts.[82] Although the Communist Party tried to chart a more moderate course, this radical-left contention scared the civilian opposition even more; it had an especially consequential impact on the Christian Democratic Party (see Valenzuela 1978: 89–92, 95–8, 107). Growing sectors of this politically pivotal

---

[79] Sigmund 1977: 133–4, 147–8, 157; García 1979: 172–8; Boeninger 1997: 177–80.

[80] Arriagada 1974: 154, 184–90, 268–71; Sigmund 1977: 158–60.

[81] Arriagada 1974: 251–71; Kay 1975: 10–11; Sigmund 1977: 167–71, 206–7, 223; Maira 1979: 264–8; Arrate and Rojas 2003, vol. 2: 72–3, 115–18; Haslam 2005: 181.

[82] Sigmund 1977: 215–16, 227–8; Quiroga Zamora 2001: 95–6; Haslam 2005: 180–1, 186, 188; Winn 2010: 251–3.

grouping sided with the conservative National Party and came to support its stubborn opposition against the Popular Unity regime.[83]

As over the years both poles of the ideological spectrum dug in their heels, competitive mass mobilization, spiraling street conflict, and the ever more frequent eruption of violence eroded the institutional solidity of Chilean democracy (see the classical analysis by Valenzuela 1978: chap. 3; see also Tapia Videla 1979: 41, 45, 48, 57–8; Huneeus 1981: 262–87; Garretón 1983: 44–59). Political forces slowly lost their commitment and trust in elections as the main mechanisms for temporarily resolving political disagreements; instead, they increasingly resorted to "politics by other means" (cf. Ginsberg and Shefter 2002). Because there was a progressive politicization of crucial regime institutions, political tricks, especially obstructionist stalling tactics by the opposition (Maira 1979: 253–69) and governmental usage of "discriminatory legalism" (Tomić 1979: 227; Sunkel 1983: 83–4; cf. Weyland 2013), came to proliferate. For instance, the opposition press, led by the reactionary El Mercurio with its ideologically biased news coverage,[84] spread scary rumors (Durán 1976; Landis 1981, 1982), and the government retaliated with efforts to control the supply of printing paper (Sigmund 1977: 157, 183, 207) and other "thoughtless measures of repression" (Haslam 2005: 178). Predictably, opposition forces, especially right-wingers, condemned this harassment as a fundamental attack on democratic freedoms and an indication of the "totalitarian" intentions of the Popular Unity coalition (US Senate 1976: 176).

In a similar escalation, the attempt of the Allende government to extend state ownership and control in the economy led business sectors, which saw these measures as serious threats to their room of operation, if not their very survival, to protest through massive strikes and other forms of disruption (Tapia Videla 1979: 50–2; Huneeus 1981: 269–71). The government responded forcefully, for instance by imprisoning the leaders of these protest movements and by using the police to rein in trouble and turmoil. Business, in turn, had since the beginning of the Allende government funded ultra-right movements such as Patria y Libertad, which engaged in frequent street battles with left-wingers and used bombings, mostly of public infrastructure, to hamper the economy and sow fear (*FRUS 1969–1976*, vol. 21: 806–8; Grugel 1985: 117; Whelan 1989: 396–7, 410).[85] Thus, the sociopolitical opposition responded with drastic

---

[83] Whelan 1989: 309–12. As Fleet (1985: 136, 138, 149–50, 152) highlights, the Christian Democrats' working-class base, which was quite substantial, held rather conservative and anticommunist views.

[84] Cortés 2014: 59–62, 77–8, 83–9, 96–104; see also Sunkel 1983: 70–3, 78–97, and recently Alvear and Lugo-Ocando, forthcoming. Llewellyn's (2002: 108) thorough analysis arrives at the conclusion "that although *El Mercurio* did not directly mislead its readers with regards to UP government economic policies, it did prove to be somewhat biased, even alarmist, in its interpretation of them."

[85] In their comparison of Chile 1973 and Spain 1936, Landsberger and Linz (1979: 410) judge, however, that "the chief role of the extreme right (*Patria y Libertad*) was ultimately limited to

countermeasures to the grave threats that it saw arise from Chile's march toward socialism.

What exacerbated the political conflict by establishing a potent association with the Cuban case and reinforcing right-wing fears that Chile was sliding toward communism was an unprecedented, exceptionally lengthy state visit by Fidel Castro in late 1971 (Espinosa 2016). For a full twenty-five days, the protagonist of radicalism in the western hemisphere toured the country and "openly indicated that he thought revolutionary transformation needed speeding up, that there were merits to using violence to advance this transformation, and that Allende bestowed too much freedom on his opposition" (Harmer 2011: 133; similar 140–1; Gustafson and Andrew 2018: 413). After the representativeness heuristic had already led opposition supporters to see worrisome parallels between Allende's march toward socialism and the Cuban Revolution, the mastermind of that outstanding precedent now seemed to confirm these threatening perceptions by advocating closer emulation.[86] No wonder that Castro's visit stirred up the Chilean right (Whelan 1989: 314; Jarpa 2002: 162), "fueled counterrevolutionary hostility" (Harmer 2011: 139), "stimulated a counteroffensive by the *Unidad Popular's* adversaries" (Maira 1979: 259), and triggered the first mass protest by conservative women and right-wing paramilitaries (Baldez 2002: 76–82).[87]

Together with this rising street contention, the bold transformations of the economy, which created enormous uncertainty for producers and investors, also caused economic trouble. Predictably, business sectors fearing expropriation engaged in disinvestment out of self-defense, but also as a means to put political pressure on the Marxist-led government, hoping to stem its expropriation drive. As a result, production suffered. At the same time, the expansionary economic policies with which Allende sought to boost his mass support soon backfired and helped to plunge the country into a worsening crisis (Tomić 1979: 222, 230–1). From late 1971 onward inflation skyrocketed and citizens came to face worsening scarcities of basic products. The severe economic deterioration created a crisis atmosphere (Navia and Osorio 2015: 131–2) and inflamed conflict in society; workers struck for higher wages, while middle sectors engaged in unprecedented street protests. All of these economic problems and the growing sociopolitical contention aggravated fears that the Popular Unity coalition, especially its most radical, revolutionary currents in the

---

aggravating the climate of violence and chaos which the extreme left (MIR and Left-Socialists in Chile) were in any case vigorously fostering as part of their own policy." Note also that "the Chilean extreme left was not only larger than the extreme right, but it was also on the scene first, well before the extreme right" (Landsberger and Linz 1979: 411).

[86] In fact, Allende himself had stressed these parallels shortly before Castro's visit by stressing that "we have achieved more than Cuba in her first year" (cited in Angell 1972: 76).

[87] Concerns about the Cuba connection were reinforced in March 1972, when the opposition suspected that "thirty crates . . . unloaded from a Cuban airliner" and transferred surreptitiously to President Allende's residence contained arms (Landsberger and Linz 1979: 426).

Socialist Party and the Christian left, would make an end run and grab total power in order to push through its ideological designs in a nondemocratic fashion. Like the conservative National Party, ever more leaders of the centrist Christian Democrats were scared that the governing leftists were advancing toward "totalitarianism."[88]

Given the deepening divisions in Chilean society, the institutional mechanisms of democracy failed to bring a resolution of these conflicts. The congressional midterm elections of early 1973 yielded an inconclusive result. The fiercely fought contest left the Popular Unity in a minority position,[89] but did not give the opposition the supermajority required for passing constitutional amendments or impeaching the president (Arrate and Rojas 2003, vol. 2: 109–14). Consequently, the left was still unable to legislate socialism,[90] whereas the opposition parties would have to wait until the presidential election scheduled for late 1976 to stop the government's bold transformational project; by then, they feared, it would be too late. The continuing political stalemate thus reinforced the tendency to resort to extralegal means. The radical left renewed its push for land and factory takeovers without congressional authorization. At the same time, the right prepared new business strikes, and the opposition parties passed a resolution in Congress that accused the Allende administration of serious violations of the Constitution.[91] Moreover, status quo-oriented sectors started to besiege the military to stop the country's slide into chaos.[92]

The impact that this deepening ideological polarization and growing conflict had on the military indeed proved decisive. The rash of illegal, forceful land and factory takeovers from mid-1973 onward, which involved armed groupings of

---

[88] See Valenzuela (1978: 89–92) and Whelan (1989: 373, 401–3, 414). These fears induced a number of Christian Democrats not only to support the coup of 1973, but to switch political alignments and collaborate with the Pinochet regime. One example is William Thayer Arteaga: he had been a government minister in the Christian Democratic administration of Eduardo Frei Montalva (1964–70), but then held several advisory positions under the military dictatorship and helped found the conservative party Renovación Nacional, in many ways a direct successor of the National Party, the right-wing opposition to the Frei and Allende governments. For his fears of "total Communist control" and his approval of the coup, see Thayer (2012: 292, 294, 297–9, 312).

[89] Note also that in February of 1973, 53.1 percent of survey respondents "rejected socialism," even its democratic models (Bermeo 2003: 173).

[90] On the crucial importance of this veto power, see *FRUS* 1969–1976, vol. 11, part 2, chap. 1: 554, 634.

[91] Reprinted in Secretaría General de Gobierno 1974: 239–42; see ibid. 11, 85, 87; Whelan 1989: 413–14; and Jarpa 2002: 179, 194. On the failure of last-minute efforts to forge a negotiated compromise, see from a Christian Democratic perspective Walker (1990: 166–7).

[92] *FRUS* 1969–1976, vol. 11, part 2, chap. 1: 585–6; Thayer 2012: 288. Despite civilian encouragement and pleas, however, the military took its coup decisions completely on its own (Fontaine 1993; interviews with business leader Orlando Sáenz and with civilian conservative Arturo Fontaine in Arancibia 2006: 227, 246; transcripts of confidential interviews by Chilean academics with a right-wing leader; Vial 2003: 195; Nunn 1976: 288, 293).

peasants and workers, had especially deleterious repercussions.[93] Whereas large parts of the officer corps had long subscribed to the constitutionalist principle of accepting the elected government,[94] concern now spread that the Popular Unity coalition promoted or at least condoned radical efforts to undermine the state's monopoly over organized coercion, the core institutional interest of the military. Officers feared that worker militias, supplied with guns by communist countries such as Cuba (Whelan 1989: 382–5), could soon pose a serious threat to the armed forces and eventually push the country into a civil war.[95] After all, the overheated rhetoric of left-wing extremists, such as the violence-prone Movement of the Revolutionary Left (MIR) and the ultraradical sectors of the Cuba-inspired Socialist Party, depicted the military as the ultimate mainstay of the established order, which needed to be infiltrated, divided, or defeated in order to allow for the irreversible breakthrough to socialism.[96] In response, more and more generals and their civilian supporters came to see these radicals as a mortal threat.[97] The final straw that broke the camel's back were leftist efforts to win support among enlisted men in the navy.[98]

As in Brazil in early 1964, where radicals' challenges to military discipline and hierarchy had prompted the formation of a wide-ranging coup coalition, the proliferation of worker militias and incipient challenges from enlisted men tipped the balance inside the Chilean military.[99] A quickly growing number of officers now regarded the Allende administration as illegitimate and decided to

---

[93] *FRUS 1969–1976*, vol. 11, part 2, chap. 1: 601–2, 646; Quiroga Zamora 2001: 95–8; Schnake 2004: 186–7, 195; Sigmund 1977: 215–16, 227–8. By encouraging and supporting the most radical currents inside and outside the Popular Unity coalition, Cuban diplomats and intelligence agents inadvertently contributed to the overthrow of the Allende government (Gustafson and Andrew 2018: 409, 411, 415, 417).

[94] Nunn 1976: 254–5, 272–3; *FRUS 1969–1976*, vol. 11, part 2, chap. 1: 400–1, 432–5.

[95] As Arrate and Rojas (2003, vol. 2: 26–8) highlight, the left's military preparations under the Allende government initially had defensive purposes, driven by fears of right-wing counter-revolution. But against the wishes of President Allende, the MIR from 1972 onward tried to build up "popular power" in order to put pressure on the state itself and push forward the socialist transformation of society (Arrate and Rojas 2003, vol. 2: 72, 86, 98).

[96] See recently Marchesi 2018: 121. Note that already in 1967, the radicalized Socialist Party had declared in its (in)famous "Resolution of Chillán" that "only by destroying the bureaucratic and military apparatus of the bourgeois state can the socialist revolution be consolidated" (reprinted in Huneeus 1981: 176).

[97] Valenzuela 1978: 99–103; Vial 2003: 173; Prats 1987: 380, 428, 440, 459–60, 502; Merino 1998: 126, 128–45, 195, 207; interviews in Arancibia 2006: 147–8, 151, 154; 188–9; 431, 437–8.

[98] Merino 1998: 209–11, 224–7; Whelan 1989: 410, 417–18; Jarpa 2002: 193; Secretaría General de Gobierno 1974: 25; see Tapia Videla 1979: 61; Huneeus 1981: 285–6; Arrate and Rojas 2003, vol. 2: 133, 140. Moreover, the coup mongers insistently claimed that the Allende administration had prepared a total power grab via a self-coup (Secretaría General de Gobierno 1974: 21, 23, 41–65; Merino 1998: 147–51), but this "Plan Z" was most likely a forgery (Winn 2010: 266–7, 270).

[99] Valenzuela 1978: 99–103; Arriagada 1974: 311, 314–15, 318–20; see in general Linz 1978: 60.

combat the threats to their own institution with open force. After some reactionary generals had plotted for a long time (*FRUS* 1969–1976, vol. 21: 810, 812), now many officers jumped onto the bandwagon. The urge to evict the Popular Unity coalition was especially intense among the middle ranks (Whelan 1989: 391). After one rogue officer started an ill-considered coup attempt in late June 1973, the leading generals and admirals worried that midranking officers would soon act on their own again to overthrow the Marxist-led government, yet in the process overturn the military hierarchy as well.[100] Thus, the institutional structure of the armed forces now seemed threatened both from the outside and the inside, namely by the proliferation of armed left-wingers in society, by their efforts to win adherents inside the military, and by the eagerness of conservative officers to combat these problems with all means.

Because the navy had discovered what it saw as a dangerous leftist infiltration effort (Haslam 2005: 201–2), admirals took the lead in organizing a serious coup plan;[101] soon they reached out to the air force and army as well. Given the rapidly growing discontent inside the armed forces, the remaining constitutionalist generals faced ever greater difficulty in trying to sustain the Allende administration until the presidential elections of 1976. Numerous officers changed sides in mid-1973. As the pivotal figure, Augusto Pinochet, newly appointed as army commander, had long stayed loyal to his hierarchical superiors and the elected president.[102] But on September 9, 1973, pressured by the leading conspirators, he finally swung his support behind the coup,[103] setting in motion the overthrow of Chilean democracy two days later.[104]

In conclusion, the Popular Unity's determination to force a march toward socialism, the most emblematic product of the groundswell of the Cuba-inspired radicalization in Latin America, aggravated sociopolitical polarization in Chile and put enormous strain on democratic institutions. Predictably, this bold project, which never found majority support among the citizenry (cf. Bermeo 2003: 173; see also Valenzuela 1978: 42–3), threatened the core interests of powerful socioeconomic elites, conservative and even centrist politicians, and – eventually – the military. No wonder that these forces fought back with growing fierceness. And because the armed forces

---

[100] Merino 1998: 194–7, 209–14, 225; similar Prats 1987: 423, 425, 433–4, 441, 484.

[101] Merino 1998: 233–4; transcript of confidential interviews by Chilean academics with navy leader; Whelan 1989: 374, 421, 458.

[102] González 2000: 238, 241–2, 247, 250–3, 256–8, 286, 289, 305, 310, 317.

[103] The crucial document, which Pinochet signed on that day, is reproduced in Merino (1998: 230–1).

[104] Pinochet's halting decision-making process is extensively analyzed and documented in Vial (2003: 183–218). In retrospect, however, Pinochet claimed that he started plotting in mid-1972 (Pinochet 1990: 242–3; see also Whelan 1989: 468–70, 607–8) – probably to justify the leadership position that he grabbed right after the coup. Like most observers, González (2000: 260) sees these claims as a falsification of history.

commanded much more firepower than their leftist challengers, reaction decisively squashed revolution. The coup faced strikingly little resistance. The military took control of the whole country within a few hours, disproving its exaggerated fears of civil war (Whelan 1989: 457, 471, 498–9, 515). In retrospect, these outcomes are not surprising; what is surprising is how late the opposition ousted Marxist President Allende and how long they let him and his radical supporters pursue their profound transformational project.

Clearly, the danger that the radical left posed to status quo-oriented sectors and the costs that elites had already incurred were much higher in Chile (1970–3) than they had ever been in Brazil and in Argentina, at least until the mid-1970s. As an Allende minister claimed in early 1973, "The bases of Chilean capitalism have been destroyed" (cited in Whelan 1989: 375). Consequently, Chile's conservatives had much more reason to fight back and evict their political enemies from power. By "finally" overthrowing the Allende administration in 1973,[105] the military acted less rashly and precipitously than in the other instances of the Latin American coup wave. In the real world of politics, their intervention was "inevitable," as even a leader of Chile's renovated socialists acknowledges in retrospect.[106] The military and its civilian backers, who according to centrist witnesses commanded majority support,[107] had already suffered substantially greater losses than their counterparts elsewhere in the region. In other words, it took a much greater challenge, namely a determined march to socialism that was well under way, to induce the Chilean military to overthrow democracy. While morally condemnable and terrible in its human and political repercussions, the Chilean coup was the product of less tightly bounded rationality than in Brazil and Argentina.

On the other hand, the Chilean armed forces did display distortions arising from cognitive shortcuts and asymmetrical loss aversion. Their perceptions and actions deviated from the standards of full rationality – just not as far as in

---

[105] Scholars highlight "the hesitancy and delay of the military," which had "take[n] steps to avoid intervention" (Landsberger and Linz 1979: 431).

[106] Núñez y el Golpe de Estado 2004. See the very similar overarching judgment by Brands (2010: 127).

[107] Boeninger (1997: 214–15); interview with Renán Fuentealba in Arancibia (2006: 210). See also historian Fermandois (2003: 21). Opinion polls show that from April–June 1972 to February 1973, citizen support for establishing a military government had increased from 17 percent to 26 percent (Bermeo 2003: 167). In subsequent months, the country's economic and sociopolitical crisis deteriorated gravely; for instance, inflation surged from 78 percent in calendar year 1972 to 235 percent during the first eight months of 1973 alone, and scarcities spread. As a result, popular assessments of the country's situation worsened drastically (Navia and Osorio 2015: 131–2), and these evaluations were significantly correlated with presidential approval (Navia and Osorio 2017: 793–4; the data analysis documents this finding, although Navia and Osorio [2017: 795–6] draw different conclusions). These developments make claims of majority support for the military intervention plausible. Of course, like most politicians, citizens probably expected a quick restoration of democracy.

Brazil and Argentina. Above all, the Chilean coup makers overestimated the acuteness of the leftist threat. By mid-1973, the Allende government faced multiple pressures and lurched from crisis to crisis, rather than preparing an end run on power. Yet many generals and civilian opponents were overly impressed by the extremist rhetoric of the Popular Unity's ultraradical wing, which had no realistic chance to unleash armed mass struggle.[108] Swept up by fear, the military carried out the coup with excessively brutal, "unnecessary" repression (Harmer 2011: 232, 244–6, 254, 271, 273). Chile specialist Paul Sigmund (1977: 256, 258) highlights the armed forces' "paranoia," and historian Tanya Harmer (2011: 254) stresses their "wildly exaggerated fears." Similarly, historian Peter Winn (2010: 267) argues that "the counterrevolutionary violence of the coup and the terror that followed were unnecessary." After all, "the plotters were not faced by a civil war with an unknown outcome that might have justified such extreme measures, but rather a military coup whose outcome was never in doubt."

Moreover, in combating these threats, the armed forces overreacted considerably, as strikingly evident in the bloody determination of the coup and the brutality of the subsequent purge, which were "greater than necessary" for accomplishing the coup makers' goals (Fermandois 2003: 21; Huneeus 2007: 32, 43–6). The bombing and strafing of the presidential palace, forever enshrined in iconic images, were a rare occurrence, even in a continent where military takeovers used to be common. Because the armed forces overestimated the strength of the left, especially of its armed formations (e.g., Merino 1998: 241),[109] they proceeded with full force when – after long hesitation – they eventually did decide to act. This overreaction was remarkable because during the months preceding the coup, the armed forces had systematically confiscated weapons from left-wing groupings, and in these raids also managed to assess the limited organizational and military strength of their adversaries (Kay 1975: 21–2; Whelan 1989: 385, 403, 416). Nevertheless, they cracked down with unprecedented severity during their takeover of power.

Even more tragic was the forceful crackdown that the left, particularly its radical wing, suffered in subsequent months. The extralegal killings, mass imprisonment, sadistic torture, and expulsions of citizens from their own country reflected the deep fears that the new power holders harbored against their ideological foes. As the coup makers expected armed resistance and saw a risk of civil war (Whelan 1989: 499, 515), they were determined to nip any

---

[108] The risk of a popular insurgency was especially low because in the weeks preceding the coup, the military had rigorously enforced the Arms Control Law of 1972 and had confiscated a good deal of the weaponry that left-wing workers held, as even the Pinochet-friendly account of Whelan (1989: 385, 403, 416) mentions.

[109] Of course, leftist grandiloquence about "armed struggle" and "popular power" (cf. Carlos Altamirano in Arancibia 2006: 173) fueled these misperceptions. The radical left greatly overestimated its strength (interview with socialist leader Jaime Gazmuri in Arancibia 2006: 415, 425) – and so did the right, therefore cracking down especially hard.

possible challenges to the new autocracy in the bud. But given that the armed forces so quickly established unchallenged control (Huneeus 2007: 43–4), there was no rational reason for atrocities like the "caravan of death" that – weeks after the coup – left a bloody trail of extrajudicial executions across the length of the country (Hurtado 1990; Huneeus 2007: 48–50). After all, its victims were prisoners, not combatants in active fighting; and it is unclear why this variegated set of people, who had not offered violent resistance to the coup, were selected for elimination (Verdugo 2001: 14–15, 31, 41, 65, 94, 111, 144–5). In the unscrupulous and cruel way that the military junta crushed its enemies and consolidated its hold on power, the coup of 1973 and its aftermath clearly were excessive; this overkill reflected bounded rationality as well.

In relative terms, however, the bounds of rationality were relatively loose in Chile, as the contrast with Brazil and Argentina suggests. While the Chilean coup mongers and their civilian supporters deviated from the probability estimates and cost assessments that comprehensive rationality would have suggested, they deviated to a lesser extent than their counterparts did in the rest of Latin America. Their fears of leftist radicalism were excessive, but they had much better reasons to harbor fear than Brazilian and Argentine conservatives. What was the reason for the less tightly bounded rationality that prevailed in Chile?

HOW ORGANIZATIONAL STRUCTURES MEDIATE THREAT PERCEPTIONS

The preceding case studies of the installation of reactionary dictatorships in Brazil, Argentina, and Chile have mustered ample evidence for the crucial role of fears about leftist radicalization and communist subversion. The concerns that the Cuban Revolution made acute, and that inferential heuristics intensified, induced a growing range of political forces to despair about the resilience of liberal democracy and to seek protection against extremism in the strong arms of military autocracy. As Castro's success unleashed a groundswell of radicalization across Latin America, more and more countries therefore installed dictatorships, sometimes repeatedly, such as Argentina.

Yet while threat perceptions fueled by cognitive shortcuts provided the fundamental motive for the Latin American coup wave, their intensity and their political impact were not uniform; instead, they were mediated by the organizational structures enveloping the main political forces. As highlighted throughout this study, the bounds of rationality vary, depending on individual-level knowledge and expertise and – of special relevance for political analysis – depending on institutional patterns. Weak organization leaves cognitive shortcuts and disproportionate loss aversion free rein; inbred, sect-like organization can even exacerbate these deviations from comprehensive rationality. By contrast, broad-based, internally pluralistic organizations engage in better information processing and promote fairly open debates, which tend to filter out the worst misperceptions. Discussion and criticism subject the prevailing fears to reality checks and thus diminish distortions in judgment and choice. As a result, broad-based organizations proceed with a higher level of political rationality.

The impact of organizational structures becomes obvious in a comparison of autocracy's imposition in Brazil and Argentina versus Chile. In Brazil, the Goulart government and the populist and radical forces pushing to the left were demanding "basic reforms," but had not yet enacted many bold changes by the time they were dislodged from power. In other words, conservative sectors feared facing serious costs, but had not actually suffered many real losses. Similarly, in Argentina the Frondizi administration (1958–62) and especially the Illia government (1963-6) had not imposed costly policies, though the recent experience of Peronist rule (1946–55) kept fears of radicalization alive. And after their return to power in 1973, Juan and Isabelita Perón (1973–6) raised serious worries not by what they did, but by failing to prevent political chaos and growing violence. In all of these instances, the perceived threat arose from weakness, ungovernability, and the power vacuum that radical forces seemed ready to use to their advantage; it did not emerge from governmental initiatives themselves.

How different were the Allende years in Chile (1970–3)! After an avowed Marxist (Allende in Debray 1971: 62, 67, 81, 118) captured the presidency in late 1970, the Popular Unity embarked on a determined march to socialism, speeding up land redistribution, completing the nationalization of copper, and expropriating more and more private businesses, both domestic and transnational. From late 1972 onward, partly in response to reactionary countermobilization, ideological polarization deepened in dangerous ways, and political contention and violence spread. Left-wing worker militias and extremist groupings increased their activities and pushed the president, who preferred greater caution, toward increasing radicalism, spearheading ever more illegal takeovers of farms and enterprises. From mid-1973 onward, a growing range of status quo-oriented sectors, extending into the center-left Christian Democratic Party, came to regard the situation as fundamentally untenable (Fleet 1985: 167–9).

What is noteworthy in the Chilean case, and what the comparison with Brazil and Argentina highlights, is not that the military ended up unseating the Popular Unity in a bloody coup. Instead, it is interesting that this coup occurred comparatively late; for a long time, conservative and centrist forces, both among civilians and inside the military, remained reluctant to interrupt Chilean democracy. Clearly, the process of radicalization in Chile was much more advanced than in Brazil and Argentina. Three years of profound redistributive reforms and disastrous economic policies had created serious costs for many elites and middle sectors; intense popular mobilization and sociopolitical polarization had thoroughly disrupted everyday life and undermined state control; and the emergence of armed formations was challenging the military's monopoly over organized coercion. Thus, leftist radicalization had imposed actual losses on a range of powerful sectors, and the magnitude of these costs was unprecedented in Latin America, if not in any democracy in world history. This experience of losses was concrete and dramatic – no comparison to the potential costs that could arise from the demands for basic reforms in Brazil and the worrisome consequences of power vacuums in Argentina. Thus, to bring democracy down in Chile, it took a much clearer, bigger, and more painful challenge than in the other countries.

Obviously, the greater consolidation of Chilean democracy and the apolitical professionalism of the military played a major role in the differential thresholds of threat that triggered the reactionary backlash.[110] The breakpoint was comparatively high in Chile because, by persisting for more than three decades since the last transition from authoritarianism in 1932, democracy had gained a great deal of resilience;[111] the relevant political forces had become habituated to resolving political and ideological conflicts through free competitive elections.[112] In Brazil and Argentina, by contrast, democracy was much more precarious. In the lusophone country, the military had on several occasions acted as a veto player during presidential successions in the 1950s and early 1960s. Even worse, Argentina's polity had been rocked by frequent coups since the 1930s. And when the armed forces restored democracy in 1958 and 1963, they insisted on proscribing the main political and electoral movement, Peronism, and exercised constant tutelage over the semidemocratic governments, for instance by pushing around President Arturo Frondizi (1958–62) with their demands (Potash 1980; Wynia 1978: 93–4, 107–10; Halperin Donghi 2010: 120–1, 126, 130).

Because liberal democracy was exceedingly precarious in Argentina and weak in Brazil, it did not take very profound threats and the actual imposition of losses to induce status quo defenders to call on the armed forces. In their eyes, civilian competitive rule was so vulnerable to radical subversion and revolutionary assaults that the iron fist of autocracy was required for guaranteeing sociopolitical stability. By contrast, the relative strength of Chilean democracy gave conservative and especially centrist forces greater confidence that they could contain extremist challenges inside the established institutional framework. Consequently, these

---

[110] Landsberger and Linz (1979: 402–7) highlight Chile's long history of constitutionalism and the relatively low levels of political violence in a very interesting and insightful comparison of "Chile, 1973/Spain, 1936."

[111] While arguments about democratic consolidation have often been criticized as imprecise and analytically unhelpful, if not quasi-tautological (O'Donnell 1996), Svolik's impressive study (2015: 719–23) recently found a substantial reduction in the risk of breakdown about seventeen to twenty years after a democratic transition, which indicates democratic consolidation.

[112] This is why the 1967 proclamation in which the Socialist Party committed to armed struggle had come as such a surprise, as mentioned in Chapter 5.

forces long trusted in conflict resolution via the electoral arena, for instance by hoping to inflict a clear defeat on the Popular Unity government in the congressional midterm elections of 1973.

An additional reason for the relatively long survival of Chile's democracy under Marxist President Allende was the institutional strength and ideological breadth of the country's party system. This organizational factor, which contrasts especially with the notorious weakness of rightist parties in Argentina, long helped to reinforce confidence that civilian politics could resolve the deepening crisis, especially via elections. Whereas Argentine conservatives lacked significant representation in the party system, Chile's National Party had come close to defeating Allende in the 1970 contest and hoped to win enough votes in the upcoming 1976 elections to unseat the Popular Unity in peaceful ways.[113] By contrast, their electoral weakness seemed to leave Argentine right-wingers few options but to "pull the emergency brake" by instigating military interventions (cf. Gibson 1996: 61–70).

In sum, the relative consolidation of democracy in Chile and the institutionalization of its party system created a "political opportunity structure" (cf. Tarrow 2011: chap. 8) that goes a long way toward explaining why Chilean status quo defenders submitted to much greater losses than their counterparts in Brazil and Argentina. These institutional and organizational factors, which shaped the configuration of parameters facing the main political forces, help account for why the reactionary backlash and the imposition of autocracy came comparatively late.

But in the world of bounded rationality, objective constellations do not automatically shape the perceptions and subsequent actions of the relevant political forces. Instead, commonly used inferential heuristics can lead to cognitive distortions, cause misunderstandings, and entail costly mistakes, as this book amply shows. With respect to this subjective, perceptual filter, Chile's broad-based, internally pluralistic parties also ensured that the main political actors engaged in better information processing than their weaker, more haphazard counterparts in Brazil and Argentina. Constant deliberation and debate, inside and among parties, subjected the scary inferences fueled by cognitive shortcuts to more thorough evaluations and cross-checking. As a result, Chilean centrists and even most right-wingers had a reasonable understanding of the threats that left-wingers posed. In Brazil and Argentina, by contrast, misperceptions ran wild, as the dire warnings about "the revolutionary war" in the lusophone country (Brasil 1964: 25–52; Pinto 1964: 136, 141, 146–7, 150, 166–7) and the baseless charges about President Frondizi's communist leanings (*FRUS 1961–1963*: 386; Rouquié 1985: 170–1,

---

[113] The fact that Chile's left-wing parties had for many years participated in democratic politics also enhanced hopes in a nonviolent, electoral resolution of the growing crisis.

176–7, 180, 220; Brown 2017: 236) suggest. Chile's status quo defenders never diverged that far from realistic assessments of the challenges they faced.

Most importantly, the pivotal party located at the median of Chile's left-right spectrum, Christian Democracy, drew on its broad-based organization and held frequent discussions among its different currents and wings (Fleet 1985: chap. 4). For a long time, these debates kept the worst fears in check and led the party to trust in electoral mechanisms.[114] Only when from June 1973 onward illegal factory takeovers proliferated and worker militias seemed to spread did Christian Democracy finally conclude that they could not wait for the presidential elections of 1976. Because left-wingers apparently broke with legality, centrist leaders came to believe that a military intervention was necessary. Therefore, in August 1973 the party fully sided with the right-wing National Party and passed a joint congressional resolution that declared the Allende government in violation of the constitution (reprinted in Secretaría General de Gobierno 1974: 239–42).

Interestingly, a large majority of Chile's armed forces showed a good deal of caution and restraint as well. Far from acting as power-hungry coup makers who take advantage of the opportunity to oust civilians, many generals tried hard to avoid the downfall of Chilean democracy. While small right-wing coteries of generals did plot for years, the bulk of the organization long remained loyal to the elected government (*FRUS 1969–1976*, vol. 11, part 2, chap. 1: 400–1, 476, 514, 540–2). Military leaders deliberately helped stabilize the regime by entering the Allende administration both after the reactionary protests of late 1972 and after the ill-prepared coup attempt of June 1973. Top commander Carlos Prats, in particular, undertook every effort to preserve democracy (Prats 1987: 397, 407, 423, 431–52, 463). Remarkably, even later dictator Augusto Pinochet, who during and after the coup took advantage of his command over the army to establish his personal predominance, long supported Allende's constitutional government; in August 1973 still, he threatened opposition demonstrators with military repression! Notably, Pinochet was the last commander of Chile's four military branches to sign on to the coup plot,[115] and he did so only under pressure from other top generals, less than two days before the bloody overthrow (Vial 2003: 183–218).

In line with the organizational argument advanced in this book, the military's hesitation reflected not only the constitutionalist norms inculcated for decades in the armed forces, but also organizational mechanisms that allowed for structured debate and deliberation, such as the Council of Generals in the

---

[114] Bermeo (2003: 171–4) stresses the failure of Chile's strong parties to uphold political rationality. But what is more noteworthy in the real world of bounded rationality, especially in a comparative perspective, is that despite a grave crisis, Chile's parties for so long remained committed to electoral mechanisms in trying to resolve their severe conflicts.

[115] In Chile, the main police force, the *Carabineros*, are a part of the military; therefore, they had their own seat in the military junta that governed the country from 1973 to 1990.

army (Prats 1987: 243–5, 413–14, 425, 456). In fact, to deal with the growing crisis unleashed by Allende's march to socialism and the right and center's increasingly obstinate resistance, the three main branches created a special organization for open discussion. In mid-1973, when the ever more dangerous polarization forcefully drew them into politics, the army, navy, and air force formed a committee to which each branch sent five representatives. This group of fifteen regularly debated the deteriorating political situation and assessed how best to preserve the military's fundamental institutional interests (Vial 2003: 178–9, 199; *FRUS 1969–1976*, vol. 21: 884–5).

While many observers depict this committee of fifteen as the core of the coup conspiracy, it started out as an institutional mechanism representing the diversity of orientations inside the armed forces (Prats 1987: 423, 435–6; González 2000: 181–7). Accordingly, the discussions aired a plurality of views and brought many direct and frank exchanges, which were rather unusual for an institution resting on hierarchy. Although numerous committee members were highly critical of the Allende administration and tended toward forceful moves, the top leaders, especially commander-in-chief Carlos Prats, upheld constitutionalist principles of obedience to civilian authority and sought a compromise between the Popular Unity and the opposition that would preserve democracy.[116] Reflecting these different orientations inside the military, the committee of fifteen first drew up the bases of a national agreement that could have stabilized the polity (reprinted in González 2000: 184–7, 501–7).

Thus, due to the open debates in this organizational forum, the scary inferences suggested by cognitive heuristics did not hold unimpeded sway among Chile's armed forces. Consequently, the committee of fifteen did not immediately embrace a worst-case scenario and advocate a coup. Instead, the assembled generals first tried out a more cautious and prudent course of action by pushing civilian politicians to contain the crisis. Yet Prats' exhaustive and increasingly desperate efforts to win support for a national agreement from the feuding political parties, interest associations, and even militarized radical groupings did not yield success (Prats 1987: 397, 407, 423, 431–52, 463). As deepening polarization stimulated further radicalization among the left and the right, members of the committee of fifteen concluded, more or less reluctantly, that only the military could forestall a violent collapse.

---

[116] Interestingly, Augusto Pinochet as army commander sought to prohibit his branch's participation in the committee's deliberations, which he seems to have seen as undue interference in politics. Pinochet relented only because commander-in-chief Carlos Prats, the mainstay of professionalism in the Chilean military, had authorized the formation of this coordination mechanism (González 2000: 187). Prats himself faced the tragic dilemma of getting drawn into politics in order to keep the military out of politics, as he highlighted in his memoirs (Prats 1987: 397).

Interestingly, growing support for a coup did not just reflect a generic fear of Chile turning into a second Cuba (González 2000: 206), but specific threats to the military as the last bulwark of political order, as mentioned in the preceding section. Committee members worried especially that worker militias and ultraradical groupings were trying to entrench themselves among the popular sectors and to infiltrate the armed forces as well. During the preceding years, the military had understood that rhetorical celebrations of political violence and sporadic incidents, which were all too common in Chile during the late 1960s and early 1970s, did not pose a real threat to their control over organized coercion. But when evidence appeared that leftist preparations for violence seemed to spread and to target the military itself, the alarm lights went on: the military feared the creation of parallel armed forces and the corrosion of its internal discipline and hierarchy, which could end up leading to civil war.[117] While these threat perceptions were exaggerated,[118] as proven by the quick defeat of the armed left following the coup, they had much more basis in fact than the worries that ran wild among Brazilian and Argentine generals before the 1964 and 1966 takeovers. Thus, helped by the committee of fifteen and its unusually frank deliberations and debates, in Chile even the military – normally a conformity-seeking institution susceptible to cognitive shortcuts and distortions – achieved a higher degree of political rationality than in other Latin American countries.[119]

In conclusion, organizational structures mediated the political effect of the threat perceptions that cognitive shortcuts derived from the precedent of the Cuban Revolution. Fears of radicalism had a direct and powerful impact on a wide range of political forces in Brazil and Argentina, which had institutionally weak political parties and lacked mechanisms of deliberation inside the military.[120] As a result, the military in Brazil and Argentina responded to left-wing radicalization comparatively quickly and overthrew democracy precipitously. By contrast, Chile's political parties and even the military had stronger organizational structures that guaranteed better information processing, and thus kept worries about radicalization in check for a surprisingly long time. Only after Allende's bold march to socialism had

---

[117] Prats (1987: 380, 428, 440, 459–60, 502); interview with General Ernesto Videla Cifuentes in Arancibia (2006: 147–8, 151, 154); right-wing leader Sergio Onofre Jarpa (in Arancibia 2006: 188–9) and civilian conservative Hermógenes Pérez de Arce shared these concerns (in Arancibia 2006: 431, 437–8); see also González 2000: 203–5, 221–2, 305–6.

[118] Faúndez (1988: 267–77, espec. 277) claims that the worker groupings sprouting up in industrial areas were only lightly armed. On the limited strength of the Popular Unity's military groupings, see also Arrate and Rojas (2003, vol. 2: 129).

[119] Commenting on the 1980s, when he served in high-level positions under the military regime, Cáceres (interview 2007) claimed that Chile's armed forces followed a rather rational process of decision making, considering all the possible scenarios and attaching probability estimates to them.

[120] As a result, Argentina's deeply divided military sometimes carried out its internal conflicts with armed violence, as in 1962–3.

advanced quite far, after the president himself had lost control of the strong radical currents inside his coalition, and after leftist preparations for violence were making headway did the military finally stop this spiraling challenge, which had imposed much greater actual costs on establishment forces than in the other two countries.

Thus, institutions of deliberation and debate loosened the bounds of rationality and brought a less precipitous reaction to the concerns fueled by a striking revolutionary precedent. Chilean political actors, both among civilians and inside the military, had a better understanding of the political opportunity structure, which due to the long-standing consolidation of democracy and the strength of political parties facilitated more and longer tolerance for left-wing radicalism. For those subjective and objective reasons, when the reactionary backlash finally occurred with the autocratic coup of September 1973, it was prompted by more realistic threats than the overthrow of democracy in Brazil and Argentina. While Chile's armed forces were under the spell of exaggerated threat perceptions as well and therefore overshot with excessive brutality, they had much more reason to worry than their counterparts across the Andes. Their probability estimates about the danger emerging from the radical left clearly had more basis in facts and was closer to the target than in the rest of Latin America.

CONCLUSION

Through in-depth analyses of the cases of Brazil, Argentina, and Chile, this chapter has corroborated that the installation of institutional autocracies during the 1960s and 1970s was fundamentally a reaction to the perceived threat of leftist radicalism that the Cuban Revolution made acute (similar Brands 2010: 96–7, 127–8). My novel contribution was the argument that status quo-oriented sectors derived these threat perceptions via cognitive shortcuts which fueled excessive fears. Specifically, the availability heuristic induced conservative forces to overrate the significance of Castro's success, and the representativeness heuristic made them believe in its easy replicability across the region: established regimes came to look brittle and precarious. While the same inferential shortcuts fired up the hopes and illusions of leftists, and thus gave rise to the tremendous radicalization of Latin American politics, they instilled deep fears in the right and, increasingly, in centrist sectors. These concerns triggered disproportionate loss aversion, which motivated conservatives to combat the perceived danger of communism with all means. Scared about turning into a second Cuba, they appealed to the military for protection and sacrificed liberty to preserve or restore sociopolitical stability.

In line with the central thesis of this book, the Latin American coup wave thus was a process of counterdiffusion. To prevent the Cuban Revolution from spreading, status quo defenders sought or endorsed a counterrevolutionary fortification of the political order. To avoid a dramatic move toward the left, they made a determined move to the right. The striking precedent of Communist Cuba thus prompted a strong backlash which pushed many countries in the opposite direction. Precisely because Castro's success inspired many emulation efforts by left-wing extremists and radicalized a much broader set of progressives and populists, right-wingers and – depending on the depth of the perceived threat – centrist forces embraced determined countermeasures. In an interactive dynamic, illusionary hopes bred paranoid fears, and ill-considered revolutionary efforts prompted disproportionately harsh reactions. As the left uniformly lost out to the right, deterrent effects proved most powerful.

Distorted by cognitive shortcuts, the fears of communism that prompted such draconian countermeasures were excessive. Leftists' efforts to emulate the Cuban Revolution rarely had chances of success; the professional militaries, institutionalized states, and liberal or democratic regimes prevailing in South America were much less vulnerable than Batista's Sultanistic dictatorship had been (Wickham-Crowley 1992: 166, 169, 173, 184–92). As many Latin Americans came to endorse and support unaccountable autocracy, they acted rashly and made serious mistakes. Yet contrary to the rationalist accounts that attribute these exaggerated threat perceptions to the self-interested machinations of reactionary elites (or the United States – see Chapter 7), the present study takes them seriously as honest mistakes fueled by cognitive shortcuts. While right-wingers certainly tried to proselytize and used scary rumors and deliberate misinformation for this purpose, the available evidence suggests that many conservatives held deep and genuine fears of the radical left (similar Brands 2010: 127); they did not invent this scarecrow to promote their instrumental interests and ideological causes.

Instead, a wealth of internal documents demonstrate how deep and widespread fears of radicalism were. Given the stunning events in Cuba, cognitive shortcuts that people commonly use and that psychologists have thoroughly documented provide a sufficient explanation for these threat perceptions. In the same way that many Americans were scared about plane rides after 9/11, many Latin Americans were frightful about communist revolution after Castro's success. Conservative manipulation reinforced these fears but was not their root cause. Latin Americans fell prey to misperceptions in holding such excessive dread, but they were not victims duped by conniving reactionaries.

As the penultimate section with its comparison of democracy's overthrow in Brazil, Argentina, and Chile shows, however, inferential heuristics and the loss aversion they can trigger are not uniform in their operation, strength, and impact. In particular, the distortions caused by these cognitive mechanisms vary with the political-organizational context. Human rationality is bounded, but the stringency of these bounds depends on the setting. In the realm of politics, organizations play an important role. Accordingly, Chile's institutionalized party system produced better information processing and less distorted decision making than the inchoate political arenas of Brazil and

Argentina. As a result, political rationality in Chile was less tightly bounded than in the other two countries. Chileans overreacted less drastically than Brazilians and Argentines. It therefore took a much clearer and stronger challenge from the radical left, namely three years of a determined march toward socialism promoted by a Marxist-led government, to trigger a reactionary coup; the Brazilian and Argentine military, by contrast, evicted democratic administrations for much lower challenges (at least until the mid-1970s in Argentina).

With this argument, the chapter embeds the cognitive microfoundations that shape human perceptions and decisions in an institutional and organizational macrostructure. This analytical move is crucial for disentangling the interaction of diffusion and counterdiffusion highlighted in this study, and for building a bounded rationality theory of politics more broadly.

7

Horizontal Diffusion and Vertical Promotion in the Autocratic Wave

Chapter 6 has shown that the proliferation of harsh military rule in Latin America arose from a counterrevolutionary backlash: the coup wave of the 1960s and 1970s was prompted by intense fears of communism's spread, which status quo defenders derived via the availability and representativeness heuristics from Fidel Castro's revolutionary success. As these perceptions of danger activated asymmetrical loss aversion, conservative sectors led by the armed forces crushed the radical left in order to forestall the specter of a communist takeover. Thus, deterrent effects proved crucial: intense concern about revolutionary diffusion drove reactionary counterdiffusion.

Yet in addition, counterrevolutionary demonstration effects also helped to propel the coup wave and the subsequent institution of bureaucratic-authoritarian rule. Nested in the region-wide backlash against the Cuban Revolution, a new regime model spread that promised reliable protection against the perceived menace of communism. Brazil's institutional military regime, which promoted economic development to cement sociopolitical stability, drew admiration and influenced the imposition of similar autocracies in the region, especially in Argentina (1966 and 1976), Chile (1973), Uruguay (1973), Bolivia (1971, albeit with limited success), and in Peru (1968, though with an initially different ideological orientation). All of these dictatorships followed in Brazil's footsteps by trying hard to transform their countries in order to preclude the spread of communism. Thus, the deterrent effect of the Cuban revolution was crucial for turning the Brazilian model attractive. To combat the communist virus, countries swallowed the bitter yet effective medicine invented in Brazil. In sum, counterdiffusion provided the fundamental impulse for the diffusion of a new right-wing regime type.

However, because this secondary diffusion unfolded in parallel with the deterrent effects of the Cuban Revolution, it did not make a big difference. To understand the limited impact of the Brazilian model, a comparison with the reverse wave of the interwar years is instructive. During the 1920s and 1930s, the strikingly novel and highly ambitious model of Italian fascism deeply shaped the wavelike advance of autocracy, as my next book will examine (preview in Weyland 2017 and in Chapter 8). This impact arose from the mixture of attractions and risks that Mussolini's innovation held for powerful establishment sectors.

After all, the Italian strongman forged a particularly potent antidote to communism, yet it revolved around a violent, plebeian mass movement led by a single overbearing leader. Moreover, fascism installed a totalitarian system that differed fundamentally from the more restrained demobilizational, hierarchical authoritarianism preferred by conservative elites (Linz 1976: 12–23; Paxton 2005: chap. 4). The powers that be therefore held profoundly ambivalent views about fascism. On the one hand, this new regime model offered special opportunities for combating communism, but on the other hand, it posed threats to their own interests and causes. Consequently, the rise of fascism prompted shifting alignments and frequent conflicts among right-wing forces (Blinkhorn 1990). This new model thus turned the reverse wave of the 1920s and 1930s into a jumble of crosscurrents and undertows that gave rise to a variety of "twisted paths" (Gerwarth 2007) – quite different from the rather uniform wave of reactionary backlash triggered by the Cuban Revolution.

Compared to bureaucratic authoritarianism, fascism was a much more innovative regime type, yet also much riskier. Accordingly, fascism exuded enormous attraction, but it also provoked a great deal of concern and even fear among status quo defenders. Mussolini's – and later Hitler's – success helped to stimulate the rise of energetic, brutal fascist movements in a wide range of countries; this contentious mass mobilization profoundly shook up politics and jeopardized the predominance of entrenched elites. The Brazilian model, by contrast, unambiguously appealed to many establishment forces: rather than threatening the sociopolitical power constellation, it restored and cemented this hierarchy. Bureaucratic authoritarianism embodied a conservative project, whereas fascism pursued more transformative, profoundly reactionary goals. Contrary to the dramatic change pushed by fascism, the restoration sought by the Brazilian generals and their emulators did not stir up trouble and conflict among the right-wing advocates of autocratic rule.

By regional standards, Brazil's developmental dictatorship certainly was novel, and therefore served as a model for coup mongers across Latin America. But by comparison to the originality of fascism, the Brazilian innovations were limited. The institutional nature of the lusophone military regime guaranteed greater solidity and infrastructural power than Latin America's personalistic dictatorships had commanded. But this institutionalization was in line with the modernization process that the region was undergoing, rather than moving in a divergent direction, as fascism with its hyperpersonalistic, charismatic leadership had done. The developmental quest for socioeconomic transformation went beyond Latin America's earlier pattern of short-term, merely corrective military dictatorships, sought to institute authoritarianism for the long run, and gave the armed forces an unusually broad range of responsibilities (Stepan 1971; Stepan 1973; Linz 2000: 205–8). But this ambitious project mainly sought to push economic growth and social improvement forward, rather than tracing a very different path, as Hitler's plan for a warrior-peasant state and a racial empire in Eastern Europe foresaw.

Because it embodied a comparatively limited departure, the Brazilian model of bureaucratic authoritarianism shaped the Latin American reverse wave less strongly than fascism affected – and shook up – the proliferation of autocracy during the interwar years. The lusophone innovation reinforced existing trends and played into the hands of powerful elites, exerting demonstration effects of moderate force. Because it did not stimulate any independent, challenging mass mobilization, it fundamentally differed from fascism by not provoking its own deterrent effects, which made the reactionary groundswell of the 1920s and 1930s so complex. For these reasons, the spread of dictatorship during the 1960s and 1970s in Latin America unfolded in a straightforward fashion, driven by a direct backlash against the radicalization inspired by the Cuban Revolution. Comparatively speaking, the Brazilian model provided mere reinforcement for conservative rescue efforts and did not have a big formative impact, as the following section of the present chapter shows.

Besides this horizontal diffusion of secondary importance, the Latin American reverse wave received another impulse from a vertical direction: as the great power in the western hemisphere, the United States helped to foment the region-wide reaction to the Cuban Revolution. The South American riptide thus allows for an empirical assessment of the impact of international power structures, which the theories of vertical promotion and imposition discussed in Chapter 2 highlight. Indeed, analysts of the spread of authoritarianism during the 1960s and 1970s used to charge the United States with a great deal of responsibility for the coup wave. According to these claims, the self-proclaimed leader of the western world in the Cold War pushed for and participated in the installation of anticommunist dictatorships among the "penetrated" client states in its region (cf. Black 1977; McSherry 2005; references mentioned in A. Pereira 2018: 6–7).

The analysis below, however, which comprises most of this chapter, finds that US influence and involvement played a fairly limited role. Diplomatic documents and thorough historical investigations show that the northern giant did indeed reinforce perceptions of the danger of communism, encourage counterrevolutionary coups, and support reactionary military regimes. But essentially, US officials usually preached to the converted: they nudged Latin American conservatives in directions in which those status quo defenders were already moving on their own. There was a convergence of perceptions and interests[1] rather than one-sided US promotion. The United

---

[1] For a US assessment of the Brazilian case, see US 1964: 12; similar A. Pereira 2018: 11.

States did not need to exert much pressure. Accordingly, US influence did not have much independent causal impact and made only a modest difference. Arguably, the Latin American reverse wave would have unfolded even without US involvement.

In fact, the initial stimulus for antileftist measures came more often from Latin America than from the northern superpower. On a number of occasions, Latin American conservatives took it upon themselves to alert Washington to the danger of radicalism and asked insistently for protection and support. For instance, Brazilian right-wingers managed to persuade US diplomats and intelligence agents of the threat posed by the populist government of President João Goulart. As historian Jonathan Brown (2017: 454–5; similar 244–5, 296–7) highlights, "US policymakers bought into the anticommunist rhetoric of the Brazilian right wing [and] believed the opposition's improbable contention that President Goulart was planning a left-wing coup d'état" (similar Leacock 1990: 59, 164, 167). Similarly, Agustín Edwards, owner of Chile's main newspaper, the staunchly conservative *El Mercurio,* in early 1970 "began to lobby the influential Americans he knew to press for aggressive US intervention" designed to "'prevent [Salvador] Allende's election.'" After that project failed, this Chilean right-winger "sought to push US covert operations toward plotting a military coup to stop Allende from assuming the presidency" (Kornbluh 2003a: 16). Through a personal meeting with leading US officials, including National Security Advisor Henry Kissinger, Edwards apparently provided important inspiration for the disastrous "Track II" operation set in motion by President Nixon on that same day (Sigmund 1977: 115; on "Track II," see discussion in the section on the Chilean coup).

The efforts of Latin American reactionaries to mobilize the United States against the radical left even assumed a transnational dimension. In 1971, for instance, Brazilian dictator Emílio Garrastazu Médici used a state visit with President Nixon to urge greater pressure on Chile's Allende administration.[2] In sum, rather than acting like an imperialist great power that pushed political forces in its client states into attacks against its ideological enemies, Washington was often the target of persistent lobbying by Latin American status quo defenders who asked their northern ally for help in protecting *their* self-interests and ideological causes. Thus, conservatives in the region used the United States and its external influence to advance their own projects against their domestic adversaries and enemies. Instead of the unidirectional influence – not to speak of imposition – postulated by vertical diffusion theories, a complex reciprocal relationship prevailed. Influence flowed both ways, based on a broad and solid convergence of perceptions and concerns.

---

[2] US White House 1971: 4–7; Harmer 2011: 101, 103, 106, 127–9.

After all, the acute fears of leftist radicalism unleashed by the Cuban Revolution had firm roots inside Latin America and were certainly not a product of North American indoctrination. Employing cognitive shortcuts, Latin American conservatives derived from Castro's success the same scary inferences that their US counterparts did. Both sides shared these fears and anticipated serious threats to sociopolitical stability, which both sought to maintain. Due to asymmetrical loss aversion, their goals and strategies coincided as well. As radicalism swept across the Americas during the 1960s and 1970s, anticommunism also spread in the north and in the south. Reactionary orientations in Latin America did not originate from US propaganda, but primarily from domestic perceptions and concerns. In fact, when the US military promoted its national security doctrine from the early 1960s onward, Latin America's armed forces, especially in the Southern Cone, had already sought and received similar teachings before, from French experts in counterrevolutionary warfare (Brands 2010: 47–8, 78–82). Yet France lacked any power over the region; and even at that earlier time, Latin American militaries were already fearful of radicalism and averse to communism.

In sum, great power promotion did not make a big difference for the autocratic wave of the 1960s and 1970s. US influence merely reinforced tendencies and trends that had their origins inside Latin America. The claims and insinuations that the CIA played a major role in coup preparations (Bandeira 1983: 126–9, 136, 140, 153, 166, 174–5; Haslam 2005: 169, 182, 211, 219, 230; Kornbluh 2003b, 2014) do not find support in the growing number of documents that have become available through declassification and the opening of archives. Instead, in each instance of authoritarian imposition, Latin Americans clearly took the lead; while they felt encouraged by US endorsement and support, they made the crucial decisions on their own. They certainly saw sufficient reasons to combat the perceived threat of radicalism; the Brazilian and Chilean militaries, for instance, only overthrew democracy in 1964 and 1973 when they found their own institutional integrity jeopardized, as Chapter 6 showed. In all likelihood, these generals and their civilian supporters would have acted in fairly similar ways even if the United States had not played any role at all. In particular, the military would eventually have stopped the descent into polarized conflict and acute crisis, which afflicted Brazil in early 1964 and especially Chile in mid-1973.

In conclusion, vertical diffusion strengthened the impetus behind counterdiffusion, but it was not the root cause or the primary force propelling these processes. Like the horizontal diffusion of the Brazilian model, great power influence did not have a big impact. The authoritarian wave that washed across Latin America during the 1960s and 1970s unfolded mainly as a direct backlash against the perceived threats emanating from the Cuban Revolution.

THE LIMITED ROLE OF HORIZONTAL DEMONSTRATION EFFECTS: BRAZIL'S MODEL OF BUREAUCRATIC AUTHORITARIANISM

While arising from a common reaction to a rash of leftist challenges, authoritarian rule spread across Latin America for a second, albeit distinctly secondary reason, namely the emergence of Brazil's military regime. This new model of autocracy helped propel the regional reverse wave both due to the way in which the generals took power and due to the ambitious project they ended up pursuing with this power. A "successful" military takeover in the largest nation was bound to encourage coup mongers throughout the region. Moreover, the moves toward institutionalization and the developmental drive of the Brazilian regime held considerable appeal for other conservative sectors and armed forces in Latin America. As a result, powerful status quo defenders took inspiration from the lusophone giant when moving forcefully against left-wingers inside their own countries.

In South America during the 1960s, military coups tended to stimulate emulation efforts. A regime overthrow was a dramatic event to which the availability heuristic drew attention. The Brazilian coup of 1964, for instance, found ample press coverage across the region (e.g., Silveira 2012). Conservatives in other countries who feared communism and who were discontented with democracy inferred from such a striking "success" that coup mongers could count on participation from powerful sectors in the armed forces and from civilian elites; that they would find support or at least acquiescence among the broader public; that few opponents would actively resist; and that those who did fight back were easily defeated and suppressed. Perceptions of similarity derived from the representativeness heuristic suggested the feasibility of coups and their replicability elsewhere. Consequently, Latin American politicians and US foreign policy makers firmly believed that the overthrow of democracy in one country would encourage similar assaults in other nations of the region (*FRUS 1961–1963*: 368–72, 865, 872).

These demonstration effects contributed to the proliferation of autocracy. For instance, the Uruguayan coup of mid-1973 had an impact on anti-Allende conspirators in Chile (Prats 1987: 409–10, 457). Yet it was the early Brazilian takeover of 1964 and the subsequent installation of bureaucratic authoritarianism that served as a particularly influential model (Bermeo 2003: 69), especially in Argentina (Mainwaring and Pérez-Liñán 2013: 143), Chile (Harmer 2012: 660–2, 680–1), Uruguay (Kaufman 1979: 18, 20, 59–60, 75; Gaspari 2003: 348–52), and Bolivia (Dunkerley 1984: 118). Systematic data collection and statistical analysis suggest that during this time period, when the Cuban Revolution made perceived threats to sociopolitical stability particularly salient, there was such a "coup contagion" (Lehoucq 2016: 8–9; see also Li and Thompson 1975).[3]

---

[3] However, the analysis of Latin American coups across the whole twentieth century by Lehoucq and Pérez-Liñán (2014: 1115–17) finds that the precedent of a coup has a deterrent effect on coup

But because military interventions had a reactive, counterrevolutionary purpose, and because radical challenges became acute in different Latin American countries at different points in time, Brazil's high-profile coup of 1964 did not unleash an immediate riptide of emulation efforts. Instead, the Latin American coup wave unfolded at a measured pace, bringing takeovers in 1966 in Argentina, 1968 in Peru, 1971 in Bolivia, 1973 in Uruguay and Chile, and 1976 in Argentina again. Thus, the armed forces did not precipitate the overthrow of democracy.

After all, most Latin American militaries had a high level of professionalism and institutionalization, which allowed for some discussion and deliberation. Despite the uniformity pressures that prevail inside the armed forces and that fueled exaggerated fears of communism, generals therefore had some capacity to filter out the starkest misperceptions. Consequently, they pursued courses of action that reflected a reasonable grasp of the domestic and international power constellation. Because Latin America's armed forces managed to broaden their bounds of rationality to some extent, they did not rush into imitation efforts right after the Brazilian power grab of 1964. Instead, they waited until left-wing challenges or political violence had turned particularly intense – and when they could therefore count on strong support from elites and substantial segments of the citizenry.

For the same reason, when militaries did decide to follow their lusophone colleagues, combat the left, and overthrow democracy, they were usually successful. Whereas rash, precipitous attempts at emulation often fail (Weyland 2014), South America in the 1960s and 1970s saw relatively few unsuccessful coups.[4] When the armed forces decided to strike, they managed to oust democratic governments and install dictatorships that held power for years. The one exception that proved the rule was Bolivia with its weakly institutionalized military, which experienced a series of coups and countercoups from 1964 to 1971 and again from 1978 to 1981 (Corbett 1972: 408–9, 416–25; Malloy and Gamarra 1988). In sum, secondary diffusion from the Brazilian model contributed to a sequence of coups executed by institutionalized militaries that proceeded with lower speed, yet higher success than the rash and ill-considered guerrilla challenges undertaken by radical left groupings.

Country experiences evince the influence of the Brazilian coup and the model of bureaucratic authoritarianism. Accordingly, the Argentine officers who overthrew democracy in mid-1966 took a good deal of inspiration from their

---

mongers in neighboring countries, and the thorough, global investigation by Miller, Joseph, and Ohl (2016) shows that in general there is no coup contagion.

[4] Interestingly, one of these exceptions, the failed *Tancazo* in Chile in June 1973, motivated the formation of the three-branch coordination mechanism by Chile's armed forces that Chapter 6 examined. Military leaders sought to learn from this failure and to design a more effective response to the country's severe crisis. One goal was to ensure that if the armed forces were to intervene, they would act in an effective manner.

northern neighbors (e.g., Rapoport and Laufer 2000: 86). After all, the Brazilian dictatorship provided a recipe for stabilizing and strengthening a conflict-ridden country, an accomplishment of particular interest and concern for Argentina, Brazil's traditional rival in the Southern Cone (Silveira 2016: 673–4, 680–5). To learn from the northern neighbor, General Juan Carlos Onganía, who ended up leading the 1966 coup, visited the Brazilian generals in mid-1965 already.[5] After a meeting with War Minister Artur da Costa e Silva, leader of the hard-line faction that was pushing the Brazilian dictatorship in a more autocratic and repressive direction, Onganía advocated a cross-national "alliance" that had a clear anticommunist bent.[6] This unusual move, which bypassed the foreign policy officials of Argentina's democratic government, shows how much the country's army leadership wanted to follow Brazil's lead in combating any perceived danger from the left.

When the Argentine coup makers then proceeded to evict President Arturo Illia in June 1966, they felt encouraged by the ease with which their Brazilian counterparts had ousted President João Goulart two years earlier. These inferences derived from the Brazilian "success" also extended to the international front, namely the role of the United States as a potential veto player. From that side, the Argentine generals anticipated no serious constraint either; after all, they had noticed that despite its professed commitment to democracy, the northern giant had quickly recognized the lusophone dictatorship in 1964 and had offered its strong support thereafter (*FRUS 1964–1968*: 302–4). Applying the representativeness heuristic, the Argentine coup mongers therefore expected US approval as well and grabbed power without hesitation. The Lyndon Baines Johnson (LBJ) administration indeed recognized Argentina's new dictatorship soon. Certainly, US diplomats initially condemned the coup and pushed hard for a quick return to democracy, because they did not see the acute leftist threat in Argentina that they had perceived under President Goulart in Brazil (*FRUS 1964–1968*: 300–2, 304, 307, 315–20, 322). But President Onganía's anticommunism, which he had already proclaimed in a high-profile speech at West Point in 1964 (excerpt in Cavarozzi 1983: 100; see also Lanusse 1977: 4–5; Rouquié 1985: 231–2), won over the US government.

The Brazilian model of bureaucratic authoritarianism also provided inspiration for the structure and goals of Argentina's new dictatorship (see De Riz 2010: 29). President Onganía instituted an autocratic regime with similar developmentalist ambitions as his lusophone counterparts. Determined to impose a sequence of economic, social, and political transformations, and

---

[5] Dame (1968: 107) also mentions an Onganía trip to Brazil in 1964, in which he incurred a "commitment . . . to Gen. Castello Branco [Brazil's authoritarian president] . . . to cooperate in stamping out Communism in the two countries."

[6] Rouquié 1985: 232–3; Marchesi 2018: 45. Onganía approached the Uruguayan military with the same proposal (Kaufman 1979: 16).

thus overcome his country's decades-long instability, Onganía rejected US pressures for the restoration of free elections and planned to stay in office indefinitely. Interestingly, Argentina's authoritarian leader overshot in his learning. Whereas the Brazilian regime kept Congress open most of the time, held legislative elections on schedule, and allowed two newly created, moderate parties to compete, President Onganía – like all later imitators of the Brazilian model – closed down politics in the public sphere completely (Laguado 2006: 253).[7] Because Brazil's evolving regime had considerable difficulties making authoritarian realities compatible with a semidemocratic façade, its emulators in the rest of Latin America preferred a clean break by outlawing civilian political activities. This determination to impose harsh, full-scale dictatorship was especially strong in cases in which the preceding democracy had faced the most acute threats and had suffered from chaotic misgovernance, as in Chile up to 1973 and in Argentina before 1976.

Another reason why secondary diffusion became more sinister over time was the gradual hardening of the Brazilian autocracy. Thus, the model itself changed significantly. In response to student and labor protests and a challenge from Congress, the Brazilian regime turned more dictatorial and repressive in the late 1960s, as Chapter 6 explained. The government of Emílio Garrastazu Médici, in particular (1969–74), engaged in large-scale torture and embarked on brutal campaigns against guerrilla movements. Therefore, the Chilean and Argentine generals followed the Brazilian model not only in the institutionalization of military rule, but also in the nasty techniques to crush the radical left (on Chile, see Lyles 2016: 369–70, 397–401; see also Huneeus 2007: 67, n. 101). Once again, however, the emulators overshot in their learning, due to the graver threats they faced. The Chilean and Argentine dictatorships of the 1970s employed torture, assassinations, and forced disappearances on a vastly larger scale than the Brazilians ever did.

Besides serving as a source of inspiration for conservative sectors, Brazil's fiercely anticommunist autocracy under General Médici also sought actively to spread authoritarian rule by combating the left and supporting reactionary forces in other South American countries. In this vein, Brasília allegedly helped to prevent an election victory by Uruguay's radical leftist coalition, Frente Amplio (Broad Front), in 1971 (Gaspari 2003: 351; NSA 2002). Similarly, Brazil's ambassador in Chile, Antônio Cândido da Câmara Canto, channeled subsidies from Brazilian businesses to Chile's right-wing parties and cooperated with Chilean generals in preparing the coup of 1973 (Davis 1985: 331–2; Gaspari 2003: 348, 355). After Allende's overthrow, Brazilian torturers allegedly interrogated compatriots who in earlier years had fled into exile in Santiago (Burns 2014). Brazil's most consequential involvement occurred in Bolivia, where Colonel Hugo Banzer used direct Brazilian (and US) support to

[7] Some politicians in Argentina's authoritarian coalition, however, "suggested a two-party system similar to the system tried in Brazil" (Jordan 1970: 88).

evict the socialist Juan José Torres regime and grab power in 1971.[8] Thus, adding to the demonstration effects of the Brazilian coup and the appeal of the resulting military regime, the Médici government took direct steps to help install similar autocracies in other countries of the region.

In sum, the demonstration effects of the "successful" coup of 1964, the dissemination of the new regime model that emerged in Brazil during the 1960s, and the deliberate promotion efforts spearheaded by Brasília in the early 1970s reinforced and shaped the spread of reactionary autocracy. Because the military took and usually exercised power as an institution, these dictatorships had much firmer organization and greater infrastructural power than the personalistic despotism that had earlier prevailed in Latin America. As a result, they commanded considerable capacity to propel economic modernization, enact some social programs to alleviate poverty and envelop poorer strata in clientelistic dependencies, and reorient the education system and cultural life, not only through censorship and purges, but also by propagating their own conservative and anticommunist mentalities. Driven by the fundamental goal to impose controlled change from the top down in order to forestall uncontrollable revolution from the bottom up, and determined to prevent the reemergence of radicalism in the future, these institutional autocracies pursued greater ambitions than the "men on horseback" of yesteryear.

Besides the concrete demonstration effects of the Brazilian precedent, this new type of military regime had its theoretical foundation in the National Security Doctrine that gained widespread support across Latin America (Pion-Berlin 1989; Rivas Nieto 2008). In the 1960s, the Brazilian regime turned into the prototype advocated by this doctrine. This strategy of proactive defense against left-wing radicalism originated in the French writings about "the revolutionary war," which found immediate resonance in countries such as Argentina, Brazil, Chile,[9] and Peru, and later received important US inputs as well. As the northern superpower drew lessons from its increasing involvement in unconventional warfare in Vietnam, it developed systematic tactics of counterinsurgency, including rather unpleasant methods for forcibly extracting information from captured enemy fighters. The United States heavily promoted this National Security Doctrine, especially by training thousands of Latin American military officers (Gill 2004). Yet the fact that the Brazilian regime actually began to put these ideas into practice, and that it seemed to achieve a great deal of "success," was crucial for validating this

---

[8] On Brazil's role, see Gallardo Lozada 1972: 401–3, 411–12; Dunkerley 1984: 183, 197–8, 201; Malloy and Gamarra 1988: 68, 80, 91–4. Given the deep divisions inside the Bolivian military and the risk of a total breakdown of state authority, the United States seems to have had closer connections to coup plotters than in other Latin American countries, which had much higher levels of institutionalization (*FRUS* 1969–1976, vol. E-10, docs. 76a, 101, 102, 104, 106).

[9] While Nunn (1976: 261–6) claimed that – unique in South America – the Chilean military had not embraced an ideology focused on internal security, Bawden (2012) found evidence that French teachings on "the revolutionary war" did have an impact.

doctrine in the eyes of military officers and for propelling its widespread dissemination.

While pursuing fundamentally conservative goals, the National Security Doctrine included important modernizing elements, especially in its effort to stimulate socioeconomic development and in the technocratic approach it employed for this purpose (Stepan 1971: chap. 8; O'Donnell 1979: 76–85). Clearly, one reason why Brazil's dictatorship looked successful and attracted imitators was that from 1968 to 1974, it achieved sky-high rates of economic growth, which it advertised as a "miracle." But this developmental promise and temporary achievement never gave Latin America's bureaucratic-authoritarian regimes much intrinsic normative appeal, as fascism had eradiated it during the interwar years (Weyland 2017). Accordingly, the new dictatorships did not claim genuine legitimacy as permanent alternatives to democracy (O'Donnell and Schmitter 1986: 15). Instead, led again by Brazil, they sought to reorganize domestic politics and lay the ground for more resilient, "stronger" forms of democracy in the future.[10] Thus, compared to earlier rounds of reactionary autocrats, the Latin American coup makers of the 1960s and 1970s had relatively limited ambitions.

In conclusion, Brazil's model of bureaucratic authoritarianism gave an additional impulse to the autocratic wave of the 1960s and 1970s, which resulted primarily from a backlash against the left-wing radicalism strengthened by the Cuban Revolution. The lusophone coup exerted demonstration effects, and the development-oriented dictatorship inspired emulation as well. But Brazil's military regime was not nearly as novel, ambitious, and controversial as fascism. Therefore, its impact remained limited. This precedent and model reinforced ongoing trends to some extent, but did not cause the cleavages among right-wingers that fascism provoked. Therefore, Latin America's process of counterdiffusion in the 1960s and 1970s unfolded rather smoothly, by contrast to the refracted, jumbled reverse wave of the interwar years.

THE LIMITED ROLE OF VERTICAL PROMOTION: US INFLUENCE IN THE LATIN AMERICAN COUP WAVE

Vertical clout, namely the involvement and machinations of the regional "hegemon" United States, also reinforced the proliferation of reactionary autocracy in Latin America. But like horizontal diffusion from Brazil, great power influence was not the decisive cause for the reverse wave. Instead, domestic initiatives prompted by the deterrent effects of the Cuban Revolution were crucial in every case of democratic breakdown. Certainly, the United States encouraged, facilitated, and supported this reactionary

---

[10] Conselho de Segurança Nacional 1968: 2; interview with Brazilian ex-President Ernesto Geisel in
    D'Araujo and Castro (1997: 395–6, 443–5); Rouquié 1987: 345–50.

counterdiffusion. But Washington's influence did not make a big difference in the imposition of military autocracy. The following sections substantiate these arguments, which diverge from viewpoints that long had widespread support among Latin America specialists.

Many left-wing critics have claimed that the main impulse for the reverse wave emanated from the US determination to protect its client states by combating Cuba-inspired radicals and by pushing for anticommunist authoritarianism (see, e.g., Bandeira 1983: 126–9, 136, 140, 153, 166, 174–5; Teixeira 1992: 8). This line of reasoning embodies the theoretical logic of external pressure approaches, which attribute to great powers the capacity and will to shape regime developments in their sphere of influence. Accordingly, the threat posed by the irruption of communism into the western hemisphere induced the United States to suspend its proclaimed preference for liberal democracy and to impose right-wing authoritarianism as a protective device against the political fallout of the Cuban Revolution. In this view, the rash of right-wing coups arose from Washington's defensive machinations in the Cold War against the Soviet Union.

Adherents of external pressure arguments highlight the shift in the US posture in 1964, when the LBJ administration moved to support anticommunist autocracy. President Kennedy had responded to the Cuban Revolution with his reformist Alliance for Progress, advocating democracy and denouncing military interventions, as mentioned in Chapter 4. In line with this reformist policy orientation, the United States tried to prevent the coup in Argentina in 1962 (Brown 2017: 239), condemned the military takeover in Peru in 1962 (Naftali 2001: 17, 26), and pushed hard for a quick restoration of democracy in the Andean nation.[11] This vertical pressure was one crucial reason why interventionist sectors in both militaries lost out. In Argentina, where violent conflict inside the armed forces erupted, legalist currents defeated hard-liners who saw Peronist populism as paving the ground for communist extremism and who therefore advocated long-term military rule. In Peru, developmentalist sectors, who sought longer-lasting authoritarianism to impose solutions for the country's socioeconomic problems and thus take the wind out of the sail of radicalism, also lost out (Kuczynski 1977: 44–8). Thus, in the early 1960s, the United States provided unusually strong and consistent support for democracy and thereby helped to forestall the spread of military regimes that wanted to combat the diffusion of communism with a potent mixture of repression and developmental efforts.

But with Fidel Castro's ever firmer embrace of communism and the remarkable radicalization gripping many other Latin American countries, US foreign policy makers started to back away from this prodemocratic posture. Under President Kennedy already, diplomats and foreign policymakers questioned this principled stance and suggested greater acceptance of military

---

[11] *FRUS* 1961–1963: 859–61, 864–7, 870, 873, 876; Walter 2010: 19–23; Packenham 1973: 71–3.

interventions, which might be required for stemming the advance of extremism in Latin America (*FRUS* 1961–1963: 150–3; Packenham 1973: 73–5).

President Johnson then completed this change of course and embraced reactionary rule as the lesser evil to forestall communism (Smith 1995: 226–7; Wright 2001: 69–70). Specifically, Thomas Mann, Assistant Secretary of State for Inter-American Affairs, announced this new "doctrine" in March 1964 (Szulc 1964; Parker 1979: 61–3; Packenham 1973: 95–7) – not coincidentally, just a couple of weeks before the military coup in Brazil. After all, as the embassy personnel stationed in the lusophone giant had advised, the growing opposition to President Goulart seemed to need prior indication of US endorsement to strengthen its spine (Gaspari 2002: 97–101). In particular, the legalist tradition prevailing among Brazilian officers (*FRUS* 1961–1963: 497) made it important for the United States to guarantee that it would not condemn an effort to preempt the perceived threat of President Goulart's radical power grab with forceful means. The Mann Doctrine and the suspiciously quick US recognition of the Brazilian coup regime sent a clear signal and encouraged antileftist conspirators across the region.[12]

According to a view that used to be widely embraced by Latin America experts, the Mann Doctrine then led the United States from the mid-1960s onward to play a crucial role in preparing and helping to organize military coups designed to oust leftist governments and crush radical movements in the region (see, e.g., Rapoport and Laufer 2000; Sanchez 2003: 224–5). For this purpose, the northern hegemon drew on its long-standing connections to Latin American militaries, which it systematically strengthened after the Cuban Revolution through extensive training programs for officers, the propagation of the National Security Doctrine, and generous subsidies for the armed forces throughout the southern subcontinent (Gill 2004; McSherry 2005: chap. 2). The United States allegedly used the resulting influence to promote the spread of reactionary autocracy in the region.[13] In fact, many scholars claim that North American diplomats, military officers, or intelligence agents directly participated in conspiracies, encouraged repressive crackdowns against the left, and helped to forge coup coalitions (see, e.g., Bandeira 1983: 126–9, 136,

---

[12] Thyne's statistical analysis of Latin American coups indeed finds a powerful effect of hostile US signals (Thyne 2010: 453–5, 459). But his study does not consider domestic opposition by powerful forces, including the military, which is crucial for coups – and which is probably highly correlated with hostile US signals. Given the frequent anticommunist convergence between domestic sectors and US foreign policy officials, the actual causal effect of US signals is therefore unclear.

[13] In his critical analysis of the Kennedy administration, Rabe (1999: 63, 68, 71, 197) attributes a great deal of powerful agency to the United States and emphasizes its deleterious impact in destabilizing left-wing governments and preparing the ground for anticommunist military coups. Applying a similar line of reasoning, Winn (2010: 267–8) emphasizes "the involvement or complicity of the US government in the events leading up to the coup" of 1973 in Chile.

140, 153, 166, 174–5; Haslam 2005: 167, 169, 182, 211, 219, 230; see also Kornbluh 2003b, 2014).

In theoretical terms, these claims point to several mechanisms of vertical diffusion.[14] Adherents of the great power approach highlight direct pressures and leverage, such as economic sanctions and the denial of aid, which in the Chilean case have given rise to the common accusation of an "economic blockade" against the Allende government (Farnsworth 1974: 131–4; Kornbluh 2003b: 82–6). Other arguments emphasize linkages, especially US support for opposition forces in politics and society and close connections with many military leaders. Allegedly, these connections allowed for direct influence, including actual participation of US diplomats or CIA agents in the organization of coups (see, e.g., Bandeira 1983: 126–9; Haslam 2005: 169, 182, 211, 219, 230). Adherents of great power arguments also emphasize the impact of US values and ideas, which extend from the promotion of anticommunism to propaganda against specific leftist and populist leaders and to the teaching of counterinsurgency techniques, including torture (e.g., Black 1977: chaps. 9–13). In line with vertical diffusion arguments, critics allege that these flows of ideas and values were predominantly unidirectional: they originated in the United States and shaped the thinking of Latin American conservatives.

Contrary to these frequent claims and suspicions,[15] however, the historical evidence, reinforced by the recent declassification of documents, shows that the US role in the Latin American coup wave was distinctly limited. In every country, the main initiative for overthrowing left-leaning democracies lay with domestic actors. US pressures helped to weaken some of these administrations, especially the Allende government in Chile, but their problems arose mainly from internal resistance and their own problematic policy decisions. Similarly, US support for opposition forces was limited and avoided involvement with the most radical and disruptive forces.

The United States did have close connections with military officers and frequently discussed the threats posed by left-wing administrations. But contrary to vertical pressure arguments, these exchanges were far from one-way streets. Instead, Latin American generals had their own independent reasons for intense concern about domestic radicalism; given that Fidel Castro had fusilladed their Cuban colleagues, they needed no warnings from Washington. Anticommunism was not an invention of the United States but had a long tradition inside Latin America. Latin American militaries' urge to

---

[14] However, the United States rarely employed the strongest means of great power influence, namely direct coercion, not to speak of military occupation, which Washington had used in Austria, Germany, Italy, and Japan after World War II. In Latin America during the Cold War, the invasion of the Dominican Republic remained an exception; and this US-led military intervention did not dislodge an established government, as the country was racked by civil war at the time (Smith 1995: 228–31).

[15] See, e.g., Rapoport and Laufer 2000: 71, 77; Gill 2004: 79, 113; Kornbluh 2004, 2014; Schmitz 2006: 94–102; Hershberg and Kornbluh 2014; see criticism in Fermandois 2003: 8.

combat left-wing extremists did not originate in the National Security Doctrine that the United States promoted from the early 1960s onward. Indeed, years before, armed forces in the region had already begun to absorb French teachings about "the revolutionary war" derived from the brutal struggles in Vietnam and Algeria. Thus, the strong anticommunism prevailing inside Latin America during the 1960s and 1970s was not a product of US influence. Instead, it arose from a coincidence of perceptions, values, and concerns. Latin American conservatives and centrists did not need the United States to alert them to the danger posed by radical leftism.[16]

As anticommunism had firm domestic roots in Latin America and as internal political forces, especially military leaders, took the main initiative in overthrowing radical governments, the most direct responsibility of the United States was that the northern hegemon did not seek to forestall coups, as President Kennedy had tried to do in the early 1960s. Instead, US acceptance allowed for military interventions and provided encouragement for combating left-wing extremism. Yet the United States did not hold direct responsibility for any of these coups, and was far from providing the main impetus for the overthrow of democracy. In all cases, Latin American actors, especially military officials, conservative politicians, and business leaders, bore the primary responsibility. Driven by powerful loss aversion activated by the advance of leftist radicalism, they took the initiative in plotting coups and played the leading role in executing them. In all likelihood, these coups would have happened sooner or later, even if the US had stayed neutral.

This emphasis on Latin American responsibility does not deny US influence.[17] US acquiescence and support did matter, especially by allowing for the proliferation of lasting authoritarian regimes. Whereas under President Kennedy's pressure, the Peruvian military, for instance, had quickly relinquished power after the 1962 coup, they retained control of the government for more than a decade after evicting democracy again in 1968. One crucial reason was that by the end of the 1960s the protagonist of the "Free World" no longer ostracized coup makers. Thus, the change in the US position in 1963–4 and its codification in the Mann Doctrine was clear, marked, and influential. As a permissive cause for authoritarian rule, it had a significant impact – less on the coup wave as such than on the institution of anticommunist dictatorships thereafter. Acquiescence and support by the regional great power helped to pave the way for the spread of reactionary autocracy during the 1960s and 1970s.

[16] See for Colombia's democratic governments, for instance, Maullin (1971: 86–8) and Randall (1992: 219).

[17] This subsection focuses on the role of US government officials. For a comprehensive analysis of the multiple ways in which a host of US-based actors, including private business and the media, "penetrated" Brazil and thus contributed to the overthrow of democracy and the consolidation of authoritarian rule after 1964, see Black (1977).

Under the shock of the Cuban Revolution, the northern giant also provided a great deal of financial support and military assistance to its southern clients (Rouquié 1987: 131–4; Sanchez 2003). Moreover, the United States helped shape the ideational climate for the diffusion of authoritarianism by systematically disseminating the National Security Doctrine, which it enriched with lessons from its frustrating experiences in Vietnam. Over the years, thousands of Latin American officers underwent training in US institutions, both in the mainland and the Panama Canal Zone (Gill 2004). Even in the promotion of ideas and values – particularly anticommunism – the US role was more limited than often assumed. For instance, a surprisingly small number of Brazilian officers participated in US courses on counterinsurgency; most visitors took classes on standard military topics, such as artillery, radar technology, and engineering (Martins Filho 1999: 77–8; Lyles 2016: 298, 315–18, 327; see also *FRUS 1961–1963*: 477).

Furthermore, as mentioned above, the roots of the national security doctrine lay in French teachings about counterinsurgency derived from Algeria and Indochina (Martins Filho 2012),[18] which had an early impact on the Argentine military (Mazzei 2002), quickly diffused to Brazil and Peru, and soon affected other Latin American countries as well.[19] Moreover, these original French ideas exerted a much stronger effect than their later US elaborations. Interviewed about the motivations of the 1964 coup against President Goulart, for instance, Brazilian generals highlighted the French teachings, not US contributions.[20] One main reason was that the French doctrine had a much more comprehensive scope than its US counterpart. Above all, it assigned the military an expansive role in politics and thus offered a powerful justification for Latin American generals' long-standing tendencies toward political interventionism (Martins Filho n.d.: 7–9; Novaro and Palermo 2003: 91; Brands 2010: 79–80). Whereas US teachings sought to uphold democracy, the tougher French version directly questioned liberal restraints on the exercise of power, which Latin American militaries also saw as problematic obstacles to the effective fight against communism (Lyles 2016: 309–10, 363–5).

Altogether, despite its significance, Washington's influence was by no means the decisive factor propelling the authoritarian wave (Stepan 1971: 124–33; Rouquié 1987: 130–50; Harmer 2011; Shiraz 2011). Latin American right-wingers were the main protagonists, who would probably have installed anticommunist autocracies even without US involvement. After all, most

---

[18] I owe this point and reference to David Pion-Berlin, personal communication, February 6, 2013.
[19] Martins Filho (n.d.: 4–5, 15). For instance, in the late 1950s already, Peruvian officers sought training in "antisubversive techniques" in France and visited Algeria in the midst of the brutal colonial war (Monteforte Toledo 1973: 39; see also Einaudi 1971: 27, 32; Nunn 1979: 416). For the impact of French teachings among the Chilean military, see Bawden (2012: 13–14).
[20] General Octávio Costa in D'Araujo, Dillon Soares, and Castro 1994: 78; see Rouquié 1987: 143, 283; Ferreira 1963: 25–6; Oliveira 1964: 30, 36, 38, 45.

Latin American militaries commanded professional autonomy and institutional strength (Stepan 1971). They had long embraced and constitutionally enshrined the mission to safeguard their country's national security. Moreover, these coercive state agencies had for decades embraced an anticommunist orientation that the Cuban Revolution turned virulent and that was not the product of US sermons. For all of these reasons, Latin American militaries acted largely on their own account in forcefully confronting the perceived threat of Castro-inspired radicalism.[21] The Latin American coup wave was not primarily the result of vertical promotion by the regional "hegemon."

Methodologically, of course, it is difficult to prove the absence or weakness of influence. Given obvious incentives for secrecy, how to show convincingly, for instance, that US diplomats and CIA operatives did not instigate and organize coups? When archives were largely closed, widely held theories of US hegemony and Latin American dependency gave rise to ample suspicions. Yet as more and more historical sources have been declassified, long-standing conjectures can be checked against the evidence. Interestingly, the opening of archives has yielded very few if any "smoking guns" concerning direct US involvement.[22] Due to this unexpected and striking null finding, academic historians and other thoroughgoing observers hailing from the United States, Europe, and Latin America have distanced themselves from earlier analyses that put the primary blame for Latin America's reactionary wave on the northern powerhouse (Brands 2010: 81, 257–62).

With respect to the Brazilian case, for instance, journalist Elio Gaspari (2002: 102) concludes from decades of painstaking research about Brazil's military regime, including unprecedented access to leading decision makers and to a wealth of confidential documentation: "Not one Brazilian, civilian or military, participated in the ouster of João Goulart because the United States wanted that." Similarly, historian Jonathan Brown derives from his comprehensive, careful archival studies the finding that "rather than Washington, it was the Brazilians themselves who set the agenda and the pace for the overthrow" of President Goulart. "US diplomats resembled fans cheering for the team on the right, while [the Brazilian] players on the field actually determined the ultimate victors" (Brown 2017: 304; see also 220–1, 244–5, 296–7).

---

[21] Accordingly, Lyles' (2016: 187, 190, 196–7, 206, 215, 291, 298–300, 313–23, 368–9, 373, 376–7, 397, 460–2) wide-ranging, thorough analysis of "US army internal security training . . . in the 1960s" documents with how much "agency" the political leaders of many Latin American countries responded to US suggestions, recommendations, and pressures.

[22] Note that the CIA extensively chronicled the disastrous Track II Plan of September to November 1970 in a memorandum of November 18, 1970, which included the open admission that the "CIA focused on provoking a military coup" (*FRUS 1969–1976*, vol. 11, part 2, chap. 1: 211; see also 215–18). Conversely, it is telling that despite the wide-ranging declassification of documents in recent decades, no reference to any equivalent involvement in Allende's overthrow in 1973 has appeared.

The US did not help plot the overthrow of Argentine democracy in 1966 either.[23] As a wealth of documents show, its diplomats were not even well-informed about the coup preparations, not to speak of encouraging them. On the contrary, the embassy responded to rumors about military conspiracies by expressing "our position of strong opposition to coup against Illia government" (*FRUS 1964–1968*: 300; see also 301–2, 315, 326). The limits of US influence became obvious when the generals struck anyway. In fact, once army leader Juan Carlos Onganía had grabbed power, he proved impervious to insistent US demands to convoke new elections quickly. Disregarding American threats of sanctions, the dictator made it clear that he intended to stay in power for a long time so he could transform his country and prevent the resurgence of Peronist or leftist radicalism in the future (*FRUS 1964–1968*: 317–22). Thus, Argentina's armed forces acted with a great deal of independence in toppling a democratic government and installing an ambitious dictatorship. Their "embrace of . . . the counterrevolutionary ideology was not imposed from the outside" by the United States. "The myth of the Latin American officer brainwashed in Fort Gulick [a US training camp for Latin American officers] does not withstand a comparative assessment," as Alain Rouquié (1985: 353), a leading expert on the Argentine military, emphasized.

In the same vein, the Argentine military clearly acted in an autonomous fashion when planning and executing the coup of 1976. Chastened by the rather critical Senate investigation of US covert action against Chile's Salvador Allende (US Senate 1976; cf. *FRUS 1969–1976*, vol. 11, part 2, chap. 1: 106–7), US diplomats and CIA agents made every effort to stay on the sidelines when Argentina's democracy was teetering close to collapse in the mid-1970s. To avoid even the impression of involvement, they went so far as to turn away Argentine informants who wanted to update them about the coup preparations (*FRUS 1969–1976*, vol. 11, part 2, chap. 1: 2, 90–1, 106–7, 113–14). Accordingly, Perelli (1993: 27) categorically "refuses to consider the armed forces . . . as an armed robot blindly following directives coming from the center of power in Washington, D.C."

As regards the most-discussed coup in Latin America's autocratic wave of the 1960s and 1970s, namely the 1973 ouster of President Allende in Chile, historian Tanya Harmer (2011: 272) finds in her thorough study that "the United States did not manipulate or force its Chilean contacts to do anything that they did not want to." Instead, the coup makers expressed "'extreme pride that they managed their own coup without the assistance of the USG [US government] or other nations.'" Long-standing country specialists Simon Collier and William Sater concur, after highlighting US efforts to undermine

---

[23] Similarly, the United States sought to prevent the military overthrow of President Arturo Frondizi in 1962, and only reluctantly accepted the subsequent government, which constituted a civilian façade for effective military domination (*FRUS 1961–1963*: 362–3, 366–7, 371–2, 375–9, 390).

the Chilean economy and back opposition groupings: "It may be doubted, however, whether the CIA made very much difference: sad as it is to have to say this, the real 'destabilization' of Chile was the work of Chileans" (Collier and Sater 1996: 355). Accordingly, the outstanding analysis by political scientist Arturo Valenzuela (1978) focuses first and foremost on internal dynamics, especially the deepening polarization among political parties and social forces inside Chile; after its clumsy efforts to prevent Allende's assumption of power in 1970, the US government played a limited role (Valenzuela 1978: 48–9, 56–7, 120, n. 42).

While opponents of these views continue to suggest much greater US involvement (Kornbluh 2014), their dogged efforts to uncover actual evidence have failed (Fermandois 2003: 12, 22), as the archival material dug up by these critics themselves shows (see, e.g., Kornbluh 2003b; see also *FRUS 1969–1976*, vol. 21). With the increasing opening of archives and the continuing declassification of documents, this remarkable failure to find incriminatory documentation is telling and casts ever more doubt on their claims.[24]

Altogether, the tremendous power of the United States and its great concern about the spread of radicalism in Latin America helped to open the door for the Latin American coup wave of the 1960s and 1970s. But Americans did not play a leading role and often stayed on the sidelines while Latin Americans proceeded to overthrow one democracy after the other. Accordingly, vertical clout had significantly less impact than the horizontal dynamics that drove the spread of military regimes, especially the backlash against Castroite communism, which was reinforced to some extent by the promise of the Brazilian model as a protective mechanism.

THE UNITED STATES AND THE BRAZILIAN COUP OF 1964

To offer some in-depth substantiation of the claim that Latin American status quo defenders held primary responsibility for the imposition of reactionary authoritarianism, attention turns to the prototypical case of Brazil, which then provided an additional impetus for the autocratic wave in the region. How deeply was the United States involved in the ouster of President Goulart? Interestingly, long before the overthrow of Brazilian democracy, US foreign policy makers discussed a wide range of contingencies and options, which included pressure on Brazil's populist leader to retreat from radicalism, a military coup, and even a direct US military intervention (US NSC 1962; US State Department, Latin American Policy Committee 1963; Excerpts 1963; see Leacock 1990: 187, 213–14; Loureiro 2017: 67–73).

---

[24] Focusing on Brazil in the early 1960s, A. Pereira (2018: 6, 11, 16) similarly argues that newly available documents show significantly less US involvement in coup machinations than has often been claimed.

The latter scenario was foreseen for the outside possibility that President Goulart might "really institute, or try to institute, a revolutionary regime, a Fidelista type of a regime if you will" (Excerpts 1963: 7–9); or "if there were clear evidence of Soviet Bloc or Cuban intervention on the other side" (US 1964: 5). In this kind of case, the northern hegemon could feel compelled to prevent a second Cuba or, as US diplomats framed it in recognition of Brazil's continental size and geostrategic significance, "the China of the 1960s" (Gordon 1964a: 8; see also *FRUS 1964–1968*: 430, 438). But Washington regarded it as exceedingly unlikely that the task of suppressing the radical left would fall directly to the United States. Instead, Brazilian status quo defenders would surely take the lead in such a counterrevolutionary initiative.

Accordingly, US foreign policy makers estimated the probability of a military coup as fairly high and discussed extensively how their government should respond to the ongoing conspiracies spearheaded by a variety of Brazilian elites (Leacock 1990: 131, 177–83, 191–2, 198). In their view, the strongest groupings of conservatives sought to defend the existing democratic regime against the feared power grab by Brazil's increasingly vocal and mobilized radical sectors.[25] The biggest risks would arise from a forceful takeover by procommunist groupings or from a self-coup with which President Goulart might try to perpetuate himself in power (Muricy 1993: 506–7, 514; *FRUS 1961–1963*: 509; Fico 2008: 90, 93–4, 98).

Overestimating the strength of extremist forces in society and inside the government and military, US planners feared that conservative attempts to block these risks could provoke substantial violence, if not a full-scale civil war (Parker 1979: 67–70). Given this anticipated danger, US diplomats in March 1964 discreetly strengthened the spine of the opposition to Goulart (cf. Leacock 1990: 198). Washington also prepared potential support operations by the US military, which included a naval task force sailing toward Brazil and carrying fuel and ammunition. In these ways, the United States communicated to Brazilian coup mongers that it endorsed their efforts and would back them up in case of need (Gaspari 2002: 97–101; A. Pereira 2018: 14–15). Clearly, then, the western superpower was indirectly involved in the termination of the lusophone democracy.

But the ample available documentation also makes it very clear that the coup was overwhelmingly the result of internal Brazilian initiatives. US officials were certainly not the ringleaders in the drama. The initial conspiracies, which started immediately after President Goulart's assumption of power in 1961, came from a few renegade generals or small right-wing groupings, which did not command much clout inside the armed forces.[26] US diplomats kept their

---

[25] The US was, however, critical of right-wingers that were "too fanatically anti-Goulart," especially Governor Carlos Lacerda of Guanabara (the city of Rio de Janeiro), and rejected "the reactionary proposals of the far right" (*FRUS 1961–1963*: 506 and 512, respectively).

[26] For instance, many officers did not hold Marshal Odylio Denys, one of the early protagonists (Denys 1967), in very high esteem (Muricy 1993: 504–5).

distance from this early plotting (Parker 1979: 10–11; Excerpts 1963: 10; *FRUS 1961–1963*: 510) and were unwilling to support military intervention (US Government 1963: 3, 6), especially because President Kennedy's Alliance for Progress condemned coup mongering (US 1964: 1). In fact, until right before the eventual overthrow of President Goulart, US Embassy officials hoped for a formally legal denouement to the growing crisis,[27] such as pressure on Goulart to back off from radicalism or the more or less "induced" resignation of Brazil's chief executive.[28] A military coup, which in the eyes of US diplomats held a substantial risk of failure or of unleashing considerable violence, if not a civil war,[29] was not their preferred option; instead, until right up to the coup, they "hope[d] the ship of state can stay afloat until the [presidential] elections" scheduled for 1965.[30] Moreover, the Mann Doctrine, which announced US toleration of coups, was adopted only in mid-March 1964, when coup plotting by Brazilian generals was already long under way.

Interestingly, US officials deliberately stepped aside as the likelihood of a coup increased ever more obviously. In March 1964, domestic escalation, especially governmental acceptance and apparent encouragement of the corrosion of military hierarchy and discipline (Denys 1967: 11), prompted the formation of a broad coup coalition that began to make President Goulart's ouster viable. Highly respected General Humberto Castello Branco left behind his legalistic scruples and took the lead in the effort to unseat the populist president and his radical allies (Dulles 1978: 306, 321–6, 330–42, 349–50, 378; Gordon 1964a: 5–8; Parker 1979: 57–61). Only at that point (not before: cf. CIA 1963) did the overthrow of democracy turn into a realistic option (Stepan 1978a: 120–9). Yet exactly at this moment, US diplomats reduced their contacts inside the Brazilian military, confining it to information gathering (cf. Walters 1964; Dulles' interview with Walters 1975: 7);[31] they deliberately forwent advice and influence. As US Ambassador Lincoln Gordon informed Washington, "I have had no direct contact with military plotters" (Gordon 1964b: 1; similar Gordon 1975: 1–3).

The purpose of this self-restraint was to avoid giving President Goulart any opportunity to invoke nationalism and anti-Americanism and thus shore up his ever more precarious hold on power (see US 1964: 1, 5). US military attaché Vernon Walters, in particular, who had the closest connections to Brazilian generals due to the lasting legacies of joint cooperation in World War II,

---

[27] Gordon 1964a: 2; US NSC 1964: 1; *FRUS 1964–1968*: 398.

[28] US NSC 1962; Gordon 1963; US State Department, Latin American Policy Committee 1963: 4; see A. Pereira 2018: 12.

[29] Excerpts 1963: 7; CIA 1964a: 2; Gordon 1964a: 7, 10; see also A. Pereira 2018: 14, 16.

[30] *FRUS 1964–1968*: 409; similar 413 – a document from March 28, 1964! See also Smith 2015: 263, 265; and from a Brazilian perspective, Fico 2008: 77.

[31] Accordingly, the weekly report by the US Embassy in Rio written on March 25, 1964, just a few days before the coup, gives no indication of US awareness that a military intervention was imminent (US State Department 1964, document A-1152).

intentionally loosened his contacts with his long-standing friend Castello Branco.[32] As Walters emphasizes (1978: 382, 390–1, 396), Brazilian generals were far too independent-minded and insistent on national sovereignty to look kindly on any trace of US pressure or involvement. Even mere insinuations, Walters claims (1978: 382), would have risked backfiring and ruining his close relationship with the new head of the conspiracy, who ended up becoming president (similar Dulles' interview with Gordon 1965).[33]

This deliberate self-limitation is noteworthy because coup preparations advanced at a feverish pace, and the loyalties of good parts of the Brazilian military, at all levels of hierarchy, remained unclear. Moreover, many of the leading conspirators expected a coup to unleash armed struggles in various regions of the country. Thus, the United States refrained from involvement not because the whole affair was wrapped up and success was already assured; on the contrary, uncertainty ran very high. In fact, like domestic conspirators (see Dulles' interview with Kruel 1975: 4), North American diplomats feared that the Goulart government had gotten wind of the plotting and would dismiss or even imprison prospective coup leaders. Yet on the other hand, a precipitous move designed to prevent the government's self-protection efforts risked challenging the president with insufficient support, which could easily result in failure. Thus, the exact timing of the attempt to unseat President Goulart involved a variety of high-stakes gambles (Dulles 1978: 350–3, 356, 366–7).

When the coup did happen, it indeed unfolded in a haphazard way (Muricy 1993: 527, 533, 540; see also Leacock 1990: 207–10). One general forged ahead before Castello Branco had given the signal, ushering in a drama in which important military groupings unexpectedly switched allegiance and narrowly avoided violent clashes. At this critical juncture, when Brazil's fate seemed to hang in the balance, US diplomats desperately tried to keep track of the fast-changing developments; but there is no indication at all that they took a direct role in the showdown and brought any influence or pressure to bear.[34] As Ambassador Gordon (1975: 3) emphasized, "the Brazilian revolution [coup] of 1964 was a 100 percent Brazilian movement – not 99 44/100 percent, but 100 percent" (similar *FRUS 1964–1968*: 457).

In sum, this examination of the Brazilian military takeover shows that the United States did not organize this affair (Parker 1979: 102–4), despite the tremendous importance that the northern hegemon attributed to its biggest South American ally. American diplomats realized that their influence was

---

[32] US State Department 1964, Telegram March 27: 2; Dulles 1978: 332, 345–8, 377; confirmed by Muricy 1993: 522; see also *FRUS 1964–1968*: 438. As a result, the United States learned less than four days before the coup that "General Castello Branco finally accepted leadership of forces determined to resist Goulart coup or Communist takeover" (US State Department 1964, Telegram March 27: 1). Yet even at that point, US officials believed that "plotters do not appear to be ready to go into action now" (ibid. 2).

[33] Walters resumed his contacts with Castello Branco right after the coup, however (Diuguid 1976).

[34] *FRUS 1964–1968*: 422, 427, 433, 437; Gordon 1964a: 6–7, 11; Dulles 1978: 377.

limited (cf. Smith 2015: 278–9), and that direct involvement in the machinations against Goulart could backfire.[35] The US did give Brazilian conspirators assurances, especially concerning diplomatic recognition and potential support in case the coup would fail to oust the government and unleash a civil war (Gordon 1964b: 2–3; see A. Pereira 2018: 14–15).[36] But these promises of support merely shaped the parameters of internal decision making by lowering the costs and risks of antigovernment moves. Inside these broad parameters, Brazilian actors had great latitude as to whether to strike or not. Accordingly, domestic officers, politicians, and businesspeople made the principal decisions, and their interactions determined the conflict's outcome. Theories of vertical pressure, not to speak of coercion, clearly cannot explain the overthrow of President Goulart in 1964.

Similarly, US influence on the military dictatorship emerging from the coup remained limited. While the northern superpower embraced the new regime, it did so under the assumption that the armed forces would relinquish power after a quick purge and hold the democratic presidential elections scheduled for late 1965.[37] After all, the first military president, Humberto Castello Branco (1964–7) "had a reasonably liberal-democratic program" (Soares 1979: 453), which coincided with US preferences (CIA 1964b: 5). But as explained in Chapter 6, Castello Branco lost out to hard-core factions in the intramilitary struggle over the severity of the new regime, which gradually turned into a full-scale dictatorship and used ever harsher methods for strengthening its hold over power.

From the beginning, Washington tried hard to forestall this dictatorial turn – but without success (Leacock 1990: 215–17, 221–30, 236, 249). From April 1964 onward, US officials opposed the severity of the postcoup crackdown and over the subsequent years sought to prevent the hardening of authoritarianism (*FRUS 1964–1968*: 459–60, 489–90, 493–4; see already US 1964: 6). In particular, the US government objected to the institutionalization of the dictatorship via ever more autocratic "institutional acts," and disapproved especially of the drastic measures of 1968, which established full-scale despotism (*FRUS 1964–1968*: 523–6). But these divergences did not seem to make a significant difference for the regime involution in Brazil; the United States was unable to impede the repressive moves

---

[35] US Government 1963: 3, 6; US 1964: 1, 5. The fear that US involvement could turn counterproductive and unintentionally strengthen hard-left governments imposed self-restraint on US diplomats and secret service agents even in Bolivia, where – due to the internal fragmentation of the military and the utter weakness of the Bolivian state – US actors were more deeply involved in coup preparations than in the rest of South America (*FRUS 1969–1976*, vol. E-10, docs. 104, 106, 107).

[36] Note, however, that the US naval task force that was supposed to guarantee logistical support to the coup makers sailed so late that the military leadership already had a firm grip on power "before the fleet had neared Brazilian waters" (Leacock 1990: 214). This underappreciated fact shows that the United States was not very well informed about the coup decision, not to speak of participating in it.

[37] See three reports from the US State Department 1964, namely document A-134: 2; document A-139: 1; and document A-1211: 2.

of its lusophone allies (*FRUS 1964–1968*: 495, 530, 535–6). In sum, both during and after the coup of 1964, Brazilian generals acted with a great deal of independence; they were certainly not agents controlled by the western superpower.

THE UNITED STATES AND THE CHILEAN COUP OF 1973

The most prominent episode in which many scholars and other observers, especially in prior decades, charged the United States with responsibility for Latin American coups against left-wing governments concerned Chile in the early 1970s. For the thesis advanced in this study, namely that the US role in the rise of anticommunist authoritarianism was rather limited, the overthrow of Salvador Allende thus constitutes a "least likely case." Yet an analysis of primary documents and the rich and thorough secondary literature, especially major recent contributions, suggest that the violent ouster of the Marxist-led Popular Unity (UP) coalition was first and foremost a Chilean initiative; most likely, the United States did not participate in the plotting of Allende's eviction from power. While it is by nature difficult to prove a null hypothesis, namely the absence of direct US involvement, it is noteworthy that the massive declassification of documents in recent years and the opening of long-inaccessible archives, for example in former communist countries, has not yielded any evidence of US participation in the coup.[38] Instead, the new sources suggest less US involvement, and less impact of this involvement, than used to be commonly suspected.[39] Indictments of "US imperialism," which carried some plausibility when many sources remained closed, are therefore finding diminishing support among academic specialists (Fermandois 2003; Gustafson 2007; Harmer 2011).

Suspicions against the United States are fueled by the fact that the democratic electoral victory of the leftist UP coalition threw President Nixon and his National Security Adviser Henry Kissinger into a spasm of paranoia and prompted the anticommunist president to order an all-out effort to prevent Allende's assumption of power (Sigmund 1977: 120–3; Sigmund 1993: 48–55, 82). Nixon did not only want to "make the [Chilean] economy scream" (document reprinted in Kornbluh 2003b: 36) and was prepared to bribe deputies in the Chilean Congress to initiate a convoluted paralegal obstruction maneuver, but he also urged the CIA to push the Chilean military into stepping in.[40] This ultrasecret plan, the infamous "Track II," which

---

[38] See note 22 above. In his most recent book, even critic Greg Grandin (2015: 147–53) makes no claim that Henry Kissinger, for instance, was involved in the Chilean coup of 1973.

[39] Gustafson 2007: 80, 114, 146, 204, 210, 225, 235–6, 239; see also Devine 2014.

[40] This plan, according to which the "CIA focused on provoking a military coup," is chronicled rather openly and extensively in a CIA memorandum of November 18, 1970 (*FRUS 1969–1976*, vol. 11, part 2, chap. 1: 210–18; quote from p. 211).

remained hidden from US diplomats,[41] was so rash and ill-prepared that it unfolded disastrously. (Fermandois 2003: 18–20). CIA agents quickly concluded that their Chilean contacts were unreliable and that the whole project was unworkable. Therefore, they pulled back and exited from this conspiracy (Gustafson 2007: 122–7, 130–4). Their Chilean counterparts, however, went ahead anyway, yet botched the operation so badly that it backfired and unintentionally guaranteed Allende's installation as president. In sum, the United States had helped to launch this initiative and had clearly communicated its hostility to the new left-wing leader, but it had inadvertently played into his hands at this early point.

After this embarrassing fiasco, which resulted from top foreign policy makers pushing an ill-conceived last-minute operation against all odds, the United States did not undertake any direct effort to overthrow Chile's new president. In his first year in office, Allende was in a strong position: his expansionary economic policies fueled a boom and allowed for increased social expenditures, which strengthened his political and electoral support and protected him against any machinations (*FRUS 1969–1976*, vol. 11, part 2, chap. 1: 239–53, 287–97, 393–413). The United States, however, helped to bring this favorable yet clearly unsustainable conjuncture to an end by greatly reducing bilateral and multilateral credit to the UP government (*FRUS 1969–1976*, vol. 11, part 2, chap. 1: 301, 382–4, 419–20, 425, 440–2). Political goals contributed to this hostile stance, such as retaliation for Chile's uncompensated expropriation of US companies and the effort to weaken the Popular Unity's chances in upcoming electoral contests, but it was also driven by economists' belief that Allende's big-spending policies were unsustainable and that his administration was therefore not creditworthy.[42] This so-called "invisible blockade" (Kornbluh 2003b: 82–6; see also Farnsworth 1974: 131–4) significantly exacerbated the difficulties facing Chile's left-wingers in 1972 and 1973 and hurt Allende's coalition in the congressional midterm elections of 1973. But this economic squeeze, which was not as stringent as is often claimed,[43] did probably not constitute a deliberate US effort to prepare Allende's overthrow. At least until mid-1973, the United States clearly preferred a constitutional path and hoped that the UP coalition could be stopped or unseated democratically, especially via elections.[44]

---

[41] Korry 1998: 25–8; Davis 1985: 310–16; Gustafson 2007: 121–2. Ambassador Korry strongly opposed any efforts to stimulate a military coup as unrealistic and ineffective (see document in Kornbluh 2003b: 47–8).

[42] Sigmund 1974: 143–8; Whelan 1989: 333–9; Gustafson 2007: 149–52; Kedar 2017: 678–83.

[43] Kedar 2015: 668–72; Kedar 2017: 735–9, 742, 745. Moreover, Chile could draw on a substantial backlog of development credits that had already been approved (*FRUS 1969–1976*, vol. 11, part 2, chap. 1: 391).

[44] *FRUS 1969–1976*, vol. 21: 814, 869. In a discussion with President Nixon about the US response to Allende's uncompensated expropriations of US businesses, however, Treasury Secretary John Connally said with reference to the Chilean leader, "he's an enemy . . . And the only thing you can

For this purpose, the United States channeled large sums to opposition forces in Chile, especially centrist and right-wing parties, which jointly held a majority in Congress (*FRUS 1969–1976*, vol. 11, part 2, chap. 1: 283–7, 455–62). The northern superpower also subsidized the country's main newspaper, *El Mercurio*,[45] an outspoken mouthpiece for conservatism and anti-Allende voices.[46] The US foreign policy apparatus believed that this support was crucial to preserve these independent voices. After all, with its large-scale nationalizations, the UP government threatened to cut off business support for the opposition parties (*FRUS 1969–1976*, vol. 11, part 2, chap. 1: 456, 555, 632–3), and with its harassment and pressure on *El Mercurio*, it seemed intent on stifling press freedom.[47] Thus, from the US perspective, the funding for opposition forces had partly a defensive purpose; it was destined to preserve liberty and democracy in Chile, not to contribute to their termination.[48] Yet of course, US backing was also meant to enable these forces to resist Allende's socialist revolution with greater strength and determination (*FRUS 1969–1976*, vol. 11, part 2, chap. 1: 562), and to boost the opposition's electoral fortunes, for instance in the congressional midterm elections of 1973. While this US involvement skewed Chile's democratic process, the underlying hope was to terminate the UP experiment with constitutional means – without recourse to a coup.

With these goals in mind, the United States systematically targeted its financial backing to democratic forces and excluded the most reactionary sectors that fomented unrest and violence, and that seemed determined to prepare the ground for a military coup. As ample diplomatic documents and the scholarly literature show, the United States therefore kept at bay business groupings that tried to force the Allende government to its knees by inciting large-scale, disruptive strikes and protests.[49] In particular, the United States seems to have refrained from subsidizing the truckers' strikes of late 1972 and of

---

ever hope is to have him overthrown." But interestingly, Nixon did not acknowledge or endorse this suggestion, and the conversation immediately turned toward more limited retaliatory measures (*FRUS 1969–1976*, vol. 11, part 2, chap. 1: 441).

[45] *FRUS 1969–1976*, vol. 11, part 2, chap. 1: 429–31; US Senate 1976: 155, 176. Landis' (1982: 6, 9) claim, however, that "the CIA took over" this newspaper and used it for "psychological warfare" is exaggerated and not confirmed by other analyses (Kornbluh 2003a, Cortés 2014, Alvear and Lugo-Ocando, forthcoming), especially Llewellyn's (2002) thorough investigation, which shows that *El Mercurio* was *not* "deliberately disseminating false information," as Landis (1981: 76) claims.

[46] *FRUS 1969–1976*, vol. 11, part 2, chap. 1: 562; Sunkel 1983: 70–3, 78–97; Kornbluh 2003a; Cortés 2014.

[47] Korry 1998: 30–3; Davis 1985: 336–7, 339, 342; Devine 2014: 29; see also Haslam 2005: 178 and document in Kornbluh 2003b: 130–1. The defense of press freedom was the main plank that the newspaper used in its outspoken criticism of the Allende government (Sunkel 1983: 82–4).

[48] *FRUS 1969–1976*, vol. 21: 887–8, 922–3; Davis 1985: 319–20, 336–44, 398; Gustafson 2007: 156, 159–61.

[49] *FRUS 1969–1976*, vol. 21: 810, 867–77, 892–3; Gustafson 2007: 164–8.

mid- to late 1973 (US Senate 1976: 157, 177–8; Sigmund 1993: 78), which did a great deal of additional damage to the Chilean economy, fostered further ideological polarization, and dramatically inflamed the political crisis plaguing the country. While some seepage of US funding is possible, as suggested by Haslam (2005: 140, 149–50, 192–4), the available evidence indicates that the truckers' strike was mostly financed by Chilean and other Latin American businesses (Davis 1985: 324–7; Gustafson 2007: 167–8).

Similarly, after some initial funding in 1970 and early 1971 (Sigmund 1993: 77–8), the United States avoided the reactionary Patria y Libertad (Fatherland and Liberty) movement, which began to confront UP supporters with increasingly violent contention. In a dangerous escalatory dynamic, this far-right grouping engaged the ultraradical fringes of the governing coalition in nasty street battles and committed acts of sabotage and terrorism (Landsberger and Linz 1979: 410–11; Kay 1975: 15). From mid-1971 onward, the United States turned down several pleas to fund this thuggery and tried to ensure that the financial support given to other opposition forces would not in sinuous ways end up with Patria y Libertad. In one instance, the CIA did discover such an unauthorized transfer – and promptly sanctioned the offending grouping. The $2,800 involved in this leakage was unlikely, however, to have had a significant impact on the increasing economic chaos and political turmoil in Chile.

Most importantly, the United States cautiously stayed away from direct participation in coup plotting, as even the very critical Senate investigation of US involvement in Chile concludes.[50] As the Chilean economy started to take a nosedive from late 1971 onward and as conservative protest movements erupted, such as pot-banging marches (*Cacerolazo*) modeled in part on the anti-Goulart protests in Brazil in 1964,[51] sectors in the Chilean military began to engage in variegated "contingency planning," and some officers proceeded toward active conspiracies (*FRUS 1969–1976*, vol. 11, part 2, chap. 1: 291, 434, 476, 514–17, 541–2, 634). Though frequently approached, US personnel confined itself to intelligence gathering and avoided giving encouragement to Chilean plotters, not to speak of pushing them into action.[52] After all, the firm, entrenched constitutionalism of the Chilean military kept conspirators marginalized and for a long time made their plans unrealistic; sheer prudence thus induced CIA agents and US diplomats to keep their distance.

---

[50] US Senate 1976: 16, 149, 175; see also Sigmund 1993: 74; Harmer 2011: 130, 183, 206–7, 218, 220–1, 229–39. After the CIA's disastrous coup mongering in 1970, which contributed to the unprecedented assassination of its commander, René Schneider, the Chilean army had also deliberately distanced itself from the United States (Vial 2003: 151). Chilean socialist Erich Schnake (2004: 209) also acknowledges that the CIA did not engage in coup plotting.

[51] Power 2015: 113–14. The possibility of direct Brazilian involvement is suggested by cryptic comments by Henry Kissinger to President Nixon (*FRUS 1969–1976*, vol. 11, part 2, chap. 1: 521).

[52] *FRUS 1969–1976*, vol. 21: 814, 819–20; *FRUS 1969–1976*, vol. 11, part 2, chap. 1: 592–3, 600–2, 611–14, 642–5; see also Kornbluh 2003b: 106–8, 139–40, 145.

Even as Chile's crisis worsened in mid-1973 and broader sectors of the armed forces, especially in the navy and air force, started to conspire against the Popular Unity experiment (*FRUS 1969–1976*, vol. 21: 857), the United States deliberately stayed on the sidelines.[53] As a coup seemed to become ever more imminent, the United States even reduced its intelligence gathering because contact could create an impression of active encouragement and expose the northern hegemon to embarrassing disclosures and revelations (Whelan 1989: 495, 587–8). Any indication of US support, in turn, would play into the hands of the Allende government, which could claim the mantle of nationalism and thus discredit, if not politically destroy its enemies as lackeys of the northern hegemon (*FRUS 1969–1976*, vol. 21: 876, 892). Because Chilean coup mongers were aware of the same risk, they in turn refrained from approaching the United States once the plot to oust Allende entered into its operational phase (Davis 1985: 347–8, 363–4). Instead, they made sure that their coup clearly was a Chilean affair.[54]

Due to this caution on both sides, the United States actually had only limited knowledge of the machinations under way in Chile (*FRUS 1969–1976*, vol. 21: 881–2, 889, 914, 917, 921; Whelan 1989: 587–8). Foreign policy makers received warnings about the coup only at the last minute;[55] Ambassador Nathaniel Davis, for example, almost missed this crucial event by departing for an unrelated visit back to Washington, DC (Davis 1985: 354–60). US understanding of the coup makers' goals was deficient as well. Like Chile's opposition parties, the US mistakenly assumed that after ending the Marxist project and, perhaps, prohibiting the left-wing parties, the military junta would soon reinstitute democracy and convoke new elections.[56] Consequently, for months after Allende's overthrow, the United States kept funding centrist and right-wing parties, even after the new government had quickly "suspended" their activities. The United States did not expect General Pinochet, who had supported the constitutionalist wing of the Chilean military until late August 1973, to insist on keeping power for many years and on initiating a profound transformational project (Gustafson 2007: 212–18). This limited knowledge further corroborates that the United States was not the mastermind of the coup against Popular Unity.

---

[53] Davis 1985: 348–9, 357–8; Gustafson 2007: 175–7, 204, 210, 212–22, 225–6, 235.

[54] Based on a single, confidential interview source and some newspaper reports, Haslam (2005: 167, 169, 182, 211, and espec. 219) claims that US officials, led by General Vernon Walters, then deputy director of the CIA, actually masterminded the coup from Santiago de Chile. But there does not seem to be any documentary evidence for this claim, which the ongoing declassification of documents makes ever more implausible. In fact, as Lockhart (2014) argues, Walters' private diaries (Walters 1973) demonstrate clearly that he was not in Santiago in late August and early September of 1973; these diaries contain no evidence of Walters' involvement in the Chilean coup. Therefore, I do not follow Haslam's interpretation.

[55] *FRUS 1969–1976*, vol. 21: 917; Devine 2014: 26–7; Gustafson and Andrew 2018: 414.

[56] Devine 2014: 33–4; Haslam 2005: 194, 222–3; Gustafson 2007: 228–31; Harmer 2011: 274.

Recent historical scholarship confirms this conclusion, which Sigmund's (1977: xii) thorough early study reached as well. Based on a comprehensive investigation of CIA documents, Gustafson (2007: 210), for instance, concludes: "For certain, all of these stages on the road to the coup were domestically driven and resulted in domestic plotting only. In none of the text, in not one of the CIA documents, can one find reference to American involvement, passive or active, in coup plotting." Harmer (2011: 265) similarly concludes her well-researched investigation by emphasizing that "the United States' power to *control* events . . . was more limited than is commonly suggested" (emphasis in original).

An important and only recently investigated factor that limited the impact of covert actions by the United States – and that makes this interference appear in a somewhat different light, namely less as an unprovoked intervention – is the equally long-standing and active involvement of Russian and Cuban intelligence agencies in Chilean politics. For instance, subsidies from communist countries for the left-wing parties counterbalanced US subsidies for its domestic allies; in 1970, the Communist Party received more funds from the USSR than the Christian Democratic Party, Washington's preferred partner, from the CIA (Gustafson and Andrew 2018: 411–13). Moreover, throughout the Allende years, even when confrontation and polarization inside Chile worsened and a coup seemed to become more likely, US officials deliberately limited their contacts to the country's military for fear of being detected by Cuban and Russian intelligence agents, who provided a great deal of security assistance to the Popular Unity government (Gustafson and Andrew 2018: 414). In sum, the northern superpower felt constrained and saw its influence diminished by the global rivalry with the USSR and its Caribbean ally (see also Haslam 2005; Gustafson 2007; Harmer 2011).

Interestingly, whereas the United States does not seem to have had direct participation in the ouster of the Allende administration, there is growing evidence about some involvement from other Latin American countries, especially the anticommunist regime of Brazil (Davis 1985: 331–2, 348). In 1971 already, President Emílio Garrastazu Médici had urged President Nixon during a high-profile state visit in Washington, DC, to take a tougher stance against the Marxist-led UP coalition (as well as against other radical leftists in Latin America, particularly in Uruguay).[57] Brazil's ambassador in Santiago, Antônio Cândido da Câmara Canto, was a sworn enemy of Allende and actively participated in antigovernment maneuvers (Burns 2014). As the Brazilian dictatorship emerging after the 1964 coup had turned into the model of a successful anticommunist regime, Chilean coup plotters did not only take clear inspiration from the lusophone giant (Harmer 2011: 184–6, 228–9, 273), but also cooperated directly with Brazilian government officials and military officers (Haslam 2005: 138; Gaspari 2003: 348, 355). In particular,

[57] US White House 1971: 4–7; Harmer 2011: 101, 103, 106, 127–9.

they secured help in case the effort to unseat Allende would provoke armed resistance and trigger a civil war. The Brazilian regime also reassured the Chilean generals that hostile neighbor Peru would not take advantage of domestic trouble arising from a coup.[58] Notwithstanding this Brazilian involvement, the Chilean military seems to have acted on its own in overthrowing the UP government, and the coup was so brutally effective that the Brazilian lifeline proved unnecessary.

Thus, although many Brazilian sources, especially from the military, remain closed, it seems that to the limited extent in which Chilean coup plotters received foreign assistance, it came from Brazil, rather than from the United States. Whether this Brazilian involvement in Chile was coordinated with the United States remains unclear. At their meeting in 1971, Presidents Nixon and Médici had agreed to establish a direct confidential connection in order to collaborate in their efforts to contain and "reverse" the spread of leftism in South America (Harmer 2012: 670). While no documentary evidence of CIA or State Department collaboration with Brazil in the runup to the Chilean coup is available (Davis 1985: 332; see also Ferraz 1985), it is possible that this top-level presidential link was activated. What is noteworthy, however, is that it was the Brazilian president, not anticommunist Nixon, who had emphasized in 1971 the threat posed by the Allende government and urged more determined countermeasures (Harmer 2012: 663, 667–70). Moreover, throughout the early 1970s, Brazil's ambassador in Santiago engaged much more directly in anti-Allende activities than his US colleague (Davis 1985: 332). Consequently, it seems that Brazilian help for the Chilean coup plotters emerged primarily from Brazilian initiatives, rather than from "subimperialism" on behalf of the northern hegemon. As in Bolivia in 1970–1, the lusophone autocracy had sufficient reasons of its own to undermine left-wing governments in its sphere of interest. Involvement by a Latin American country mattered more than vertical pressure from the United States.

In sum, the United States indirectly contributed to the downfall of Allende by helping to undermine his economic performance and by supporting opposition parties and media. Moreover, Nixon and Kissinger's hostility to Chile's leftist regime was clear, providing encouragement and reassurance to coup mongers. Certainly, the United States was prudent enough to keep its distance from the most radical and disruptive opposition sectors, such as the violence-prone

---

[58] Diez episodios desconocidos sobre el golpe 2008: 9; Harmer 2011: 220–1, 228, 273. The memo that the military's committee of fifteen sent to President Allende as a virtual ultimatum in July 1973 (reprinted in González 2000: 502–3) and transcripts of confidential interviews by Chilean academics with a right-wing leader indicate that fear of a Peruvian attack on a Chile weakened by economic collapse and sociopolitical polarization and contention helped to motivate the coup. Right before the military takeover, however, conspirators were concerned that Peru could take advantage of the civil war that a coup attempt might provoke; the effort to avert this foreign threat was probably another reason for the heavy-handed crackdown on the left, which was designed to impose "order" as quickly as possible.

Patria y Libertad movement and the striking truckers;[59] similarly, the United States did not respond to the entreaties of the most reactionary generals, whose limited following inside the armed forces long made a coup attempt unrealistic.[60] But the history of US support for other anticommunist military regimes in Latin America, such as the Brazilian dictatorship, the precedent of the disastrous machinations to block Allende's inauguration in 1970, and the many conflicts of the northern superpower with the Allende government (especially over nationalizations), gave Chilean conservatives every reason to believe that they could count on US acquiescence and backing in case they managed to topple the UP administration. Most likely, the Nixon administration was also prepared to assist the coup makers in case they encountered armed resistance (Kornbluh 2003b: 112, 137); the United States definitely preferred a "white" over a "red" victory in any potential civil war.

Yet while Washington helped prepare the ground for the Chilean tragedy, there is no evidence that US officials were directly involved in Allende's ouster (as even Kornbluh 2003b: 114, admits). The Chilean generals deliberately acted on their own in order not to enable the left-wing parties to invoke anti-US nationalism. Moreover, counterfactual reasoning suggests that sooner or later, Chile's armed forces would have stepped in, even without US involvement. By 1973, their country was in a tailspin heading toward chaos, suffering from hyperinflation and fierce sociopolitical contention. Left-wing militias and armed worker groupings seemed to sprout up, undermining the military's cherished monopoly on organized coercion.[61] And the ever more cohesive opposition parties were practically advocating a military intervention by passing a congressional declaration on August 22, 1973, that accused the Allende administration of systematic violations of the Chilean constitution (text in Secretaría General de Gobierno 1974: 239–42). Given that despite last-minute mediation efforts the leftist president refused to change course, the generals were bound to remove him, with or without Brazilian help and indirect US encouragement.

THE BOUNDED RATIONALITY OF US INVOLVEMENT IN LATIN AMERICAN COUPS

From the theoretical perspective of this book, it is interesting that whatever US involvement in Latin America's coup wave existed was also driven by cognitive shortcuts and disproportionate loss aversion. The Cuban Revolution grabbed the attention of Washington's foreign policy makers via the availability heuristic, and the representativeness heuristic suggested that radicalism could

---

[59] A CIA report suggests implicitly that the United States was not involved in the truckers' strike (*FRUS 1969–1976*, vol. 11, part 2, chap. 1: 640–1).
[60] *FRUS 1969–1976*, vol. 21: 810, 814, 819–20, 829, 876–7, 885–6, 892–3.
[61] Haslam 2005: 148, 180–1, 186, 188, 209; Valenzuela 1978: 68–71, 98–103.

easily spread in Latin America. Consequently, US diplomats often fell prey to a tendency to see left-wing reformism in Latin America as a prelude or preparation for revolutionary moves that held a high risk of ending up in communism. Because they overrated the political savvy and support of radicals, they saw any evidence of communist leanings or infiltration as a serious danger.

These distorted views shaped US–Latin American relations throughout the 1960s and early 1970s and caused frequent tensions and a number of conflicts with left-leaning governments. Due to these exaggerated threat perceptions (see, e.g., *FRUS 1961–1963*: 451–3, 501–3),[62] for instance, President Kennedy in late 1962 sent his brother Robert, then the Attorney General, to press Brazilian President Goulart hard on pockets of communist influence inside his government (Gordon 1962: 2, 11–13). Taken aback by this blunt interrogation, which reflected the intensity of US fears,[63] "President Goulart reacted somewhat sharply," as even Ambassador Lincoln Gordon recorded.[64] In fact, Brazil's chief executive was "furious" (Loureiro 2017: 73; similar Parker 1979: 19–20, 30–1; Leacock 1990: 134–9; Fico 2008: 78).

As this unusually undiplomatic initiative suggests, leading US politicians relied on the availability and representativeness heuristics and inferred from the Cuban Revolution similar threat perceptions as status quo-oriented sectors in Latin America did. Fear of a second Cuba ran high in Washington – the regional version of the "domino theory" that held US foreign policy makers in its grip worldwide (cf. Slater 1987; Fagen 1975: 301–3). These doomsday scenarios rested on a distinct overestimation of communist agency and on excessive doubt in the solidity and resilience of US-friendly regimes – typical products of the cognitive shortcuts highlighted in this book.

Even more than President Kennedy, "[Lyndon] Johnson proved to be . . . susceptible to the 'Cuban Syndrome' . . . After all, as administration officials high and low were fond of noting, Fidel Castro had launched *his* successful revolution with only twelve men" (Grow 2008: 85). Accordingly, LBJ stated in the runup to the US invasion of the Dominican Republic in 1965, "They [his own foreign policy advisors] don't think [Juan] Bosch [the DR's ex-president][65] is [a Communist]. They think he's just a stooge for the deal. But nobody thought Castro was either" (Transcript of Tape No. 2 1965: 3–4). The depth of LBJ's

---

[62] These misperceptions seem to have induced US officials to misunderstand President Goulart's bargaining ploy for extracting greater financial assistance from the northern superpower as a serious threat to turn away from the United States and toward the Soviet Union (Loureiro 2017: 69–71, 74–8).

[63] US policy makers deliberately sought to "confront" President Goulart with their concerns, as they stressed several times in their internal deliberations (*FRUS 1961–1963*: 482–5; see Loureiro 2017: 72–3).

[64] Gordon 1962: 13; see also Smith 2015: 251; *FRUS 1961–1963*: 486–8.

[65] After left-wing populist Bosch had been deposed in a coup in 1963, his military supporters started an uprising in 1965, which caused serious concerns in Washington.

fears became obvious in 1967, when he and his top advisors discussed aid for Peru, which at that time was not facing any subversive challenges: "The President [considered] . . . what could happen if we weren't able to help these countries. The President said there will be many other Cubas in Latin America unless we do" (*FRUS 1964–1968*: 1020).[66]

These exaggerated assessments of danger, which were prompted by the Cuban precedent, then activated powerful loss aversion among US foreign policy makers. Many politicians and government officials therefore advocated all-out efforts to forestall communism's further spread. Because they foresaw a serious risk in Brazil in the early 1960s, the Kennedy and Johnson administrations were willing to send US troops in the unlikely case that radicals were about to defeat US-friendly moderates in a potential civil war, as mentioned above. The Brazilian military, however, easily subdued left-wingers with its 1964 coup – suggesting how overblown US concerns had been. Then, in the Dominican Republic, where conservatives were weaker and more disorganized, the US did overreact to the eruption of armed unrest with a full-scale invasion in 1965 (Grow 2008: 79–86). US officials such as Vernon Walters (1978: 399, 402–3) saw this intervention as crucial for "resist[ing] a brutal Communist takeover" – a threat perception not validated by country specialists (see, e.g., Hartlyn 1991: 76).

In sum, leading US foreign policy makers shared the profound fears and intense loss aversion of status quo-oriented sectors in Latin America. Washington therefore stood ready to prevent the worst-case scenario of communist takeovers in the region. Yet this commonality of perceptions and concerns among elites in the north and south also meant that in countries with firmly institutionalized militaries, Washington did not have to take the lead in this anticommunist crusade. Instead, Presidents Johnson and then Nixon could let locals spearhead the charge against leftist radicalism, as they did in the cases of Brazil, Argentina, and Chile that this book has examined in some depth.

The prevalence and impact of cognitive mechanisms among US officials is surprising, given the unusually open, pluralistic structure of the foreign policy apparatus and the participation of a great variety of agencies, which bring diverse perspectives to bear. As highlighted by the literature on bounded rationality (Simon 1976; March and Simon 1993; Jones 2001; Bendor 2010) and as explained in Chapter 3, this kind of organizational structure should help to filter out misperceptions, correct problematic inferences, and thus ensure more rational decision making.

---

[66] Interestingly, US foreign policy makers also worried that leftist experiments inspired in part by the Cuban precedent would inspire their own emulation efforts. This fear of further, "secondary" diffusion intensified the concerns that Henry Kissinger, for example, expressed about the election of Salvador Allende in Chile (Haslam 2005: 55–7; see also *FRUS 1969–1976*, vol. 11, part 2, chap. 1: 480).

But at the very apex of the foreign policy apparatus of a global superpower, these beneficial tendencies may be undermined by important problems and limitations. After all, US presidents and their top aides are in charge of a vast range of responsibilities and face a mountain of tasks, often under considerable time pressure. Yet human attention is distinctly limited, hindering the thorough, systematic processing of the massive stream of information that would be required for properly attending to all of these tasks (Jones and Baumgartner 2005). This disjuncture between human cognitive capacities and the information processing demands they face, which Herbert Simon compared to a wide-open pair of scissors (Bendor 2010: 2–3), is particularly stark for top officials, creating a temptation to resort to cognitive shortcuts.

Accordingly, while the leading decision makers can, in principle, listen to diverse sets of well-trained experts, in practice they may not have the time to do so. Moreover, these top officials are often generalists, do not have much experience in foreign affairs,[67] and lack thorough knowledge of specific issues and regions of the world. As regards US relations with Latin America, the cultural and historical distance between the northern colossus and its southern allies inhibited more rational decision making. After all, presidents and their top aides had only spotty knowledge of the region, its political evolution, and the changing power constellation prevailing in each country. Moreover, steeped in the "liberal tradition in America" (Hartz 1955), most US foreign policy makers lacked familiarity with left-wing forces and tended to take their frequent rhetorical posturing and bold pronouncements too literally. After all, Latin American radicals often proclaimed overambitious goals or uttered threats that they had no way of realizing.[68] Yet to leading US policy makers, such bravado, which was common in the fifteen years after the Cuban Revolution, sounded worrisome indeed.

Due to the heavy burden of their ample agenda, Washington's top foreign policy officials paid only sporadic attention to specific Latin American countries. When a crisis did erupt, they were ill prepared, hastily resorted to cognitive shortcuts, and risked making rash, problematic decisions (Pastor 2001: 17–19, 33–4, 191–3). This deleterious pattern is particularly obvious in the case of Chile, where President Nixon and Henry Kissinger had initially underestimated the risks posed by the 1970 election. Yet then, when Marxist Salvador Allende unexpectedly won, they fell into a panic and ordered ill-considered machinations to forestall his assumption of power, disregarding all expert advice (Gustafson 2007: 80–1, 113–18).

---

[67] As Saunders' analysis (2017: S226-27) suggests, US presidents are unlikely to command a great deal of foreign policy experience, especially in recent decades; George H. W. Bush (Saunders 2017: S238-41) was unusual in the number of high-level positions he had held before assuming the presidency.

[68] In retrospect, Latin American left-wingers, including Carlos Altamirano, the most radical leader of Chile's Socialist Party, acknowledge these rhetorical excesses (see interview with Altamirano in Arancibia 2006: 173; see also Schnake 2004: 174, 180, 183, 199).

Their lack of country knowledge induced the United States' top foreign policy makers to look at "the big picture" in dealing with Latin American left-wingers. Given the recent trauma of Cuba, which the availability heuristic kept salient, this ungrounded perspective exposed them to distortions. Unfamiliarity with specific circumstances gave the representativeness heuristic considerable sway and fueled exaggerated fears of a repeat of Castro's revolution.[69] The reflexive response was to try to forestall that scary outcome at all cost. Consequently, Washington commonly employed the lens of the Cold War, seeing specific issues from the perspective of the West's struggle against communism.[70]

For all these reasons, cognitive heuristics and asymmetrical loss aversion played a surprisingly important role at the apex of the US foreign policy apparatus. The very top of this massive organizational structure was in some ways disjointed from the vast range of agencies it commanded. After all, country specialists, intelligence agents, and diplomats on the ground often had a fairly thorough, reasonable understanding of local political tendencies and developments inside specific Latin American nations.[71] Therefore, these lower-level officials arrived at measured assessments of the problems and threats posed to the United States by the left-leaning governments of João Goulart in Brazil,[72] Salvador Allende in Chile,[73] and other cases.[74] Their ample access to relevant information and their fairly solid background knowledge limited the impact of distortions arising from inferential heuristics,[75] which shone through only in the disproportionate attention paid to left-wingers and in the "automatic" tendency to see radicals as cryptocommunists.[76]

---

[69] Fears of diffusion also arose from other outstanding advances of radical leftism, especially Salvador Allende's democratic electoral victory and his rapid march toward socialism (*FRUS 1969–1976*, vol. 11, part 2, chap. 1: 372; see also 378–9).

[70] See, for instance, JFK's surprising question about a small state in the Brazilian northeast that he could not identify: "How strong are the communists there?" (reproduced in Naftali 2001: 12).

[71] Even Rabe's (1999: 138–9) critical analysis of foreign policy making under the Kennedy administration recognizes this contrast.

[72] See, e.g., US State Department, Latin American Policy Committee 1963; Excerpts 1963: 1–4; US 1964; US State Department 1964, document A-1116; see also Parker 1979: 79, 103.

[73] *FRUS 1969–1976*, vol. 21: 591–617, 812–14; *FRUS 1969–1976*, vol. 11, part 2, chap. 1: 393–413; US Senate 1976: 20–1, 195; Gustafson 2007: 85–8, 241–2; see also Harmer 2011: 191, 213–14.

[74] See, e.g., analyses of Brazil in the early 1970s (CIA 1972) and of Argentina in the mid-1970s (see *FRUS 1969–1976*, vol. 11, part 2, chap. 1: 10–18, 34–8, 53–5).

[75] Even friendly observers, however, argue that these officials often held exaggerated threat perceptions as well (see, e.g., Smith 2015: 242, 247).

[76] Long-standing Brazil expert Vernon Walters (1978: 374, 377–8, 380, 388–9), however, did have clearly excessive concerns about the advances of communism in Brazil during the early 1960s. For instance, he was "convinced that if the revolution [the military coup of 1964] had not occurred, Brazil would have gone the way of Cuba" (Walters 1978: 389).

Leading US officials, by contrast, such as Presidents Johnson and Nixon, and even International Relations specialist Henry Kissinger, the main protagonist of "realism" in US foreign policy, could for obvious reasons have only a tenuous grasp of the internal situation inside different Latin American countries. Therefore, they tended to rely more heavily on the representativeness heuristic and to overrate the similarities between local leftist movements and the striking, scary Cuban precedent (see, e.g., US Senate 1976: 174–5). While the chief executive and his top advisors usually received high-quality information[77] and engaged in extensive, frank debates, their cultural distance and lack of regional expertise prompted heavy reliance on cognitive mechanisms.

The resulting tendency to "jump to conclusions" caused significant problems and failures in US relations with important Latin American countries. This overreaction drove President Kennedy's abovementioned decision to send his brother Robert to Brazil and press President Goulart hard on communist tendencies in his administration. The overestimation of similarities also came to the fore when LBJ overrode his advisors' assessment of a populist leader in the Dominican Republic based on a telling analogy to Fidel Castro,[78] as discussed above.

Similarly, after Salvador Allende's electoral victory in Chile in late 1970, "[t]he hysterical reaction of Nixon and Kissinger differed sharply from the view articulated by the foreign policy bureaucracy and the CIA."[79] These lower-level officials produced thorough, well-informed, and very reasonable assessments of the issues and risks facing the United States – which were in fact limited (e.g., Korry [1970] 1998). But suddenly driven by excessive fear and intense loss aversion, the president and his top advisor insisted on trying to prevent Allende's assumption of power with all means (Gustafson 2007: 80–1, 113–15), against the explicit opposition of US Ambassador Edward Korry (see document in Kornbluh 2003b: 47–8). Due to this ill-considered determination, the US government helped to launch an amateurish coup attempt that backfired dramatically.

In sum, US involvement in the struggle against communism in Latin America was significantly shaped by inferential heuristics and stark loss aversion, which affected especially the decision making of presidents and their top advisers.

---

[77] As a remarkable exception, however, in the midst of the Brazilian coup the CIA gave President Johnson superficially based information in its daily briefings, which relied on several "press reports" (CIA 1964c: 2–3). Thus, it seems that during this high-stakes showdown, in which the United States was eventually prepared to intervene as a last resort to forestall the country's slide into communism, the agency did not have well-placed informants on the ground.

[78] Transcript of Tape No. 2 1965: 3–4; similar Walters 1978: 399, 402–3.

[79] Sigmund 1993: 56; similar Schmitz 2006: 99–100.

CONCLUSION

Chapters 5 and 6 showed that the proliferation of military dictatorships in Latin America during the 1960s and 1970s was driven primarily by inordinate fears of Cuban communism and domestic radicalism. The present chapter then explained that the powerful deterrent effects of Castro's revolution found some reinforcement from two diffusion processes of secondary importance. First, the Brazilian coup of 1964 and the subsequent institution of bureaucratic authoritarianism exerted demonstration effects across the region. The "successful" military takeover itself suggested to the armed forces of other countries that the overthrow of democracy was feasible and would not founder on domestic or international opposition. Thereafter, the institutional strength and the ambitious development project of the lusophone dictatorship served as a model, especially for status quo defenders in the Southern Cone. In these ways, the lessons of the Brazilian precedent provided additional impulses for the reverse wave of the 1960s and 1970s.

Second, the vertical influence of the United States strengthened the regional counterrevolution against the specter of Cuba-inspired communism as well. The northern superpower persistently warned its Latin American allies against the danger of radicalism, put pressure on left-wing governments, encouraged and condoned military interventions, and supported the resulting dictatorships. Consequently, the United States holds some responsibility for the overthrow of democracy among its client states.

But in every case of autocratic imposition, the main initiative clearly lay with domestic actors. After all, Latin American status quo defenders had powerful reasons of their own to be concerned about the threats emanating from revolutionary Cuba. Militaries, for instance, needed no wake-up calls from Washington; the shots with which the guerrilla fighters on the Caribbean island had executed many old regime generals had rung loud enough. As Latin American elites drew on the same cognitive shortcuts as their US counterparts, they shared intense threat perceptions. Consequently, asymmetrical loss aversion induced them to defend their interests and causes with all means at their disposal. They therefore took the lead in combating domestic left-wingers and radicals. In particular, they conspired and organized the military coups that ushered in authoritarian rule without direct US involvement. Moreover, hard-line factions in the armed forces then pressed relentlessly for the installation of harsh, long-term dictatorships, against the explicit wishes of the United States.

Thus, as the in-depth analysis in this chapter has shown, the spread of bureaucratic authoritarianism was first and foremost the product of Latin American agency, not of US machinations. Vertical pressure was certainly not the main cause driving this powerful wave of counterdiffusion. Instead, the scary precedent of Castro's Cuba and the powerful backlash it provoked were decisive.

PART III

COMPARATIVE PERSPECTIVES AND THEORETICAL
CONCLUSIONS

8

Reactionary Waves across History

Why have there been important time periods when history has seemed to move backwards and to undo earlier advances toward political liberalism and democracy? To shed light on these reversals of progress, this study of the main wave of reactionary rule in Latin America has proposed a backlash interpretation, which the concluding Chapter 9 will review in depth. In a nutshell, the spread of right-wing autocracy constituted a panicked response to the overestimated danger of communism, which raised doubts about the defensive resilience of political liberalism and democracy. Across Latin America, radical-left efforts inspired by the Cuban Revolution prompted forceful, broadly supported counterdiffusion designed to fortify the body politic through the installation of dictatorship.

Is this new theory valid only for the reverse wave investigated in this book, or does it have broader applicability? The first section of this chapter discusses the single most momentous spread of reactionary rule in the modern world, namely the wide-ranging proliferation of authoritarianism and fascism during the interwar years. Interestingly, this autocratic riptide in the core of the world system unfolded in strikingly similar ways as the later rash of coups in Latin America. Like the Cuban Revolution, Russia's October Revolution of 1917 inspired the radical left, yet sent shivers down the spines of conservative and centrist sectors. Consequently, isomorphic efforts to replicate the armed power grab of Lenin's Bolsheviks quickly erupted, but these uprisings suffered brutal repression. Because left-wing extremists eventually learned from these defeats, they came to adjust their strategy and focused on organizational and electoral efforts, and the Soviet Union supported this agitation and promoted the spread of world revolution. For these reasons, intense threat perceptions persisted on the right side of the ideological spectrum and contributed mightily to the imposition of autocratic rule in many countries of Europe and beyond. Thus, the causes and processes of the reverse wave of the interwar years resembled the spread of military dictatorship in Latin America. The theory designed in this book does have broader validity.

There was one crucial difference, however, which made the frequent downfall of democracy during the 1920s and 1930s even more complex than the Latin American coup wave of the 1960s and 1970s. Intense fears of communism contributed to the emergence of a new reactionary regime model, namely fascism. Fascism had important affinities with the authoritarian projects embraced by conservative elites, namely deep enmity against the left, an advocacy of powerful authority, and fervent nationalism. But fascism also differed significantly from conservative authoritarianism in its violent dynamism, its bottom-up, plebeian mobilization, and its reliance on omnipotent charismatic leadership. Consequently, powerful elite sectors, especially conservative politicians, military generals, and big businesspeople, were wary of the threats that fascism's transformational impetus and its quest for total control posed to their own power and privileges. The specific processes and outcomes of the interwar reverse wave therefore depended on the power balance between conservative establishment sectors and rising fascist movements. In fact, in a number of cases, the overthrow of democracy resulted from efforts to preempt a fascist takeover. Thus, the spread of reactionary autocracy during the 1920s and 1930s was driven by a double deterrent effect – namely, the effort to forestall communism, yet also fascism.

After the first section explains these complex developments, attention turns to other wave-like moves toward right-wing authoritarianism. Yet because these reversals affected mostly countries that had not installed liberal democracy, they did not entail full-scale regime change. Instead, they were clusters of regime hardening in which conservative autocracies pushed even farther away from political liberalism and democracy. Authoritarian incumbents tightened control over society, cracked down on opposition movements, and tried to cement their own political predominance and command. Interestingly, these waves of intensified oppression, which occurred both in the distant past and during recent decades, also arose in reaction to revolutionary challenges. Thus, the mechanisms of my theory hold more general validity.

THE MASSIVE REVERSE WAVE OF THE INTERWAR YEARS

In the same way that the spread of military dictatorships in Latin America arose from the deterrent effects of the Cuban Revolution, so the downfall of many democracies during the 1920s and 1930s had a crucial root cause in the Russian Revolution of 1917 (Linz 1976: 7, 16–17, 26; Payne 1995: 76–8; Pasteur 2007: 12–14; Paxton 2009: 550–5). Just like Castro's success forty-two years later, the violent takeover by Lenin's Bolsheviks immediately drew enormous attention and stimulated expectations of replication. That these perceptions and beliefs were shared by political sectors across the ideological spectrum, especially the left and the right, demonstrates the operation of cognitive shortcuts rather than wishful thinking among the left or fear-mongering by the right. As my next book project demonstrates in depth, the heuristics of availability and representativeness inspired radicals to undertake a spate of isomorphic emulation efforts. But these inferential shortcuts also instilled deep fears among status quo defenders and activated asymmetrical loss aversion, which motivated determined, often brutal countermeasures. The communist challenges and uprisings that erupted in many countries, ranging from Finland to Germany, Hungary, and northern Italy (Priestland 2016: 88-89), therefore suffered harsh repression and uniformly went down to defeat. Like the rash of guerrilla struggles that exploded in Latin America after the Cuban Revolution, the immediate efforts to follow in Lenin's footsteps by taking power through armed assaults therefore ended in colossal failure (Tökés 1967; Carsten 1988: chap. 12; Gerwarth and Horne 2012).

As in Latin America during the 1960s, these decisive victories of counterrevolution eased the initial panic among status quo defenders and forestalled the immediate imposition of reactionary autocracy in most countries (except Hungary and later Italy). Indeed, centrist and social-democratic parties designed a political strategy that sought to preempt or contain communist advances through preemptive reforms, such as land redistribution (see, e.g., Jörgensen 2006). While less comprehensive and while lacking external funding and support, these efforts pursued the same pacifying goals as the Alliance for Progress proposed by President Kennedy in response to the Cuban Revolution. In many countries, especially in Eastern Europe, these measures prevented the radical left from gaining strong backing in rural areas (Kasekamp 2010: 114). Also, because the reform approach proclaimed less ambitious goals (no "Revolution in Liberty," as in Chile after 1964), it did not have the unintended consequences of the Alliance for Progress analyzed in Chapters 4 and 5, namely to stimulate the very radicalization that it was intended to forestall.

Neither the quick defeat of isomorphic emulation efforts nor the preemptive reform measures, however, managed to extinguish the threat that a broader set of radical forces seemed to pose to the established order. After all, communists eventually learned from their initial failures, gave up isomorphic emulation efforts, and switched from insurgency to an organizational and electoral strategy (see, e.g., Weitz 1997: chaps. 4–7). Their persistent and concerted efforts to win support for radical transformations in a wide range of countries received intensive backing from the Russian Bolsheviks, whose new regime had survived counterrevolutionary attacks and eagerly sought to foment world revolution. That this assistance remained secretive and that domestic communists often hid their "subversive" activities behind façade organizations reinforced the threat perceptions of establishment sectors, who feared being undermined by devious, invisible enemies.

Yet whereas in Latin America, exaggerated fears of such radical challenges prompted one military coup after the other, the reverse wave of the interwar years advanced in less straightforward ways. The backlash was more complex and heterogeneous, because a new model for countering the supposed communist threat arose, namely fascism (Kallis 2016; comprehensive overviews in Payne 1995 and Bosworth 2009). Because Mussolini's novel regime type had been forged in struggles against the radical left in northern Italy, it promised particularly strong, reliable protection against the specter of revolution. After all, the fascist movement mobilized fervent mass support for reactionary causes, proved willing and able to crush its enemies with sustained violence, and gave its overbearing autocratic leader a supremely powerful tool for cementing "order," stability, and hierarchy. The rise of fascism therefore held tremendous appeal for a wide range of right-wing sectors (Bauerkämper 2006: chap. 3). Mussolini seemed to have developed the potent medicine that could definitively eradicate the virus of communism.

But while holding great attraction for conservatives and reactionaries, the new regime type of fascist totalitarianism also caused unease among many rightist establishment sectors (Blinkhorn 1990). For conservative elites, this weapon against the perceived threat from the radical left contained its own dangers. What if this medicine against communism amounted to an overdose that would end up damaging the patient's health? After all, the mobilizational energy of fascist mass movements and the ambitious, comprehensive goals of their overbearing charismatic leaders risked undermining the privileges and power of currently dominant sectors. With its forceful bottom-up impetus and its quest for absolute command, fascism jeopardized the hierarchy and top-down control that conservative politicians, military generals, and societal elites were determined to maintain. Therefore, these sectors strenuously wanted to avert the installation of full-scale fascism. Instead, they intended to use fascist movements merely as auxiliaries for pursuing their own, limited goals.

Due to the tension between authoritarian conservatives and totalitarian fascists,[1] the reverse wave of the interwar years was propelled by a double deterrent effect. On the one hand, all right-wing groupings sought to combat the radical left and embraced autocracy as essential protection against the perceived communist threat. Yet on the other hand, conservative elites also feared fascists and tried hard to keep them under control, especially after the striking precedent of Hitler's ruthless power grab in Germany (Mann 2004: 238; Weyland 2017). Accordingly, in a number of countries, such as Brazil, Portugal, and Spain, right-wingers used support from reactionary radicals to impose or harden authoritarian rule – but then subordinated their fascist allies to the yoke of this demobilizational, top-down dictatorship, repressing any protest against this "betrayal" (Payne 1995: 274–6, 312–16). Indeed, in countries where fascist movements gained particular strength, as in Austria, Estonia, and Romania, conservative leaders overthrew liberal regimes precisely in order to prevent the radical right from wining or taking power (Payne 1995:

---

[1] On the conceptual and theoretical differences fueling this tension between the advocates of authoritarianism and of totalitarianism, see especially Linz (2000).

248–52; Von Rauch 1995: 148–54). Thus, in several cases, the direct trigger of democratic breakdown was the deterrent effect of fascism, which in turn had its origin in the deterrent effect of communism.

After Mussolini's installation of fascism in Italy, there was only one other country that instituted this type of right-wing totalitarianism, namely Germany (interesting analysis of these parallels in Knox 2007). Given that this Central European nation had a higher degree of modernization and societal mobilization than Eastern and Southern Europe, where authoritarianism proliferated, conservative elites commanded lower strength and support (Peukert 1993). Conversely, a novel outsider movement, National Socialism, managed to boost its mass backing, especially when the Great Depression caused catastrophic socioeconomic problems. Hitler's party therefore ballooned to a size that blocked the imposition of authoritarian rule during this crisis (classical analysis by Bracher [1955] 1978; see recently Mommsen 2016). Then, when conservative elites reluctantly ceded the premiership to the fascist leader, he quickly succeeded in breaking their supposed stranglehold over his government and in brutally pushing toward full-scale totalitarianism (Bracher 1979; Sauer 1974). This unusual case, in which the most drastic countermodel to communism gained total predominance, in turn sent shockwaves through right-wing circles across the world and thus reinforced the deterrent effect of fascism that induced conservative elites in many countries to impose authoritarian rule, with an anticommunist as well as an antifascist edge.

In sum, the rise of fascism made the reverse wave of the interwar years more complex and heterogeneous than the proliferation of military dictatorships in Latin America. Of course, both of these clusters of reactionary regime changes received a fundamental impulse from the communist revolutions in Russia and Cuba, respectively. As a powerful right-wing backlash propelled the move toward autocracy, deterrent effects played a decisive role in these processes of counterdiffusion. But whereas in Latin America these reactionary moves advanced in a straightforward way and brought the spread of authoritarian regimes, the rise of fascism gave the right-wingers of the 1920s and 1930s two different options for replacing liberal democracy. In many countries, in fact, it was the tension-filled relationship between the conservative adherents of authoritarianism and the fascist advocates of totalitarianism that directly produced the overthrow of liberalism and democracy. My next book will analyze these complex developments in depth.

CLUSTERS OF REACTIONARY REGIME HARDENING

Besides the rash of coups in Latin America and the spread of authoritarianism and fascism during the interwar years, there have been no other broad riptides in which political liberalism or democracy have fallen to assaults from the conservative or reactionary right. In Latin America, for instance, the end of

World War II brought a region-wide trend toward political liberalization and democracy (Bethell and Roxborough 1992: 1–13), but the inception of the Cold War in 1947–8 did not prompt a correspondingly widespread cascade of authoritarian reversal.[2] In the late 1940s, fledgling democracies fell to right-wing coups only in Peru and Venezuela; and the abortion of the mobilizational *trienio* in Venezuela "did not seem to be strongly influenced by the international conjuncture" (Collier 1994: 85; see also 86–7). In general, most reactionary regime replacements have occurred selectively, in different countries at different times, not in distinctive clusters.[3]

In line with the main argument of the present study, this absence of further reverse waves reflected the dearth of dramatic revolutionary precedents that shook up liberal or democratic countries. Note that the Cuban Revolution erupted at a time when most of South America featured liberal, democratic or democratizing regimes, and the Russian Revolution occurred as many democracies emerged in Europe after the end of World War I. Thus, the shockwaves emanating from these radical challenges affected numerous open, nonrepressive regimes that in the eyes of conservative elites were particularly vulnerable to communist subversion. To gain greater protection, establishment sectors therefore came to embrace regime change and advocated the overthrow of democracy.

Most other revolutionary upheavals, however, occurred at times and in regions where democracy, even liberal rule, were rare or absent. Thus, there simply were no pluralist, open regimes that conservative elites would have seen as fragile and assailable and that the fear of revolution's spread would have induced them to overthrow. No democracy existed, for instance, when the French stormed the Bastille and then beheaded their king. Similarly, with the exception of Turkey (and Israel), the Middle East almost uniformly chafed under authoritarian rule when the Iranian Revolution of 1978–9 toppled the mighty Shah. Obviously, a reverse wave of democratic overthrow can only occur if there had been prior progress and there are democracies to overthrow.

In general, major revolutions are exceedingly infrequent, as a long line of scholarship has shown (Skocpol 1979; Goldstone 1991; Katz 1997; Goodwin 2001; Foran 2005; see also Wickham-Crowley 1992). In particular, revolutions

---

[2] Rock (1994: 34) argues, however, that in the late 1940s "incumbent regimes moved sharply to the right, launching repressive campaigns against the Communist parties in each country, repressing the labor unions, and silencing the reformers" (similar Bethell and Roxborough 1992: 16–30). As these measures were clearly driven by domestic and international fears of communism, which seemed exaggerated, they were in line with the core argument of the present book. But they were not drastic enough to bring political regime change.

[3] One important reason is that right-wing assaults on democracy tend to be spearheaded by establishment sectors that command organizations. In line with the theoretical approach of this book, these organizations act with fairly loose bounds of rationality. Therefore, they base their political actions primarily on the domestic opportunity structure and are much less influenced by foreign developments (cf. Weyland 2014: 53–8).

rarely if ever shake up liberal democracies themselves.[4] The profound transformations that did erupt during the last few decades happened mostly in Africa and Asia, especially during conflictive processes of decolonization (Goodwin and Skocpol 1989; Foran 2005: chap. 3). But in the neighborhoods of these anti-colonial revolutions, free, competitive regimes could exist only in countries that had already undergone decolonization. For this reason, the revolutionary precedent no longer held relevance in these newly independent countries and could not easily serve as an imitable model; a new, more legitimate state had already established its domination. In fact, in much of Africa and Asia liberal democracy was rare to begin with. Few if any countries were democratic in Southeast Asia from the 1950s to the 1970s, in the Maghreb during the 1950s and early 1960s, or in sub-Saharan Africa during the 1970s. Because there was little political progress to reverse, the revolutions in Vietnam, in Algeria, and in Angola and Mozambique, respectively, simply could not prompt the widespread replacement of democracy by right-wing autocracy. Therefore, the world has not seen additional riptides of democratic breakdown.

There have been several reactionary waves, however, that have brought a significant hardening of existing autocratic regimes. In these instances, nondemocratic incumbents in a range of countries have moved further away from political liberalism and have taken determined steps to tighten their hegemonic control over politics and society. These measures have turned hybrid regimes closer to full-scale authoritarianism, exacerbated the repressive features of unambiguous autocracies, or cemented the durability of nondemocratic rule. As this deepening of autocracy has been regionally clustered, it reflected diffusion processes. Established nondemocracies learned from their neighbors when and how to tighten the reins, and they responded to deterrent effects that had acute salience in the vicinity.

Interestingly, these clusters of authoritarian tightening have occurred in response to revolutionary challenges that have erupted in high-profile countries, especially regional great powers (cf. Katz 1997: 13, 26). In line with the main argument of this study, these profound, violent upheavals in particularly visible settings instilled intense, arguably exaggerated fears among incumbent rulers and their core supporters. These concerns then prompted crackdowns on (potential) opposition forces and a further intensification of authoritarian controls. Thus, these moves toward harsher autocracy arose from backlashes that resembled the sequences of diffusion and counterdiffusion highlighted in this book.

Typically, this series of right-wing regime fortifications started with the epic French Revolution of 1789, which stimulated numerous emulation efforts, but

---

[4] Foran (2005: 20, 158–63) highlights the exceptional case of Chile, but the socialist transformation spearheaded by Marxist president Salvador Allende was brutally aborted, as Chapter 6 discussed and as Foran himself (2005: 174–81) analyzes.

whose radicalization soon exerted powerful deterrent effects as well. Besides giving birth to conservatism as an ideological doctrine and political current (Burke [1790] 1999), the violent overthrow of Europe's most powerful monarchy motivated repressive countermeasures across the continent, which included distinctive setbacks to the incipient liberalism arising in Great Britain. Moreover, the slave revolution in France's colony Haiti, a spillover from the upheaval in the motherland, prompted an intensification of slavery in Brazil, Cuba, and the southern United States.

A similar reactionary wave gathered steam in 1848, when established princes faced a revolutionary wildfire sparked by the overthrow of "Citizen King" Louis Philippe in Paris. After initially promising liberal openings, rulers in Central and Eastern Europe gradually yet forcefully took back their initial concessions, reasserted coercive control with more or less violence, and then, despite some formal-institutional advances (such as Prussia's royally imposed, "octroyed" constitution), turned to more heavy-handed and severe repression during the 1850s (see Weyland 2016).

The twentieth century also saw waves of autocratic hardening, which sought to suppress the risk of radical challenges. In this vein, Iran's Islamist Revolution of 1978–9 prompted many Middle Eastern despots, especially in the Persian Gulf region, to tighten their stranglehold over civil society and to stamp out any opposition. To the present day, Arab rulers have skillfully used the perceived threat arising from religious fundamentalism for engineering domestic acquiescence to continued authoritarianism and for winning ample subsidies and support from the United States (Brownlee 2012). The same kind of reactionary backlash occurred after the "color revolutions" in the postcommunist world, which brought a sequence of challenges to competitive-authoritarian regimes and their crony capitalism (Beissinger 2007). From 2005 onward, reigning nondemocrats, most importantly Russia's Vladimir Putin and most brutally Uzbekistan's Islam Karimov, forestalled contagion by harassing or repressing the opposition, imposing ever tighter restrictions on civil society and public opinion, and employing governmental influence and state resources to create subservient organizations of regime supporters (Koesel and Bunce 2013).

While this deepening of autocracy crossed regime thresholds in few cases, it brought noteworthy political deterioration by cementing antiliberal, nondemocratic rule and by making future progress even more difficult. These repressive measures entailed clear reversals in short-term political trends in Central Europe in 1848–9, where the protest wave unleashed in France had initially induced princes to include political liberals in their governments and to promise constitutions; the reactionary backlash then quickly dashed these hopes of advancement. Similarly, a medium-term setback occurred under the Putin administrations in Russia. After the downfall of communism and the introduction of free elections had pointed the country in a democratic direction during the 1990s, Putin's efforts to concentrate power, which took a more sinister turn in response to the color revolutions, aborted this trend and pushed the country toward authoritarian rule (Bunce 2017: 26–7).

By contrast, the durability of authoritarianism in the Middle East had foreclosed liberal openings in the first place; thus, there was not much progress to reverse. But it is striking how little that region was affected by the "third wave of democratization," which brought numerous advances in all other regions of the world (Markoff 2009: 59, 69). From a comparative perspective, the very lack of progress in the Middle East – the unusual ineffectiveness of an otherwise powerful trigger – is remarkable (Bellin 2004: 142). The fear of Islamic fundamentalism and fierce opposition to "revolutionary" Iran help to account for the exceptional resilience of autocracy in this region (Rubin 2014).

Typically, and in line with the central argument of this book, the counterrevolutionary backlash was most forceful and repressive where the challenge was most profound, shocking, and fear-inspiring. In this respect, the French Revolution of 1789 and the Iranian Revolution of 1978–9 stand out because they toppled the seemingly most powerful autocracies after long stretches of political stagnation and stability. Moreover, these uprisings brought unprecedentedly deep, multidimensional change that extended far beyond political regime issues and revamped the material or spiritual foundations of society. Following upon the precedent of 1789 and the revolutionary waves of 1820–1 and 1830–1 and targeting primarily political change, the 1848 revolution posed a less stunning threat. The postcommunist color revolutions were even less dramatic; after all, protesters merely invoked the formal rules of the game against the illegitimate authoritarian realities. With the resort to protest and mass contention, however, and with the plan to dismantle massive corruption and crony capitalism, these daring initiatives were more radical than simple democratic transitions and arguably had a revolutionary dimension.

Depending on the depth of the revolutionary challenge, the reactionary response differed in fierceness and excess as well. Accordingly, the French Revolution of 1789 prompted heavy-handed repression, for instance in the Habsburg Empire (Michel 1989: 272–3; Reinalter 1988: 109–10) and even in England (Harvie 2010: 487, 492–3; see more detailed analyses below). The Iranian revolution provoked crackdowns in the regional neighborhood as well (Esposito 1990a: 33–5). Moreover, excesses abounded during the barricade fighting in 1848, both in Berlin and in Vienna, as evident in the extralegal execution of parliamentarian Robert Blum (Reichel 2007: 170–8; for Berlin, see Wolff 1898: 37, 46–8, 51–2, 57–8). Due to the comparatively lower threat, however, the postrevolutionary imposition of order was less uncontrolled. In the color revolutions, brutal counterattacks as perpetrated by the dictator of Uzbekistan (Fumagalli and Tordjman 2010: 171–3) were even rarer. Russia's Vladimir Putin, for instance, tightened the reins in a notoriously calculated vein. Thus, the hardening of autocracy proceeded with the greatest excess where incumbent rulers confronted the most profound revolutionary challenges.

A number of these fortified, harsher authoritarian regimes are not easy to classify in ideological terms – a result of the vague mentalities prevailing under this regime type (Linz 1964). Overall, however, a right-wing tendency prevailed. This reactionary orientation is evident, for instance, in President Putin's alliance with the Orthodox Church, his revival of traditional Russian nationalism, and his appeals to cultural traditionalism. A conservative tendency also underlies the alliance of many Middle Eastern despots with the United States, which is reminiscent of US support for Latin American dictatorships during the 1960s and 1970s. Certainly, in all of these cases the main rationale of authoritarian hardening was the effort to protect the status quo (ante). There was a reactionary impetus, namely to foreclose or undo political change; and the principal strategy was to reverse, block, and reliably forestall radical impulses.

In sum, as the central argument of the present study expects, these determined efforts to fortify autocracy were prompted by profound threats to established regimes and states. The four main clusters of authoritarian tightening that the following sections examine in some depth arose from fearful responses to revolutionary challenges and constituted reactionary efforts at counterdiffusion – similar to the two reverse waves discussed so far. In all of these cases, a stunning revolutionary precedent or a sequence of successful challenges seemed to unleash strong impulses toward the (further) diffusion of contentious threats to autocratic incumbents. In similar ways as during the interwar years and the 1960s and 1970s in Latin America, conservative elites employed all the necessary means to squash this perceived danger – and political liberty suffered even more.

REACTIONS TO THE FRENCH REVOLUTION OF 1789

The gathering storm in France, which erupted into a full-scale revolution in 1789, drew enormous attention and elicited a great deal of admiration all over the globe (Hobsbawm 1996: 77–81; for the Habsburg Empire, see Michel 1989: 266–70, 273–4). While the challenges to royal absolutism and to feudal society that this upheaval posed deepened gradually until 1794, from the beginning the intensifying reform efforts inspired emulation efforts across Europe and beyond. In the Austrian Netherlands (the later Belgium) and in many German territories, for instance, citizen protests and peasant revolts began to erupt right from 1789 onward (Aretin 1980: 65; Reinalter 1988: 73–86). The French attempts to institute a constitutional monarchy, as codified in the liberal charter of 1791, held tremendous appeal as well and stimulated heated debates in various German state parliaments (Braubach 1974: 11). In Hungary (then under Austrian Habsburg domination), the revolutionary transformation in France propelled constitutional changes, but the deputies in Budapest followed primarily the English model (Gergeley 1989: 649–52).

Even the radicalization of the early 1790s, which culminated in the Jacobin rule and *terreur* of 1793–4, elicited sympathies among groupings across the continent. In fact, Jacobin clubs formed in some polities of the Holy Roman Empire and beyond (Hobsbawm 1996: 79–81), as far away as the newly independent United States (Fox-Genovese and Genovese 2005: 13, 24). While these radical stirrings were stronger in the regions bordering on France (Fehrenbach 1981: 154–9; Hoyer 1989: 369–77; Thiele 1989: 531–51; Timmerman 1989: 561–8), especially when some of these areas were conquered by revolutionary armies sent from Paris,[5] they also took hold in unpropitious settings, such as Vienna (Aretin 1980: 64–6; Reinalter 1988: 104–9) and Warsaw (Polasky 2015: 129–34). Indeed, French mercenaries founded a Jacobin club as far away as India! (Hunt 2010: 21)

All of these emulation efforts achieved little success, however. Where the attempt to replicate France's constitutional transformation went the farthest, namely in Poland, the resulting turmoil and conflict provided the pretext for external intervention (Polasky 2015: 131–4). After two rounds of military invasion, neighboring autocracies Austria, Prussia, and Russia simply divided up the rebellious country and erased heroic Poland from the European map for more than 120 years (Zgórniak 1989). Attempts to imitate the more radical currents of the French Revolution held particularly low prospects of success. For instance, the Jacobin clubs that sprouted up across Europe consisted merely of small groupings of intellectuals and lacked both firm organization and any mass support (Reinalter 1988: 67; Press 1989: 223–6). Without the backing of Parisian-style *Sansculottes* they had no chance at all to effect political change. Their hopeless activities were probably inspired by the heuristics of availability and representativeness, which instilled wildly unrealistic assessments about the replicability of Danton and Robespierre's feats.

As the efforts to emulate the French Revolution occurred in objectively unpropitious settings, they also ran afoul of particularly determined opposition. After all, the convulsion in Paris and its diffusion effects instilled strong concern among conservative sectors, such as feudal landowners, clergymen, and especially princes (Hoyer 1989: 377; Schultz 1989: 386); given the monumental impact of the revolutionary precedent, this fear and the resulting counterrevolutionary reflex reached as far as Spain's colony in Peru (Rodríguez Toledo 2011: 188–96). Early on, when the political changes in France seemed to bring a constitutional monarchy as it already existed in England, some rulers, such as Austria's Emperor Leopold II, responded pragmatically with reform efforts (Michel 1989: 265–6) – a faint forerunner of JFK's Alliance for Progress.

---

[5] On revolutionary France's armed export of revolution, see Bayly (2004: 96–9) and recently Polasky (2015: chap. 8).

Yet as soon as the French uprising turned into a frontal attack against the king, intense loss aversion motivated a reactionary switch to clampdowns on oppositionists and the fortification of autocratic rule (Aretin 1980: 67–8; Reinalter 1988: 101–3; Hroch 1989: 53–8; Schultz 1989: 386–7). For instance, the Viennese Jacobins were put on trial for high treason, which resulted in several death sentences and lengthy prison terms (Michel 1989: 272–3). The severity of this repression reflects the depth of fear and the resulting loss aversion; after all, the government employed capital punishment even though Joseph II's reforms had officially abolished the death penalty (Reinalter 1988: 109–10). In addition to this targeted counterattack against the worst troublemakers, the imperial administration tightened its political control mechanisms and created a system of domestic espionage to stamp out any revolutionary ferment emanating from the French precedent.

Interestingly, reactionary counterdiffusion also took hold in Great Britain, which had initially served as a model for the efforts of French revolutionaries to replace royal absolutism with a liberal, constitutional monarchy. In turn, the changes in France inspired ambitious demands in England, such as the proposal of universal suffrage, which found unprecedented support among broader sectors of the citizenry ranging beyond the elite, such as artisans and workers (Maurer 2007: 311–12). While conservative Edmund Burke ([1790] 1999) had from the beginning worried about the political risks inherent in strident reform efforts guided by abstract rationalist doctrines, more and more Englishmen turned sour on the French Revolution when it slid into ever greater radicalism (Harvie 2010: 485–6). The execution of the king and the dictatorship of the self-appointed vanguard of Jacobins created a strong backlash across the English Channel (Maurer 2007: 316).

Paradoxically, yet in line with the main argument of this book, the defense of Britain's incipient liberalism employed some rather illiberal mechanisms. The French *terreur* provoked the British Prime Minister's own "'reign of terror' in 1793/94" (Harvie 2010: 487). Indeed, the government in London suspended habeas corpus in 1794, restricted the rights of assembly and of free speech in 1795, and outlawed trade unions in 1799. As these control measures drove French-inspired radicals underground, the administration responded by building up its apparatus for gathering internal intelligence. The intense concerns for guaranteeing sociopolitical stability demonstrated the depth of the fears unleashed by the French Revolution in Europe's most liberal country, which were arguably exaggerated (Harvie 2010: 492–3). Due to these reactionary countermeasures, "the English freedom, about which one had spoken everywhere in Europe with admiration during the eighteenth century, seemed definitively destroyed," as a historian comments (Maurer 2007: 313). Remarkably, these restrictions began to be lifted only from 1825 onward, long after all remnants of the French Revolution had been replaced by a reactionary restoration regime in its home country (Harvie 2010: 494).

The French Revolution also stimulated unrest in France's colonies in the Caribbean, where ample black populations took inspiration from the calls for "*liberté, égalité, fraternité*" to shake off the yoke of slavery and protest against stringent racial discrimination. While rebellions erupted throughout the region (Gaspar and Geggus 1997), they sooner or later suffered suppression on the small islands, such as Guadeloupe and Martinique. In Saint Domingue, however, the western third of Hispaniola, where France held rich plantations of sugar, coffee, and other lucrative crops, contentious movements triggered a massive slave uprising in 1791 that quickly turned into a major revolution and cruel race war (Landers 2010: chap. 2; Polasky 2015: 147–58). After many years of brutal civil conflict and various foreign interventions, the devastated country managed to defeat an army sent by Napoleon Bonaparte and to gain independence in 1804. Thus, Haiti became a rare case in which an emulative revolution achieved a lasting victory.

The Haitian precedent in turn caused tremors in the western hemisphere, stimulating waves of unrest and uprisings, both after the outbreak of the slave rebellion in the 1790s and after the country's independence in 1804 (Geggus 1989: 108–16; Ferrer 2015: 213–23). Specifically, "the French and Haitian revolutions sparked a series of conspiracies and revolts throughout [the] America[s] that sought slave emancipation and equality for freedmen . . . Such was the case of the so-called tailors' conspiracy in Bahia in 1798 . . . [and a] series of Islamic rebellions in Bahia from 1808 to 1835 . . . [including] a massive attack of three hundred *quilombolas* [runaway slaves] . . . in 1809 that was repressed with much bloodshed" (Klein and Luna 2010: 209; see also 301; and Adelman 2006: 91–4, 100, 222–3). Eventually, the Brazilian government employed so much violence against the rebels that it managed to stop the further proliferation of uprisings (Klein and Luna 2010: 208, 210).

As the reaction of the Brazilian authorities shows, the radical challenge in Haiti, its unusual triumph, and the imitation efforts it stimulated also exerted strong deterrent effects across the western hemisphere. The mass slaughter that engulfed and destroyed the crown jewel of the French colonial empire sent shivers down the spines of slaveholders throughout the Caribbean and beyond, especially in Cuba, Brazil, and the southern United States.[6] As emulative revolts erupted in a variety of settings, the masters strengthened the defensive mechanisms designed to cement their racial superiority and to perpetuate the oppressive exploitation of their captive work force (Fox-Genovese and Genovese 2005: 235; Blackburn 2006: 654–5, 673; Ferrer 2015: 10, 17, 173, 212–14). Moreover, the authorities imposed additional restrictions on "Cuba's free people of color . . . [who] were feared as potential abettors of rebellious slaves" (Cottrol 2013: 51).

---

[6] Landers 1997: 156; Fox-Genovese and Genovese 2005: 14–15, 18, 35–7, 746; Hunt 2010: 27; Cottrol 2013: 71, 94; Ferrer 2015: 8, 42–3, 47, 80–1.

In a tragic twist, the Haitian Revolution also prompted an expansion of slavery in Cuba, Brazil, and the southern United States. After all, the violent destruction of the plantation system in western Hispaniola and the freed slaves' preference for subsistence agriculture caused a drastic permanent reduction in Haiti's sugar and coffee exports. Consequently, the laws of supply and demand created strong incentives for extending the plantation system elsewhere. The planters of Cuba, Brazil, and the US South eagerly responded to these unexpected profit opportunities: they augmented their own production and substantially increased the corresponding use of slaves (see for Cuba Ferrer 2014: 4–5, 10, 17, 36–43). In Brazil, for instance, the forceful import of slaves almost doubled from the 1790s to the 1820s (Klein and Luna 2010: 77; see also 74, 78–80, 90–1; see also Adelman 2006: 84–5). Haitians' gain in personal freedom thus entailed a loss for Africans in other areas of the Americas (Geggus 2010: 84–5; Cottrol 2013: 50).

To conclude, in the typical backlash dynamic highlighted in this study, the Haitian Revolution stimulated the reinforcement and expansion of oppressive slavery in the western hemisphere. Fear of the diffusion of slave revolts prompted determined counterdiffusion, which clearly carried the day. Sadly, even Haiti, where the emulation of the French Revolution achieved an exceptional, permanent success, made no advances toward political liberalism. While the abolition of slavery brought a quantum leap in personal freedom, the political leaders who spearheaded Haitian independence "were unapologetically dictatorial . . . Far from driven by 'democratic ideals,' the revolution that grew out of the slave uprising was authoritarian from beginning to end" (Geggus 2010: 97; see also 97–100). Thus, in the Americas as in Europe, the French Revolution and its spinoff effects provoked a hardening of oppressive rule.

THE BACKLASH AGAINST LIBERAL CONTENTION IN 1848-1849

In 1848, the contentious impulse unleashed in Paris shook some polities much more profoundly than others. Louis Philippe's overthrow had limited, specifically political significance in the liberal nation states of western and northern Europe, where neither the internal social order nor the external shape of the state drew acute, grave conflict. Because a number of these countries, such as Belgium, England, and the Netherlands, already were constitutional monarchies, even the political demands that protesters advanced were fairly contained (Dowe, Haupt, et al. 2001).

By contrast, the revolutionary tsunami spreading eastward from Paris posed much more profound challenges to established rulers in Central and Eastern Europe, where absolutist autocracy prevailed, where ethnic conflicts brewed and the territorial shape of polities was hotly contested, and where important elements of feudalism had survived the French Revolution of 1789–1815. Consequently, the political spark from the West threatened to light the dynamite formed by the complex intersection of political, socioeconomic, and national issues. For instance, the armed rebellion that erupted in Hungary in March 1848 jeopardized the whole Habsburg Empire. And in Berlin, emulative protests raised the acrimonious issue of Prussia's role in the ever more widely demanded unification of Germany. Moreover, Austrian Galicia had experienced violent *jacqueries* in 1846, which the new wave of contention risked reigniting. The profound and multifaceted nature of these challenges, which went far beyond issues of suffrage extension and political rights, made a variety of sociopolitical groupings in Central and Eastern Europe fear substantial costs. Consequently, as this profound contention advanced toward the east, it prompted intense loss aversion. Panicked autocrats and their close counselors desperately groped for countermeasures to prevent the collapse of their rule and forestall the sociopolitical combustion it would likely entail.[7]

Initially, the sudden, surprising eruption of mass contention after many years of quiescence instilled in stunned princes a paralyzing sense of consternation and weakness, which made them vacillate between direct confrontation and tactical concessions. Believing that they faced radical provocateurs and foreign conspirators, they initially called out the troops for violent repression, which was conducted with excessive brutality and produced many vengeful executions (Hohenlohe-Ingelfingen 1897: 32–3, 39; Wolff 1898: 37, 46–8, 51–2, 57–8).

But when these monarchs realized that a broad cross-section of the population, including many upstanding citizens, filled the streets in swelling crowds, they shied away from ordering a bloodbath and instead proposed compromises (Prittwitz 1854: 95–7; Hohenlohe-Ingelfingen 1897: 31, 50; Hachtmann 1997: chap. II.1–2). In Austria and Prussia, the two European great powers engulfed by massive protests in March 1848, rulers quickly withdrew their – militarily undefeated – troops and handed public safety over to newly forming citizen militias. In this way, they temporarily capitulated to the contentious masses, while keeping the forces of organized coercion intact. In Prussia, reactionary sectors, such as the young Otto von Bismarck and the king's own brother Wilhelm, were appalled at this lack of backbone and pushed for a crackdown. In fact, some generals sought to organize the forced removal of the indecisive king (Bismarck 1898: 25–6, 30; cf. L. Gerlach 1891: 193; E. Gerlach 1903, vol. 1, 517–18, 525; Gall 1983: 70–1), but this coup plan foundered on traditional notions of hierarchy. When the monarch tried to explain his hesitant approach to an assembly of leading officers, many responded with sabre rattling, in the most striking demonstration of open military discontent in Prussian history.

But the fear of sharing Louis Philippe's fate by falling prey to escalating crowd protests induced perplexed incumbents to focus first and foremost on ensuring their political survival by any means. To calm the upsurge of contentious fervor among broad sectors of the citizenry, they saw themselves

---

[7] This section draws on materials and arguments presented in Weyland (2016).

forced to offer concessions. The Prussian king and Austrian emperors reformed their governmental cabinets and dismissed notorious conservatives who drew popular ire, most prominently the mainstay of the European restoration era after 1815, Austrian Prince Clemens Metternich. As replacements for these scapegoats they appointed well-known liberals, who loosened autocratic rule and adopted a number of moderate reforms. Furthermore, the monarchs convoked constituent assemblies that would codify the abandonment of absolutism, guarantee fundamental civil rights, and institute limited electoral participation. By making these concessions, the challenged rulers sought to take the wind out of the sail of emulative revolutions and help to demobilize mass contention, which for lack of organization would be difficult to sustain over time.

At the same time, these monarchs, who managed to survive the onslaught of French-inspired revolution, insisted on maintaining exclusive control over the principal forces of coercion, especially the military and the police. As a result, they commanded the instruments of power that would allow them to reassert their autocratic control later on. Indeed, the citizen militias that had mushroomed at the height of the contentious wave faced great difficulty establishing a disciplined organization. Many of these civilians sooner or later tired of their guard duties. Moreover, they were certainly no match for the well-oiled military machine of a European great power. Also, divisions quickly arose among the contentious crowds. Professional and middle-class sectors feared and despised workers and poor artisans, who pushed controversial social demands. Political cleavages also ran deep, both over the proper extent of regime change and over nationality issues, such as the extremely complicated question of how to unify Germany while respecting the interests and needs of Austria and Prussia.

As the wave of popular protest predictably ebbed, princes saw increasing opportunities to reassert their interests and used coercive means to rescind their initial promises and take back concession after concession. A mere two weeks after yielding to the upsurge of mass contention, Prussian King Friedrich Wilhelm IV, for instance, was itching to smother the revolution and reestablish coercive control over his capital.[8] But in order not to reignite bottom-up challenges, princes moved slowly and gradually, targeting first peripheral areas (such as the West Prussian province of Posen) rather than their capitals, the real hotbeds of rebellion. In these ways, autocratic rulers steadily tightened their grip again.

The use of large-scale counterrevolutionary violence started in June 1848 in Prague, which Austrian general Alfred zu Windischgraetz shelled into

---

[8] See his letter of April 6, 1848, to interim Minister of War, Lieutenant General Karl von Reyher, reproduced in Haenchen (1930: 64–6). See also his letter in June to his sister, Tsarina of Russia (in Haenchen 1930: 114), and his comments on a letter from Count Senfft of Pilsach (in Haenchen 1930: 116).

submission. This backlash then received a powerful impulse from the bloody suppression of the June uprisings in Paris: in the very epicenter of the revolutionary wave, conservative sectors crushed a protosocialist challenge at the cost of thousands of lives and thus broke the back of radicalism. Based on this new, reactionary precedent in France, princes across Europe inferred that the wind had changed and felt encouraged to proceed toward dismantling liberal advances at home (for Prussia, see Varnhagen 1862, vol. 5: 88, 95–6, 103, 106; Hachtmann 1997: 555, 654–5, 661). After the spark of contention from France had lit the initial wildfire in early 1848, the ice bucket of repression now similarly helped to extinguish the flames. Signals from Paris had first inspired protesters, but new impulses now energized their mortal enemies. Thus, as in the main wave of autocracy examined in this book, revolutionary diffusion was soon followed by reactionary counterdiffusion.

Besides feeling inspired by the effective defeat of radicalism in Paris, princes actively encouraged each other to crack down in their own country. The fascinating correspondence of Prussian King Friedrich Wilhelm IV, for instance, reveals that some rulers of other German states heavily criticized this monarch for his early concessions and urged him to take them back with force. They clearly hoped that the reassertion of autocracy in this European great power would have spillover effects and strengthen their own hands vis-à-vis their subjects. Thus, they wanted to help create another precedent of repression that would reinforce the "reverse wave" of reactionary counterdiffusion.[9] The hesitant sovereign in Berlin, however, waited until October, when the resurgent Habsburgs harshly crushed a renewed uprising in Vienna. Violating parliamentary immunity, the victorious Austrian army court-martialed and executed Robert Blum, a famous leader of the left in the German National ("Paulskirchen") Assembly (Reichel 2007: 170–8).

While deputies of the Prussian national assembly, another product of the 1848 revolution, called for military support for the Viennese insurgents, King Friedrich Wilhelm IV and his reactionary kitchen cabinet (*camarilla*) took inspiration from their adversaries (E. Gerlach 1903, vol. 2: 4, 13, 15, 17, 21, 23–4, 30, 32; L. Gerlach 1891: 231–4, 239, 242, 254). Moreover, the Prussian monarch's uncle, King Ernst August of Hannover, repeatedly urged him to "make a similar example" in Berlin as well (in Haenchen 1930: 234, 236–7). Soon after the Austrian precedent, Friedrich Wilhelm IV ordered his military to occupy the capital, declared martial law, and forcefully evicted the recalcitrant constituent deputies. Then he reaffirmed autocracy by decreeing a constitution from the top down. Although this charter had a surprisingly liberal content, the reascendant sovereign soon tightened censorship, limited freedom of assembly, and turned the 1850s into a decade of stifling political stagnation.

---

[9] See letters from King Ernst August of Hannover, reproduced in Haenchen (1930: 70–3, 109–10, 233–4), from Grand Duke Georg of Mecklenburg-Strelitz (in Haenchen 1930: 241–2, 288–9), and from King Friedrich August II of Saxony (in Haenchen 1930: 242–4).

Following in the footsteps of great powers Austria and Prussia, princes in many other parts of Germany, especially the north and east, soon aborted liberal openings and reestablished firm, coercive control as well (Engehausen 2007: 232–5). The revolutionary fire kept smoldering, however, especially in southwestern Germany and in Hungary. Early 1849 in fact saw renewed mobilization, with armed uprisings in the most contentious regions. By the summer, however, another round of repression extinguished the flames. Notably, in several cases challenged incumbents relied on external help; accordingly, Prussian troops squashed rebellions in the Rhineland and Baden, while the Russian tsar helped the Austrian Emperor subdue Hungary with massive force.

Thus, open military assistance by powerful autocrats helped their weaker counterparts finally to suppress remaining challenges. Solidarity and cooperation among princes brought the revolution to an end. After the reactionary backlash had first unfolded via a process of counterdiffusion, it was actual collaboration that brought it to completion. This eventual move to effective cooperation was the product of coalition-building efforts that had started very early, namely in the immediate aftermath of Louis Philippe's overthrow in February 1848. Within days, German princes foreseeing the spread of the contentious challenge began feverish efforts to forge an antirevolutionary alliance. Prussia's Friedrich Wilhelm IV, for instance, sent a close confidant, Josef von Radowitz, to Vienna to prepare a conference of German princes that would deliberate on countermeasures (Radowitz 1922: 6, 10, 14–17, 19, 22–5, 30, 33, 47, 50). In addition to the fear of an imminent war with France, which memories of the first French Revolution (specifically, 1792–1815) reflexively evoked, the goal to organize the collective protection of domestic stability motivated this attempt at coordination.

This ambitious plan, in line with the whole spirit of the post-1815 restauration period, was swept aside by the revolutionary tsunami that it was designed to prevent, however. Before the panicked rulers could convene for their conference, Count Metternich, the cornerstone of autocracy in Germany, fell to escalating crowd protests, which made the Viennese court promise liberal reforms. A few days later, mass contention engulfed Berlin and paralyzed Germany's second great power, depriving other challenged rulers of any external military support. Greatly weakened, King Friedrich Wilhelm IV now had to hope for emergency assistance from the Russian tsar, but his fear of a direct challenge to his throne never materialized. Throughout 1848, therefore, connections among autocrats were confined to learning and diffusion, rather than concrete cooperation.

THE IRANIAN REVOLUTION AND THE TIGHTENING OF MIDDLE EAST AUTOCRACIES

Compared to the overthrow of the French King in 1848, the Iranian upheaval of 1978–9 constituted an even more profound challenge to incumbent rulers.

By contrast to the protests of 1848, the downfall of the Shah ushered in a full-scale social revolution, even by Theda Skocpol's exacting standards (Skocpol 1982). Moreover, the revival of militant Islam, especially the violent power grab by Muslim fundamentalists, constituted a virulent threat to neighboring leaders (Rubin 2014: 1, 13, 41, 46–7, 54–6, 99-100). As the Russian Revolution of 1917 had greatly boosted the luster of Lenin's activist brand of revolutionary Marxism, so the establishment and consolidation of the new theocracy in Iran energized Muslim fundamentalism, drawing considerable sympathy in the Arab world and beyond. This appeal reached as far as Malaysia and Indonesia (Von der Mehden 1990: 247–8) and prompted a wave of emulation efforts (Katz 1997: 26–8, 35–7, 51–2, 61–2, 107-15). For established states and societies, the Iranian Revolution called into question a whole way of life and threatened a radical overhaul of basic cultural norms and practices. No wonder, then, that this earthquake quickly shook up the Middle East and instilled hope in some sectors, yet intense loss aversion in others. The regime change in Tehran inspired contentious stirrings in a number of countries, especially along the Persian Gulf; these challenges in turn provoked determined repression and a hardening of authoritarian rule (Ramazani 1988; Esposito 1990b).

These immediate repercussions, which resemble the outbreak of guerrilla uprisings in Latin America after 1959, were shaped by the cognitive shortcuts documented in this study. The availability heuristic drew enormous attention to the unexpected collapse of the Shah's glitzy empire. The stunning overthrow of this self-appointed reincarnation of Cyrus the Great made news across the globe. After all, it was amazing that swelling crowds of common people had managed to evict an apparently all-powerful monarch protected by a well-equipped military. This surprising success of largely unarmed mass contention activated the representativeness heuristic and induced a wide range of people and political forces of divergent persuasion to question the solidity of the other autocrats in the Middle East. Maybe these potentates were also giants on feet of clay: perhaps a determined challenge could bring down these dictators as well!

As in Europe in 1848 and in Latin America during the early 1960s, the inference that incumbent rulers were in a precarious position quickly spread, on all sides of the ideological spectrum. This perception of fragility gave hope to oppositional sectors, regardless of whether they were motivated by fundamentalist Islam, leftist worldviews, or secular liberalism (Bill 1984: 117; Abdelnasser 1997: 26–33). The very same perception of instability instilled fear in adherents of the established order, who saw the ground crumble under their feet (Ramazani 1988: 24, 32, 131, 162, 173, 199, 235–6, 243, 246; Anderson 1990: 157–8, 166; Esposito and Piscatori 1990: 4, 7–15; Von der Mehden 1990: 239–42).

As it happened in Latin American after the Cuban Revolution, the representativeness heuristic triggered a rash of precipitous, ill-prepared emulation efforts across the Middle East, which drew a repressive response and uniformly failed. Right in 1979, Saudi Arabia faced protests in its main oil-producing region in the east, which lies directly across the Persian Gulf from Iran. Moreover, Muslim militants took hostages at the annual pilgrimage in Mecca that fall. Contentious stirrings also occurred in 1979 and early 1980 in Bahrain, which Iran claims as a province. Moreover, in 1981 that monarchy suffered a coup attempt inspired – and perhaps supported – by the theocratic regime in Tehran (Ramazani 1988: 50–1). Also in 1979, "the Kuwaiti ruling family . . . felt threatened . . . by an Iranian-inspired, if not Iranian-sponsored, act to incite political unrest in Kuwait" (Ramazani 1988: 118–19). Similarly, "Islamists in Jordan capitalized on the Iranian Revolution" as well as domestic grievances "to gain popular support" (Lust-Okar 2004: 167) during the early 1980s. Most dramatically, a terrorist cell in the Egyptian military assassinated President Anwar el-Sadat in 1981, invoking lessons drawn from the Iranian Revolution. Its leader, Lieutenant Colonel Abbud Zumur, had hoped to unleash a popular uprising because "Iran taught us that the army and police cannot stand against an insurgency of the masses" (quoted in Akhavi 1990: 143; see also Meijer 2011: 152–3). This inference derived from Ayatollah Khomeini's success provides a striking indication of the representativeness heuristic and its impact in spurring imitation efforts.

Due to the same cognitive shortcuts, the cataclysmic Iranian Revolution caused panic among established rulers. Therefore, this rash of diffusion attempts activated strong loss aversion and provoked a repressive backlash (Bill 1984: 123; Esposito 1990a: 33, 35; Esposito and Piscatori 1990: 6, 9; Anderson 1990: 166–7; Von der Mehden 1990: 243, 245, 251). Throughout the Middle East and beyond, the police and military squashed open contention and took preemptive steps to forestall its eruption. The Bahraini, Kuwaiti, and Saudi authorities quelled unrest and punished its real or potential instigators. Proceeding with his notorious brutality, Saddam Hussein in 1980 executed Shiite cleric Muhammad Baqr al-Sadr and many of his followers, whom he suspected of stirring up trouble among coreligionists in southern Iraq (Robins 1990: 86–7, 95–6). Furthermore, incumbent regimes tightened censorship and deepened their surveillance of civil society, especially of Islamist groupings. In all of these ways, many Middle Eastern autocracies hardened, reversed any halting steps toward political liberalization, and moved further away from democracy.

In fact, the deterrent effect of the Iranian revolution may also have contributed to one full-scale regime change in the Middle East, namely the 1980 overthrow of democracy by a military coup in Turkey. One of the factors motivating the imposition of authoritarian rule was the rise of a domestic Islamic movement during the 1970s, which was beginning to challenge the secular orientation imposed by the armed forces since the times of Mustafa Kemal Atatürk. Khomeini's stunning success seems to have exacerbated the concerns about Muslim fundamentalism, both among Turkish generals and their supporters in the US government.[10] In conclusion, as in the other instances of counterdiffusion

---

[10] Birand's (1987: 24, 65–7, 102, 122–3, 139–41, 182, 187, 192, 215) in-depth journalistic investigation emphasizes, among other motivations for the coup, the military's fear of resurgent

analyzed in this book, an outstanding revolutionary precedent prompted a potent reaction, which turned history "in the wrong direction."

Given the resource abundance that the oil rentier states in the Gulf region commanded, however, incumbent authoritarian regimes did not confine themselves to sheer repression but often let carrots follow the stick. Averting political trouble through generous economic benefits and plentiful patronage has been a well-oiled mechanism that has greatly helped make Middle Eastern autocracy so durable (Bellin 2004: 144, 147–8; see recently Brownlee, Masoud, and Reynolds 2015: 51–5). Thus, petroleum wealth allows reactionary stabilization efforts motivated by asymmetrical loss aversion to go beyond pure repression; incumbent rulers can skillfully use their windfall rents to buy political acquiescence. Yet this greater tactical latitude does not alter the goal nor the outcome of these fear-driven measures, namely to cement authoritarian rule.

As the initial panic subsided, however, it became obvious that the Iranian Revolution unleashed less broad and powerful impulses for imitation efforts than proestablishment sectors, both at the domestic and international level, had feared in the beginning. This limited diffusion is noteworthy because in addition to the inherent impetus emanating from the Shah's overthrow in the world of bounded rationality, Iran's new leadership actively sought to export its brand of Muslim fundamentalism (Ramazani 1988: 24–7). But both the demonstration and contagion effects of the upheaval in Tehran and the new theocracy's attempts to spread its gospel faced several important obstacles (Rajaee 1990: 72, 76–7; Long 1990: 102, 104, 106, 114).

Although Ayatollah Khomeini deliberately sounded universalistic themes and depicted his regime as the revival of Islam in general (Tibi 1986: 34–5; Esposito 1990a: 30–4; Rajaee 1990: 71–5), the longstanding, bitter sectarian divide between Shiites and Sunnis severely restricted receptivity for these appeals (thorough analysis in Sivan 1989). Even eager novices who traveled to Iran to receive instruction quickly found out that the Mullah regime's worldview was deeply shaped by Shiite particularism; feeling betrayed, Sunnis therefore departed soon (Rajaee 1990: 75–7). Ethnic differences, especially the gulf between Persians and the Arabs populating most of the Middle East, created additional barriers and acquired acute salience with the bloody Iran – Iraq war that erupted in 1980 and dragged on for nearly a decade.

Islamism and its resentment against Islamist leader Necmettin Erbakan; US officials shared these concerns, perhaps even more intensely, due to the geopolitical perspective of the global superpower. Harris (2011: 209) and Orhon (2012: 297, 301) also highlight the generals' concern about Turkey's domestic Islamists, but draw no connection to the Iranian Revolution. Demirel (2003: 254), however, who "relies heavily on documentary analysis and interviews with General Kenan Evren," the mastermind of the 1980 coup, does not mention fears of Islamism at all. And Turan's overview analysis (2015: 105–14) mentions "left-right polarization" in general, but not the rise of Islamism.

Moreover, as with the *terreur* of the French Revolution of 1789, the excesses committed by Iran's new dictatorship antagonized many early sympathizers. Mass executions, brutal torture, the capture of US hostages, and the totalitarian imposition of traditional social norms caused widespread revulsion and gave defenders of the established order great opportunities to discredit the Iranian precedent and thus help forestall its spread. For all of these reasons, the spontaneous fear that Muslim fundamentalism would diffuse widely and prompt a wave of emulative revolutions receded, especially in nations more distant from the epicenter of this upheaval.

Accordingly, during this wave of diffusion and counterdiffusion, the threat posed by the Iranian Revolution was especially severe for the Gulf monarchies, for four reasons. First, they are located directly across the Persian Gulf from Iran. Geographic proximity facilitates diffusion, even in the era of globalization. An impulse that is territorially close tends to have particular force. Second, a significant proportion of their citizens, in Saudi Arabia at least in a strategic province, are Shiites; yet Sunnis have long monopolized political power and discriminated against Shiites, who could therefore be susceptible to Khomeini's "populist" appeals to the downtrodden and disadvantaged (Bill 1984: 108–12; Ramazani 1988: 23–4). Third, the leader of the Iranian Revolution heavily criticized these monarchies, declaring them as fundamentally illegitimate and incompatible with Islam (Esposito 1990a: 33). Fourth, many of the Gulf states were close allies of the United States, whom Khomeini vilified as the "Great Satan." The dependence on US support and perceived subservience to the global superpower made these polities look very similar to prerevolutionary Iran, which the Shah had turned into the United States' auxiliary sheriff in the Gulf region. No wonder that the Gulf monarchies became favorite targets of Iran's revolutionary propaganda and that they lived in fear of spillover effects.

In response, these Arab kingdoms took particularly determined steps to preclude contagion and to combat the slightest efforts to emulate the Iranian Revolution. Indeed, the leader among the Gulf monarchies, Saudi Arabia, encouraged its neighbors to take a hard line against contentious stirrings inspired or supported by its Persian adversary (Bill 1984: 123). To institutionalize these coordination efforts, the Gulf monarchies organized the collective protection of their entrenched autocracies by forming the Gulf Cooperation Council (GCC) on the heels of the Iranian Revolution in 1981. While this new body had several purposes, incumbent rulers' intention to forestall infection by the revolutionary virus was most important (Bill 1984: 122–3; Ramazani 1988: 114–27, 242–3). The kings in the region sought to guarantee firm support from their counterparts in case they had to confront sudden challenges – which were most likely to come in the form of Islamic fundamentalist efforts to imitate the radical transformation across the Gulf. The GCC thus sought to fulfill the same function that the Concert of Europe (created at the Vienna Congress in 1815) had discharged for many years and that the hasty alliance sought by the Austrian emperor, Prussian king, and Russian tsar in early March 1848 was designed to realize. Like these precursors, the GCC arranged for the collective defense of established rulers against current waves of contention and prepared systematic measures to forestall future wildfires.

Interestingly, this mechanism for protecting autocracy has operated with considerable reliability for decades. During the Arab Spring, the GCC under Saudi leadership dispatched troops to help the embattled monarch of Bahrain suppress the uprising focused on Pearl Roundabout (Niethammer 2013: 269, 281, 284–6; Kneuer et al. 2018: 7–9). Moreover, this council of conservative princes brokered a compromise deal in Yemen that replaced long-ruling Ali Abdullah Saleh by his vice president, yet left the entrenched power structure intact (Worth 2014). Moreover, the GCC took steps to include Jordan and Morocco and thus stabilize fellow monarchs against domestic opposition (Yom 2016: 28–32). Thus, antirevolutionary cooperation and authoritarian solidarity in the Gulf region have remained alive and well over the long run. While the luster of the Iranian Revolution has faded and direct emulation efforts have ceased, fears among established leaders have persisted; new challenges continue to be viewed through the lens of this striking precedent (Rubin 2014: 118–22; see also Schwedler 1998); and the institutional instrument for protecting established despots against this threat has continued to function. Thus, the mechanisms of counterdiffusion have outlived the impulses of diffusion – another indication of asymmetrical loss aversion and its lasting power.

In general, memories of the Persian upheaval have continued to feed the specter of Muslim fundamentalism in Middle East politics (Wright 1992: 133, 144; Posusney 2004: 128–9). Autocrats keep genuinely fearing this threat, but also use it to justify their refusal to initiate or sustain political liberalization. Facing protests in 1984, for instance, King Hassan II of Morocco leveled accusations against the opposition while "waving a picture of Khomeini" (Lust-Okar 2004: 164), the spiritual leader of the Iranian Revolution. Thus, rulers have invoked the Iranian precedent to discredit domestic challenges.

A particularly tragic instance in which the Iranian experience colored and exacerbated perceptions of an acute challenge occurred in Algeria in the early 1990s, where an Islamist party took advantage of a political opening and achieved impressive electoral majorities in local and national elections. Yet its victory in the parliamentary contest of late 1991 unleashed intense concerns among elites, middle sectors, and foreign powers such as France and the United States. The Iranian Revolution, which served as an inspiration for the more radical wing of the Islamist Salvation Front (Front Islamique de Salut – FIS), aggravated the fears among status quo-oriented circles (Cavatorta 2002: 33, 36–7). This outstanding precedent continued to spur efforts at diffusion and at counterdiffusion. As one side seemed to seek an Islamic state and even embraced armed jihad to attain it (Viorst 1997: 90–1, 95), the other side was determined to forestall this outcome at all costs, and therefore organized a military intervention to abort the democratic experiment that had gone awry. This desperate countermeasure, designed to preclude another Iranian-style theocracy, plunged the country into a lengthy and bloody civil war. Predictably, profound loss aversion prompted an excessively harsh response to the Islamist threat, which included many indiscriminate massacres. This brutality reflected in part the specter of the Iranian Revolution, which with its own excesses had branded common perceptions of Islamist rule and instilled lasting fear among incumbent rulers, their domestic and foreign supporters, and even many citizens throughout the Middle East (Wright 1992: 133, 144; cf. Shirley 1995).

As in the Algerian case, the threat of antimodern, Iranian-style theocracy has frequently guaranteed Middle Eastern autocrats the more or less begrudging support of western democracies led by the United States (Brownlee 2012). Loss aversion, which gives negative news special salience and disproportionate weight, has helped to keep the traumatic downfall of the Shah on the radar screen of regional and extraregional decision makers. Recent studies confirm the lingering impact of the Iranian Revolution, which keeps posing an ideational threat, at least in the eyes of fearful, eternally suspicious autocrats, their domestic coteries, and their uncertainty-plagued foreign backers. While incumbent despots certainly play up these concerns and invoke them strategically to stabilize their domination, there is every indication that they genuinely see considerable danger (Rubin 2014). Thus, notwithstanding deliberate exaggeration, there also is a strong core of real fear, derived in part from the Iranian precedent. As memories of the dramatic French Revolution of 1789, especially of Robespierre's *terreur*, shaped European politics during the whole first half of the nineteenth century, so recollections of the Persian earthquake have influenced Middle Eastern politics for decades. The impact of these legacies was obvious during the Arab Spring, when they gave special resonance to the widespread concerns that Islamists would take advantage of the political openings arising from successful protests.

In conclusion, the Iranian Revolution provided the stunning impulse that set in motion a typical wave of diffusion and counterdiffusion, as examined in this book. Once again, cognitive shortcuts shaped the perceptions of both sympathizers and adversaries of this profound transformation. This striking precedent grabbed observers' attention via the availability heuristic, and the representativeness heuristic then suggested its widespread replicability. As some sectors therefore felt inspired to undertake emulation efforts, status quo-oriented sectors perceived grave threats which activated their loss aversion. Intent upon defending their power and privileges and to safeguard stability, elites, middle sectors, and even mass actors supported crackdowns on contentious stirrings and a tightening of autocratic control. As a result, the Iranian Revolution set back the cause of political liberalism and democracy and contributed to the remarkable durability of authoritarian rule in the Middle East. For instance, this area proved most resistant to the massive third wave of democratization, which reshaped all other regions of the world. By many accounts, the deterrent effect of Islamic fundamentalism, which gained special salience with the theocratic power grab in Iran, contributed to this unusual persistence of authoritarianism.

THE COLOR REVOLUTIONS AND THE AUTHORITARIAN
REACTION IN THE FORMER SOVIET UNION

The color revolutions that advanced in the postcommunist world around the turn of the millennium also set in motion the typical sequence of diffusion and counterdiffusion. This pattern of advances and reactions is noteworthy because these challenges to competitive-authoritarian regimes (cf. Levitsky and Way 2010; Bunce and Wolchik 2011) emerged from a less dramatic precedent than the Iranian cataclysm. The Shah's eviction had unleashed a profound social and religious revolution that not only overturned politics, the state, and society, but also transformed the everyday lives of common citizens.

By contrast, the Eastern European crowds pursued no radical goals and rarely used violent means. Instead, they merely protested against stolen elections and pushed for evicting the corrupt cronies who unfairly sought to perpetuate their power. In fact, the discontented masses invoked the officially valid formal rules against chief executives who violated these laws in order to maintain a competitive authoritarian regime behind a democratic façade. Thus, while these oppositionists engaged in street contention and boldly defied the powers that be, they actually defended the existing constitutional order against the manipulations and infractions committed by chief executives. They pushed hard for change, but sought only to achieve the faithful implementation of the laws that the incumbents had pledged to uphold. Accordingly, their challenge, which mainly employed "contained" contention (McAdam, Tarrow, and Tilly 2001: 7–8), was less profoundly disruptive than the Iranian Revolution had been. This largely nonviolent defiance followed the established institutional calendar and targeted an institutional solution, though with the underlying goal of replacing the corrupt "political class" and overhauling its crony capitalism.

As this postelectoral contention was less extraordinary and dramatic than other precedents examined in this book, it is not even clear which event really triggered the color revolutions. Scholars disagree about the precedent that set in motion this wave of regime challenges. Most observers highlight the postelectoral protests that triggered the overthrow of Serbian thug Slobodan Milošević in late 2000. But Bunce and Wolchik (2011: chap. 3) point to earlier cases in which electoral defeats forced semiauthoritarian governments to back down and open the way for democratic advances, namely Slovakia in 1998 and Croatia in 2000. This disagreement over the precipitating event suggests that the wave of color revolutions gathered steam gradually, rather than being propelled by one clear-cut, outstanding precedent, as it happened in the other diffusion processes examined in this book. There certainly was no equivalent to the epochal Russian and Cuban Revolution, nor the surprising Iranian collapse.

In fact, these postelectoral challenges took time to gather steam, produce broader reverberations, and exert a significant impact. Only after a while did the color revolutions, which emerged in Eastern European hybrid regimes, move toward the East, threaten more unambiguously autocratic incumbents, and affect the former Soviet Union. In particular, the rulers of Russia, who were turning this mutilated and diminished great power into the mainstay of competitive authoritarianism in the region, did not initially seem to expect significant spillover from these crowd protests. Even when Georgia, which had been a peripheral part of the USSR, evicted its nondemocratic incumbent in late 2003, President Putin and his entourage wrote off this episode as an anomaly that was unlikely to have further consequences.

But then, with the Orange Revolution in Ukraine, defiance erupted close to the core of the former superpower; and it engulfed a major urban center that was similar to Moscow and St. Petersburg. As the contentious wave was shaking up the old empire's heartland, alarm bells went off in the Kremlin.[11] President Putin was determined to prevent further contagion and protect the nondemocratic regime that he himself was installing. In fact, Ukraine's division between a more liberal west that was looking toward "Europe," and a Russian-leaning, crony-capitalist, and authoritarian east had induced the new tsar to strengthen his friends inside the neighboring country. Accordingly, Putin had in various ways supported the autocratic incumbent's handpicked successor in the fraudulent elections of late 2004 that drew protesters' ire (Petrov and Ryabov 2006; Horvath 2013: 23–30). Due to his massive involvement, the Russian president saw himself as a direct target of the mass contention in Kiev. Precisely because he had openly taken sides in Ukraine and thus shown his true colors, he feared that his own manipulations in Russia would soon provoke domestic challenges as well. For these reasons, the Ukrainian upheaval dramatically impressed on the Russian leadership the potential threat posed by the advance of the color revolutions. Unusually, it was not the first precedent, but a later step in this sequence of contentious experiences that emitted the strongest shock waves and made the architect of Russia's competitive authoritarianism tremble.

Yet because the color revolutions lacked a single outstanding trigger and did not seek a profound, comprehensive overhaul, the hopes and fears they evoked were – in relative terms – less intense and widespread than after the Russian, Cuban, and Iranian Revolutions. Stirred up primarily by educated youth activists who were linked into transnational networks, the protesting crowds seemed to come disproportionately from the middle class; lower-class people pressing socioeconomic or religious demands were strongly underrepresented. What was at stake was authoritarian control over the political regime and cronyism and corruption in the economy, not the fundamental structure of state and society. Because the challenge was less deep-reaching, the threat perceptions on the incumbent side – while typically overblown and exaggerated – were less severe as well. Established rulers, their entourages,

---

[11] Ambrosio 2009: 40, 72, 79, 111, 137, 143, 159; Silitski 2010: 342–4; Wilson 2010: 29; Finkel and Brudny 2012b: 15; Horvath 2013: 5, 22, 31–84.

and their underlings certainly feared for their perks, privileges, and sinecures, if not their political survival. But these acute concerns found less automatic resonance in society at large.

To strengthen their defensive efforts, chief executives tried hard to win broader support and persuade public opinion to share their genuine threat perceptions. They denigrated protesters as hooligans and troublemakers and depicted them as lackeys of foreign powers, especially the United States, which incumbent autocrats blamed for fomenting this unrest (Ambrosio 2009: chaps. 4–5; Horvath 2013: chaps. 4–7). In this way, authoritarian governments sought to enlist nationalism and invoke the rights of sovereignty. For this purpose, President Vladimir Putin coined the concept of "sovereign democracy" and claimed that Russia should be allowed to pursue its own, native version of democracy without outside interference. By implying the inapplicability of the liberal-pluralist notions embraced by the West, Russia's powerful leader tried to immunize the nondemocracy he was establishing against foreign criticism (Ambrosio 2009: 71–84; Wilson 2010: 22, 31; Finkel and Brudny 2012b: 28). And by depicting this competitive-authoritarian regime as autochthonous and homegrown, Putin appealed to Russian pride in order to garner internal backing. In these ways, he wanted to inoculate his country against the color revolutionary virus, rally his compatriots around him, and thus win acceptance and support for his domestic backlash.

Strengthened in these ways, Putin responded to the color revolutions by systematically tightening restrictions on the opposition, intensifying control over and surveillance of the media, disarticulating independent groupings in civil society, and building up his own support organizations (Silitski 2010; Wilson 2010; Koesel and Bunce 2013: 756–8). For instance, real or potential adversaries faced petty restrictions and constant harassment, which made it impossible for them to engage in serious electoral competition – the very precondition of a color revolution: as Putin engineered lopsided victories for his own candidates, postelectoral protests lost any credibility and became unpromising (Bunce 2017: 26–7). In fact, by establishing firm command over the media, the incumbent autocrat obstructed the opposition's ability to "reach" substantial parts of the citizenry and mobilize for contention. Moreover, the Russian president used carrots and sticks to intimidate business "oligarchs" and prevent them from taking an oppositional stance. In all of these ways, the Russian leadership moved steadily and systematically in an ever more authoritarian direction. While this trend had preceded the Orange Revolution, it became more marked and obvious thereafter. Typically, this wave of diffusion prompted determined counterdiffusion as well; prodemocratic contention triggered "preemptive authoritarianism" (Silitski 2010).

This backlash was not confined to Russia, but also unfolded in several other countries that had emerged from the breakup of the Soviet Union (see in general Beissinger 2007: 268–74). In Belarus, Alexander Lukashenko responded to the color revolutions, especially the Ukrainian upheaval, by fortifying his autocratic stranglehold over a fairly developed society. When the "last dictator of Europe" faced postelectoral protests in 2006, he reacted with heavy-handed repression. He was more willing than Putin's regime to impose prison sentences and even make some leading opponents "disappear" (Markus 2010: 122–5). In subsequent years, Lukashenko further reduced the political space for the domestic opposition, cemented his alliance with Russia, and thus inoculated his openly authoritarian regime against the growing chorus of criticism from Europe and the United States. By building such an unassailable fortress, Lukashenko precluded any serious unrest after the coerced elections of 2008 and 2010. In sum, while Belarus had already suffered under authoritarian rule before the Orange Revolution, the mass contention in Kiev prompted a further deterioration.

Another backlash occurred in Uzbekistan, where a longstanding autocrat responded fiercely to an uprising that looked like a spillover of the Kyrgyz Tulip Revolution of 2005. As spiraling protests quickly drove out the authoritarian incumbent in Bishkek, the Tashkent government harshly repressed the unrest erupting in an Uzbek province. Scared by the neighbor's unexpected downfall and warned by the evicted autocrat of Georgia, President Islam Karimov and his cronies predictably overreacted and applied excessive force to restore "order" (Fumagalli and Tordjman 2010: 171–3). As is common in the world of bounded rationality, geographic proximity facilitated activation of the availability heuristic, and the representativeness heuristic suggested that what had occurred in one "Stan" could happen among its neighbors as well. To forestall this severe threat, Karimov cracked down hard, shelved his efforts to win greater international autonomy, and aligned more closely with Russia again. While not facing an open challenge and therefore not responding with stern repression, the autocrats of Kazakhstan, Tajikistan, and Turkmenistan tightened their command over political society as well (Isaacs 2010: 206–7; Kevlihan and Sherzamonov 2010: 185–8; Ó Beacháin 2010: 224–6).

Furthermore, as the Iranian Revolution spurred an effort at collective defense among anxious autocrats, so the color revolutions stimulated the strengthening of a similar body, the Shanghai Cooperation Organization. To guarantee economic and political stability in Central Asia, Kazakhstan, Kyrgyzstan, Turkmenistan, and Uzbekistan had joined with Russia and China right after the turn of the millennium to form the SCO. When the Tulip Revolution in Kyrgyzstan seemed to reveal the fragility of authoritarian regimes in the region, the SCO turned into a political mechanism for preserving Central Asia's dictatorships against any challenges (Melnykovska, Plamper, and Schweickert 2012: 77). The organization condemned "extremist forces" and "terrorism," the code words its officers used to delegitimize prodemocratic manifestations (Ambrosio 2008: 1332–6). While the exact functions and attributions of this collective security mechanism remain vague, and while the SCO stopped short of preparing for interventions in the domestic affairs of a challenged autocracy, the overall purpose of this collaborative venture was clear, namely to preserve the established authoritarian regimes in the area (Ambrosio 2008; 2009, chap. 8).

In sum, fearful nondemocratic governments in a number of post-Soviet republics countered the danger emanating from the color revolutions by taking further steps in an autocratic direction (Bunce and Wolchik 2011: chap. 7). Observers often marvel at the fierceness of these responses, which seem excessive in light of the actual challenge. For instance, Jeanne Wilson comments:

> On the face of it, the heavy-handed tactics of the Kremlin against a marginalized and unpopular opposition in the 2007 parliamentary and 2008 presidential elections seem irrational . . . The right-wing parties did not pose even a remote electoral threat to Putin . . . The fear that the West could devise a Color Revolution scenario of infiltration and penetration making use of this small stratum of Russian right-wing politicians explains the virulence of the Kremlin's reaction to these liberal parties, a reaction that was highly disproportionate to their domestic influence. (2010: 25)

Yet this overshooting is understandable from the perspective of the theory developed in this book: The color revolutionary threat activated powerful loss aversion among authoritarian incumbents, which made them go to striking lengths to ensure their political survival.

Similarly, autocrats' reactionary moves were surprisingly indiscriminate and undifferentiated – another indication that cognitive heuristics and skewed choice mechanisms were at work. A rationally calculating posture would have assessed the specific challenges confronting each ruler and would have prudently calibrated the response to a thorough evaluation of the prevailing power constellation. Yet contrary to such distinctive, well-targeted responses, panicked autocrats proceeded in a uniformly heavy-handed fashion. Koesel and Bunce (2013: 755–6, 760–2) establish this unexpected finding by comparing the ways in which the Russian and Chinese regimes dealt with the color revolutions and the Arab Spring. Based on specific regime type, geographic location, and religious background, pragmatic interest calculations would have predicted differential, carefully adjusted responses. But in fact, both countries reacted in remarkably similar and remarkably harsh ways to both of these contentious waves.[12] This finding corroborates the central arguments of this book that cognitive shortcuts and asymmetrical loss aversion provoked undifferentiated overreactions to efforts at emulative contention.

Due to all of these domestic and international reactions, the color revolutions – like the other contentious waves discussed in this section – had a negative net effect on the prospects for political liberalization and democracy

---

[12] Whereas the Chinese regime took determined defensive steps, its own autocratic model, bolstered by the country's amazing economic performance over the last three decades, has not begun to exude appeal on the international stage; foreign observers also doubt its broader applicability. For these reasons, the "China model" has not set in motion a diffusion process (Ambrosio 2012).

in their region, as many observers argue (Silitski 2010: 339, 349; Finkel and Brudny 2012a: 7; see also Kalandadze and Orenstein 2009). Due to loss aversion, progressive actions drew much more determined and powerful reactions. Demands for freedom made little headway and often provoked repression, which ended up producing setbacks.

CONCLUSION

The preceding examination of the reverse wave of the interwar years and of four clusters of autocratic hardening shows that the central argument designed in this study of the proliferation of military dictatorship in Latin America has more general validity. All of these reactionary riptides emerged from responses to revolutionary challenges that seemed to threaten the political and socioeconomic status quo in a wide range of countries. By imposing authoritarianism and fascism during the interwar years, and by moving further away from political liberalism and democracy in the other four episodes, right-wing sectors sought to combat real or potential challengers inspired by high-profile precedents of profound transformations that had recently occurred in their regions. Fear of contentious diffusion thus prompted conservative or reactionary counterdiffusion. To avoid being swept up in a revolutionary wave, conservative elites sought protection under authoritarian rule, and reigning autocrats fortified restrictive and repressive mechanisms for preserving their domination.

Thus, the backlash mechanism highlighted in the present study holds explanatory power beyond the rash of coups in Latin America. The new theory can also account for the impulse behind the massive reverse wave of the interwar years and for several clusters of illiberal changes that have made nondemocratic regimes even more undemocratic. As all of these reactionary moves were prompted by the perceived threat of revolution, the argument developed in this study holds broader applicability.

9

Conclusion: Theoretical Reflections

REVERSE WAVES AS BACKLASH PHENOMENA

As Chapters 4 through 7 have amply documented, the Latin American reverse wave of the 1960s and 1970s was essentially a backlash phenomenon. The Cuban Revolution stimulated daring and persistent diffusion efforts by radicals across a wide range of countries, but this dramatic event also scared conservative and centrist sectors and induced them to combat the leftist promotion of revolution with all means. This interactive dynamic of revolutionary diffusion and reactionary counterdiffusion drove the forceful crackdown against the isomorphic imitation of the Cuban Revolution via the rash of guerrilla movements during the 1960s. Yet the inspirational impact of Castro's success was so powerful that left-wing efforts to foment socialist revolution persisted, despite the brutal crushing of these precipitous ventures at direct replication. As Latin America experienced a profound process of radicalization during the 1960s and early 1970s, the challenge-reaction dynamic highlighted in this book brought the proliferation of autocratic regimes in more and more countries. The imposition of bureaucratic authoritarianism sought to forestall the spread of revolutionary transformations definitively.

Invariably, thus, left-wing attempts at diffusion prompted right-wing and centrist counterdiffusion. The transformational optimism of the left instilled deep fear among the other side of the ideological spectrum and provoked a fierce determination to foil these hopes, block profound change, and fortify the polity against radical projects. Due to the intensity and depth of this backlash, reactionary counterdiffusion did not only stop the advance of revolutionary projects, but also sought to prevent the recurrence of renewed "communist" threats forever. Thus, counterdiffusion went beyond maintaining the status quo and tried to reinforce the existing system by eradicating the radical left, often with a great deal of repression. From the perspective of the progressivism shared by modernization theory and mainstream constructivism, these counterrevolutionary initiatives sought to turn the clock back by trying to root out the very potential for future challenges.

By demonstrating and highlighting this backlash dynamic, the present study contributes to the diffusion literature in theoretical and conceptual terms. Most of this burgeoning body of writings, particularly the analysis of policy diffusion, conceives of the spread of innovations as involving the choice between adoption and nonadoption; where the original model or precedent undergoes modifications, those fall in between full emulation and the preservation of the status quo. But where a transformation is so drastic and deep-reaching that it threatens the core interests and fundamental values of many powerful elite sectors, its high-profile realization in one country provokes resolute efforts at self-protection in a wide range of other nations. To forestall what they see as a very costly change, establishment groupings impose thorough countermeasures and attack their extremist enemies with full force. The strength of these fortification efforts blocks the spread of the initial stimulus. A radical precedent thus has a strong deterrent effect. Imitation attempts backfire and provoke forceful moves in the opposite direction. As diffusion is overwhelmed by counterdiffusion, the protagonists of the initial precedent achieve the opposite of their broader goals. In taking power in Cuba and pushing for socialism, Fidel Castro hoped to trigger a region-wide revolution – but he ended up provoking the most massive proliferation of reactionary autocracy that Latin America has ever seen.

A BOUNDED RATIONALITY ACCOUNT

To explain the interactive dynamic of diffusion and counterdiffusion that drove the Latin American reverse wave, this study has applied and extended the bounded rationality approach developed in my analysis of the main cascades of democratic contention (Weyland 2014). The clustering of political regime change, including both struggles for democracy and the imposition of autocracy, arises from inferences that political actors draw from relevant precedents via cognitive shortcuts. Due to these inferential heuristics, observers of all ideological stripes usually pay disproportionate attention to dramatic, vivid events, such as the sudden overthrow of a longstanding autocracy, as in France in 1848 or Tunisia in 2011 (Weyland 2012), or the stunning power grab by a minority of radical revolutionaries, as in Cuba in 1959. Applying the availability heuristic, actors assign enormous importance to such high-profile feats and come to overestimate the likelihood that this kind of event could happen again in similar settings. Consequently, such an unexpected political change suddenly reshapes actors' probability assessments and decision calculus.

Moreover, the representativeness heuristic induces political actors to overrate apparent similarities and to discount relevant context factors such as statistical base rates and the possibility of chance factors. By exaggerating the significance of resemblances and parallels, this common cognitive shortcut makes people jump to the conclusion that a precedent event has a high likelihood to recur in a wide range of additional settings. Accordingly, prodemocratic forces across Europe in 1848 and in the Arab world in 2011 inferred from the surprising success of revolutionaries in France and Tunisia, respectively, that they could successfully contest their own autocratic rulers as well (Weyland 2012). This rash inference, which saw the initial precedent as "representative" of the political situation prevailing in a whole region of the world, motivated an outburst of replication efforts. But in most cases, the hopes of repeating the French or Tunisian success quickly ran afoul of the significant differences that actually existed across these diverse political settings; in most of the other polities, incumbent autocrats sat much more firmly in the saddle and managed to deflect or repress this precipitous wave of emulative crowd challenges.

In very similar ways, many left-wing groupings inferred from the unlikely success of the Cuban Revolution that they could emulate Fidel Castro's example and foment successful revolutions in their own countries as well. Status quo defenders, in turn, also overrated this stunning precedent. Therefore, they foresaw the spread of communist uprisings, saw profound threats to the maintenance of the established order, and took drastic countermeasures to combat leftist challenges. This book thus demonstrates that cognitive shortcuts shaped and distorted the information processing, probability calculations, and political actions not only of prodemocratic forces, as documented in Weyland (2014), but also of their political enemies, whether they came from the radical left or the reactionary right. The historical analysis of Chapters 4 through 7 thus extends central findings of the earlier book and corroborates through an out-of-sample investigation the more general applicability of my bounded rationality theory of waves of political regime change.

The present study then adds a crucial additional mechanism to this bounded rationality theory in order to account for the interactive dynamic of diffusion and counterdiffusion that propelled the Latin American reverse wave. As mentioned above, the spread of autocratic rule arose from a backlash against the revolutionary projects of the left. Thus, radical action provoked forceful reaction. What is noteworthy in this polarizing dynamic is its stark asymmetry: status quo defenders uniformly ended up winning these all-out contests; they managed to forestall revolutionary replication efforts and suppressed the protagonists. While the obvious resource advantages of sociopolitical elites contributed significantly to these heavily skewed outcomes, establishment forces in most cases also had numerical advantages: status quo defenders outnumbered radicals, not rarely by wide margins.

This uneven alignment of political forces is remarkable given that according to rationalist accounts, Latin America's stark social inequality would have predicted overwhelming support for bold redistributive change by the large majority of "the poor" against the few "rich" (cf. Acemoglu and Robinson

2005; Boix 2003). Real mortals, however, often deviated from these rational expectations as many people from the disadvantaged sectors of society disapproved of radical efforts at change. Moreover, besides their frequent numerical superiority, establishment forces usually demonstrated greater intensity and determination in their political action as well. This unconditional will to prevail drove the striking brutality and unnecessary overkill with which they wielded coercion, as many historians and other observers have bemoaned.

What accounts for these surprising imbalances? This study invokes what is perhaps the most fundamental mechanism uncovered by cognitive psychology, namely people's disproportionate aversion to losses. As innumerable laboratory experiments and field studies have documented (see recently Zamir 2014), individuals subjectively weight losses much more heavily than gains of equal objective magnitude. Due to this clear asymmetry, people try much harder to avert losses than they are eager to achieve gains. Whoever sees a threat goes to great lengths to combat it (see also Stenner 2005 and Stein 2013). Indeed, larger numbers of people are likely to perceive losses in the complexity of fierce political struggles compared to those who expect gains; after all, the overweighting of losses distorts the ledger of cost-benefit analysis. This skewed accounting mechanism thus helps explain why Castro's disciples and admirers tended to win fewer supporters than the adversaries they encountered. Groupings of relatively limited size sought to replicate the Cuban Revolution, whereas a larger – often, much larger – phalanx of forces combatted these emulation efforts; and these status quo defenders employed all means to achieve their conservative goal, including cruel repression.

For these reasons, people's disproportionate aversion to losses lies at the root of the interactive dynamic of diffusion and counterdiffusion. As the Cuban Revolution inspired fairly small groups of radical left-wingers to foment revolutions that in their eyes promised gains, ample conservative and centrist forces that foresaw losses countermobilized with great energy. The uneven valuation of gains versus losses is crucial for explaining why in this polarization, status quo defenders clearly carried the day. The ambitious attempts to follow Castro's footsteps universally failed. They provoked painful repression and, sooner or later, led to the downfall of liberal democracy and the imposition of reactionary autocracy in many countries. Communist revolution backfired; Castro's success did not make revolution in Latin America more likely, but on the contrary induced establishment forces to block this prospect with all means. Because radical transformation beckoned, right-wing reaction proliferated. Marxist efforts to abolish exploitation, alienation, and oppression provoked the installation of hierarchical, exclusionary police states. Due to the loss aversion documented by cognitive psychology, the overoptimism of the radical left drew the wrath of the conservative right. Deterrent effects proved much more powerful than demonstration effects.

ORGANIZATIONAL FACTORS AND COGNITIVE MECHANISMS

How do the mechanisms of bounded rationality, which shape the information processing and choices of individuals, affect political decisions and outcomes, considering that in politics, collective groupings, crowds, and institutions play major roles? In other words, how do the microprocesses elucidated by cognitive psychology aggregate up to the macro level of politics? Just as in the struggle for democracy (Weyland 2014: 52–65), organizational factors operate as crucial intervening variables, mediating the impact that individual-level heuristics and asymmetrical loss aversion exert on collective action and political decision making.

As the classical literature on bounded rationality emphasizes (Simon 1976; March and Simon 1993) and recent contributions confirm (Bendor 2010; Hafner-Burton, Haggard, et al. 2017: S5, S20), in principle organizational structures can compensate for the inferential deficiencies and distorted choices of individuals. Open, critical debate casts doubt on the most problematic conclusions derived via cognitive shortcuts and questions particularly unthinking, skewed choices. Moreover, well-constructed organizations, such as meritocratic bureaucracies, promote experienced cadres or technical experts to leadership positions, whose ample base of knowledge and solid understanding anchor their perceptions and choices and thus make them less susceptible to the whirlwind of heuristic shortcuts. The experience that comes with sequential organizational advancement serves as an additional safeguard (see recently Saunders 2017). Cadres who have already suffered a series of defeats may get less "bent out of shape" by another loss – or a sudden victory – than inexperienced youngsters who are still convinced of their own invincibility.

The type of organization and its strength thus affect how tight the bounds of rationality are – one of the cutting-edge issues at the intersection of cognitive psychology and political science (Stein 2017: S256). As the analysis of democratic contention showed (Weyland 2012), spontaneously forming, unorganized, and leaderless crowds are particularly subject to rash inferences suggested by the heuristics of availability and representativeness. Accordingly, in the amorphous societies of Europe in 1848 and the Arab world in 2011, the striking precedents of autocrats' downfall set in motion amazingly quick and wide-ranging waves of emulation. But because these imitative protests were driven by cognitive shortcuts rather than prudent probability assessments and rational cost-benefit calculations, they mostly failed, as has become so painfully clear over the last few years in the Middle East (Brownlee, Masoud, and Reynolds 2015).

By contrast, as Chapter 3 has argued, broad-based, pluralistic organizations that institutionalize internal mechanisms of discussion and deliberation manage to loosen the bounds of rationality and make decisions that are better attuned to the actual political opportunity structure. While their decision making is still shaped to some extent by cognitive shortcuts and skewed loss aversion, they consider the constellation of power more carefully and therefore initiate externally inspired efforts at regime change only when the political situation is fairly propitious. Acting in this vein, the Social-Democratic Party of Germany in 1918–19 and Chile's democratic parties in the 1980s achieved a relatively high degree of success in bringing (back) liberal democracy (Weyland 2014: 137–48, 194–221).

Compared to the politics of democratic contention, organizations play an even greater role in autocratic reverse waves, in which spontaneous crowds rarely act as protagonists. Instead, establishment sectors that tend to have some degree of organization usually take the lead in the overthrow of democracy. Above all, with the professionalization of militaries across the globe, the hierarchically structured wielders of organized coercion have become more and more decisive, as amply evident during the Latin American coup wave of the 1960s and 1970s (Stepan 1971; Potash 1980; Rouquié 1987). While the armed forces with their quest for cohesion and discipline are far from being paragons of pluralistic debate, and are often swayed by exaggerated threat perceptions, they do tend to engage in internal discussions before taking action. As Chapter 6 showed, for instance, generals in Brazil and Chile intensely discussed the political crisis and the various decision options before ousting democratically elected governments in 1964 and 1973, respectively.[1] Moreover, political parties, which often do engage in a good deal of pluralistic debate, played a major role in the politics of democratic breakdown, as the Brazilian and Chilean cases show as well (Valenzuela 1978; Cohen 1994; Ferreira and Gomes 2014). Where such parties guaranteed governability and therefore established a good deal of civilian control over the military, as in post-1958 Colombia and Venezuela, looser bounds of political rationality prevailed, and democracy survived surprisingly persistent attacks from the radical left.

Due to these organizational factors and the resulting extension of the bounds of rationality, autocratic reverse waves unfolded much less quickly and indiscriminately than many waves of democratic contention, which swept like riptides across whole regions of the world (Weyland 2014: chaps. 4, 8). In particular, the Cuban Revolution and the outburst of guerrilla movements it spawned did not provoke the immediate imposition of autocracy; instead, military dictatorships emerged in response to specific challenges that affected different countries at different times, over the course of more than a decade. The proliferation of authoritarian rule therefore advanced at a relatively moderate pace compared to other regime change cascades (see also Hale 2013).

For the same reason, namely because the protagonists of reactionary backlash targeted specific threats arising in each country, they were quite "successful" in their goal achievement – vastly more successful in advancing their own interests and causes than the guerrilla insurgencies inspired by the

---

[1] In the early 1960s, the Argentine military also had an interbranch committee of twelve generals that discussed political issues (Potash 1980: 361–4).

Cuban Revolution. As conservative sectors drew on their organizations to respond to perceived challenges from the radical left, they weighed opportunities and constraints, designed effective (though drastic and brutal) countermeasures, and traced courses of action that in many cases proved politically viable and that suppressed the threats they saw, at the cost of destroying liberal democracy. While there certainly were many unrealistic conspiracies, some failed coup attempts, and the occasional volatile, unstable autocracy (Bolivia), overall the right was clearly more successful in its assaults on political liberty than the radical left was in its innumerable attempts to unleash revolution.

After all, admirers of Fidel Castro often had less well-structured organizations than their conservative adversaries did. Most guerrilla groupings, in particular, were notorious for their loose structure. These mostly young fighters also lacked experience (cf. Saunders 2017), which allows for a better grasp of the political opportunity structure. Furthermore, these armed insurgencies were spearheaded by tiny minorities: the few people whom heuristic inferences from the Cuban Revolution had swept off their feet (Wickham-Crowley 1992: 30–6; Wickham-Crowley 2014: 226). Thus, guerrilla struggles resulted from participants' self-selection based on emulative radicalism. Due to the powerful impact of cognitive shortcuts on some youngsters in numerous countries, these violent challenges spread rather indiscriminately across Latin America, with little regard for the domestic constellation of power. Precipitous and ill-considered, the long series of rebel uprisings during the 1960s resulted in one catastrophic failure after the other.

What is particularly striking in this riptide of insurgencies is the lack of learning. Despite the wholesale repression of earlier guerrilla movements, new challenges erupted in Argentina, for instance, over and over again (Brown 2017: chap. 13). Obviously, cognitive shortcuts had such a grip over these weakly organized bands of imitative ultraradicals that each new grouping was confident in its capacity to replicate Castro's stunning precedent, despite the sorry fate of a growing number of similarly misguided emulation efforts. As tight bounds constrained the political rationality of these self-selected youthful fighters, realistic assessments and prudent calculations were conspicuous by their absence.

A much larger number of left-wingers, however, who tended to have more political experience and some rooting in the partisan arena, pursued a range of alternative strategies for taking power that were better adapted to the political constellation prevailing in different countries. While under the influence of the Cuban Revolution, these progressive forces underwent a great deal of radicalization; they promoted revolutionary goals with more conventional means, combining political mobilization, electoral campaigning, and, sometimes, preparations for potential armed struggle, which – in their view – a conservative backlash might make necessary. The specific mix of these strategies and tactics and the political success resulting from their use depended on the party system of each country, especially its level of institutionalization (cf. Mainwaring 2018). Accordingly, in nations with strong left-wing parties such as Chile, party organizations took the lead in the push for profound transformations. As the end of Chapter 6 showed, Salvador Allende's march toward socialism, which was calibrated to the political opportunities and constraints prevailing in that country, advanced rather far – much farther than the less determined reform efforts undertaken by populist President João Goulart in Brazil's more fluid party system, for instance.

This difference reflected the fact that in the rest of Latin America, political parties were much weaker than in Chile (see data for 1965 in Dix 1992; see also Kaufman 1977; Mainwaring and Scully 1995). In a number of countries, such as Argentina and Brazil, weakly organized populist movements prevailed. Organizationally amorphous and dominated by personalistic leaders, these populist movements did not manage to extend the bounds of rationality as much as Chile's well-structured parties did. Due to their organizational deficiencies, cognitive shortcuts continued to hold considerable sway, giving political actors a tenuous grasp of the prevailing constellation of power. In retrospect, one marvels at the groundswell of radicalization that "carried away" so many Latin Americans during the 1960s and early 1970s. Reformists turned revolutionary and regarded quick, comprehensive, and profound transformations as feasible that look distinctly unrealistic in light of the elite dominance entrenched in their countries.

In line with the organizational argument of this book, this extremism inspired by the Cuban Revolution had a more striking impact on weakly institutionalized populist movements, such as Argentine Peronism, than on disciplined parties, such as the communists. Even in Chile, the fractionalized Socialist Party was swept away much more by revolutionary voluntarism than its main partner in the Popular Unity coalition, the communists. In sum, because in line with theories of bounded rationality, organizational factors conditioned the impact of cognitive shortcuts, the fluidity prevailing on the left side of the ideological spectrum, combined with the self-selection based on emulative radicalism, often kept the bounds of rationality tight and produced a number of utopian projects. Inspired by the epic Cuban Revolution, this overambitious quest for profound transformation lacked political feasibility – and resulted in failure after failure, sooner or later.

Interestingly, the conservative right, while certainly stricken by excessive fears that sometimes bordered on panic and paranoia, seemed somewhat less detached from reality, at least in assessing the chances for pursuing its counterrevolutionary goals. While Castro's surprising success activated the heuristics of availability and representativeness and instilled exaggerated threat perceptions, status quo defenders tended to be better organized than their leftist adversaries, commanded greater experience, and therefore had a better grasp of the constellation of power.[2] The grounding in organizations, especially the military, also hindered precipitous action by reactionary extremists and forced coordination and compromise with more moderate right-wingers. Accordingly, the most eager coup mongers usually did not strike on their own, and never successfully; instead, they had to wait until worsening polarization and deepening crises convinced the large legalistic, institutionalist sectors of the armed forces, most prominently Marshal Humberto Castello Branco in Brazil and new army commander Augusto Pinochet in Chile,[3] of the need for military intervention. On the conservative side of the spectrum, organization thus tended to forestall the self-selected hyperactivism that was more common on the left, as evident especially in the innumerable guerrilla attacks.

For these reasons, the countermeasures of the right reflected bounds of rationality that were somewhat less tight than those shaping the challenges of the radical left. Although status quo defenders often overreacted, they pursued their own interests and causes with more cold-blooded calculation than did their political enemies. No doubt that under the thrall of cognitive shortcuts, conservatives overestimated the threats they actually faced. Consequently, they often proceeded with "unnecessary roughness" and a clear overdose of brutality, which – given their command over organized coercion – led to disproportionate bloodletting.

Yet despite this overkill in the execution of their goals, right-wing sectors designed a modulated strategy for counteracting left-wing initiatives. In particular, they did not respond to the initial rash of isomorphic attempts to replicate the Cuban Revolution by rushing immediately into the imposition of defensive autocracy. The struggle to suppress guerrilla movements in the 1960s did not usher in transitions to authoritarian rule. Instead, in addition to repressing precipitous rebel assaults, status quo defenders sought to take the wind out of the sails of the radical left by enacting more or less significant programs of preemptive reforms, especially democratization and land redistribution, as supported by the United States through the Alliance for Progress. Thus, while the overestimation of the communist threat prompted cruel crackdowns, it also spurred a more sophisticated counterstrategy, which pursued reformist change to avoid radical revolution. This two-sided approach was particularly well-developed and ambitious in countries governed by broad-based parties, such as Venezuela (Miller 2016), where it achieved a great deal of

---

[2] For an earlier instance in which counterrevolutionaries, based on their organizations and experience, operated with looser bounds of rationality than their progressive opponents, see Weyland (2016).

[3] In insisting on and sticking to the constitution that he got passed in 1980, even when it was not to his immediate political advantage in the runup to the plebiscite of 1988, Pinochet maintained this firm legalism during the political struggles of the 1980s, which eventually culminated in redemocratization (interviews with Fernández 2007 and with Rodríguez 2007).

political success and helped consolidate a fledgling democracy (Levine 1973: 47, 56, 61, 208).

Only when and where this first line of proactive defense ran into difficulties and failed to appease the transformative demands and expectations unleashed by the Cuban Revolution, did more and more status quo defenders lose faith in liberal democracy and seek protection from dictators. As shown toward the end of Chapter 4, the Alliance for Progress did little to moderate the push for change and paradoxically added fuel to the fire of radicalization in a number of countries. Especially in Latin America's Southern Cone, a growing range of leftist and populist forces insistently came to demand drastic reform, if not revolution. It was this broader push for profound transformations, which in Argentina and Uruguay escalated to large-scale urban violence in the early 1970s, that then prompted the installation of autocracy. Thus, democracy suffered breakdown only under the weight of real challenges from an increasingly radical left. While conservative forces clearly exaggerated the threats and to some extent propagated fear to advance their own self-interests, their concerns were arguably less detached from reality than the unrealistic expectations of their radical enemies. Because status quo defenders tended to have a more developed organizational infrastructure than their left-wing adversaries and foes, they acted with somewhat looser bounds of rationality. Certainly, their decisions were marred by many deviations from the standards of comprehensive rationality – but to a lesser extent than the transformational or revolutionary hopes of the left.

In sum, organizational factors mediated the operation of cognitive mechanisms and shaped collective action and political decision making in the Latin American reverse wave. Because many status quo defenders who spearheaded the imposition of reactionary autocracy were based in fairly structured organizations, they tended to operate with looser bounds of rationality compared to the more fluid, fractured left-wing forces that tried eagerly to follow in Guevara's footsteps or that sought to approximate Castro's success through more conventional political means.[4] Accordingly, conservative sectors calibrated their actions more to the configuration of power prevailing in each country, and therefore managed to achieve their opportunistic goals in many cases. Organizational differences thus contributed to the defeats of the radical left and the frequent victories of the right, which drove the Latin American reverse wave.

---

[4] Note also that according to Olson (1965) and to Offe and Wiesenthal (1985), elite actors, who tend to be status quo defenders, have a greater ease in – and perhaps a lower need for – forming and sustaining collective organizations than mass actors, which the left sees as the main constituents of its transformational projects.

BROADER THEORETICAL CONCLUSIONS

The bounded rationality approach of this book diverges significantly from the ideal-typical postulates of conventional rational choice. As the historical chapters amply documented and as the preceding sections highlighted, political actors of all stripes often deviated from systematic information processing and careful cost-benefit calculations, to a greater or lesser extent. Due to the availability and representativeness heuristics, radical left-wingers were carried away by Castro's precedent and initiated a host of ill-considered attempts at isomorphic imitation, which predictably failed. So many overeager revolutionaries paid for these problematic inferences and the resulting rash decisions with their lives. A crucial reason for this string of defeats was that status quo defenders also overestimated the probability of emulative revolution; therefore, due to pronounced loss aversion, they cracked down hard against their leftist challengers, often proceeding with unnecessary harshness.

Continuing revolutionary efforts by the left kept exaggerated fears alive among conservative sectors. Because status quo defenders navigated conjunctures of uncertainty by resorting to cognitive mechanisms, they often overreacted and "pulled the emergency brake" by spearheading military coups and the installation of authoritarian rule. Thus, the distortions of bounded rationality provided crucial impulses for the proliferation of counterrevolutionary autocracy in Latin America during the 1960s and 1970s. As political actors across the ideological spectrum deviated from prudent rational assessments, democracy fell in one country after the other. Insights derived from cognitive-psychological microfoundations explain this reverse wave much better than conventional rational choice.

Bounded rationality also offers a more convincing account than constructivist approaches that highlight the diffusion of ideas and values. Obviously, the spread of autocratic regimes that had a distinctly conservative, if not reactionary orientation contradicts the progressivist premises underlying predominant currents of constructivism, which emphasize the attraction and appeal of advanced, modern principles and norms. Whereas many constructivists tend to believe in the forward movement of history, the 1960s and 1970s in Latin America saw a series of striking reversals. History turned in the wrong direction, away from the trend toward gradual progress that the twentieth century had brought; in particular, the regional coup wave undid the substantial advance of political liberty that the region had enjoyed after World War II (Smith 2012: 27, 35; Mainwaring and Pérez-Liñán 2013: 3, 73–4).

Even historicist versions of constructivism, which do not assume unilinear, irreversible progress but acknowledge fundamental changes in the *Zeitgeist,* are not fully persuasive. The Latin American reverse wave was not preceded and driven by a distinct ideational downturn, such as the spread of cultural pessimism and the questioning of reason that occurred in Europe from the late nineteenth century onward (Burrow 2000). When liberal democracy did become the target of fundamental questioning, these doubts emerged in response to the Cuban Revolution, which stimulated the rejection of "bourgeois democracy" by revolutionary activists of the radical left; these attacks, in turn, caused concerns about the resilience of pluralist democracy to "communist" challenges, which became ever more intense among the conservative right. Thus, ideational developments were not "independent variables" that shaped politics; instead, they were (ideologically mediated) responses to the specific political developments that this book has highlighted as the main trigger of the proliferation of autocracy in Latin America.

Moreover, contrary to historicist versions of constructivism, the military regimes that sprouted up across the region lacked ideational foundations in a distinctive edifice of authoritarian principles. In fact, these dictatorships acknowledged the absence of inherent normative appeal by depicting themselves as mere housecleaners preparing the eventual restoration of democracy. Right-wing alternatives to democracy had lost their genuine claim to legitimacy with the catastrophic downfall of fascism in World War II (O'Donnell and Schmitter 1986: 15). The ideational hollowness of conservative and reactionary autocracy prevailed especially in the western hemisphere, where the United States officially embraced political liberalism and democracy (Smith 1995: chaps. 7–9). In fact, President Kennedy reinforced these antiauthoritarian commitments by responding to the Cuban Revolution with his Alliance for Progress.

The counterrevolutionaries of the 1960s and 1970s therefore stood on weak ground in the ideological arena. While there were some diehards who embraced authoritarianism as a viable regime type for the long run (for Chile, e.g., see Grugel 1985: 117–20), many supporters of counterrevolutionary coups sought only the repression or elimination of the radical left, which would then open the door for eventual redemocratization (Rouquié 1987: 345–50). Thus, the protagonists of autocracy in Latin America were aware of the threadbare foundations of their rule. As mentioned in Chapter 2, Latin America's authoritarian rulers claimed to head "strong democracies" and allergically rejected disqualification as dictators, a title that a number of interwar autocrats had openly, even proudly, adopted.[5]

Strikingly, however, the weak legitimacy of authoritarianism did not preclude its proliferation. Concrete fears drove a rash of coups, autocratic rescue efforts, and brutal repression which blatantly diverged from prevailing normative principles. Obviously, major political decisions and their institutional outcomes were at odds with well-established moral ideas and maxims. Contrary to constructivist assumptions, ideational orientations did not guide actual behavior. Evidently, developments in the realm of ideas operate

---

[5] This aversion persisted even after the return of democracy, as Wendy Hunter noticed during the field research (1988–90) for her doctoral dissertation on the military in Brazil, published as Hunter (1997).

as soft, loosely probabilistic causes and leave ample margins for more concrete factors to shape specific political decisions and collective action.

For these reasons, constructivist lines of reasoning are not fully convincing. While intellectual currents and the normative *Zeitgeist* do exert some influence by orienting political projects and actions in certain directions, by no means do they shape choices and their outcomes in a direct and tight fashion. In particular, political actors have a great deal of latitude to pursue and advance their own interests and causes, even when those run counter to strong ideational trends. Certainly, it is easier to swim with the predominant normative current; but swimming against this current and nevertheless reaching one's intended destination is not enormously difficult.

Great power theories, which argue that mighty countries can mold political regime developments in their spheres of influence, make only limited contributions as well. Clearly, the "strongest" arguments in this vein, which highlight forceful pressure and coercion, cannot account for the Latin American reverse wave. As Chapter 7 showed, the United States did not impose dictatorship in Latin America during the 1960s and 1970s. Instead, internal actors took the main initiative and spearheaded the overthrow of democracy in nation after nation. While after the Cuban Revolution, the United States worried about the spread of Castroite communism and therefore supported moves toward autocracy as a presumed defensive necessity, an ample gamut of Latin American elites, middle classes, and even popular sectors held exactly the same perception and therefore embraced dictatorship out of their own volition. Thus, there was a strong coincidence of situational assessments, political interests, and dispositions for action across the Rio Grande.

Arguably, in every case of the regional coup wave of the 1960s and 1970s, the domestic military would have overthrown struggling liberal democracies even without US involvement. While North American diplomats and CIA agents backed the ouster of left-wing presidents and nudged Latin American officers along, they merely condoned conspiracies that were already ongoing. After all, the heuristics of availability and representativeness led domestic actors to overrate the communist threat as well, and loss aversion induced them to fight back with all means; obviously, the stakes were much higher for southern elites than for their northern allies, as Fidel Castro's mass fusillade of old regime generals had made so strikingly clear. Therefore, Latin American status quo defenders needed no encouragement to crush guerrilla movements and, later, to safeguard the sociopolitical order through the institution of authoritarian rule.

Yet although the United States had limited causal impact on the proliferation of dictatorship, it does hold considerable historical responsibility for enabling the destruction of democracy. If the United States had continued to employ its economic, political, and military clout to promote its stated preference for liberal democracy, as it did at the very beginning of the Alliance for Progress, it may well have managed to prevent the imposition of brutal dictatorships that abused their countries for many years. President Kennedy's forceful response to the Peruvian coup of 1962, for instance, pushed the local armed forces to shelve more ambitious dictatorial projects and to initiate steps toward redemocratization quickly.

The Mann Doctrine of early 1964, however, abandoned this principled defense of democracy and effectively accepted authoritarian rule as the presumed lesser evil. As the United States backed away from threats of economic sanctions and diplomatic isolation and confined itself to exhortations behind closed doors, it gave Latin American militaries much freer hand to crush their enemies, usher in harsh autocracies, and monopolize power for the long run. In sum, while the northern superpower holds limited responsibility with its acts of commission, which did not make a big difference, it incurred a great deal of historical guilt through its acts of omission, namely by neglecting the energetic defense of democracy.

In conclusion, both great power arguments and constructivist lines of reasoning help explain some aspects of the Latin American reverse wave, but do not capture the main causal impetus behind the proliferation of right-wing autocracy, namely the backlash to left-wing revolution. The principal impulse arose from the deterrent effect of Castro's success, which exerted a disproportionate impact on the perceptions and choices of many establishment sectors due to cognitive heuristics and asymmetrical loss aversion. Therefore, a bounded rationality approach is crucial for understanding why, during certain time periods, namely in the aftermath of stunning revolutionary precedents, history seemed to move backwards.

DIVERSITY, COMPLEXITY, AND THEIR METHODOLOGICAL IMPLICATIONS

This study draws on a few basic findings from cognitive psychology to elucidate a fundamental backlash dynamic, namely the interaction of left-wing diffusion and right-wing counterdiffusion. Both the building blocks of the argument and the main causal mechanism that connects them are rather simple. But the historical investigation of the principal reverse wave sweeping across Latin America, conducted in Chapters 4 through 7, has uncovered a great deal of complexity and diversity.

One main reason is that even boundedly rational actors learn, sooner or later. While they do not respond to costs and benefits as directly and optimally as rational choice predicts, they do eventually adjust their behavior, especially after experiencing losses. In Latin America during the 1960s, for instance, left-wingers learned from the repeated failures of guerrilla struggles, however belatedly. On the other side of the ideological divide, status quo defenders reacted to the disappointing results of the Alliance for Progress by switching from a preemptive reform strategy to the imposition of harsh authoritarianism. Due to this boundedly rational learning, political actors over time responded to similar incentives and constraints in varying ways. This sequence of steps by each side in turn provoked reactions from the other side, which then prompted a new round of responses. Due to these conflictive interactions, the Latin American reverse wave unfolded in complex ways.

Moreover, the simple mechanisms of cognitive psychology were embedded in various structural and institutional context factors, which shaped their operation. As the literature on bounded rationality has long emphasized, organizational features were especially important. In particular, due to the differential breadth and strength of political parties, left-wing challenges and the anticommunist backlash played out differently in different countries. In Argentina with its weak partisan left, for instance, the Cuban Revolution helped inspire a series of guerrilla movements, whereas such ultraradical challenges did not occur in Chile's better-structured party system; there, Castro's feats inspired radicalization among the more loosely organized Socialist Party, yet not in the disciplined Communist Party. Similarly, variations in party strength help explain why the advance of conservative autocracy did not sweep up all countries. Above all, the breadth and firmness of Venezuela's two main parties allowed democracy to escape unscathed, and even Colombia's crisis-ridden system survived, sustained by party pacts.[6]

The confluence of boundedly rational learning and organizational differences caused further complexity. For instance, while military dictatorships were uniformly determined to forestall communism, they diverged in specific ideological orientation, depending on the main reasons for the perceived failure of the Alliance for Progress. Accordingly, the Peruvian autocracy broke the obstacles posed by liberal democratic checks and balances and initially imposed progressive reforms, whereas the Brazilian and Chilean dictatorships squashed the radicalization inadvertently unleashed by preemptive reform efforts and pursued a firmly conservative project. For all of these reasons, microfoundational simplicity gave rise to macrolevel complexity and diversity, leading to a good deal of cross-national variation in political processes and institutional outcomes.

How did these complex developments play out over time? As argued in Chapter 3, the Latin American reverse wave unfolded via two processes by which overoptimistic efforts at revolutionary diffusion provoked severe reactions by establishment sectors. First, the overwhelming impact of the Cuban Revolution quickly inspired unorganized groupings of radicals to start isomorphic imitation efforts through a rash of guerrilla movements across Latin America. A broad phalanx of status quo defenders, who were shaken up by Castro's revolutionary precedent as well and who saw it as a major threat, decisively squashed these precipitate emulation attempts. Yet because Communist Cuba survived US strangulation efforts, many winners of these early battles also sought to forestall the spread of revolution by initiating

---

[6] Paraguay also remained unaffected, though for a very different reason: the country chafed under authoritarian rule throughout the 1950s to 1980s.

preemptive reforms, especially democratization and controlled redistributive change, such as land reform. Thus, the immediate upsurge of radical-left challenges drew a dual response, namely harsh repression against its direct protagonists, combined with reformist concessions for nonviolent left-wingers and for the population sectors whom revolutionaries could potentially win over. Interestingly, these responses did not include the imposition of bureaucratic authoritarianism. Instead, domestic status quo defenders, encouraged and supported by the United States via the Alliance for Progress, gave liberal democracy a chance.

In many countries, however, preemptive reforms did not succeed in fostering political moderation and democratic stability. Instead, deepening polarization and the radicalization of the left were more likely outcomes. As a result, a wide range of progressive sectors energetically pursued ambitious, often revolutionary goals through party politics and electoral contests, and through mass mobilization and street pressure. As this persistent agitation showed, the effort at controlled change had not managed to contain and ban what conservatives saw as the menace of communism, which Castro's Cuba promoted energetically. Because pluralist democracy allowed for these left-wing efforts and therefore seemed weak and vulnerable, worried militaries in more and more countries imposed autocratic rule, which promised firm protection against the specter of radical threats. As political liberalism did not seem to guarantee reliable defensive capacity, the persistent danger of left-wing extremism prompted the installation of dictatorships. Thus, the proliferation of institutional authoritarianism in Latin America resulted primarily from the backlash against this broad-based radicalization.

The complexity and diversity in the unfolding of diffusion and counterdiffusion and the corresponding differences in institutional outcomes create methodological complications. It would be difficult for statistical models to capture these intersecting demonstration and deterrent effects. In the search for regularities, large-N analyses tend to rely on restrictive assumptions. Investigations of diffusion, for instance, usually postulate short and uniform time lags between the precedent and the resulting imitation efforts and their outcomes (see the particularly sophisticated analysis in Elkink 2013). But rural and urban guerrilla movements took inspiration from the Cuban Revolution from the late 1950s through the mid-1970s, more than a decade after Castro's triumph. Moreover, the complexity of regime developments would require the analysis of multiple interaction effects, which create problems of multicollinearity (Ragin 1987: 61–7). Consequently, statistical models cannot easily disentangle the diffusion phenomena examined in this book.

Small-N analysis and process tracing are much less rigorous than statistical investigations and cannot yield broad generalizations. But their attention to specificity turns into a strength when it comes to analyzing processes and outcomes as complex and multifaceted as the Latin American reverse wave. Because these methods are well suited for capturing qualitative differences, they can map diverse paths of regime development and reconstruct how inspirations and demonstration effects travel across various stretches of time. Moreover, small-N analysis and process tracing can capture the instances in which causality operates in less than straightforward ways, namely via anticipated reactions or deterrent effects.

With its focus on specificity, however, process tracing risks sliding into mere description of particular cases. To avoid this problem, qualitative studies need guidance from clear theoretical ideas (Beach and Pedersen 2013: chap. 4; Checkel and Bennett 2015: 269–72). The assessment of competing arguments in Chapter 2 and the bounded rationality approach developed in Chapter 3 try to serve this purpose. Inferential heuristics and asymmetrical loss aversion constitute fundamental components of humans' cognitive architecture and therefore provide causal mechanisms that shape perceptions and decisions, at the individual yet also the collective level. These mechanisms give rise to probabilistic regularities, including the tendency for political processes to advance in temporal waves and to form cross-national groupings. This temporal and regional clustering allows and calls for middle-range generalizations, which this study has sought to establish by examining each turning point through comparison and contrast.

FUTURE PROSPECTS: AN IMPENDING REVERSE WAVE?

This book has investigated Latin America's major reverse wave in depth; thereafter, Chapter 8 examined four additional clusters of authoritarian hardening. All of these backlash processes disrupted the forward march of history postulated by modernization theory and mainstream constructivism. Is a similar kind of reflux gathering steam now, as the 2010s approach their end? During the last few years, concerns about the fate of liberal democracy in the world have run ever higher (Diamond 2016; Levitsky and Ziblatt 2018; Mounk 2018). Many pluralist democracies in the Global North have confronted challenges and constraints reinforced by the dramatic depression of 2008, and the commodities boom as well as its collapse have created serious problems for many democracies in the Global South.

More fundamentally, contemporary democracy faces increasing cross-pressures arising from economic globalization and the perceived need for technocratic decision making on the one hand (see, e.g., Ezrow and Hellwig 2014), and from growing substantive demands and participatory expectations among the citizenry on the other (e.g., Dalton, Farrell, and McAllister 2011: 228–30). Due to these contradictory challenges (Mounk 2018), and due to the emergence of new avenues for interest articulation, such as the internet, many party systems have fragmented or eroded. As a result, political uncertainty has risen and opened up space for populism. Exemplified by the unlikely triumph of Donald Trump in the United States, the spread of personalistic plebiscitarian leadership sustained by unorganized mass support – my definition of populism

(Weyland 2001: 12–14) – has exacerbated political volatility. The election of populist outsiders has also inspired skepticism in the essential premise of liberal democracy, namely that individuals are the best judges of their own interests and that they know how to vote for the candidate who most faithfully represents these interests. Most worrisome are the inherent tendencies toward illiberalism and authoritarianism that populism harbors and that have born undemocratic fruits in countries ranging from Venezuela to Hungary, Turkey, and the Philippines (Weyland 2018). As democratically elected chief executives have strangled democracy from the inside, observers have started to worry about the specter of Adolf Hitler (Maier 2017; Wirsching, Kohler, and Wilhelm 2018), who charted this very same course in 1933.

At the same time that liberal democracy has suffered from a host of problems and has seen its luster dim, countermodels have arisen that have begun to exude some appeal on the global stage. Above all, China's phenomenal success on the economic front and the resulting boost in international standing have impressed many current or aspiring autocrats, especially in Africa and Asia. The Chinese accomplishments have rekindled interest in the notion of a "developmental state" that combines state-guided economic development with nondemocratic political stability. Certainly, it is doubtful that many potential imitators could recreate the comprehensive, penetrating organizational network of the Chinese Communist Party or the meritocratic features of the Chinese state (see the sympathetic treatment in Bell 2015). But as the comparative analysis in Chapter 8 mentioned, fascism provided major impulses to the reverse wave of the interwar years, although Mussolini's model only exceptionally found full emulation. As authoritarian forces did during the 1920s and 1930s, their counterparts in the twenty-first century could install or harden autocracies by importing bits and pieces of the novel tool kit. In this way, China's nondemocratic model could contribute to the proliferation and consolidation of authoritarian rule (see Gunitsky 2017: 238–44; NED 2017). In sum, there seem to be good reasons for concern about the future prospects of liberal democracy.

But the main argument of this book inspires hope that a major, wide-ranging reverse wave is unlikely to happen.[7] As demonstrated in Chapters 4 through 7 and as corroborated in Chapter 8, the fundamental impulse behind the diffusion of right-wing authoritarianism was the deep fear of revolution which arose from the shocking success of Fidel Castro and other contentious leaders. At present, however, a political earthquake that could provoke such a powerful backlash effect, especially a riptide extending to the advanced democracies of the Global North, is not on the horizon. As regards recent challenges, Hugo Chávez's

---

[7] See Cornell, Møller, and Skaaning (2017) for a similar conclusion focused on the longstanding democracies in advanced industrialized countries (the "Northwest"). While my reasoning highlights the absence of dramatic challenges, their arguments stress the defensive resilience of consolidated democracies.

Bolivarian revolution, which even the United States saw more as an irritant than a serious threat, has self-destructed so disastrously that it no longer finds imitators (cf. De la Torre 2017). Al Qaeda, ISIS, and their offshoots have remained marginal fringe phenomena due to their fanatical penchant for bloody terrorism; therefore, they do not pose a political threat to established regimes, even in most of the Islamic world. The only risk of a major collapse concerns Saudi Arabia, but the direct repercussions would probably remain confined to the Middle East, as the experience of Iran's Islamic Revolution (analyzed in Chapter 8) suggests.

Theoretically speaking, there is no reason to expect the eruption of a new revolutionary challenge that would have wide-ranging consequences.[8] Modern societies, both in the Global North and in the Global South, are enormously complex and heterogeneous, and therefore lack the clear and sharp cleavages that could prompt the citizenry to divide into hostile camps and initiate a fundamental conflict. Indeed, the post-Marxian search for a revolutionary subject that would rock the established order has turned up empty-handed; none of the possible candidates that theorists and activists considered along the way, ranging from the peasantry to squatter settlers, antiglobalization protesters (e.g., Evans 2008), and the indigenous, proved capable and willing to take on this historical task.

While Francis Fukuyama's (1989) "end of history" thesis has drawn withering criticism, the fundamental claim that liberal, pluralist democracy lacks intellectual and political alternatives with universal appeal has proven correct. For instance, the Chinese model of a politically disciplined "developmental state" holds little attraction for societies that have achieved some degree of political mobilization and openness – which includes most countries in the world. Moreover, populism, seen as a particular threat in recent years, revolves around the opportunistic goals of personalistic leaders and is devoid of ideological definition and programmatic content (Weyland 2001). And direct, participatory democracy, which holds normative appeal for progressive sectors, is of very doubtful feasibility in the era of globalization and therefore lacks a real-world example; to the chagrin of progressives, Switzerland, the democracy with the most participatory features, is a thoroughly conservative country: the Alpine nation adopted female suffrage at the federal level in 1971 only! Consequently, there do not seem to be any grand ideologies and millenarian visions that could incite fervent commitment and induce people to incur the tremendous risks and hardships involved in pushing for profound, revolutionary overhauls.

---

[8] In his provocative essay "on political reaction," Lilla (2016: 99) agrees that there is no prospect of revolution, but claims "the enduring vitality of the reactionary spirit even in the absence of a revolutionary political program" (Lilla 2016: xiv). At the level of collective action and political decision making, this study of a major reverse and other backlash processes disagrees, finding in line with Newtonian reasoning: no action – no reaction.

Given the current absence and future unlikelihood of a revolutionary or deeply transformative challenge, the proliferation of conservative autocracy is not to be expected. In particular, it is exceedingly unlikely that true reverse waves will sweep across regions where pluralist democracy has become widespread, such as the Americas and Western Europe. Without a severe threat that would activate stark loss aversion among the principal establishment sectors, liberal democracy with its safeguards against the abuse of political power and the resulting protection it offers to elites is not at risk of falling. Why adopt nondemocratic rule as the lesser evil when no big evil is on the horizon? Why suffer the risks posed by unaccountable autocracy when one does not see the need for its iron fist to enforce sociopolitical stability and to combat the specter of dangerous internal enemies?

Certainly, cognitive heuristics can induce many actors to overrate threats and fall prey to excessive fear, as this book has shown repeatedly. But bounded rationality differs from irrationality and does not lose all touch with reality. While cognitive distortions lead people to overestimate danger, they do not see ghosts and fight against windmills. During the Latin American reverse wave and the four clusters of regime hardening, perceptions of challenges had some base in facts. While blown out of proportion, the Cuban Revolution, for instance, did pose real problems and some risks for political regimes across Latin America. Boundedly rational actors do not fall into panic without any reason at all. Yet currently, there is no broadly salient, striking precedent that could be overrated as a fundamental threat and that could give rise to powerful reactions and overreactions; nor does such a precedent seem to be on the horizon, as just explained. Consequently, the heuristics of availability and representativeness are unlikely to produce distorted inferences that would trigger asymmetrical loss aversion and stimulate panicked overreactions.

As mentioned above, the main threat that contemporary observers highlight, especially as a potential problem for established democracies, is populism, above all in its reactionary, exclusionary right-wing version. The unexpected electoral triumph of Donald Trump stoked particular fears (see Levitsky and Ziblatt 2018). If even the United States with its entrenched "liberal tradition" (Hartz 1955) and pluralist society could fall prey to the uncivil appeals of an overbearing outsider, how vulnerable would other countries be? In turn, given that populist leaders in a number of nations have undermined political liberalism or gone so far as to strangle democracy (Weyland 2018), did the United States now face risks of a similarly dire fate?

But these concerns overestimate the virulence of populism and the uniformity of diffusion processes, which – as this book has shown – go beyond contagion and demonstration effects and include deterrent effects as well. The shock of Trump's election, for instance, served as a warning for citizens in other advanced democracies. This alarm contributed to the defeat of populist candidates in the Netherlands and France in early 2017, thus giving a boost to liberal, pluralist democracy. As affinities with the US president hurt right-wing populists, his stunning rise has helped precipitate the fall of plebiscitarian leaders elsewhere, which in the French case of Marine Le Pen has ushered in a virtual self-destruction (Nossiter 2017).

Moreover, President Trump's experience in the United States suggests that even a determined, headstrong populist leader is unlikely to undermine an entrenched democracy. The billionaire tycoon has faced a number of obstacles, especially institutional checks and balances; a party that he does not fully control; ideological polarization that limits his support base; and the absence of an acute crisis that would allow him to win mass backing by bringing dramatic relief. For these reasons, Donald Trump is unlikely to win the concentrated power with which he could do serious damage to democracy (Weyland and Madrid 2018). Indeed, even Silvio Berlusconi in Italy, who governed for years in an institutional setting with lower barriers against populist power grabs, did not make a lasting dent in democracy (Verbeek and Zaslove 2016). Liberal, pluralist regimes in countries with strong civil societies seem to be quite resilient to the dangers arising from right-wing populism (for a broadly similar conclusion, see Cornell, Møller, and Skaaning 2017).

Admittedly, the rise of populism has caused a number of setbacks for democracy in regions where political liberalism has weaker roots and where civil society commands less vibrancy. But these precedents of democratic backsliding, which have occurred in countries as diverse as Venezuela, Hungary, and Turkey, have not stimulated powerful waves of emulation. For instance, admirers of Venezuela's Hugo Chávez have won government power and strangled democracy only in a few minor countries, namely Bolivia, Nicaragua, and Ecuador (Weyland 2013), and a liberal recovery is already under way in Ecuador, while massive protests have shaken the rule of autocrat Daniel Ortega in Nicaragua. In fact, as in the case of Donald Trump, the triumph of populism in some countries has unleashed deterrent effects in others. For instance, Chávez's efforts to promote his "Bolivarian" model across Latin America backfired in Peru in 2006 and in Honduras in 2009; and in order not to have his electoral chances hurt by perceived affinities to the Venezuelan firebrand, Mexican populist Andrés Manuel López Obrador has felt compelled to moderate his stances greatly (cf. O'Boyle 2017). As in the Global North, the emergence of populism has thus had a self-limiting dynamic in the Global South.

In conclusion, this book's explanation of the Latin American reverse wave and of the main processes of authoritarian hardening instills hope that humankind can avoid a wide-ranging political setback in the foreseeable future. While the *Zeitgeist* has turned skeptical on liberal pluralism, the bounded rationality approach of this study suggests that dire political consequences can be avoided as long as no earth-shattering challenge erupts. Although ideational and normative tendencies, which are currently unfavorable to representative democracy, have an impact, political interests and cost-benefit calculations, however distorted by cognitive mechanisms, end up being much more important. Because democracy guarantees a great deal of liberty and political protection, and because the western paragons of democracy enjoy a high standard of living, democracy's replacement by a wave of "forms of government" that are even worse – to invoke Winston Churchill's famous characterization – is unlikely.

Bibliography[*]

Abdelnasser, Walid. 1997. Islamic Organizations in Egypt and the Iranian Revolution of 1979. *Arab Studies Quarterly* 19 (2) (Spring): 25–39.

Acemoglu, Daron and James Robinson. 2005. *Economic Origins of Dictatorship and Democracy*. Cambridge: Cambridge University Press.

Acta de la Revolución Argentina. 1966. *Boletín Oficial* (July 8).

Adelman, Jeremy. 2006. *Sovereignty and Revolution in the Iberian Atlantic*. Princeton: Princeton University Press.

Adler, Gerhard, ed. 1970. *Revolutionäres Lateinamerika: Eine Dokumentation*. Paderborn: Ferdinand Schönigh.

Akhavi, Shahrough. 1990. The Impact of the Iranian Revolution on Egypt. In John Esposito, ed. *The Iranian Revolution: Its Global Impact*, 138–56. Miami: Florida International University Press.

Albertus. Michael. 2015. *Autocracy and Redistribution: The Politics of Land Reform*. Cambridge: Cambridge University Press.

Alexander, Robert. 1964. *The Venezuelan Democratic Revolution*. New Brunswick: Rutgers University Press.

Almeida, Ângelo Nolasco de. 1990. Depoimento 1986. Rio de Janeiro: Centro de Pesquisa e Documentação de História Contemporânea do Brasil (CPDOC), Fundação Getúlio Vargas.

Alvear, Francisco and Jairo Lugo-Ocando. Forthcoming. When Geopolitics Becomes Moral Panic: El Mercurio and the Use of International News as Propaganda Against Salvador Allende's Chile (1970–1973). *Media History*.

Ambrosio, Thomas. 2012. The Rise of the "China Model" and "Beijing Consensus": Evidence of Authoritarian Diffusion? *Contemporary Politics* 18 (4) (December): 381–99.

2010. Constructing a Framework of Authoritarian Diffusion. *International Studies Perspectives* 11 (4) (November): 375–92.

2009. *Authoritarian Backlash: Russian Resistance to Democratization in the Former Soviet Union*. Farnham: Ashgate.

---

[*] Where a text was originally published long before the edition that I used and where this earlier publication date holds historical significance, I list it in parenthesis.

2008. Catching the "Shanghai Spirit": How the Shanghai Cooperation Organization Promotes Authoritarian Norms in Central Asia. *Europe-Asia Studies* 60 (8) (October): 1321–44.

Anderson, Lisa. 1990. Tunisia and Libya: Responses to the Islamic Impulse. In John Esposito, ed. *The Iranian Revolution: Its Global Impact*, 157–76. Miami: Florida International University Press.

Angell, Alan. 1972. Allende's First Year in Chile. *Current History* 62 (366) (February): 76–80.

Ansell, Ben and David Samuels. 2014. *Inequality and Democratization*. Cambridge: Cambridge University Press.

Arancibia Clavel, Patricia, ed. 2006. *Cita con la Historia*. Santiago de Chile: Editorial Biblioteca Americana.

Araujo, Rodrigo Nabuco de. 2012. L'Art Français de la Guerre: Transferts de la Doctrine de la Guerre Révolutionaire au Brésil (1958–1974). *Cahiers des Amériques Latines* 70: 39–58.

Archer, Ronald. 1995. Party Strength and Weakness in Colombia's Besieged Democracy. In Scott Mainwaring and Timothy Scully, eds. *Building Democratic Institutions*, 164–99. Stanford: Stanford University Press.

Aretin, Karl Freiherr von. 1980. *Deutsche Geschichte*, vol. 7: *Vom Deutschen Reich zum Deutschen Bund*. Göttingen: Vandenhoeck & Ruprecht.

Arnove, Robert. 1980. Education Policies of the National Front. In Albert Berry, Ronald Hellman, and Mauricio Solaún, eds. *Politics of Compromise: Coalition Government in Colombia*, 381–411. New Brunswick: Transaction.

Arrate, Jorge and Eduardo Rojas. 2003. *Memoria de la Izquierda Chilena*, 2 vols. Barcelona: Javier Vergara.

Arriagada, Genaro. 2007. Author interview with Christian Democratic politician. Santiago: July 20.

  1988. *Pinochet: The Politics of Power*. Boston: Unwin Hyman.

  1974. *De la "Vía Chilena" a la "Vía Insurreccional."* Santiago de Chile: Editorial del Pacífico.

Arrubla, Mario. 1980. Síntesis de historia política contemporánea. In Mario Arrubla, Jesús Bejarano, et al. *Colombia, hoy*, 6th edn, 186–220. Bogotá: Siglo XXI Editores de Colombia.

Assunção, Vânia. 2005. No Princípio, Era o Medo: As Bases do Pensamento Conservador do General Golbery do Couto e Silva. *Verinotio – Revista On-line de Educação e Ciências Humanas* 1 (2) (April): 1–22.

Astiz, Carlos. 1969. The Argentine Armed Forces: Their Role and Political Involvement. *Western Political Quarterly* 22 (4) (December): 862–78.

Astiz, Carlos and José García. 1972. The Peruvian Military: Achievement Orientation, Training, and Political Tendencies. *Western Political Quarterly* 25:4 (December): 667–85.

Azevêdo, Fernando. 1982. *As Ligas Camponesas*. Rio de Janeiro: Paz e Terra.

Bagley, Bruce and Matthew Edel. 1980. Popular Mobilization Programs of the National Front. In Albert Berry, Ronald Hellman, and Mauricio Solaún, eds. *Politics of Compromise: Coalition Government in Colombia*, 257–84. New Brunswick: Transaction.

Baldez, Lisa. 2002. *Why Women Protest: Women's Movements in Chile*. Cambridge: Cambridge University Press.

Bandeira, Moniz. 1983. *O Governo João Goulart: As Lutas Sociais no Brasil, 1961–1964*, 6th edn. Rio de Janeiro: Civilização Brasileira.

Baskind, Irwin, Enrique Lerdau, and Theodore Mesmer. 2008. *The Alliance for Progress in Chile and Colombia*. Washington, DC: Interamerican Development Bank.

Bauerkämper, Arnd. 2006. *Der Faschismus in Europa 1918 – 1945*. Stuttgart: Reclam.

Bawden, John. 2012. Gazing Abroad: The Chilean Military's Reading of International Events. *The Latin Americanist* 56 (3) (September): 5–30.

Bayly, Christopher. 2004. *The Birth of the Modern World, 1780–1914*. Malden: Blackwell.

Beach, Derek. 2017. Process-Tracing Methods in Social Science. In *Oxford Research Encyclopedia on Politics*, forthcoming.

Beach, Derek and Rasmus Pedersen. 2013. *Process-Tracing Methods*. Ann Arbor: University of Michigan Press.

Beissinger, Mark. 2007. Structure and Example in Modular Political Phenomena. *Perspectives on Politics* 5 (2) (June): 259–76.

Béjar, Héctor. 1970. *Peru 1965: Notes on a Guerrilla Experience*. New York: Monthly Review Press.

Bejarano, Ana. 2011. *Precarious Democracies: Understanding Regime Stability and Change in Colombia and Venezuela*. Notre Dame: University of Notre Dame Press.

Bell, Daniel. 2015. *The China Model: Political Meritocracy and the Limits of Democracy*. Princeton: Princeton University Press.

Bellin, Eva. 2004. The Robustness of Authoritarianism in the Middle East. *Comparative Politics* 36 (2) (January): 139–57.

Bendor, Jonathan. 2010. *Bounded Rationality and Politics*. Berkeley: University of California Press.

Bennett, Andrew and Jeffrey Checkel, eds. 2015. *Process Tracing*. Cambridge: Cambridge University Press.

Bergstrand, Kelly. 2014. The Mobilizing Power of Grievances: Applying Loss Aversion and Omission Bias to Social Movements. *Mobilization* 19 (2) (June): 123–42.

Bermeo, Nancy. 2003. *Ordinary People in Extraordinary Times*. Princeton: Princeton University Press.

Bethell, Leslie and Ian Roxborough. 1992. Introduction: The Postwar Conjuncture in Latin America. In Leslie Bethell and Ian Roxborough, eds. *Latin America between the Second World War and the Cold War, 1944–1948*, 1–32. Cambridge: Cambridge University Press.

Bill, James. 1984. Resurgent Islam in the Persian Gulf. *Foreign Affairs* 63 (1) (Fall): 108–27.

Bismarck, Otto von. 1898. Das Jahr 1848. In *Gedanken und Erinnerungen*, vol. 1. Stuttgart: Cotta.

Birand, Mehmet. 1987. *The Generals' Coup in Turkey*. London: Brassey's Defense Publishers.

Black, Jan Knippers. 1977. *United States Penetration of Brazil*. Philadelphia: University of Pennsylvania Press.

Blackburn, Robin. 2006. Haiti, Slavery, and the Age of the Democratic Revolution. *William and Mary Quarterly*, third series 63 (4) (October): 643–74.

Blanco, Hugo. 1972. *Land or Death: The Peasant Struggle in Peru*. New York: Pathfinder.

Blinkhorn, Martin, ed. 1990. *Fascists and Conservatives*. London: Routledge.

Boeninger, Edgardo. 1997. *Democracia en Chile*. Santiago de Chile: Editorial Andrés Bello.

Boix, Carles. 2011. Democracy, Development, and the International System. *American Political Science Review* 105 (4) (November): 809–28.

2003. *Democracy and Redistribution*. Cambridge: Cambridge University Press.

Booth, John. 1998. The Somoza Regime in Nicaragua. In Houchang Chehabi and Juan Linz, eds. *Sultanistic Regimes*, 132–52. Baltimore: Johns Hopkins University Press.

Bosworth, Richard, ed. 2009. *Oxford Handbook of Fascism*. Oxford: Oxford University Press.

Botana, Natalio, Rafael Braun, and Carlos Floria. 1973. *El régimen militar, 1966–1973*. Buenos Aires: Ediciones La Bastilla.

Bowman, Kirk. 2002. *Militarization, Democracy, and Development: The Perils of Praetorianism in Latin America*. University Park: Pennsylvania State University Press.

Bowman, Kirk, Fabrice Lehoucq, and James Mahoney. 2005. Measuring Political Democracy. *Comparative Political Studies* 38 (8) (October): 939–70.

Bracher, Karl Dietrich. 1979. *Die nationalsozialistische Machtergreifung*, vol. 1: *Stufen der Machtergreifung*. Frankfurt am Main: Ullstein.

(1955) 1978. *Die Auflösung der Weimarer Republik*, 5th edn. Königstein im Taunus: Athenäum – Droste.

Brancante, Eldino. 1965. Interview by John W. F. Dulles with military officer, November 23. Interview 250. John W. F. Dulles Papers Relating to Brazil, 1920–1979, Benson Latin American Collection, University of Texas at Austin, Box 2, Folder 1.

Brands, Hal. 2010. *Latin America's Cold War*. Cambridge, MA: Harvard University Press.

Brasil, Pedro [pseudonym]. 1964. *Livro Branco sôbre a Guerra Revolucionária no Brasil*. Pôrto Alegre: Livraria do Globo.

Braubach, Max. 1974. *Gebhardt Handbuch der deutschen Geschichte*, vol. 14: *Von der Französischen Revolution bis zum Wiener Kongreß*. Munich: Deutscher Taschenbuch Verlag.

Brazil. Ministério da Aeronáutica. Centro de Informações de Segurança da Aeronáutica (CISA). 1973. *Relatório Especial de Informações – Mar 73/CISA*. N.p.: Ministério da Aeronáutica, CISA.

Bresser Pereira, Luiz. 1985. *Desenvolvimento e Crise no Brasil, 1930–1983*, 14th edn. São Paulo: Brasiliense.

Brill, William. 1967. *Military Intervention in Bolivia: The Overthrow of Paz Estenssoro and the MNR*. Washington, DC: Institute for the Comparative Study of Political Systems.

Brinks, Daniel and Michael Coppedge. 2006. Diffusion Is No Illusion: Neighbor Emulation in the Third Wave of Democracy. *Comparative Political Studies* 39(4) (May): 463–89.

Brown, Jonathan. 2017. *Cuba's Revolutionary World*. Cambridge, MA: Harvard University Press.

2012. The Tsunami of Military Counterrevolutions in the 1960s. Paper for 30th International Congress, Latin American Studies Association, San Francisco, May 23–26.

2011. *A Brief History of Argentina*, 2nd edn. New York: Lexington.

Brownlee, Jason. 2012. *Democracy Prevention: The Politics of the U.S.-Egyptian Alliance*. Cambridge: Cambridge University Press.

Brownlee, Jason, Tarek Masoud, and Andrew Reynolds. 2015. *The Arab Spring: Pathways of Repression and Reform*. Oxford: Oxford University Press.

Bunce, Valerie. 2017. The Prospects for a Color Revolution in Russia. *Daedalus* 146 (2) (Spring): 19–29.

Bunce, Valerie and Sharon Wolchik. 2011. *Defeating Authoritarian Leaders in Postcommunist Countries*. Cambridge: Cambridge University Press.

Burke, Edmund. (1790) 1999. *Reflections on the Revolution in France*. Oxford: Oxford University Press.

Burnier, João Moreira. 2005. Depoimento 1993. Rio de Janeiro: Centro de Pesquisa e Documentação de História Contemporânea do Brasil (CPDOC), Fundação Getúlio Vargas.

Burns, Mila. 2014. Dictatorship across Borders: The Brazilian Influence on the Overthrow of Salvador Allende. Paper presented at the 32nd International Congress, Latin American Studies Association, Chicago, IL, May 22–24, 2014.

Burrow, John. 2000. *The Crisis of Reason*. New Haven: Yale University Press.

Cáceres, Carlos. 2007. Author interview with former finance and interior minister under the Augusto Pinochet regime. Santiago: July 18.

Campbell, Leon. 1973. The Historiography of the Peruvian Guerrilla Movement, 1960–1965. *Latin American Research Review* 8 (1) (Spring): 45–70.

Campos, Esteban. 2013. Entrevista a Ignacio Vélez: Del catolicismo renovador a la lucha armada. In Patricia Pensado Leglise, ed. *Experimentar en la izquierda: Historias de militancia en América Latina, 1950–1990*, 77–99. Buenos Aires: CLACSO – Consejo Latinoamericano de Ciencias Sociales.

Cardoso, Fernando Henrique. 1986. Entrepreneurs and the Transition Process: The Brazilian Case. In Guillermo O'Donnell, Philippe Schmitter, and Laurence Whitehead, eds. *Transitions from Authoritarian Rule: Comparative Perspectives*, 137–53. Baltimore: Johns Hopkins University Press.

Carsten, Frances. 1988. *Revolution in Central Europe, 1918–1919*. Aldershot: Wildwood House.

Carvalho, Ferdinando de. 1964. A Guerra Revolucionária Comunista no Brasil. Reprinted in Exército (Brazil), ed. 1966. *A Revolução de 31 de Março*, 84–103. Rio de Janeiro: Biblioteca do Exército – Editora.

Castañeda, Jorge. 1993. *Utopia Unarmed: The Latin American Left after the Cold War*. New York: Knopf.

Castello Branco, Humberto de Alencar. 1964. Circular do Chefe do Estado-Maior do Exército. Reprinted in Exército (Brazil), ed. 1966. *A Revolução de 31 de Março*, 17–20. Rio de Janeiro: Biblioteca do Exército – Editora.

Cavalcanti, Newton. 1963. Recordando. *A Defesa Nacional* 50 (584) (April): 67–9.

Cavalheiro, Almoré Zoch. 2011. *A Legalidade, o Golpe Militar, e a Rebelião dos Sargentos*. Porto Alegre: Editora AGE.

Cavarozzi, Marcelo. 1983. *Autoritarismo y Democracia (1955–1983)*. Buenos Aires: Centro Editor de América Latina.

Cavatorta, Francesco. 2002. The Failed Liberalisation of Algeria and the International Context. *Journal of North African Studies* 7 (4) (Winter): 23–43.

Chaplin, David, ed. 1976. *Peruvian Nationalism: A Corporatist Revolution*. New Brunswick: Transaction.

Chaplin, David. 1968. Peru's Postponed Revolution. *World Politics* 20 (3) (April): 393–420.

Checkel, Jeffrey, and Andrew Bennett. 2015. Beyond Metaphors: Standards, Theory, and the "Where Next" for Process Tracing. In Bennett and Checkel, eds. *Process Tracing*, 260–75. Cambridge: Cambridge University Press.

Cheibub, José Antonio. 2007. *Presidentialism, Parliamentarism, and Democracy*. Cambridge: Cambridge University Press.

Chirio, Maud. 2003. El Golpe de Estado de 1964: ¿Sobresalto contrarrevolucionario o revolución militar? In Marianne González Alemán and Eugenia Palieraki, eds. *Revoluciones imaginadas*, 73–86. Santiago de Chile: RIL Editores.

CIA (Central Intelligence Agency). 1972. *The New Course in Brazil: NIE (National Intelligene Estimate) 93–72*. Langley: CIA. http://nsarchive.gwu.edu/NSAEBB/ NSAEBB282/Document%20146%201.13.72.pdf, accessed January 17, 2016.

  1964a. Intelligence Information Cable: Plans of Revolutionary Plotters in Minas Gerais. http://nsarchive.gwu.edu/NSAEBB/NSAEBB118/bz04.pdf, accessed January 12, 2016.

  1964b. *Memorandum: Effects of the Brazilian Revolution*. Langley: Directorate of Intelligence, July 29. Brown Digital Repository. Opening the Archives: Documenting U.S.-Brazil Relations, 1960s-80s. nsfco_br_4–64_68.pdf, accessed May 14, 2018.

  1964. *The President's Intelligence Checklist – 1 April 1964*. Langley: CIA.

  1963. Current Intelligence Memorandum. Subject: Plotting Against Goulart. OCI No. 0503/63. Langley: CIA. http://nsarchive.gwu.edu/NSAEBB/NSAEBB465/docs/ Document 7 Plotting against Goulart.pdf, accessed January 15, 2016.

Cohen, Youssef. 1994. *Radicals, Reformers, and Reactionaries: The Prisoner's Dilemma and the Collapse of Democracy in Latin America*. Chicago: University of Chicago Press.

  1989. *The Manipulation of Consent*. Pittsburgh: University of Pittsburgh Press.

Collier, David. 2011. Understanding Process Tracing. *PS – Political Science & Politics* 44 (4) (October): 823–30.

  ed. 1979. *The New Authoritarianism in Latin America*. Princeton: Princeton University Press.

Collier, David and Ruth Collier. 1991. *Shaping the Political Arena*. Princeton: Princeton University Press.

Collier, Ruth. 1994. Labor Politics and Regime Change. In David Rock, ed. *Latin America in the 1940s*, 59–88. Berkeley: University of California Press.

Collier, Simon and William Sater. 1996. *A History of Chile, 1808–1994*. Cambridge: Cambridge University Press.

Conselho de Segurança Nacional (Brazil). 1968. Ata da Quadragésima Terceira Sessão. Rio de Janeiro, December 13. Archived in Centro de Pesquisa e Documentação de História Contemporânea do Brasil, Fundação Getúlio Vargas, Rio de Janeiro.

Coppedge, Michael. 1994. *Strong Parties and Lame Ducks*. Stanford: Stanford University Press.

Corbett, Charles. 1972. Military Institutional Development and Sociopolitical Change: The Bolivian Case. *Journal of Interamerican Studies and World Affairs* 14 (4) (special issue, November): 399–435.

Cornell, Agnes, Jørgen Møller, and Svend-Erik Skaaning. 2017. The Real Lessons of the Interwar Years. *Journal of Democracy* 28 (3) (July): 14–28.

Cortés, Denisse. 2014. *Salvador Allende y el diario El Mercurio: Caricatura de una caída.* Saarbrücken: Editorial Redactum.

Costa, Octávio Pereira da. 1964. Compreensão da Revolução Brasileira. Reprinted in Exército (Brazil), ed. 1966. *A Revolução de 31 de Março*, 61–83. Rio de Janeiro: Biblioteca do Exército – Editora.

Cotler, Julio. 1978. A Structural-Historical Approach to the Breakdown of Democratic Institutions: Peru. In Juan Linz and Alfred Stepan, eds. *The Breakdown of Democratic Regimes*, 178–206. Baltimore: Johns Hopkins University Press.

Cottrol, Robert. 2013. *The Long, Lingering Shadow: Slavery, Race, and Law in the American Hemisphere.* Athens: University of Georgia Press.

Cousins, Cyrus. 2008. General Onganía and the Argentine Military Revolution of the Right: Anti-Communism and Morality, 1966–1970. *Historia Actual Online* 17 (Fall): 65–79.

Crozier, Michel, Samuel Huntington, and Joji Watanuki. 1975. *The Crisis of Democracy.* New York: New York University Press.

Dalton, Russell, David Farrell, and Ian McAllister. 2011. *Political Parties and Democratic Linkage.* Oxford: Oxford University Press.

Dame, Hartley. 1968. Argentina, A Violent Society? Part II. *World Affairs* 131 (2) (July–September): 101–13.

Danneman, Nathan and Emily Hencken Ritter. 2014. Contagious Rebellion and Preemptive Repression. *Journal of Conflict Resolution* 58 (2) (March): 254–79.

D'Araujo, Maria and Celso Castro, eds. 1997. *Ernesto Geisel.* Rio de Janeiro: Editora da Fundação Getúlio Vargas.

D'Araujo, Maria, Gláucio Dillon Soares, and Celso Castro, eds. 1994. *Visões do Golpe.* Rio de Janeiro: Relume-Dumará.

Davis, Nathaniel. 1985. *The Last Two Years of Salvador Allende.* Ithaca: Cornell University Press.

Debray, Régis. 1971. *The Chilean Revolution: Conversations with Allende.* New York: Pantheon.

1967. *Revolution in the Revolution?* New York: Grove Press.

De Janvry, Alain. 1981. *The Agrarian Question and Reformism in Latin America.* Baltimore: Johns Hopkins University Press.

De la Puente Uceda, Luis. 1964a. Nuestra Posición. www.marxistsfr.org/espanol/delapuente/1964/posicion.htm, accessed December 10, 2017.

1964b. La Revolución Peruana: Concepciones y perspectivas. www.marxistsfr.org/espanol/delapuente/1964/rev-peru.htm, accessed December 10, 2017.

De la Torre, Carlos. 2017. Hugo Chávez and the Diffusion of Bolivarianism. *Democratization* 24 (7) (December): 1271–88.

Delgado, Lucília de Almeida Neves. 1986. *O Comando Geral dos Trabalhadores no Brazil, 1961–1964*, 2nd edn. Petrópolis: Vozes.

Demirel, Tanel. 2003. The Turkish Military's Decision to Intervene: 12 September 1980. *Armed Forces & Society* 29 (2) (Winter): 253–80.

Denys, Odylio. 1967. *Denys Conta Tudo.* Rio de Janeiro: N.p.

De Riz, Liliana. 2010. *Historia Argentina 8: La Política en Suspenso, 1966/1976*, 2nd edn. Buenos Aires: Paidós.

Derpic, Jorge. 2012. The (Im)Possible Revolution: Ideology, Framing and Historical Events in the Making of the Bolivian Popular Assembly of 1971. MA thesis, University of Texas at Austin.

Deutsch, Sandra McGee. 1999. *Las Derechas: The Extreme Right in Argentina, Brazil, and Chile, 1890–1939*. Stanford: Stanford University Press.

Devine, Jack. 2014. What Really Happened in Chile. *Foreign Affairs* 93 (4) (July–August): 26–35.

Dezemone, Marcus. 2016. A Questão Agrária, o Governo Goulart e o Golpe de 1964 Meio Século Depois. *Revista Brasileira de História* 36 (71) (January–April): 131–54.

Diamond, Larry. 2016. Democracy in Decline. *Foreign Affairs* 95 (4) (July): 151–9.

Dias, Luiz Antonio. 2014. Vozes dissonantes: Análise do jornal Folha de S. Paulo e de pesquisas do Ibope no golpe civil-militar de 1964. Verinotio – Revista on-line de Filosofia e Ciências Humanas 9 (17) (April): 1–10. www.verinotio.org/conteudo/ 0.9017047937044.pdf, accessed September 23, 2016.

Díaz Bessone, Ramón. 1986. *Guerra Revolucionaria en la Argentina (1959–1978)*. Buenos Aires: Editorial Fraterna.

Diederich, Bernard. 2009. *1959: The Year that Inflamed the Caribbean*. Princeton: Markus Wiener.

Diez de Medina, Fernando. 1972. *El General del Pueblo*. La Paz: Amigos del Libro.

Diez episodios desconocidos sobre el golpe. 2008. *La Tercera*, August 3, in: Archivos Salvador Allende: 1–11. www.socialismo-chileno.org/sag/Golpe/el11/10% 20episodios%20desconocidos%20del%20Golpe.pdf, accessed October 7, 2016.

Diuguid, Lewis. 1976. U.S. Forces Stood Ready to Aid '64 Brazil Coup. *Washington Post*, December 29.

Dix, Robert. 1992. Democratization and the Institutionalization of Latin American Political Parties. *Comparative Political Studies* 24 (4) (January): 488–511.

  1990. Social Change and Party System Stability in Colombia. *Government and Opposition* 25 (1) (Winter): 98–114.

  1980. Consociational Democracy: The Case of Colombia. *Comparative Politics* 12 (3) (April): 303–21.

  1967. *Colombia: The Political Dimensions of Change*. New Haven: Yale University Press.

Documento Leex (Lealdade ao Exército). 1963. Reprinted in Hélio Silva. 2014. *1964: Golpe ou Contragolpe?* 347–52. Porto Alegre: L&PM Editores.

Domínguez, Jorge. 1998. The Batista Regime in Cuba. In Houchang Chehabi and Juan Linz, eds. *Sultanistic Regimes*, 113–31. Baltimore: Johns Hopkins University Press.

Dowe, Dieter, Heinz-Gerhard Haupt, et al., eds. 2001. *Europe in 1848*. New York: Berghahn.

Drake, Paul. 2009. *Between Tyranny and Anarchy: A History of Democracy in Latin America, 1800–2006*. Stanford: Stanford University Press.

Dulles, John W.F. 1996. *Carlos Lacerda, Brazilian Crusader*, vol. 2: *The Years 1960–1977*. Austin: University of Texas Press.

  1978. *Castello Branco: The Making of a Brazilian President*. College Station: Texas A&M University Press.

Dunkerley, James. 1984. *Rebellion in the Veins: Political Struggle in Bolivia, 1952–1982*. London: Verso.

Durán, Claudio. 1976. PsychoWar of the Media in Chile under Allende. *Canadian Journal of Communication* 2 (3) (January): 7–12.

Einaudi, Luigi. 1971. Peru. In Luigi Einaudi and Alfred Stepan, *Latin American Institutional Development: Changing Military Perspectives in Peru and Brazil*. Santa Monica: Rand.

Elkink, John. 2013. Spatial, Temporal and Spatio-Temporal Clustering of Democracy and Autocracy. Paper for 109th Annual Meeting, American Political Science Association, Chicago, IL, August 29–September 1.

Elkins, Zachary and Beth Simmons. 2005. On Waves, Clusters, and Diffusion: A Conceptual Framework. *Annals of the American Academy of Political and Social Science* 598 (March): 33–51.

Ellner, Steve. 1988. *Venezuela's* Movimiento al Socialismo: *From Guerrilla Defeat to Innovative Politics.* Durham: Duke University Press.

Engehausen, Frank. 2007. *Die Revolution von 1848/49.* Paderborn: Schöningh.

Espinosa V., Sergio. 2016. La bitácora de una extensa visita a Chile que nunca tuvo una fecha concreta de término. *El Mercurio,* November 27, A11.

Esposito, John. 1990a. The Iranian Revolution. In John Esposito, ed. *The Iranian Revolution: Its Global Impact,* 17–39. Miami: Florida International University Press.

ed. 1990b. *The Iranian Revolution: Its Global Impact.* Miami: Florida International University Press.

Esposito, John and James Piscatori. 1990. Introduction. In John Esposito, ed. *The Iranian Revolution: Its Global Impact,* 1–16. Miami: Florida International University Press.

Esser, James. 1998. Alive and Well after 25 Years: A Review of Groupthink Research. *Organizational Behavior and Human Decision Processes* 73 (2/3) (February–March): 116–41.

Estudo de Situação na Guerra Revolucionária. 1963. *A Defesa Nacional* 50 (581) (January): 51–64.

Evans, Peter. 2008. Is an Alternative Globalization Possible? *Politics and Society* 36 (2) (June): 271–305.

Excerpts from John F. Kennedy's Conversation regarding Brazil with US Ambassador to Brazil Lincoln Gordon on Monday, October 7, 1963. http://nsarchive.gwu.edu/ NSAEBB/NSAEBB465/docs/Document 9 brazil-jfk tapes-100763-revised.pdf, accessed January 15, 2016.

Ezrow, Lawrence and Timothy Hellwig. 2014. Responding to Voters or Responding to Markets? *International Studies Quarterly* 58 (4) (December): 816–27.

Fagen, Richard. 1975. The United States and Chile: Roots and Branches. *Foreign Affairs* 53 (2) (January): 297–313.

Fajardo, Luis. 2003. *From the Alliance for Progress to the Plan Colombia.* London: Crisis State Programme, Development Research Centre, London School of Economics. Working Paper No. 28.

Falcão, Luiz. 2013. Ethel Leon: Rememorando tiempos extraordinarios. In Patricia Pensado Leglise, ed. *Experimentar en la izquierda: Historias de militancia en América Latina, 1950–1990,* 303–22. Buenos Aires: CLACSO – Consejo Latinoamericano de Ciencias Sociales.

Fals Borda, Orlando. 1968. *Las revoluciones inconclusas en América Latina, 1809–1968.* Mexico City: Siglo XXI.

Farias, Ignez Cordeiro de. 1998. Um *troupier* na política: Entrevista com o general Antônio Carlos Muricy. In Marieta de Moraes Ferreira, ed. *Entre-Vistas: Abordagens e Usos da História Oral,* 124–46. Rio de Janeiro: Editora da Fundação Getúlio Vargas.

Farnsworth, Elizabeth. 1974. Chile: What Was the U.S. Role? More than Admitted. *Foreign Policy* 16 (Fall): 127–41.

Faúndez, Julio. 1988. *Marxism and Democracy in Chile*. New Haven: Yale University Press.

Fehrenbach, Elisabeth. 1981. *Oldenbourg Grundriß der Geschichte*, vol. 12: *Vom Ancien Régime zum Wiener Kongreß*. Munich: R. Oldenbourg Verlag.

Fermandois, Joaquín. 2003. The Persistence of Myth: Chile in the Hurricane of the Cold War. *Estudios Públicos* 92 (Winter): 1–26.

Fernández, Sergio. 2007. Author interview with former interior minister (1987–88) under the Augusto Pinochet regime. Santiago: July 11.

Ferraz, Silvio. 1985. Ex-embaixador dos EUA conta a "conexão brasileira" no Chile. *Jornal do Brasil*, November 8, 13.

Ferreira, João Perboyre de Vasconcellos. 1963. A Guerra Revolucionária. *A Defesa Nacional* 50 (583) (March): 13–34.

Ferreira, Jorge and Angela de Castro Gomes. 2014. *1964: O Golpe que derrubou um Presidente* . . . Rio de Janeiro: Civilização Brasileira.

Ferrer, Ada. 2015. *Freedom's Mirror: Cuba and Haiti in the Age of Revolution*. Cambridge: Cambridge University Press.

Ferro, António. 1939. *Salazar: Portugal and her Leader*. London: Faber and Faber.

Fico, Carlos. 2008. *O grande irmão: Da Operação Brother Sam aos anos do chumbo*. Rio de Janeiro: Civilização Brasileira.

Field, Thomas. 2014. *From Development to Dictatorship: Bolivia and the Alliance for Progress in the Kennedy Era*. Ithaca: Cornell University Press.

Finchelstein, Federico. 2014. *Ideological Origins of the Dirty War: Fascism, Populism, and Dictatorship in Twentieth Century Argentina*. Oxford: Oxford University Press.

Finkel, Evgeny and Yitzhak Brudny. 2012a. No More Colour! Authoritarian Regimes and Colour Revolutions in Eurasia. *Democratization* 19 (1) (February): 1–14.

2012b. Russia and the Colour Revolutions. *Democratization* 19 (1) (February): 15–36.

Finnemore, Martha and Kathryn Sikkink. 2001. Taking Stock: The Constructivist Research Program. *Annual Review of Political Science* 4: 391–416.

Fleet, Michael. 1985. *The Rise and Fall of Chilean Christian Democracy*. Princeton: Princeton University Press.

Fontaine, Arturo. 1993. El orden es lo único que importa (Interview with Mónica González). *La Nación*, September 5. www.puroperiodismo.cl/?p=26206, accessed August 12, 2016.

Foran, John. 2005. *Taking Power: On the Origins of Third World Revolutions*. Cambridge: Cambridge University Press.

Fox-Genovese, Elizabeth and Eugene Genovese. 2005. *The Mind of the Master Class: History and Faith in the Southern Slaveholder's Worldview*. Cambridge: Cambridge University Press.

Fragoso, Augusto. 1959. *Introdução ao Estudo da Guerra Revolucionária*. Rio de Janeiro: Escola Superior de Guerra. Departamento de Estudos.

Franco, Marina. 2012. *Un enemigo para la nación*. Buenos Aires: Fondo de Cultura Económica.

Frei Montalva, Eduardo. 1974. Prólogo. In Genaro Arriagada. 1974. De la "Via Chilena" a la "Via Insurreccional," 9–31. Santiago de Chile: Editorial del Pacífico.

French, John. 1992. *The Brazilian Workers' ABC: Class Conflict and Alliances in Modern São Paulo*. Chapel Hill: University of North Carolina Press.

Frey, Bruno and Jana Gallus. 2014. Aggregate Effects of Behavioral Anomalies. *Economics [E-Journal]* 8: 1–15.

FRUS *(Foreign Relations of the United States), 1961–1963*, vol. 12: American Republics. Washington, DC: US State Department, Office of the Historian. https://history.state.gov/historicaldocuments/frus1961-63v12.

FRUS *(Foreign Relations of the United States), 1964–1968*, vol. 31: South and Central America; Mexico. Washington, DC: US Government Printing Office, 2004.

FRUS *(Foreign Relations of the United States), 1969–1976*, vol. 11, part 2: Documents on South America, 1973–1976, chap. 1: Argentina. Washington, DC: US State Department, Office of the Historian. https://history.state.gov/historicaldocuments/frus1969-76ve11p2/ch1.

FRUS *(Foreign Relations of the United States), 1969–1976*, vol. E–10: Documents on American Republics, 1969–1972. Washington, DC: US State Department, Office of the Historian. https://history.state.gov/historicaldocuments/frus1969-76ve10/ch3, accessed February 11, 2016.

FRUS *(Foreign Relations of the United States), 1969–1976*, vol. E–11, Part 2: Documents on South America, 1973–1976. Washington, DC: US State Department, Office of the Historian. https://history.state.gov/historicaldocuments/frus1969-76ve11p2/ch4, accessed May 14, 2018.

FRUS *(Foreign Relations of the United States), 1969–1976*, vol. E–16: Documents on Chile, 1969–1973. Washington, DC: US State Department, Office of the Historian. https://history.state.gov/historicaldocuments/frus1969-76ve16/ch4, accessed May 14, 2018.

FRUS *(Foreign Relations of the United States), 1969–1976*, vol. 21: Chile, 1969–1973. 2014. Washington, DC: US Government Printing Office.

Fuentes, Claudio. 2012. *El pacto: Poder, constitución y prácticas políticas en Chile (1990–2010)*. Santiago de Chile: Ediciones Universidad Diego Portales.

Fukuyama, Francis. 1989. The End of History? *National Interest* 16 (Summer): 3–18.

Fumagalli, Matteo and Simon Tordjman. 2010. Uzbekistan. In Donnacha Ó Beacháin and Abel Polese, eds. *The Colour Revolutions in the Former Soviet Republics*, 156–76. London: Routledge.

Gabeira, Fernando. (1979) 1996. *O Que É Isso, Companheiro?* 2nd ed. São Paulo: Companhia das Letras.

Gall, Lothar. 1983. *Bismarck: Der weiße Revolutionär*. Frankfurt am Main: Ullstein.

Gallardo Lozada, Jorge. 1972. *De Torres a Banzer: Diez meses de emergencia en Bolivia*. Buenos Aires: Ediciones Periferia.

Gambone, Michael. 2001. *Capturing the Revolution: The United States, Central America, and Nicaragua, 1961–1972*. Westport: Praeger.

Gandhi, Jennifer. 2008. *Political Institutions under Dictatorship*. Cambridge: Cambridge University Press.

García, Pío. 1979. The Social Property Sector. In Federico Gil, Ricardo Lagos, and Henry Landsberger, eds. *Chile at the Turning Point: Lessons of the Socialist Years, 1970–1973*, 160–84. Philadelphia: Institute for the Study of Human Issues.

Garretón, Manuel. 1983. *El proceso político chileno*. Santiago: Facultad Latinoamericana de Ciencias Sociales.

Gaspar, David and David Geggus, eds. 1997. *A Turbulent Time: The French Revolution and the Greater Caribbean*. Bloomington: Indiana University Press.

Gaspari, Elio. 2003. *A Ditadura Derrotada*. São Paulo: Companhia das Letras.

2002. *A Ditadura Envergonhada*. São Paulo: Companhia das Letras.

Geggus, David. 2010. The Caribbean in the Age of Revolutions. In David Armitage and Sanjay Subrahmanyam, eds. *The Age of Revolutions in Global Context, c. 1760–1840*, 83–100. Houndmills: Palgrave Macmillan.

1989. The French and Haitian Revolutions, and Resistance to Slavery in the Americas. *Revue Française d'Histoire d'Outre-Mer* 76 (282–3) (first–second trimester): 107–24.

Genoino, José. 2006. *Entre o Sonho e o Poder: Depoimento a Denise Paraná*. São Paulo: Geração Editorial.

Gergeley, András. 1989. Versuch zur Modernisierung einer ständischen Verfassung in Europa: Ungarn 1789 – 1799. In Heiner Timmermann, ed. *Die Französische Revolution und Europa 1789 – 1799*, 645–56. Saarbrücken – Scheidt: Verlag Rita Dadder.

Gerlach, Ernst von. 1903. *Aufzeichnungen aus seinem Leben und Wirken, 1795–1877*. 2 vols. Schwerin: Fr. Bahn.

Gerlach, Leopold von. 1891. *Denkwürdigkeiten aus dem Leben Leopold von Gerlachs*, vol. 1. Berlin: Wilhelm Hertz.

Germani, Gino. 1978. *Authoritarianism, Fascism, and National Populism*. New Brunswick: Transaction.

Gerwarth, Robert, ed. 2007. *Twisted Paths: Europe 1914–1945*. Oxford: Oxford University Press.

Gerwarth, Robert and John Horne, eds. 2012. *War in Peace: Paramilitary Violence in Europe after the Great War*. Oxford: Oxford University Press.

Gibson, Edward. 1996. *Class and Conservative Parties: Argentina in Comparative Perspective*. Baltimore: Johns Hopkins University Press.

Gigerenzer, Gerd. 2006. Out of the Frying Pan into the Fire: Behavioral Reactions to Terrorist Attacks. *Risk Analysis* 26 (2) (April): 347–51.

Gill, Lesley. 2004. *The School of the Americas*. Durham: Duke University Press.

Gillespie, Richard. 1982. *Soldiers of Peron: Argentina's Montoneros*. Oxford: Clarendon.

Gilovich, Thomas, Dale Griffin, and Daniel Kahneman, eds. 2002. *Heuristics and Biases*. Cambridge: Cambridge University Press.

Gimpelson, Vladimir and Daniel Treisman. 2015. Misperceiving Inequality. Bonn: Forschungsinstitut zur Zukunft der Arbeit, Discussion Paper No. 9100.

Ginsberg, Benjamin and Martin Shefter. 2002. *Politics by Other Means: Politicians, Prosecutors, and the Press from Watergate to Whitewater*, 3rd edn. New York: W. W. Norton.

Gleditsch, Kristian Skrede and Michael Ward. 2006. Diffusion and the International Context of Democratization. *International Organization* 60 (4) (Fall): 911–33.

Goebel, Michael. 2007. A Movement from Right to Left in Argentine Nationalism? *Bulletin of Latin American Research* 26 (3) (July): 356–77.

Goldenberg, Boris. 1971. *Kommunismus in Lateinamerika*. Stuttgart: Kohlhammer.

Goldstone, Jack. 1991. *Revolution and Rebellion in the Early Modern World*. Berkeley: University of California Press.

Gomes, Gabriela. n.d. Las trayectorias políticas de los funcionarios nacional-corporativistas del Onganiato. Unpublished manuscript, Universidad de Buenos Aires.

González, Luis. 1991. *Political Structures and Democracy in Uruguay*. Notre Dame: University of Notre Dame Press.

González, Mónica. 2000. *Chile, la conjura: Los mil y un días del golpe*. Santiago de Chile: Ediciones B.

Goodwin, Jeff. 2001. *No Other Way Out: States and Revolutionary Movements, 1945–1991*. Cambridge: Cambridge University Press.

Goodwin, Jeff and Theda Skocpol. 1989. Explaining Revolutions in the Contemporary Third World. *Politics and Society* 17 (4) (December): 489–509.

Gordon, Lincoln. 1975. Recollections of President Castello Branco. Attachment to Interview by John W. F. Dulles with US Ambassador in Brazil, June 11. Interview 762. John W. F. Dulles Papers Relating to Brazil, 1920–1979, Benson Latin American Collection, University of Texas at Austin, Box 5, Folder 2.

1965. Interview by John W. F. Dulles with US Ambassador in Brazil, December 18. Interview 289. John W. F. Dulles Papers Relating to Brazil, 1920–1979, Benson Latin American Collection, University of Texas at Austin, Box 2, Folder 3.

1964a. Cable from Rio de Janeiro, March 27, 1964. http://nsarchive.gwu.edu/NSAEBB/NSAEBB118/bz02.pdf, accessed January 12, 2016.

1964b. Memorandum from Ambassador Gordon, March 29, 1964. http://nsarchive.gwu.edu/NSAEBB/NSAEBB465/docs/Document 12 top secret cable dated march 29 1964.pdf, accessed January 15, 2016.

1963. Memorandum to Mr. McGeorge Bundy. N.p.: Department of State. US Embassy in Brazil. http://nsarchive.gwu.edu/NSAEBB/NSAEBB465/docs/Document 5 political considerations affecting us assistance to brazil.pdf, accessed January 15, 2016.

1962. Airgram A-710: Minutes of Conversation between Brazilian President Joao Goulart and Attorney General Robert F. Kennedy, Brasilia, December 17, 1962. http://nsarchive.gwu.edu/NSAEBB/NSAEBB465/docs/Document 4 Airgram from Rio de Janeiro December19 1962.pdf.

Gott, Richard. 2008. *Guerrilla Movements in Latin America*, 2nd edn. Oxford: Seagull Books.

Grandin, Greg. 2015. *Kissinger's Shadow*. New York: Henry Holt.

Grow, Michael. 2008. *U.S. Presidents and Latin American Interventions*. Lawrence: University Press of Kansas.

Grugel, Jean. 1985. Nationalist Movements and Fascist Ideology in Chile. *Bulletin of Latin American Research* 4 (2) (July): 109–22.

Guerra, Lillian. 2012. *Visions of Power in Cuba*. Chapel Hill: University of North Carolina Press.

Guerrero Velázquez, Carlos. 2011. El impacto ideológico de la Escuela Francesa sobre el Ejército argentino. *Persona y Sociedad* 25 (2): 55–72.

Guevara, Ernesto "Che." (1961) 2007. *Guerrilla Warfare*. N.p.: BN Publishing.

Guglialmelli, Juan. 1967. Seguridad y desarrollo. *Temas Militares* 1 (2) (January–February): 9–16.

Gunitsky, Seva. 2017. *Aftershocks: Great Powers and Domestic Reforms in the Twentieth Century*. Princeton: Princeton University Press.

2014. From Shocks to Waves: Hegemonic Transitions and Democratization in the Twentieth Century. *International Organization* 68 (3) (June): 561–97.

2013. Complexity and Theories of Change in International Politics. *International Theory* 5 (1) (March): 35–63.

Gustafson, Kristian. 2007. *Hostile Intent: U.S. Covert Operations in Chile, 1964–1974*. Washington, DC: Potomac Books.

Gustafson, Kristian and Christopher Andrew. 2018. The Other Hidden Hand: Soviet and Cuban Intelligence in Allende's Chile. *Intelligence and National Security* 33 (3) (May): 407–21.

Hachtmann, Rüdiger. 1997. *Berlin 1848*. Bonn: Dietz.

Haenchen, Karl, ed. 1930. *Revolutionsbriefe 1848: Ungedrucktes aus dem Nachlaß König Friedrich Wilhelms IV*. Leipzig: Koehler.

Hafner-Burton, Emilie, Stephan Haggard, et al. 2017. The Behavioral Revolution and International Relations. *International Organization* 71 (Supplement): S1–S31.

Haggard, Stephan and Robert Kaufman. 2016. *Dictators and Democrats: Masses, Elites, and Regime Change*. Princeton: Princeton University Press.

Hale, Henry. 2013. Regime Change Cascades. *Annual Review of Political Science* 16: 331–53.

Halperin Donghi, Tulio. 2010. *Historia Argentina 7: La Democracia de Masas*, 2nd rev. edn. Buenos Aires: Paidós.

Harding, Colin. 1975. Land Reform and Social Conflict in Peru. In Abraham Lowenthal, ed. *The Peruvian Experiment*, 220–53. Princeton: Princeton University Press.

Harmer, Tanya. 2012. Brazil's Cold War in the Southern Cone, 1970–1975. *Cold War History* 12 (4) (November): 659–81.

2011. *Allende's Chile and the Inter-American Cold War*. Chapel Hill: University of North Carolina Press.

Harris, George. 2011. Military Coups and Turkish Democracy, 1960–1980. *Turkish Studies* 12 (2) (June): 203–13.

Hartlyn, Jonathan. 1991. The Dominican Republic: The Legacy of Intermittent Engagement. In Abraham Lowenthal, ed. *Exporting Democracy: The United States and Latin America. Case Studies*, 53–92. Baltimore: Johns Hopkins University Press.

1988. *The Politics of Coalition Rule in Colombia*. Cambridge: Cambridge University Press.

Hartz, Louis. 1955. *The Liberal Tradition in America*. New York: Harcourt Brace Jovanovich.

Harvie, Christopher. 2010. Revolution and the Rule of Law (1789–1851). In Kenneth Morgan, ed. *The Oxford History of Britain*, updated edn, 470–517. Oxford: Oxford University Press.

Haslam, Jonathan. 2005. *The Nixon Administration and the Death of Allende's Chile*. London: Verso.

Havens, Eugene, William Flinn and Susana Lastarría-Cornhill. 1980. Agrarian Reform and the National Front. In Albert Berry, Ronald Hellman, and Mauricio Solaún, eds. *Politics of Compromise: Coalition Government in Colombia*, 341–79. New Brunswick: Transaction.

Hershberg, James and Peter Kornbluh. 2014. Brazil Marks 50th Anniversary of Military Coup. https://nsarchive.gwu.edu/NSAEBB/NSAEBB465/, accessed January 15, 2016.

Heydemann, Steven and Reinoud Leenders. 2011. Authoritarian Learning and Authoritarian Resilience. *Globalizations* 8 (5) (October): 647–53.

Hilliker, Grant. 1971. The Agrarian Reform Issue. In *The Politics of Reform in Peru*, 138–56. Baltimore: Johns Hopkins Press.

Hirschman, Albert. 1991. *The Rhetoric of Reaction*. Cambridge, MA: Harvard University Press.

   1973. *Journeys toward Progress: Studies of Economic Policy-Making in Latin America*. New York: W.W. Norton.

Hobsbawm, Eric. 1996. *The Age of Revolution, 1789 – 1848*. New York: Vintage.

Hohenlohe-Ingelfingen, Prinz Kraft zu. 1897. *Aus meinem Leben*, vol. 1. Berlin: Ernst Siegfried Mittler.

Horvath, Robert. 2013. *Putin's Preventive Counter-Revolution*. London: Routledge.

Houle, Christian, Mark Kayser, and Jun Xiang. 2016. Diffusion or Confusion? Clustered Shocks and the Conditional Diffusion of Democracy. *International Organization* 70 (4) (Fall): 687–726.

Hoyer, Siegfried. 1989. Der Beginn der Französischen Revolution und Kursachsen. In Heiner Timmermann, ed. *Die Französische Revolution und Europa 1789–1799*, 369–79. Saarbrücken – Scheidt: Verlag Rita Dadder.

Hroch, Miroslav. 1989. Manipulierte Information und gegenrevolutionäre Propaganda des Alten Regimes. In Heiner Timmermann, ed. *Die Französische Revolution und Europa 1789 – 1799*, 53–63. Saarbrücken – Scheidt: Verlag Rita Dadder.

Huneeus, Carlos. 2007. *The Pinochet Regime*. Boulder: Lynne Rienner.

   1981. *Der Zusammenbruch der Demokratie in Chile*. Heidelberg: Esprint Verlag.

Hunt, Lynn. 2010. The French Revolution in Global Context. In David Armitage and Sanjay Subrahmanyam, eds. *The Age of Revolutions in Global Context, c. 1760–1840*, 20–36. Houndmills: Palgrave Macmillan.

Hunter, Wendy. 1997. *Eroding Military Influence in Brazil*. Chapel Hill: University of North Carolina Press.

Huntington, Samuel. 1991. *The Third Wave*. Norman: University of Oklahoma Press.

   1982. American Ideals versus American Institutions. *Political Science Quarterly* 97 (1) (Spring): 1–37.

   1968. *Political Order in Changing Societies*. New Haven: Yale University Press.

Hurtado, María Elena. 1990. The Caravan of Death. *Index on Censorship* 19 (5) (May): 13–14.

Idle, Nadia and Alex Nunns. 2011. *Tweets from Tahrir: Egypt's Revolution as it Unfolded*. New York: OR Books.

[Os] Inquéritos policiais-militares e a ditadura militar no Brasil (1964–1985). *Cultura e Política* www.culturaepolitica.org/ipms.html, accessed September 23, 2016.

Isaacs, Rico. 2010. Kazakhstan. In Donnacha Ó Beacháin and Abel Polese, eds. *The Colour Revolutions in the Former Soviet Republics*, 196–216. London: Routledge.

Jaquette, Jane. 1975. Belaúnde and Velasco: On the Limits of Ideological Politics. In Abraham Lowenthal, ed. *The Peruvian Experiment*, 402–37. Princeton: Princeton University Press.

Jarpa, Sergio Onofre. 2007. Author interview with former leader of Partido Nacional and interior minister (1983–85). Santiago: July 13.

   2002. *Confesiones políticas. Interviews with Patricia Arancibia Clavel, Claudia Arancibia Floody, and Isabel de la Maza Cave*. Santiago de Chile: CIDOC, Universidad Finis Terrae.

Jörgensen, Hans. 2006. The Inter-War Land Reforms in Estonia, Finland, and Bulgaria. *Scandinavian Economic History Review* 54 (1) (July): 64–97.

Jones, Bryan. 2001. *Politics and the Architecture of Choice: Bounded Rationality and Governance*. Chicago: University of Chicago Press.

Jones, Bryan and Frank Baumgartner. 2005. *The Politics of Attention*. Chicago: University of Chicago Press.

Jordan, David. 1970. Argentina's New Military Government. *Current History* 58 (342) (February): 85–90, 116–17.

Julião, Francisco. 1982. *Depoimento 1982*. Rio de Janeiro: Centro de Pesquisa e Documentação de História Contemporânea do Brasil (CPDOC), Fundação Getúlio Vargas.

Kahneman, Daniel. 2011. *Thinking, Fast and Slow*. New York: Farrar, Straus, and Giroux.

Kahneman, Daniel, and Jonathan Renshon. 2009. Hawkish Biases. In A. Trevor Thrall and Jane Cramer, eds. *American Foreign Policy and the Politics of Fear*, 79–96. London: Routledge.

Kahneman, Daniel, Paul Slovic, and Amos Tversky, eds. 1982. *Judgment under Uncertainty*. Cambridge: Cambridge University Press.

Kahneman, Daniel and Amos Tversky, eds. 2000. *Choices, Values, and Frames*. Cambridge: Cambridge University Press.

Kalandadze, Katya and Mitchell Orenstein. 2009. Electoral Protests and Democratizations Beyond the Color Revolutions. *Comparative Political Studies* 42 (11) (November): 1403–25.

Kallis, Aristotle. 2016. Fascism and the Right in Interwar Europe. In Nicholas Doumanis, ed. *Oxford Handbook of European History 1914–1945*, 301–22. Oxford: Oxford University Press.

Kasekamp, Andres. 2010. *A History of the Baltic States*. London: Palgrave Macmillan.

Katz, Mark. 1997. *Revolutions and Revolutionary Waves*. New York: St. Martin's Press.

Kaufman, Edy. 1979. *Uruguay in Transition: From Civilian to Military Rule*. New Brunswick: Transaction.

Kaufman, Robert. 1977. Corporatism, Clientelism, and Partisan Conflict: A Study of Seven Latin American Countries. In James Mallow, ed. *Authoritarianism and Corporatism in Latin America*, 109–48. Pittsburgh: University of Pittsburgh Press.

Kay, Cristobal. 1975. Chile: The Making of a Coup. *Science & Society* 39 (1) (Spring): 3–25.

Kedar, Claudia. 2017. The World Bank – United States – Latin American Triangle: The Negotiations with Socialist Chile, 1970–1973. *International History Review* 39 (4) (October): 667–90.

2015. Salvador Allende and the International Monetary Fund, 1970–73. *Journal of Latin American Studies* 47 (4) (November): 717–47.

Kevlihan, Robert and Amri Sherzamonov. 2010. Tajikistan. In Donnacha Ó Beacháin and Abel Polese, eds. *The Colour Revolutions in the Former Soviet Republics*, 177–95. London: Routledge.

Kirby, John. 1973. Venezuela's Land Reform. *Journal of Interamerican Studies and World Affairs* 15 (2) (May): 205–20.

Klein, Herbert. 1992. *Bolivia: The Evolution of a Multi-Ethnic Society*. Oxford: Oxford University Press.

Klein, Herbert and Francisco Vidal Luna. 2010. *Slavery in Brazil*. Cambridge: Cambridge University Press.

Kneuer, Marianne, Thomas Demmelhuber, Raphael Peresson, and Tobias Zumbrägel. 2018. Playing the Regional Card: Why and How Authoritarian Gravity Centres Exploit Regional Organisations. *Third World Quarterly*, forthcoming.

Knox, MacGregor. 2007. *To the Threshold of Power, 1922/33: Origins and Dynamics of the Fascist and National Socialist Dictatorships*, vol. 1. Cambridge: Cambridge University Press.

Koesel, Karrie and Valerie Bunce. 2013. Diffusion-Proofing: Russian and Chinese Responses to Waves of Popular Mobilizations against Authoritarian Rulers. *Perspectives on Politics* 11 (3) (September): 753–68.

Kornblith, Miriam and Daniel Levine. 1995. Venezuela: The Life and Times of the Party System. In Scott Mainwaring and Timothy Scully, eds. *Building Democratic Institutions*, 37–71. Stanford: Stanford University Press.

Kornbluh, Peter. 2014. Showdown in Santiago. *Foreign Affairs* 93 (5) (September–October): 168–74.

  2004. Brazil Marks 40th Anniversary of Military Coup. nsarchive.gwu.edu/NSAEBB/ NSAEBB118/, accessed January 15, 2016.

  2003a. The *El Mercurio* File. *Columbia Journalism Review* 42 (3) (September–October): 14–19.

  2003b. *The Pinochet File*. New York: Free Press.

Korry, Edward. 1998. Interview: Ambassador Edward M. Korry in CEP. *Estudios Públicos* 72 (Spring): 5–44.

  1970. Contingency Paper ("Fidelism without Fidel"). Reprinted in *Estudios Públicos* (Document appendix) 72 (Spring 1998): 10–27.

Kruel, Riograndino. 1975. Interview by John W. F. Dulles with Brazilian general, September 21. Interview 769. John W. F. Dulles Papers Relating to Brazil, 1920–1979, Benson Latin American Collection, University of Texas at Austin, Box 5, Folder 3.

Kuczynski, Pedro-Pablo. 1977. *Peruvian Democracy under Economic Stress*. Princeton: Princeton University Press.

Kuran, Timur. 1995. *Private Truths, Public Lies*. Cambridge, MA: Harvard University Press.

Kuran, Timur and Cass Sunstein. 1999. Availability Cascades and Risk Regulation. *Stanford Law Review* 51 (4) (April): 683–768.

Kurzman, Charles. 2004. Can Understanding Undermine Explanation? The Confused Experience of Revolution. *Philosophy of the Social Sciences* 34 (3) (September): 328–51.

  1998. Waves of Democratization. *Studies in Comparative International Development* 33 (1) (Spring): 42–64.

Labaki, Amir. 1986. *A Crise da Renúncia e a Solução Parlamentarista*. São Paulo: Brasiliense.

Laguado, Arturo. 2006. Onganía y el nacionalismo militar en Argentina. *Universitas Humanística* 62 (July–December): 239–59.

Lamberg, Robert. 1972. *Die Guerrilla in Lateinamerika*. Munich: Deutscher Taschenbuch Verlag.

Landers, Jane. 2010. *Atlantic Creoles in the Age of Revolutions*. Cambridge, MA: Harvard University Press.

1997. Rebellion and Royalism in Spanish Florida. In David Gaspar and David Geggus, eds. *A Turbulent Time: The French Revolution and the Greater Caribbean*, 156–77. Bloomington: Indiana University Press.

Landis, Fred. 1982. CIA Psychological Warfare Operations: Case Studies in Chile, Jamaica, and Nicaragua. *Science for the People* 14 (1) (January–February): 6–11, 29–37.

1981. Mass Media and Ideological Conflict: The Case of Chile. In Jorge Nef, ed. *Repression and Liberation in Latin America*, 76–93. N.p.: Canadian Association of Latin American and Caribbean Studies.

Landsberger, Henry and Juan Linz. 1979. Chile, 1973/Spain, 1936: Similarities and Differences in the Breakdown of Democracy. In Federico Gil, Ricardo Lagos, and Henry Landsberger, eds. *Chile at the Turning Point: Lessons of the Socialist Years, 1970–1973*, 399–438. Philadelphia: Institute for the Study of Human Issues.

Langieri, Marcelo. 2013. Lucha armada y política revolucionaria en la Argentina de los años sesenta y setenta: Entrevista a J.B., protagonista de la época. In Patricia Pensado Leglise, ed. *Experimentar en la izquierda: Historias de militancia en América Latina, 1950–1990*, 155–80. Buenos Aires: CLACSO – Consejo Latinoamericano de Ciencias Sociales.

Langland, Victoria. 2013. *Speaking of Flowers: Student Movements and the Making and Remembering of 1968 in Military Brazil*. Durham: Duke University Press.

Lanusse, Alejandro. 1994. *Confesiones de un general*. Buenos Aires: Planeta.

1977. *Mi testimonio*. Buenos Aires: Lasserre.

Lavareda, Antônio. 1991. *A Democracia nas Urnas*. Rio de Janeiro: Rio Fundo/IUPERJ.

Leacock, Ruth. 1990. *Requiem for Revolution: The United States and Brazil, 1961–1969*. Kent, OH: Kent State University Press.

Leal Buitrago, Francisco. 2011. Eficiencia legislativa. In Felipe Botero, ed. *Partidos y elecciones en Colombia*, 71–113. Bogotá: Universidad de los Andes, Departamento de Ciencia Política.

2010. La doctrina de seguridad nacional en América Latina. In Angelika Rettberg, ed. *Conflicto armado, seguridad y construcción de paz en Colombia*, 271–314. Bogotá: Universidad de los Andes, Departamento de Ciencia Política.

Lefebvre, Georges. 1979. Die Große Furcht von 1789. In Irmgard Hartig, ed. *Geburt der bürgerlichen Gesellschaft: 1789*, 88–135. Frankfurt am Main: Suhrkamp.

Lehoucq, Fabrice. 2016. Toppling Governments: Waves of Military Coups in Latin America. Paper for 33rd International Congress, Latin American Studies Association, New York, May 27–30.

2012. *The Politics of Modern Central America*. Cambridge: Cambridge University Press.

Lehoucq, Fabrice and Aníbal Pérez-Liñán. 2014. Breaking Out of the Coup Trap: Political Competition and Military Coups in Latin America. *Comparative Political Studies* 47 (8) (July): 1105–29.

Levi, Margaret. 2009. Reconsiderations of Rational Choice in Comparative and Historical Analysis. In Mark Lichbach and Alan Zuckerman, eds. *Comparative Politics*, 2nd edn, 117–33. Cambridge: Cambridge University Press.

Levine, Daniel. 1978. Venezuela since 1958. In Juan Linz and Alfred Stepan, eds. *The Breakdown of Democratic Regimes: Latin America*, 82–109. Baltimore: Johns Hopkins University Press.

1973. *Conflict and Political Change in Venezuela*. Princeton: Princeton University Press.

Levitsky, Steven and Lucan Way. 2010. *Competitive Authoritarianism*. Cambridge: Cambridge University Press.

Levitsky, Steven and Daniel Ziblatt. 2018. *How Democracies Die*. New York: Crown.

Levy, Jack. 2013. Psychology and Foreign Policy Decision-Making. In Leonie Huddy, David Sears, and Jack Levy, eds. *Oxford Handbook of Political Psychology*, 301–33. Oxford: Oxford University Press.

Li, Richard and William Thompson. 1975. The "Coup Contagion" Hypothesis. *Journal of Conflict Resolution* 19 (1) (March): 63–84.

Lichbach, Mark and Alan Zuckerman, eds. 2009. *Comparative Politics*, 2nd edn. Cambridge: Cambridge University Press.

Lilla, Mark. 2016. *The Shipwrecked Mind: On Political Reaction*. New York: New York Review Books.

Lindblom, Charles. 1965. *The Intelligence of Democracy: Decision Making through Mutual Adjustment*. New York: Free Press.

Linz, Juan. 2000. *Totalitarian and Authoritarian Regimes*. Boulder: Lynne Rienner.

1990. The Perils of Presidentialism. *Journal of Democracy* 1 (1) (Winter): 51–69.

1978. *The Breakdown of Democratic Regimes: Crisis, Breakdown, and Reequilibration*. Baltimore: Johns Hopkins University Press.

1976. Some Notes toward a Comparative Study of Fascism in Sociological Historical Perspective. In Walter Laqueur, ed. *Fascism: A Reader's Guide*, 3–121. Berkeley: University of California Press.

1973. The Future of an Authoritarian Situation or the Institutionalization of an Authoritarian Regime: The Case of Brazil. In Alfred Stepan, ed. *Authoritarian Brazil*, 233–54. New Haven: Yale University Press.

1964. An Authoritarian Regime: The Case of Spain. In Erik Allardt and Yrjö Littunen, eds. *Cleavages, Ideologies and Party Systems*, 291–342. Helsinki: Transactions of the Westermarck Society.

Linz, Juan and Alfred Stepan, eds. 1978. *The Breakdown of Democratic Regimes: Latin America*. Baltimore: Johns Hopkins University Press.

Linz, Juan and Arturo Valenzuela, eds. 1994. *The Failure of Presidential Democracy*. Baltimore: Johns Hopkins University Press.

Llewellyn, Paul. 2002. The Attitude of the Chilean Newspaper "El Mercurio" towards the Main Economic Policies of the Popular Unity Government of Salvador Allende (1970–73). Thesis, University of Oslo.

Lockhart, James. 2014. He Rode a Tank, Held a General's Rank, But Did He Direct Latin America's Coups? Vernon Walters's Diaries. *War on the Rocks* http://warontherocks.com/2014/09/he-rode-a-tank-held-a-generals-rank-but-did-he-direct-latin-americas-coups-vernon-walters-diaries/.

Long, David. 1990. The Impact of the Iranian Revolution on the Arabian Peninsula and the Gulf States. In John Esposito, ed. *The Iranian Revolution: Its Global Impact*, 100–15. Miami: Florida International University Press.

Lora, Guillermo. 1982. La clase obrera después de 1952. In René Zavaleta Mercado, ed. *Bolivia, hoy*, 169–218. Mexico City: Siglo XXI.

Loureiro, Felipe Pereira. 2017. The Alliance for Progress and President João Goulart's Three-Year Plan. *Cold War History* 17 (1) (January): 61–79.

Lowenthal, Abraham, ed. 1975. *The Peruvian Experiment: Continuity and Change under Military Rule.* Princeton: Princeton University Press.

Lowenthal, Abraham and Cynthia McClintock, eds. 1983. *The Peruvian Experiment Reconsidered.* Princeton: Princeton University Press.

Lust, Jan. 2016. The Role of the Peruvian Guerrilla in Che Guevara's Continental Guerrilla Project. *Bulletin of Latin American Research* 35 (2) (April): 225–39.

Lustick, Ian. 1996. History, Historiography, and Political Science. *American Political Science Review* 90 (3) (September): 605–18.

Lust-Okar, Ellen. 2004. Divided They Rule: The Management and Manipulation of Political Opposition. *Comparative Politics* 36 (2) (January): 159–79.

Lyles, Ian. 2016. Demystifying Counterinsurgency: U.S. Army Internal Security Training and South American Responses in the 1960s. Ph.D. dissertation, University of Texas at Austin.

McAdam, Doug, Sidney Tarrow, and Charles Tilly. 2001. *Dynamics of Contention.* Cambridge: Cambridge University Press.

McClintock, Cynthia. 1994. Presidents, Messiahs, and Constitutional Breakdowns in Peru. In Juan Linz and Arturo Valenzuela, eds. *The Failure of Presidential Democracy: The Case of Latin America,* 286–321. Baltimore: Johns Hopkins University Press.

McDermott, Rose. 2004. *Political Psychology in International Relations.* Ann Arbor: University of Michigan Press.

Machillanda Pinto, José. 1988. *Poder politico y poder militar en Venezuela, 1958–1986.* MA thesis in Political Science, Universidad Simón Bolívar. Caracas: Ediciones Centauro.

McSherry, J. Patrice. 2005. *Predatory States.* Lanham: Rowan & Littlefield.

Mahoney, James. 2012. The Logic of Process Tracing Tests in the Social Sciences. *Sociological Methods & Research* 41 (4) (November) 455–71.

Maier, Charles. 2017. In Merkel's Crisis, Echoes of Weimar. *New York Review of Books,* December 4. www.nybooks.com/daily/2017/12/04/in-merkels-crisis-echoes-of-weimar/.

Mainwaring, Scott. 2018. Party System Institutionalization, Predictability, and Democracy. In Scott Mainwaring, ed. *Party Systems in Latin America,* 71–101. Cambridge: Cambridge University Press.

  1993. Presidentialism, Multipartism, and Democracy: The Difficult Combination. *Comparative Political Studies* 26 (2) (July): 198–228.

Mainwaring, Scott and Aníbal Pérez-Liñán. 2013. *Democracies and Dictatorships in Latin America.* Cambridge: Cambridge University Press.

Mainwaring, Scott and Timothy Scully. 1995. Introduction: Party Systems in Latin America. In Scott Mainwaring and Timothy Scully, eds. *Building Democratic Institutions,* 1–34. Stanford: Stanford University Press.

Mainwaring, Scott and Matthew Shugart, eds. 1997. *Presidentialism and Democracy in Latin America.* Cambridge: Cambridge University Press.

Maira, Luis. 1979. The Strategy and Tactics of the Chilean Counterrevolution in the Area of Political Institutions. In Federico Gil, Ricardo Lagos, and Henry Landsberger, eds. *Chile at the Turning Point: Lessons of the Socialist Years, 1970–1973,* 240–73. Philadelphia: Institute for the Study of Human Issues.

Malloy, James. 1971. Revolutionary Politics. In James Malloy and Richard Thorn, eds. *Beyond the Revolution: Bolivia since 1952*, 111–56. Pittsburgh: University of Pittsburgh Press.

Malloy, James and Eduardo Gamarra. 1988. *Revolution and Reaction: Bolivia 1964–1985*. New Brunswick: Transaction.

Mann, Michael. 2004. *Fascists*. Cambridge: Cambridge University Press.

Marambio, Max. 2007. *Las armas de ayer*, 3rd edn. Santiago de Chile: La Tercera – Debate.

March, James and Herbert Simon. 1993. *Organizations*, 2nd edn. Cambridge, MA: Blackwell.

Marchesi, Aldo. 2018. *Latin America's Radical Left: Rebellion and Cold War in the Global 1960s*. Cambridge: Cambridge University Press.

Markoff, John (with Amy White). 2009. The Global Wave of Democratization. In Christian Haerpfer, Patrick Bernhagen, et al., eds. *Democratization*, 55–73. Oxford: Oxford University Press.

Markus, Ustina. 2010. Belarus. In Donnacha Ó Beacháin and Abel Polese, eds. *The Colour Revolutions in the Former Soviet Republics*, 118–35. London: Routledge.

Martinelli, Colonel. 1966. Interview by John W. F. Dulles with Brazilian military officer, October 12. Interview 327. John W. F. Dulles Papers Relating to Brazil, 1920–1979, Benson Latin American Collection, University of Texas at Austin, Box 2, Folder 5.

Martins Filho, João Roberto. n.d. A educação dos golpistas: Cultura militar, influência francesa e golpe de 1964. Ms., Universidade Federal de São Carlos.

2012. A conexão francesa, da Argélia ao Araguaia. *Vária História* 28 (48) (July): 519–36.

2008. A Influência Doutrinária Francesa sobre os Militares Brasileiros nos Anos de 1960. *Revista Brasileira de Ciências Sociais* 23 (67) (June): 39–50.

1999. Os Estados Unidos, a Revolução Cubana e a contra-insurreição. *Revista de Sociologia e Política da Universidade Federal do Paraná* 12 (June): 67–82.

Martins, José de Sá. 1963. A Estratégia Revolucionária no Quadro Mundial. *A Defesa Nacional* 50 (581) (January): 3–14.

Martz, John. 1965. Political Parties in Colombia and Venezuela. *Western Political Quarterly* 18 (2) (June): 318–33.

Maullin, Richard. 1971. *Soldiers, Guerrillas and Politics in Colombia*. Santa Monica: Rand. Advanced Research Projects Agency R-630.

Maurer, Michael. 2007. *Kleine Geschichte Englands*, 2nd edn. Stuttgart: Reclam.

May, Herbert. 1968. *Problems and Prospects of the Alliance for Progress*. New York: Praeger.

May, Rachel, Alejandro Schneider, and Roberto González Arana. 2018. *Caribbean Revolutions: Cold War Armed Movements*. Cambridge: Cambridge University Press.

Mayer, Arno. 1971. *Dynamics of Counterrevolution in Europe, 1870–1956*. New York: Harper & Row.

Mazzei, Daniel. 2002. La misión militar francesa en la Escuela Superior de Guerra y los orígenes de la Guerra Sucia, 1957–1962. *Revista de Ciencias Sociales* 13: 105–37

Meadows, Donnella, Dennis Meadows, Jørgen Randers, and William Behrens. 1972. *The Limits to Growth*. New York: Universe Books.

Meijer, Roel. 2011. The Egyptian Jama'a Al-Islamiyya as a Social Movement. In Joel Beinin and Frédéric Vairel, eds. *Social Movements, Mobilization, and Contestation in the Middle East and North Africa*, 143–62. Stanford: Stanford University Press.

Melnykovska, Inna, Hedwig Plamper, and Rainer Schweickert. 2012. Do Russia and China Promote Autocracy in Central Asia? *Asia Europe Journal* 10 (1) (March): 75–89.

Mendonça, Daniel de. 2007. O Discurso Militar da Ordem: Uma Análise dos Pronunciamentos Militares durante o Governo Goulart (1961–1964). *Teoria & Pesquisa* 16 (1) (January–June): 167–98.

Mercado Jarrín, Edgardo. 1974. Política, estrategia y subversión en América Latina. In *Seguridad, política, estrategia*, 189–221. Lima: Ministerio de Guerra.

Mercer, Jonathan. 2005. Prospect Theory and Political Science. *Annual Review of Political Science* 8: 1–21.

Mercier Vega, Luis. 1969. *Guerrillas in Latin America*. New York: Praeger.

Merino Castro, José Toribio. 1998. *Bitácora de un Almirante: Memorias*. Barcelona: Editorial Andrés Bello.

Metcalf, Lee. 1997. Institutional Choice and Democratic Consolidation: The Experience of the Russian Successor States, 1918–39. *Communist and Post-Communist Studies* 30 (3) (September): 307–20.

Michel, Bernard. 1989. La Revolution Française et l'Empire des Habsburg (1789 – 1796). In Heiner Timmermann, ed. *Die Französische Revolution und Europa 1789 – 1799*, 265–74. Saarbrücken – Scheidt: Verlag Rita Dadder.

Miller, Aragorn. 2016. *Precarious Paths to Freedom: The United States, Venezuela, and the Latin American Cold War*. Albuquerque: University of New Mexico Press.

Miller, Michael, Michael Joseph, and Dorothy Ohl. 2016. Are Coups Really Contagious? An Extreme Bounds Analysis of Political Diffusion. *Journal of Conflict Resolution*, forthcoming.

Molina, Sergio. 2007. Author interview with leader of Christian Democratic Party and former Finance Minister (1964–68). Santiago de Chile: July 11.

Mommsen, Hans. 2016. *Aufstieg und Untergang der Republik von Weimar, 1918–1933*, 4th edn. Berlin: Ullstein.

Monteforte Toledo, Mario. 1973. *La Solución Militar a la Peruana*. Mexico City: Instituto de Investigaciones Sociales, Universidad Nacional Autónoma de México.

Moore Jr., Barrington. 1966. *Social Origins of Dictatorship and Democracy*. Boston: Beacon Press.

Moraes, Dênis de. 2011. *A Esquerda e o Golpe de 64*, 3rd edn. São Paulo: Editora Expressão Popular.

Morales-Bermúdez Cerruti, Francisco. 2009. Author interview with former finance minister (1968, 1969–74) and military president of Peru (1975–80). Lima, July 16.

Morewedge, Carey, and Colleen Giblin. 2015. Explanations of the Endowment Effect. *Trends in Cognitive Sciences* 19 (6) (June): 339–48.

Motta, Rodrigo Sá. 2016. O anticomunismo nas pesquisas de opinião: Brasil, 1955–1964. *Nuevo Mundo Mundos Nuevos: Workshops: Sección 1 – El liberalismo y sus enemigos:* 1–11. http://nuevomundo.revues.org/68817, accessed September 25, 2016.

  2014. O golpe de 1964 e a ditadura nas pesquisas de opinião. *Tempo* 20: 1–21.

  2002. A "Intentona Comunista" ou a construção de uma legenda negra. *Tempo* 13 (July): 189–207.

Mounk, Yascha. 2018. *The People vs. Democracy: Why Our Freedom Is in Danger and How to Save It*. Cambridge, MA: Harvard University Press.

Moyano, María. 1995. *Argentina's Lost Patrol: Armed Struggle, 1969–1979*. New Haven: Yale University Press.

Müller, Jan-Werner. 2011. *Contesting Democracy*. New Haven: Yale University Press.

Munck, Gerardo and Jay Verkuilen. 2002. Conceptualizing and Measuring Democracy. *Comparative Political Studies* 35 (1) (February): 5–34.

Muricy, Antônio. 1993. *Depoimento 1981*. Rio de Janeiro: Centro de Pesquisa e Documentação de História Contemporânea do Brasil (CPDOC), Fundação Getúlio Vargas.

1964. *Os Motivos da Revolução Democrática Brasileira*. Recife: Imprensa Oficial.

Naftali, Timothy, ed. 2001. *The Presidential Recordings: John F. Kennedy. The Great Crises*. Vol. 1: *July 30-August 1962*. New York: W.W.Norton.

Narizny, Kevin. 2012. Anglo-American Primacy and the Global Spread of Democracy. *World Politics* 64 (2) (April): 341–73.

Navia, Patricio and Rodrigo Osorio. 2017. "Make the Economy Scream"? Economic, Ideological and Social Determinants of Support for Salvador Allende in Chile, 1970–3. *Journal of Latin American Studies* 49 (4) (November): 771–97.

2015. Las encuestas de opinión pública en Chile antes de 1973. *Latin American Research Review* 50 (1): 117–39.

NED (National Endowment for Democracy). 2017. *Sharp Power: Rising Authoritarian Influence*. Washington, DC: NED.

Needler, Martin. 1975. Military Motivations in the Seizure of Power. *Latin American Research Review* 10 (3) (Autumn): 63–79.

Niethammer, Katja. 2013. Herbst statt Frühling am Arabischen Golf: Bahrain im Ausnahmezustand. In Thorsten Schneiders, ed. *Der Arabische Frühling*, 269–87. Wiesbaden: Springer VS.

Nieto Ortiz, Pablo. 2010. *¿Subordinación o Autonomía? El Ejército Colombiano, su relación política con el gobierno civil y su configuración en la violencia, 1953–1965*. MA thesis, Departamento de Historia, Universidad Nacional de Colombia.

North, Liisa. 1983. Ideological Orientations of Peru's Military Rulers. In Cynthia McClintock and Abraham Lowenthal, eds. *The Peruvian Experiment Reconsidered*, 245–74. Princeton: Princeton University Press.

Nossiter, Adam. 2017. Le Pen Loses Luster, Signaling Far Right's Retreat in France, and Maybe Beyond. *New York Times*, June 16.

Novaro, Marcos. 2006. *Historia de la Argentina contemporánea: De Perón a Kirchner*. Buenos Aires: Edhasa.

Novaro, Marcos and Vicente Palermo. 2003. *Historia Argentina 9: La Dictadura Militar (1976-83)*. Buenos Aires: Paidós.

NSA (National Security Archive). 2002. Nixon: "Brazil Helped Rig the Uruguayan Elections," 1971. National Security Archive Electronic Briefing Book No. 71. Washington, DC: NSA. http://nsarchive.gwu.edu/NSAEBB/NSAEBB71/, accessed April 20, 2016.

Nunn, Frederick. 1979. Professional Militarism in Twentieth-Century Peru. *Hispanic American Historical Review* 59 (3) (August): 391–417.

1976. Marxism and the Military, 1970–73. In *The Military in Chilean History*, 253–308. Albuquerque: University of New Mexico Press.

Núñez, Ricardo. 2013. *Trayectoria de un socialista de nuestros tiempos. Interviews with Joaquín Fernández Abara, Álvaro Góngora Escobedo, and Patricia Arancibia Clavel*. Santiago de Chile: CIDOC, Universidad Finis Terrae.

Núñez y el Golpe de Estado "inevitable." 2004. *La Nación* (Chile), December 8.

Ó Beacháin, Donnacha. 2010. Turkmenistan. In Donnacha Ó Beacháin and Abel Polese, eds. *The Colour Revolutions in the Former Soviet Republics*, 217–36. London: Routledge.

O'Boyle, Brendan. 2017. Does AMLO Have a Venezuela Problem? *Americas Quarterly*, May 11. www.americasquarterly.org/content/does-amlo-have-venezuela-problem.

Ochoa Luna, Julio. 1996. Author interview with former Congressional deputy for *Acción Popular* (1963–68). Lima, July 20.

O'Donnell, Guillermo. 1996. Illusions about Consolidation. *Journal of Democracy* 7 (2) (April): 34–51.

   1983. La Cosecha del Miedo. *Nexos* 6 (6) (January 1).

   1982. *1966–1973: El Estado Burocrático Autoritario*. Buenos Aires: Editorial del Belgrano.

   1979. *Modernization and Bureaucratic-Authoritarianism*, new edn. Berkeley: Institute of International Studies, University of California, Berkeley.

   1978. Reflections on the Patterns of Change in the Bureaucratic-Authoritarian State. *Latin American Research Review* 13 (1): 3–38.

O'Donnell, Guillermo and Philippe Schmitter. 1986. *Tentative Conclusions about Uncertain Democracies*. Baltimore: Johns Hopkins University Press.

Offe, Claus and Helmut Wiesenthal. 1985. Two Logics of Collective Action. In Claus Offe, *Disorganized Capitalism*, 170–220. Cambridge, MA: MIT Press.

Oliveira, Kleber Frederico de. 1964. Aspectos Doutrinários da Guerra Revolucionária. *A Defesa Nacional* 50 (595) (May–June): 27–46.

Ollier, María Matilde. 1998. *La creencia y la pasión: Privado, público y político en la izquierda revolucionaria*. Buenos Aires: Ariel.

Olson, Mancur. 1971. *The Logic of Collective Action*. Cambridge, MA: Harvard University Press.

Onganía, Juan Carlos. 1967. *Discurso del Presidente de la Nación en la comida de Camaradería de las Fuerzas Armadas*. Buenos Aires: Secretaría de Difusión y Turismo, Dirección de Prensa.

Orhon, Goze. 2012. Official Memory of the 1980 Coup in Turkey. *Ethnologia Balkanica* 16: 295–313.

Osterling, Jorge. 1989. *Democracy in Colombia*. New Brunswick: Transaction.

Owen, John. 2010. *The Clash of Ideas in World Politics*. Princeton: Princeton University Press.

Packenham, Robert. 1973. *Liberal America and the Third World*. Princeton: Princeton University Press.

Palmeira, Vladimir. 2008. Os Valores de 1968. In Marco Aurélio Garcia and Maria Vieira, eds. *Rebeldes e Contestadores: 1968: Brasil, França, Alemanha*, 117–28. São Paulo: Editora Fundação Perseu Abramo.

   2008. Author interview with former student leader and leftwing politician. Rio de Janeiro: July 11.

Parker, Phyllis. 1979. *Brazil and the Quiet Intervention, 1964*. Austin: University of Texas Press.

Pasteur, Paul. 2007. *Les États autoritaires en Europe, 1919 – 1945*. Paris: Armand Colin.

Pastor, Robert. 2001. *Exiting the Whirlpool: U.S. Foreign Policy toward Latin America and the Caribbean*, 2nd edn. Boulder: Westview.

Paxton, Robert. 2009. Comparisons and Definitions. In Richard Bosworth, ed. *Oxford Handbook of Fascism*, 547–65. Oxford: Oxford University Press.

2005. *The Anatomy of Fascism*. New York: Vintage.

Payne, John, James Bettman, and Eric Johnson. 1993. *The Adaptive Decision Maker*. Cambridge: Cambridge University Press.

Payne, Stanley. 1995. *A History of Fascism, 1914–1945*. Madison: University of Wisconsin Press.

Pengl, Yannick. 2013. *Coup Contagion or Learning to Protect Oneself?* Zurich: Center for Comparative and International Studies, Eidgenössische Technische Hochschule.

Pereira, Anthony. 2018. The US Role in the 1964 Coup in Brazil: A Reassessment. *Bulletin of Latin American Research* 37 (1) (January): 5–17.

2003. Political Justice under Authoritarian Regimes in Argentina, Brazil, and Chile. *Human Rights Review* 4 (2) (January–March): 27–47.

1998. "Persecution and Farce:" The Origins and Transformation of Brazil's Political Trials, 196–1979. *Latin American Research Review* 33 (1): 43–66.

Pereira, Victor Almeida. 2018. A Inteligência Militar Espanhola na Contrainsurgência: Contribuições para a Doutrina Militar Brasileira. *Military Review: Revista Profissional do Exército dos EUA* 73 (2) (second trimester): 38–46.

Perelli, Carina. 1993. From Counterrevolutionary Warfare to Political Awakening: The Uruguayan and Argentine Armed Forces in the 1970s. *Armed Forces & Society* 20 (1) (Fall): 25–49.

Peru. Junta Revolucionaria. 1968. Manifiesto del Gobierno Revolucionario de la Fuerza Armada. In María del Pilar Tello. 1983. *Golpe o revolución? Hablan los militares del 68*, vol. 2, 283–5 Lima: Ediciones SAGSA.

Peru. Ministerio de Guerra. 1966. *Las Guerrillas en el Perú y su Represión*. Lima: Ministerio de Guerra.

Petrov, Nikolai and Andrei Ryabov. 2006. Russia's Role in the Orange Revolution. In Anders Åslund and Michael McFaul, eds. *Revolution in Orange: The Origins of Ukraine's Democratic Breakthrough*, 145–64. Washington, DC: Carnegie Endowment.

Peukert, Detlev. 1993. *The Weimar Republic*. New York: Hill and Wang.

Philip, George. 1976. The Soldier as Radical: The Peruvian Military Government, 1968–1975. *Journal of Latin American Studies* 8 (1) (May): 29–51.

Pierson, Paul. 2000. Increasing Returns, Path Dependence, and the Study of Politics *American Political Science Review* 95 (2) (June): 251–67.

Pinochet, Augusto. 1990. *Camino recorrido: Biografía de un soldado*, vol. 1. Santiago de Chile: Instituto Geográfico Militar.

Pinto, Bilac. 1964. *Guerra Revolucionária*. Rio de Janeiro: Forense.

Pion-Berlin, David. 1997. *Through Corridors of Power: Institutions and Civil-Military Relations in Argentina*. University Park: Pennsylvania State University Press.

1989. Latin American National Security Doctrines. *Armed Forces & Society* 15 (3) (Spring): 411–29.

1988. The National Security Doctrine, Military Threat Perception, and the "Dirty War" in Argentina. *Comparative Political Studies* 21 (3) (October): 382–406.

Pion-Berlin, David and George Lopez. 1991. Of Victims and Executioners: Argentine State Terror, 1975–1979. *International Studies Quarterly* 35 (1) (March): 63–86.

Polasky, Janet. 2015. *Revolutions without Borders: The Call to Liberty in the Atlantic World.* New Haven: Yale University Press.

Posusney, Marsha Pripstein. 2004. Enduring Authoritarianism: Middle East Lessons for Comparative Theory. *Comparative Politics* 36 (2) (January): 127–38.

Potash, Robert. 1996. *The Army and Politics in Argentina 1962–1973: From Frondizi's Fall to the Peronist Restoration.* Stanford: Stanford University Press.

1980. *The Army and Politics in Argentina 1945–1962: Perón to Frondizi.* Stanford: Stanford University Press.

Powell, Jonathan and Clayton Thyne. 2011. Global Instances of Coups from 1950 to 2010: A New Dataset. *Journal of Peace Research* 48 (2) (April): 249–59.

Power, Margaret. 2015. Who but a Woman? The Transnational Diffusion of Anti-Communism among Conservative Women in Brazil, Chile, and the United States during the Cold War. *Journal of Latin American Studies* 47 (1) (February): 93–119.

Power, Timothy and Mark Gasiorowski. 1997. Institutional Design and Democratic Consolidation in the Third World. *Comparative Political Studies* 30 (2) (April): 123–55.

Prada, Francisco. 1999. El alzamiento de 1992 se entendió como necesario para el bienestar nacional. In Alberto Garrido, ed. *Guerrilla y conspiración militar en Venezuela: Testimonios de Douglas Bravo, William Izarra, Francisco Prada*, 71–110. Caracas: Fondo Editorial Nacional.

Prats González, Carlos. 1987. *Memorias: Testimonio de un soldado.* Santiago de Chile: Pehuén.

Press, Volker. 1989. Die Französische Revolution und das Heilige Römische Reich. In Heiner Timmermann, ed. *Die Französische Revolution und Europa 1789 – 1799*, 219–39. Saarbrücken – Scheidt: Verlag Rita Dadder.

Priestland, David. 2016. The Left and the Revolutions. In Nicholas Doumanis, ed. *Oxford Handbook of European History 1914–1945*, 77–96. Oxford: Oxford University Press.

Prieto Celi, Federico. 1996. *Regreso a la democracia: Entrevista biográfica al General Francisco Morales Bermúdez Cerruti, Presidente del Perú (1975–1980).* Lima: Realidades.

Prittwitz, Karl Ludwig von. 1854. Beiträge zur Geschichte des Monats März 1848. In Gerd Heinrich, ed. *Berlin 1848.* Berlin: Walter de Gruyter.

Quartim, João. 1970. Régis Debray and the Brazilian Revolution. *New Left Review* 59 (January): 61–82.

Quiroga, Hugo. 2004. *El Tiempo del "Proceso."* Rosario: Homo Sapiens.

Quiroga Zamora, Patricio. 2001. *Compañeros. El GAP: La escolta de Allende.* Santiago de Chile: Aguilar.

Rabe, Stephen. 1999. *The Most Dangerous Area in the World: John F. Kennedy Confronts Communist Revolution in Latin America.* Chapel Hill: University of North Carolina Press.

Radowitz, Josef von. 1922. *Nachgelassene Briefe und Aufzeichnungen zur Geschichte der Jahre 1848 – 1853*, ed. Walter Möring. Stuttgart: Deutsche Verlags-Anstalt.

Ragin, Charles. 2000. *Fuzzy-Set Social Science.* Chicago: University of Chicago Press.

1987. *The Comparative Method.* Berkeley: University of California Press.

Rajaee, Farhang. 1990. Iranian Ideology and Worldview: The Cultural Export of Revolution. In John Esposito, ed. *The Iranian Revolution: Its Global Impact*, 63–80. Miami: Florida International University Press.

Ramazani, Rouhollah. 1988. *Revolutionary Iran: Challenge and Response in the Middle East.* Baltimore: Johns Hopkins University Press.

Ranaletti, Mario. 2011. Una aproximación a los fundamentos del terrorismo del Estado en la Argentina: la recepción de la noción de "guerra revolucionaria" en el ámbito castrense local (1954–1962). *Anuario del Centro de Estudios Históricos "Prof. Carlos S. A. Segreti"* 11 (11): 261–78.

Randall, Stephen. 1992. *Colombia and the United States.* Athens: University of Georgia Press.

Rapoport, Mario and Rubén Laufer. 2000. Os Estados Unidos diante do Brasil e da Argentina: Os golpes militares da década de 1960. *Revista Brasileira de Política Internacional* 43 (1): 69–98.

Reato, Ceferino. 2012. *Disposición Final: La Confesión de Videla sobre los Desaparecidos.* Buenos Aires: Sudamericana.

Redlawsk, David and Richard Lau. 2013. Behavioral Decision-Making. In Leonie Huddy, David Sears, and Jack Levy, eds. *Oxford Handbook of Political Psychology*, 130–64. Oxford: Oxford University Press.

Reh, Hans-Ulrich. 1970. *Der Staatsstreich in Peru 1968.* Mainz: Hase & Koehler.

Reichel, Peter. 2007. *Robert Blum: Ein deutscher Revolutionär 1807–1848.* Göttingen: Vandenhoeck & Ruprecht.

Reinalter, Helmut. 1988. *Die Französische Revolution und Mitteleuropa.* Frankfurt am Main: Suhrkamp.

Reis, Daniel Aarão. 2006. Introdução. In Daniel Aarão Reis and Jair Ferreira de Sá, eds. *Imagens da Revolução: Documentos Políticos das Organizações Clandestinas de Esquerda dos Anos 1961–1971*, 2nd edn, 15–32. São Paulo: Editora Expressão Popular.

2005. Interview with Angélica Muller and Ana Paula Goulart. Projeto Memória do Movimento Estudantil.

Reis, Daniel Aarão, and Jair Ferreira de Sá, eds. 2006. *Imagens da Revolução: Documentos Políticos das Organizações Clandestinas de Esquerda dos Anos 1961–1971*, 2nd edn. São Paulo: Editora Expressão Popular.

Reis, Levy Aarão. 1965. Interviews by John W. F. Dulles with Brazilian admiral, December 13 and 15. Interview 278. John W. F. Dulles Papers Relating to Brazil, 1920–1979, Benson Latin American Collection, University of Texas at Austin, Box 2, Folder 2.

Remmer, Karen. 1991. *Military Rule in Latin America.* Boulder: Westview.

Remmer, Karen and Gilbert Merkx. 1982. Bureaucratic-Authoritarianism Revisited. *Latin American Research Review* 17 (2): 3–40.

Rempe, Dennis. 1995: Guerrillas, Bandits, and Independent Republics: US Counter-Insurgency Efforts in Colombia. *Small Wars and Insurgencies* 6 (3) (Winter): 304–27.

Rénique, José. 2010. "People's War," "Dirty War": Cold War Legacy and the End of History in Postwar Peru. In Greg Grandin and Gilbert Joseph, eds. *A Century of Revolution: Insurgent and Counterinsurgent Violence during Latin America's Long Cold War*, 309–37. Durham: Duke University Press.

2006. De la "traición aprista" al "gesto heroico:" Luis de la Puente Uceda y la guerrilla del MIR. *Ecuador Debate* 67 (April): 77–98.

Rey Tristán, Eduardo. 2005. *La izquierda revolucionaria uruguaya, 1955–1973*. Sevilla: Universidad de Sevilla.

Ridenti, Marcelo. 2007. Esquerdas revolucionárias armadas nos anos 1960 – 1970. In Jorge Ferreira and Daniel Aarão Reis, eds. *Revolução e Democracia: 1964 . . .*, 23–51. Rio de Janeiro: Civilização Brasileira.

  1993. *O Fantasma da Revolução Brasileira*, 2nd edn. São Paulo: Editora da Universidade Estadual Paulista.

Risse, Thomas, Stephen Ropp, and Kathryn Sikkink, eds. 1999. *The Power of Human Rights*. Cambridge: Cambridge University Press.

Rivas Nieto, Pedro. 2008. *Doctrina de Seguridad Nacional y Regímenes Militares en Iberoamérica*. San Vicente (Spain): Editorial Club Universitario.

Roberts, Kenneth. 1998. *Deepening Democracy? The Modern Left and Social Movements in Chile and Peru*. Stanford: Stanford University Press.

Robins, Philip. 1990. Iraq: Revolutionary Threats and Regime Responses. In John Esposito, ed. *The Iranian Revolution: Its Global Impact*, 83–99. Miami: Florida International University Press.

Rocha, Graciliano. 2016. Para CIA, paranoia excessiva de militares resultou no AI-5. *Folha de São Paulo*, January 14.

Rock, David. 1994. War and Postwar Intersections: Latin America and the United States. In David Rock, ed. *Latin America in the 1940s*, 15–40. Berkeley: University of California Press.

  1993. *Authoritarian Argentina: The Nationalist Movement, Its History, and Its Impact*. Berkeley: University of California Press.

Rodríguez, Ambrosio. 2007. Author interview with former *Procurador General* (1986–90) and legal counsel of President Augusto Pinochet. Santiago: July 12.

Rodríguez Toledo, José. 2011. El impacto de la Revolución Francesa en el Perú a través de las páginas del *Mercurio Peruano*, 1791–1794. *Historia 2.0* 2 (August): 184–97.

Rollemberg, Denise. 2001. *O Apoio de Cuba à Luta Armada no Brasil*. Rio de Janeiro: Mauad.

Rouquié, Alain. 1987. *The Military and the State in Latin America*. Berkeley: University of California Press.

  1985. *Poder militar y Sociedad política en la Argentina*, vol. 2: *1943–1973*. Buenos Aires: Emecé.

Rubin, Lawrence. 2014. *Islam in the Balance*. Stanford: Stanford University Press.

Rueschemeyer, Dietrich, Evelyne Huber Stephens, and John Stephens. 1992. *Capitalist Development and Democracy*. Chicago: University of Chicago Press.

Ruhl, Mark. 1981. Civil-Military Relations in Colombia. *Journal of Interamerican Studies and World Affairs* 23 (2) (May): 123–46.

  1980. The Military. In Albert Berry, Ronald Hellman, and Mauricio Solaún, eds. *Politics of Compromise: Coalition Government in Colombia*, 181–206. New Brunswick: Transaction.

Salas, Ernesto. 2003. *Uturuncos: El origen de la guerrilla peronista*. Buenos Aires: Biblos.

Sales, Jean Rodrigues. 2007. *A Luta armada contra a Ditadura militar*. São Paulo: Editora Fundação Perseu Abramo.

Sanchez, Peter. 2003. Bringing the International Back In: US Hegemonic Maintenance and Latin America's Democratic Breakdown in the 1960s and 1970s. *International Politics* 40 (2) (June): 223–47.

Santos, Wanderley Guilherme dos. 1986. *Sessenta e Quatro: Anatomia da Crise*. São Paulo: Vértice.

Sauer, Wolfgang. 1974. *Die nationalsozialistische Machtergreifung*, vol. 3: *Die Mobilmachung der Gewalt*. Frankfurt am Main: Ullstein.

Saunders, Elizabeth. 2017. No Substitute for Experience: Presidents, Advisers, and Information in Group Decision Making. *International Organization* 71 (Supplement): S219–S247.

Schafer, Mark and Scott Crichlow. 2010. *Groupthink versus High-Quality Decision Making in International Relations*. New York: Columbia University Press.

Schattschneider, Elmer. (1960) 1975. *The Semisovereign People: A Realist's View of Democracy in America*. Hinsdale: Dryden.

Schedler, Andreas. 2013. *The Politics of Uncertainty: Sustaining and Subverting Electoral Authoritarianism*. Oxford: Oxford University Press.

Schmidli, William. 2013. *The Fate of Freedom Elsewhere: Human Rights and U.S. Cold War Policy toward Argentina*. Ithaca: Cornell University Press.

Schmitter, Philippe. 2010. Twenty-Five Years, Fifteen Findings. *Journal of Democracy* 21 (1) (January): 17–28.

Schmitz, David. 2006. *The United States and Right-Wing Dictatorships*. Cambridge: Cambridge University Press.

Schnake, Erich. 2004. *Un socialista con historia: Memorias*. Santiago de Chile: Aguilar.

Schrad, Mark. 2010. *The Political Power of Bad Ideas*. Oxford: Oxford University Press.

Schultz, Helga. 1989. Gesellschaftliche Strukturen und geistig-politisches Klima in Berlin 1789 – 1799. In Heiner Timmermann, ed. *Die Französische Revolution und Europa 1789 – 1799*, 381–92. Saarbrücken – Scheidt: Verlag Rita Dadder.

Schwedler, Jillian. 1998. A Paradox of Democracy? Islamist Participation in Elections. *Middle East Report* 209 (Winter): 25–9, 41.

Secretaría General de Gobierno (Chile). 1974. *Libro Blanco del cambio de gobierno en Chile, 11 de septiembre de 1973*. Santiago de Chile: Editorial Lord Cochrane.

Selcher, Wayne. 1977. *The National Security Doctrine and Policies of the Brazilian Government*. Carlisle: Strategic Studies Institute, US Army War College.

Sereza, Haroldo Ceravolo. 2016. Superestimamos nossas forças em 1964, diz José Salles, ex-integrante do comitê central do PCB. *Revista Samuel*, April 25. Posted on website *Opera Mundi*, April 29. http://operamundi.uol.com.br/conteudo/samuel/43900/superestimamos+nossas+forcas+em+1964+diz+jose+salles+ex-integrante+do+comite+central+do+pcb.shtml.

Serrano, Margarita and Ascanio Cavallo. 2006. *El Poder de la Paradoja: 14 Lecciones Políticas de la Vida de Patricio Aylwin*. Santiago: Norma.

Shapiro, Samuel. 1972. Uruguay's Lost Paradise. *Current History* 62 (366) (February): 98–103.

Shimko, Keith. 1994. Metaphors and Foreign Policy Decision Making. *Political Psychology* 15 (4) (December): 655–71.

Shiraz, Zakia. 2011. CIA Intervention in Chile and the Fall of the Allende Government in 1973. *Journal of American Studies* 45 (3) (August): 603–13.

Shirley, Edward. 1995. Is Iran's Present Algeria's Future? *Foreign Affairs* 74 (3) (May–June): 28–44.

Sigmund, Paul. 1993. *The United States and Democracy in Chile*. Baltimore: Twentieth Century Fund.

1977. *The Overthrow of Allende and the Politics of Chile, 1964–1976*. Pittsburgh: University of Pittsburgh Press.

1974. Chile: What Was the U.S. Role? Less than Charged. *Foreign Policy* 16 (Fall): 142–56.

Silitski, Vitali. 2010. "Survival of the Fittest": Domestic and International Dimensions of the Authoritarian Reaction in the Former Soviet Union Following the Colored Revolutions. *Communist and Post-Communist Studies* 43 (4) (December): 339–50.

Silva, Golbery do Couto e. 1965. Interview by John W. F. Dulles with Brazilian general and head of Serviço Nacional de Informações, December 8. Interview 272. John W. F. Dulles Papers Relating to Brazil, 1920–1979, Benson Latin American Collection, University of Texas at Austin, Box 2, Folder 2.

Silva, Hélio. 2014. *1964: Golpe ou Contragolpe?* Porto Alegre: L&PM Editores.

Silva Solar, Julio. 1979. Errors of the Unidad Popular and a Critique of the Christian Democrats. In Federico Gil, Ricardo Lagos, and Henry Landsberger, eds. *Chile at the Turning Point: Lessons of the Socialist Years, 1970–1973*, 316–27. Philadelphia: Institute for the Study of Human Issues.

Silveira, Helder Gordim. 2016. Exemplo e ameaça: A consolidação da Ditadura no Brasil nas páginas da revista argentina Confirmado (1965–1966). *Estudos Ibero-Americanos* (Porto Alegre) 42 (2) (May–August): 661–93.

2012. A notícia-acontecimento como face de uma ideologia da solução autoritária: A crise política no contexto do golpe de 1964 no Brasil sugundo o diario argentino *Clarín*. *Estudos Ibero-Americanos (Porto Alegre)* 38 (1) (January–June): 81–99.

Simmons, Beth, Frank Dobbin, and Geoffrey Garrett. 2008. Introduction: The Diffusion of Liberalization. In Beth Simmons, Frank Dobbin, and Geoffrey Garrett, eds. *The Global Diffusion of Markets and Democracy*, 1–63. Cambridge: Cambridge University Press.

Simon, Herbert. 1976. *Administrative Behavior*, 3rd edn. New York: Free Press.

Sirkis, Alfredo. 2008. Author interview with former student activist and urban *guerrillero*. Rio de Janeiro: July 9.

(1979) 2008a. *Os Carbonários*. Rio de Janeiro: BestBolso.

2008b. Os Paradoxos de 1968. In Marco Aurélio Garcia and Maria Vieira, eds. *Rebeldes e Contestadores: 1968: Brasil, França, Alemanha*, 111–16. São Paulo: Editora Fundação Perseu Abramo.

2005. Interview with Ana Paula Goulart. Projeto Memória do Movimento Estudantil.

Sivan, Emmanuel. 1989. Radicalism in the Middle East and the Iranian Revolution. *International Journal of Middle East Studies* 21 (1) (February): 1–30.

Skidmore, Thomas. 1988. *The Politics of Military Rule in Brazil, 1964–1985*. Oxford: Oxford University Press.

1967. *Politics in Brazil, 1930–1964: An Experiment in Democracy*. Oxford: Oxford University Press.

Skocpol, Theda. 1982. Rentier State and Shi'a Islam in the Iranian Revolution. *Theory and Society* 11 (3) (May): 265–83.

1979. *States and Social Revolutions*. Cambridge: Cambridge University Press.

Slater, Dan and Daniel Ziblatt. 2013. The Enduring Indispensability of the Controlled Comparison. *Comparative Political Studies* 46 (10) (October): 1301–27.

Slater, Jerome. 1987. Dominos in Central America. *International Security* 12 (2) (Fall): 105–34.

Smith, Bruce. 2015. *Lincoln Gordon: Architect of Cold War Foreign Policy.* Lexington: University Press of Kentucky.

Smith, Peter. 2012. *Democracy in Latin America,* 2nd edn. Oxford: Oxford University Press.

Smith, Tony. 1995. *America's Mission: The United States and the Worldwide Struggle for Democracy in the Twentieth Century.* Princeton: Princeton University Press.

Soares, Gláucio Dillon. 1979. Impressions of an Authoritarian Model. In Federico Gil, Ricardo Lagos, and Henry Landsberger, eds. *Chile at the Turning Point: Lessons of the Socialist Years, 1970–1973,* 450–60. Philadelphia: Institute for the Study of Human Issues.

Soares, Gláucio Dillon, Maria D'Araujo, and Celso Castro, eds. 1995. *A Abertura.* Rio de Janeiro: Relume-Dumará.

Soifer, Hillel. 2015. *State Building in Latin America.* Cambridge: Cambridge University Press.

Sowers, Jeannie and Bruce Rutherford. 2016. Revolution and Counterrevolution in Egypt. In Mark Haas and David Lesch, eds. *The Arab Spring,* 2nd edn, 40–71. Boulder: Westview.

Spektorowski, Alberto. 2003. *The Origins of Argentina's Revolution of the Right.* Notre Dame: University of Notre Dame Press.

Stallings, Barbara. 1978. *Class Conflict and Economic Development in Chile, 1958–1973.* Stanford: Stanford University Press.

Stein, Janice Gross. 2017. The Micro-Foundations of International Relations Theory: Psychology and Behavioral Economics. *International Organization* 71 (Supplement): S249–S263.

  2013. Threat Perception in International Relations. In Leonie Huddy, David Sears, and Jack Levy, eds. *Oxford Handbook of Political Psychology,* 364–94. Oxford: Oxford University Press.

Stenner, Karen. 2005. *The Authoritarian Dynamic.* Cambridge: Cambridge University Press.

Stepan, Alfred. 1978a. Political Leadership and Regime Breakdown: Brazil. In Juan Linz and Alfred Stepan, eds. *The Breakdown of Democratic Regimes: Latin America,* 110–37. Baltimore: Johns Hopkins University Press.

  1978b. *The State and Society: Peru in Comparative Perspective.* Princeton: Princeton University Press.

  1973. The New Professionalism of Internal Warfare and Military Role Expansion. In Alfred Stepan, ed. *Authoritarian Brazil,* 47–65. New Haven: Yale University Press.

  1971. *The Military in Politics.* Princeton: Princeton University Press.

Sugimoto, Luiz. 2003. O Golpe que deu IBOPE. *Jornal da UNICAMP* 204 (February 24–March 9): 3.

Summo, Marcelo and Esteban Pontoriero. 2012. Pensar la "Guerra revolucionaria." *Cuadernos de Marte* 2 (3) (July): 285–305.

Sunkel, Guillermo. 1983. *El Mercurio: 10 Años de Educación Político-Ideológica 1969–1979.* Santiago de Chile: Instituto Latinoamericano de Estudios Transnacionales.

Svolik, Milan. 2015. Which Democracies Will Last? Coups, Incumbent Takeovers, and the Dynamic of Democratic Consolidation. *British Journal of Political Science* 45 (4) (October): 715–38.

2012. *The Politics of Authoritarian Rule*. Cambridge: Cambridge University Press.

Szulc, Tad. 1964. U.S. May Abandon Effort to Deter Latin Dictators. *New York Times*, March 19. www.nytimes.com/1964/03/19/us-may-abandon-effort-to-deter-latin-dictators.html?_r=0, accessed October 23, 2016.

Taffet, Jeffrey. 2007. *Foreign Aid as Foreign Policy: The Alliance for Progress in Latin America*. New York: Routledge.

Tapia Valdés, Jorge. 1979. The Viability and Failure of the Chilean Road to Socialism. In Federico Gil, Ricardo Lagos, and Henry Landsberger, eds. *Chile at the Turning Point: Lessons of the Socialist Years, 1970–1973*, 297–315. Philadelphia: Institute for the Study of Human Issues.

Tapia Videla, Jorge. 1979. The Difficult Road to Socialism. In Federico Gil, Ricardo Lagos, and Henry Landsberger, eds. *Chile at the Turning Point: Lessons of the Socialist Years, 1970–1973*, 19–75. Philadelphia: Institute for the Study of Human Issues.

Tarrow, Sidney. 2011. *Power in Movement*, 3rd edn. Cambridge: Cambridge University Press.

Tavares, Aurélio de Lyra. 1964. A Contra-Revolução do Brasil. Reprinted in Exército (Brazil), ed. 1966. *A Revolução de 31 de Março*, 104–27. Rio de Janeiro: Biblioteca do Exército – Editora.

Taylor, Steven. 2009. *Voting amid Violence: Electoral Democracy in Colombia*. Boston: Northeastern University Press.

Teixeira, Francisco. 1992. Depoimento 1983/84. Rio de Janeiro: Centro de Pesquisa e Documentação de História Contemporânea do Brasil (CPDOC), Fundação Getúlio Vargas.

Tello, María del Pilar. 1983. *Golpe o revolución? Hablan los militares del 68*, 2 vols. Lima: Ediciones SAGSA.

Tendências – Eleições Presidenciais. 1994. *Opinião Pública* 2 (2) (December), special insert: 1–31.

Teorell, Jan. 2010. *Determinants of Democratization*. Cambridge: Cambridge University Press.

Thaler, Richard. 2002. *The Winner's Curse: Paradoxes and Anomalies of Economic Life*. Princeton: Princeton University Press.

Thayer Arteaga, William. 2012. *Memorias ajenas*, 2nd edn. Santiago de Chile: Editorial Andrés Bello.

Thiele, Gunter. 1989. Die Französische Revolution als Vorbild im grenznahen Raum. In Heiner Timmermann, ed. *Die Französische Revolution und Europa 1789–1799*, 531–53. Saarbrücken – Scheidt: Verlag Rita Dadder.

Thyne, Clayton. 2010. Supporter of Stability or Agent of Agitation? The Effect of US Foreign Policy on Coups in Latin America, 1960–99. *Journal of Peace Research* 47 (4) (July): 449–61.

Tibi, Bassam. 1986. The Iranian Revolution and the Arabs. *Arab Studies Quarterly* 8 (1) (Winter): 29–44.

Timmermann, Heiner. 1989. Die Saargegend und die Französische Revolution 1789–1793. In Heiner Timmermann, ed. *Die Französische Revolution und Europa 1789–1799*, 555–75. Saarbrücken – Scheidt: Verlag Rita Dadder.

Tocqueville, Alexis de. (1856) 1978. *Der alte Staat und die Revolution*. Munich: Deutscher Taschenbuch Verlag.

Tőkés, Rudolf. 1967. *Béla Kun and the Hungarian Soviet Republic*. Stanford: Hoover Institution.

Tomić, Radomiro. 1979. Chilean Democracy and the Government of the Unidad Popular. In Federico Gil, Ricardo Lagos, and Henry Landsberger, eds. *Chile at the Turning Point: Lessons of the Socialist Years, 1970–1973*, 209–39. Philadelphia: Institute for the Study of Human Issues.

Transcript of Tape No. 2. 1965. In *Lyndon Johnson and the Dominican Intervention of 1965*. National Security Archive Electronic Briefing Book No. 513. http://nsarchive .gwu.edu/NSAEBB/NSAEBB513/docs/Tape%2002%20transcript.pdf, accessed August 20, 2016.

Tsebelis, George. 1990. *Nested Games: Rational Choice in Comparative Politics*. Berkeley: University of California Press.

Turan, İlter. 2015. *Turkey's Difficult Journey to Democracy*. Oxford: Oxford University Press.

Ugarriza, Juan and Nathalie Pabón Ayala. 2017. *Militares y guerrillas: La memoria histórica del conflicto armado en Colombia desde los archivos militares, 1958–2016*, 2nd edn. Bogotá: Editorial Universidad del Rosario.

US. 1964. A Contingency Plan for Brazil. January 6. Reprinted in Carlos Fico. 2008. *O grande irmão: Da Operação Brother Sam aos anos do chumbo*. Rio de Janeiro: Civilização Brasileira, Appendix 1.

US Government. 1963. Memorandum: Contingency Paper on Brazil, July 17.

US NSC (National Security Council). 1964. Memorandum of Conversation of March 28. http://nsarchive.gwu.edu/NSAEBB/NSAEBB465/docs/Document%2011%20brazil-nscdocument.pdf, accessed January 15, 2016.

US NSC. 1962. Memorandum for the National Security Council Executive Committee. Meeting of December 11. Washington, DC. http://nsarchive.gwu.edu/NSAEBB/NSAEBB465/docs/Document 2 US short term policy toward brazil.pdf, accessed January 15, 2016.

US Senate. Select Committee to Study Governmental Operations with Respect to Intelligence Activities. 1976. *Covert Action in Chile, 1963–1973*. Reprinted in Ipswich by Mary Ferrell Foundation Press.

US State Department. 1964. Document A-134: Goulart's Ouster and the Military Tradition in Brazil. Brasília: April 4. Brown Digital Repository. Opening the Archives: Documenting U.S.-Brazil Relations, 1960s-80s. pol23-9braz04-04-64-134_4.pdf, accessed October 22, 2017.

1964. Document A-139: The 1965 Presidential Race: March 1–April 15, 1964. Brasília: April 15. Brown Digital Repository. Opening the Archives: Documenting U.S.-Brazil Relations, 1960s-80s. pol14braz04-15-64-139_8.pdf, accessed December 12, 2017.

1964. Document A-871: Fears of Coup at Time of Rio Gas Strike. Rio de Janeiro: January 20. Brown Digital Repository. Opening the Archives: Documenting U.S.-Brazil Relations, 1960s-80s. pol23-9braz01-20-64a-871_5.pdf, accessed October 22, 2017.

1964. Document A-1116: WeekA 12. Rio de Janeiro: March 19. Brown Digital Repository. Opening the Archives: Documenting U.S.-Brazil Relations, 1960s-80s. pol2-1braz03-19-64a-1116_19.pdf, accessed October 22, 2017.

1964. Document A-1124: Brazil: Country Internal Defense Plan. Rio de Janeiro: March 20. Brown Digital Repository. Opening the Archives: Documenting U.S.-Brazil Relations, 1960s-80s. pol23-103-20-64a-1124_31.pdf, accessed October 22, 2017.

1964. Document A-1152: WeekA 13. Rio de Janeiro: March 25. Brown Digital Repository. Opening the Archives: Documenting U.S.-Brazil Relations, 1960s-80s. pol2-1braz03-25-64a-1152_18.pdf, accessed October 22, 2017.

1964. Document A-1211: WeekA 15. Rio de Janeiro: April 9. Brown Digital Repository. Opening the Archives: Documenting U.S.-Brazil Relations, 1960s-80s. pol2-1braz04-09-64a-1211_22-1.pdf, accessed October 22, 2017.

1963. Document A-61: Brizola on a Rocky Comeback Trail. Brasília: December 12. Brown Digital Repository. Opening the Archives: Documenting U.S.-Brazil Relations, 1960s-80s. pol6braz12-12-63a-61_5.pdf, accessed October 22, 2017.

1964. Telegram. March 27. Brown Digital Repository. Opening the Archives: Documenting U.S.-Brazil Relations, 1960s-80s. pol23-9braz03-27-64armydept_3.pdf, accessed May 14, 2018.

US State Department, Latin American Policy Committee. 1963. Approved Short term Policy – Brazil (October 3). Washington, DC: State Department. http://nsarchive.gwu.edu/NSAEBB/NSAEBB465/docs/Document 8 proposed short term policy in brazil.pdf, accessed January 15, 2016.

US White House. 1971. Memorandum for the President's File: Meeting with President Emílio Garrastazú [sic] Médici of Brazil (December 9). http://nsarchive.gwu.edu/NSAEBB/NSAEBB282/Document%20143%2012.9.71.pdf, accessed January 17, 2016.

Valencia Tovar, Álvaro. 2013. *Los presidentes que yo conocí.* Bogotá: Planeta.

2009. *Mis adversarios guerrilleros.* Bogotá: Planeta.

Valenzuela, Arturo. 1978. *The Breakdown of Democratic Regimes: Chile.* Baltimore: Johns Hopkins University Press.

Van der Weid, Jean Marc. 2008. Author interview with former student leader. Rio de Janeiro: July 15.

Varnhagen von Ense, Karl August. 1862. *Tagebücher,* vols. 4 & 5. Leipzig: F. A. Brockhaus.

Vaz, Thaumaturgo Sotero. 1964. Guerrilha. *A Defesa Nacional* 50 (593) (January–February): 33–9.

Velasco Letelier, Eugenio. 1976. The Allende Regime in Chile: An Historical and Legal Analysis: Part II. *Loyola of Los Angeles Law Review* 9 (3) (June): 711–31.

Velásquez Rivera, Edgar. 2012. La noción de Guerra revolucionaria en Fernando Landazábal Reyes y sus repercusiones en el conflicto armado colombiano. *Folios,* 2nd series # 35 (first semester): 145–57.

Verbeek, Bertjan and Andrej Zaslove. 2016. Italy: A Case of Mutating Populism? *Democratization* 23 (2) (April): 304–23.

Verdugo, Patricia. 2001. *Chile, Pinochet, and the Caravan of Death.* Miami: North-South Center Press, University of Miami.

Vial, Gonzalo. 2003. *Pinochet: La biografía,* vol. 1. Santiago de Chile: El Mercurio – Aguilar.

Villamizar, Darío. 2017. *Las Guerrillas en Colombia*. Bogotá: Debate.

Viorst, Milton. 1997. Algeria's Long Night. *Foreign Affairs* 76 (6) (November–December): 86–99.

Villanueva, Victor. 1972. *El CAEM y la Revolución de la Fuerza Armada*. Lima: Instituto de Estudios Peruanos.

Villegas, Osiris. 1962. *Guerra Revolucionaria Comunista*. Buenos Aires: Círculo Militar.

Von der Mehden, Fred. 1990. Malaysian and Indonesian Islamic Movements and the Iranian Connection. In John Esposito, ed. *The Iranian Revolution: Its Global Impact*, 233–54. Miami: Florida International University Press.

Von Rauch, Georg. 1995. *The Baltic States: The Years of Independence, 1917–1940*. New York: St. Martin's.

Waisman, Carlos. 1987. *Reversal of Development in Argentina*. Princeton: Princeton University Press.

Waldman, Peter. 1974. *Der Peronismus, 1943–1955*. Hamburg: Hoffmann und Campe.

Walker, Ignacio. 1990. *Socialismo y democracia: Chile y Europa en perspectiva comparada*. Santiago de Chile: CIEPLAN – Hachette.

Walter, Richard. 2010. *Peru and the United States, 1960–1975*. University Park: Pennsylvania State University Press.

Walters, Vernon. 1978. *Silent Missions*. Garden City: Doubleday.

　1975. Interview by John W. F. Dulles with US Military Attaché in Brazil, June 12. Interview 764. John W. F. Dulles Papers Relating to Brazil, 1920–1979, Benson Latin American Collection, University of Texas at Austin, Box 5, Folder 2.

　1973. Personal calendars and diary entries, August–September. Handwritten manuscripts archived at John Hughes Library, National Intelligence University. Scan forwarded by Dr. James Lockhart, University of Arizona.

　1964. Cable to Joint Chiefs of Staff, March 30, 1964. http://nsarchive.gwu.edu/NSAEBB/NSAEBB465/docs/Document%2013.pdf, accessed January 15, 2016.

Weber, Eugen. 1976. Revolution? Counterrevolution? What Revolution? In Walter Laqueur, ed. *Fascism: A Reader's Guide*, 435–67. Berkeley: University of California Press.

Weitz, Eric. 1997. *Creating German Communism, 1890–1990*. Princeton: Princeton University Press.

Weitz, Richard. 1986. Insurgency and Counterinsurgency in Latin America, 1960–1980. *Political Science Quarterly* 101 (3) (Autumn): 397–413.

Wejnert, Barbara. 2014. *Diffusion of Democracy*. Cambridge: Cambridge University Press.

Weyland, Kurt. 2018. Populism and Authoritarianism. In Carlos de la Torre, ed. *Routledge Handbook of Global Populism*, 319–33. London: Routledge.

　2017. Fascism's Missionary Ideology and the Autocratic Wave of the Interwar Years. *Democratization* 24 (7) (December): 1253–70.

　2016. Crafting Counterrevolution: How Reactionaries Learned to Combat Change in 1848. *American Political Science Review* 110 (2) (May): 215–31.

　2014. *Making Waves: Democratic Contention in Europe and Latin America since the Revolutions of 1848*. Cambridge: Cambridge University Press.

2013. Latin America's Authoritarian Drift: The Threat from the Populist Left. *Journal of Democracy* 24 (3) (July): 18–32.

2012. The Arab Spring: Why the Surprising Similarities with the Revolutions of 1848? *Perspectives on Politics* 10 (4) (December): 917–34.

2010. The Diffusion of Regime Contention in European Democratization, 1830–1940. *Comparative Political Studies* 43 (8/9) (August–September): 1148–76.

2007. *Bounded Rationality and Policy Diffusion*. Princeton: Princeton University Press.

2005. Theories of Policy Diffusion. *World Politics* 57 (2) (January): 264–98.

2001. Clarifying a Contested Concept: Populism in the Study of Latin American Politics. *Comparative Politics* 34 (1) (October): 1–22.

Weyland, Kurt and Raúl Madrid. 2018. Liberal Democracy is Stronger than Trump's Populism. The American Interest 13 (4) (March–April): 24–8.

Whelan, James. 1989. *Out of the Ashes: Life, Death and Transfiguration of Democracy in Chile, 1833–1988*. Washington, DC: Regnery Gateway.

Whitehead, Laurence. 1972. Bolivia Swings Right. *Current History* 62 (366) (February): 86–90, 117.

Wickham-Crowley, Timothy. 2014. Two "Waves" of Guerrilla-Movement Organizing in Latin America. *Comparative Studies in Society and History* 56 (1) (January): 215–42.

1992. *Guerrillas and Revolution in Latin America*. Princeton: Princeton University Press.

Wilde, Alexander. 1978. Conversations among Gentlemen: Oligarchical Democracy in Colombia. In Juan Linz and Alfred Stepan, eds. *The Breakdown of Democratic Regimes: Latin America*, 28–81. Baltimore: Johns Hopkins University Press.

Wilson, Jeanne. 2010. The Legacy of the Color Revolutions for Russian Politics and Foreign Policy. *Problems of Post-Communism* 57 (2) (March–April): 21–36.

Winn, Peter. 2010. The Furies of the Andes: Violence and Terror in the Chilean Revolution and Counterrevolution. In Greg Grandin and Gilbert Joseph, eds. *A Century of Revolution: Insurgent and Counterinsurgent Violence during Latin America's Long Cold War*, 239–75. Durham: Duke University Press.

Wirsching, Andreas, Berthold Kohler, and Ulrich Wilhelm, eds. 2018. *Weimarer Verhältnisse? Historische Lektionen für unsere Demokratie*. Stuttgart: Reclam.

Wolff, Adolf. 1898. *Berliner Revolutionschronik*. Berlin: Dümmler.

Worth, Robert. 2014. Even Out of Office, a Wielder of Great Power in Yemen. *New York Times*, January 31.

Wright, Robin. 1992. Islam, Democracy and the West. *Foreign Affairs* 71 (3) (Summer): 131–45.

Wright, Thomas. 2001. *Latin America in the Era of the Cuban Revolution*. Revised edn. New York: Praeger.

Wynia, Gary. 1978. *Argentina in the Postwar Era*. Albuquerque: University of New Mexico Press.

Yom, Sean. 2016. Community and Collaboration amongst Mideast Monarchies. Paper for IDCAR III: Third Network Conference on International Diffusion and Cooperation among Authoritarian Regimes, Oxford University, September 29, 2016.

Zamir, Eyal. 2014. Loss Aversion: An Overview. In *Law, Psychology, and Morality: The Role of Loss Aversion*, 3-49. Oxford: Oxford University Press.

Zamosc, Leon. 1986. *The Agrarian Question and the Peasant Movement in Colombia*. Cambridge: Cambridge University Press.

Zavaleta Mercado, René. 1974. *El poder dual en América Latina*. Mexico City: Siglo XXI.

Zgórniak, Marian. 1989. Die II. und III. Teilung Polens und die Französische Revolution. In Heiner Timmermann, ed. *Die Französische Revolution und Europa 1789 – 1799*, 241–49. Saarbrücken – Scheidt: Verlag Rita Dadder.

Index